BOUND FOR AUSTRALIA

BOUND FOR AUSTRALIA

A GUIDE TO THE RECORDS OF TRANSPORTED
CONVICTS AND EARLY SETTLERS

DAVID T. HAWKINGS

The
History
Press

To the memory of the late Mollie Gillen
who so kindly shared with me her extensive
knowledge of the records of the transportation of
convicts and early settlers in Australia

Back cover image: 'On Board an Emigrant Ship – "Land,
Ho!".' (*The Graphic*, 6 May 1871, p. 413)

First published by Phillimore & Co. Ltd 1987
This updated paperback edition published 2012

The History Press
The Mill, Brimscombe Port
Stroud, Gloucestershire, GL5 2QG
www.thehistorypress.co.uk

British Library Cataloguing in Publication Data.
A catalogue record for this book is available from the British
Library.

ISBN 978 0 7524 6018 5

Typesetting and origination by The History Press
Printed in Great Britain

CONTENTS

FOREWORD

May 2012 marks the 225th anniversary of the sailing of the eleven vessels of the First Fleet from Portsmouth, Hampshire, England, bound for Australia to establish an English colony. A settlement was established at Sydney Cove on 26 January 1788. Over the next fifty-two years nearly 80,000 British and Irish convicts were transported to New South Wales, and a similar number to Van Diemen's Land between 1803 and 1853, when this colony became known as Tasmania. From 1850 to 1868, some 9,800 followed to Western Australia. In addition to those transported, hundreds of thousands of free persons emigrated from Britain and Ireland to New South Wales and the other colonies in Australia, particularly from the 1830s onwards.

In 1987, David Hawkings' first publication of *Bound for Australia* was well received. Now an entirely new work is presented in twenty chapters, together with a bibliography and index. Hawkings provides some excellent examples relating to convict trials, drawn from the Old Bailey proceedings, together with various listings found in War Office and Colonial Office documents in The National Archives at Kew, London, relating to convicts and their guards. Useful data on the military and the police, not previously published, is also included. This work is essential reading for anyone interested in the history of transportation to Australia.

There are eight new chapters – Chapter 1. The First Fleet to New South Wales; Chapter 3. Forgers of Banknotes and Coins; Chapter 7. Convicts Transported from Canada to Van Diemen's Land; Chapter 10. Guards on Convict Transportation Ships, the New South Wales Corps and Other Army Regiments in New South Wales; Chapter 11. Military Convicts at Robben Island; Chapter 16. Norfolk Island; Chapter 17. Police in New South Wales; Chapter 20. Hatton Collection – all of which provide invaluable data, in addition to the revision of the other chapters of this important reference work.

I have read this historical study with appreciation of the author's in-depth research. It is a valuable addition to Australian historical and genealogical publications, competently introduced, well set out and thoroughly indexed.

Keith A. Johnson, AM, FRAHS, FSG, FSAG
Vice Patron, Society of Australian Genealogists
Past President (and Councillor, 1969–2009)

PREFACE

Transportation overseas as the punishment for many criminal offences, next in severity to the death sentence, was first introduced into English law by the Elizabethan Act of 1597 'For the punishment of Rogues, Vagabonds, and Sturdy Beggars – to be banished out of this Realm and all other Dominions thereof —'. Further Acts were passed in 1664, 1666 and 1718, authorising the transportation of felons to America. For almost two centuries male and female convicts were shipped across the Atlantic Ocean to Virginia, Jamaica, Barbados and other places under British dominion. With the American revolt and subsequent Declaration of Independence in 1776, transportation fell, for some time, into disuse. Many criminals who would formerly have been transported were instead employed at hard labour in their native land under the terms of an Act passed in 1776. The prisons became overcrowded and prison hulks (disused warships moored in the Thames at Woolwich, and at Chatham, Portsmouth and Plymouth) were used to house those convicts who had been given a sentence of transportation. The conditions for the prisoners became worse and worse, and as an alternative the government considered transporting convicts to Gibraltar or Africa. Gibraltar was, however, found unsuitable and the Admiralty sent the sloop *Nautilaus* to explore the west coast of Africa. Africa, too, was considered unsuitable for a penal colony, although there is evidence to show that a small number of convicts were in fact sent there – twenty-two convicts were transported in the *Recovery* to Cape Coast Castle in 1785 *(TNA ref T1/619)*.

Eight years after transportation to America had ended it was felt that the large numbers of criminals given this punishment and held on board prison hulks could be more usefully employed in Britain's proposed settlement in the southern hemisphere. In 1784 another Act was passed (see Appendix 1), which, although it did not specifically mention New South Wales as a destination for transportees, ordered that transportation should resume as a regular procedure. This, the Act stated, would relieve the pressure that had built up in the gaols and prison hulks.

Eventually Botany Bay was chosen and Arthur Phillip was given the task of establishing a settlement there for both convicts and free settlers. The First Fleet, carrying 778 convicts, departed on 13 May 1787 from Portsmouth. It sailed via Tenerife, in the Canary Islands, to Rio de Janeiro, Brazil and Cape Town, South Africa. The fleet consisted of six transport vessels under contract from private owners: *Alexander* (448 tons; master, Duncan Sinclair), *Charlotte* (339 tons; master, Thomas Gilbert), *Friendship* (276 tons; master, Francis Walton), *Lady Penryn* (331 tons; master, William Sever), *Prince of Wales* (334 tons; master, John Mason), *Scarborough* (420 tons; master, John Marshall). There were also three store ships: *Borrowdale* (274 tons; master, Readthon Hobson), *Fishburn* (378 tons; master, Robert Brown), *Golden Grove* (master, Captain Sharp). The Royal Navy escort consisted of two ships: HMS *Sirius* (540 tons; commodore, Captain Arthur Phillip) and HM brigantine the

Supply (170 tons; commanded by Lt Henry Ball). On 18 January 1788 the *Supply* was the first ship to arrive at Botany Bay, two days in advance of the rest of the fleet, after a voyage of eight months.

There is often confusion about the first place of settlement of the people of the First Fleet. Captain Phillip soon discovered that Botany Bay offered no shelter from the easterly winds; that the land was swampy and the fresh water was of poor quality. He explored the coast further north and discovered what he described as, 'Without exception, the finest and most extensive harbour in the universe and at the same time the most secure, being safe from all winds that blow.' He named this place after Viscount Sydney, who was responsible for sending him on his mission. On 26 January 1788 the fleet assembled in Sydney Cove. Captain Phillip hoisted the British flag, 'and possession was taken for His Majesty'.

Since the publication of the first edition of this book, I discovered in the Treasury records at The National Archives, London, a victualling list for the First Fleet. This lists every convict and every marine. It also gives details of those who died on the voyage, and the names of all children born. It does not list the government officials or naval personnel. (See Chapter 1.)

The transportation of convicts continued uninterrupted until 1836 when there was much discontent voiced in Britain about its utility. Some believed it far too harsh a punishment, while others argued that an even more severe punishment should be enforced. In 1837 a House of Commons Select Committee was set up to enquire into transportation of convicts. The outcome of this enquiry was that those convicts sentenced to seven years' transportation, or less, should either remain in Britain or be sent to Bermuda or Gibraltar. Some male convicts who were of the right age and physical stature were given the option of joining the army or navy as an alternative to being transported.

Transportation to New South Wales continued until 1840. Up to that time many of the convicts of 'worst character' had been transferred from New South Wales to Van Diemen's Land (Tasmania). Much to the relief of the authorities and free settlers, transportation to New South Wales then ceased and in 1841 convicts were shipped directly to either Van Diemen's Land or Norfolk Island, and this continued until 1853. It was not until 1850 that convicts were transported to Western Australia, the last ship being the *Hougoumont*, with 279 male convicts on board, which arrived in 1868 (one convict had died on the voyage).

Many convicts were granted pardons in Australia after serving a period of good behaviour, a number of these taking up minor positions in government service. The prisons in Australia were almost entirely staffed by ex-convicts.

To return from transportation within the period of sentence was punishable by death until 1834, when this was reduced to transportation for life. Transportation was finally abolished in 1868 and was superseded by a system of penal servitude. It is estimated that between 1788 and 1868 about 170,000 men and women (and some children) had been transported, and for the first fifty years about 40 per cent of the total population in Australia was made up from the criminal classes.

It is the ambition of many Australians to trace their ancestry back to one of the people who arrived in Australia on board a ship in the First Fleet, and thereby qualify for membership of the Fellowship of First Fleeters, or the 1788–1820 Pioneers Association. Although the fleet brought officials, free settlers and, of course, many seamen to Australia, the largest single group was that of the 788 convicts and it is probable that most genealogists who prove their right to be a First Fleeter will do so through a convict ancestor. Many more will be able to trace their descent from one of the many thousands of convicts who subsequently found themselves bound for Australia during the first half of the nineteenth century.

Not all Australians with links back to the early nineteenth century can claim criminal ancestry. Free Settlers had decided to make a life for themselves in the new land and were encouraged to do so by government land grants and other concessions. Most officials posted by the government in London to this remote outpost served out their term of duty and returned to Britain, but not all. Some preferred to stay and their descendants are now Australians. Some naval personnel also remained in New South Wales or Van Diemen's Land when their ship sailed for home – sometimes with the permission of their captain and sometimes without. The New South Wales Corps was posted to guard the convicts, and many members of this corps also remained in New South Wales. Their descendants will find guidance for tracing their ancestry in this book.

The majority of the documentary material referred to in this book is held in The National Archives, London (hereafter referred to as TNA). As any researcher who has visited TNA will know, considerable time can be spent simply trying to identify the references to documents that contain the information required for a particular research project (TNA has over 100 miles of shelving housing historic records). This book is intended to enable anyone wishing to make use of TNA material to identify the references of the documents required in order to trace a convict from their conviction in England or Wales to their life in Australia. Each chapter gives examples of each type of document, and Appendices 4–22 list all known TNA documents relating to transported convicts and early settlers in Australia. The records at TNA reflect the work of many departments of central government and its officials, but no attempt is made here to explain the workings of the various departments or why these particular types of records were maintained. Suffice it to say that it is thanks to the bureaucracy of the time that we have such extensive and detailed documentation.

Much of the material referred to has been microfilmed and is available in Australia. Details of such microfilms up to the time of writing are given where applicable. The population census of New South Wales for the year 1828 was published by The Library of Australian History in 1980 and reprinted in 1985 (it is also available on microfilm). Many of the early musters of convicts and early settlers have also been published and these are listed in the Bibliography.

The principal aim of this work is to enable the descendants of a convict to trace their ancestor and to discover as much as possible about that individual's personal life and crime; their journey to New South Wales or other parts of Australia; and their life in the colony. Many women who were transported subsequently married and left descendants.

During research into my own family history I came across references to a John Hawkins, aged 42 years (perhaps the John Hawkins who was baptised on 17 April 1761, the brother of my ancestor Robert Hawkings), who, together with Philip Cording, was, in 1804, convicted of sheep stealing and subsequently transported to New South Wales (see Chapter 19). In order to prove or disprove that this John Hawkins was in fact a relative of my ancestor Robert Hawkings an extensive search is being carried out to find living descendants of this John Hawkins so that a DNA check can be made. It is understood that to prove conclusively that John Hawkins was a relative it is necessary to compare the DNA of my direct male line to the DNA of a male descendant through a direct male line of descendants from John Hawkins. Although some female descendants of this John Hawkins have been found, to date no living male descendants through a direct male line have been identified.

Since the publication of the first edition of this book another John Hawkins has been found who was convicted of Grand Larceny at Taunton Assizes, 30 March 1797, 'for stealing goods the value of 4 shillings of John Hancock and Richard Hancock, and was given a sentence of seven years' transportation.'[1] He was recorded as being 35 years old. He was sent to the *Fortunee* prison hulk at Portsmouth and died there on 1 February 1799.[2]

1. TNA ref ASSI 21/19; ASSI 23/8.
2. TNA ref T1/802; T1/811; T1/816; T1/819.

No record of his burial has been found at the nearby churches. The Portsmouth City Archivist has informed me that deceased convicts from the hulks were not interred in consecrated ground, but were buried on the beach near their prison hulk. Perhaps this was my lost John Hawkins and not the John Hawkins who was transported in 1806.

The records of John Hawkins and Philip Cording are used as a model in Chapter 19 to illustrate the various stages through which a convict can be traced, from their first appearance in the criminal court following their arrest, to their arrival and life in the Australian colony.

Care has been taken in transcribing these records and any peculiarities in grammar or spelling are as in the original documents. In some instances punctuation has been added to clarify the meaning of a statement.

David T. Hawkings
Taunton
2012

ACKNOWLEDGEMENTS

I am indebted to the following persons, without whose help and guidance this work would have been impossible to compile. They include the staff at the Public Record Office (now The National Archives), London, for their continued patience during my numerous visits. Those who gave me particular guidance to records relating to transported convicts were: the late Dr N.G. Cox, the late Dr Daphne Gifford, C.D. Chalmers, and Dr J.B. Post. Assistance was also provided by the staff at the State Records Authority of New South Wales, Sydney.

The librarian and staff at the Guildhall Library, London, the archivists and staff of the Berkshire, Dorset, Lancashire, Warwickshire and West Devon Record Offices, the Somerset Heritage Centre, the Surrey History Centre, the Portsmouth City Record Office and the London Metropolitan Archives, all gave help and guidance, as did the staff at the National Maritime Museum, Greenwich, London, and The National Library of Wales.

I thank Anthony Camp, one-time director of the Society of Genealogists, London, and his staff for many happy years spent working in the society's library. The staff at the British Library, and the Newspaper Library, Colindale, London, also helped me. Ron Martin, late of the Registry of Shipping and Seamen, allowed me access to the Merchant Navy Records when they were in his charge. Dr Christopher Watts assisted with merchant shipping records, and Mrs U.M. Thomas and Mrs Pat Gordon helped with Australian records in Sydney.

The late Lawrence B. Richardson gave me unceasing encouragement, as did Peter Bennett, Alan Littlefield and the late Robert Massey. The late Eileen Stage, Patricia Jones, Richard Ferrier and David Janes helped with the interpretation of pharmaceutical terms.

Special thanks must go to Frank Townsend for his constructive criticism, and to his late wife, Maureen, for typing much of the first draft of this book. I also thank Rene Coulson, Andrew Janes, John Porter and Adrian Webb for their help. In addition, I would like to thank the anonymous member of the Berkshire Family History Society, who, after one of my lectures, suggested that I should 'write it all up'.

Since the publication of the first edition of this book I have received much correspondence and many suggestions. Staff at The National Archives, London, have continued to be most helpful.

A particular thank you must go to Sara Joynes of the Australian High Commission, London, for directing me to the Bank of England where, to my surprise, the archives contain records of transported convicts who had been found guilty of forging, or dealing in forged coins and banknotes. My thanks also go to Sarah Millard, archivist at the Bank of England for her help with the records of forgers.

I also thank Keith Johnson for his help and suggestions and for so kindly writing the Foreword to the second edition of this book.

Permission for reproduction of images has been given by the following: The British Library; Cape Archive, South Africa; Greater London Record Office (now London Metropolitan

Archives); Guildhall Library, London; National Maritime Museum; The National Archives Somerset Record Office (now Somerset Heritage Centre); State Library of New South Wales; Taunton Local Studies Library.

Crown Copyright material is reproduced in the text from the Public Record Office (now The National Archives) and the National Maritime Museum by permission of the Controller of Her Majesty's Stationery Office. Abstracts from Lloyd's ship survey reports deposited at the National Maritime Museum are reproduced by permission of Lloyd's Register. Other copyright material is reproduced from the Berkshire, Dorset, Hampshire, Somerset, Surrey, Lancashire and West Devon Record Offices and Portsmouth City Record Office by permission of the respective archivists. Abstracts of shipping records at the Cape of Good Hope are reproduced by permission of the National Archives of South Africa, Cape Town. The details of John Hawkins' conditional pardon and the coroner's inquest mentioning Elizabeth Taleby are reproduced by permission of the State Records Authority of New South Wales. Abstracts of records from the Bank of England Archives are reproduced by permission of the Bank's archivist.

INTRODUCTION

This book is a guide for those wishing to trace a criminal from their conviction in England or Wales to their arrival and later life in Australia. Many records of early settlers have also been included. In order to trace a convict from their trial onwards, the relevant document references have been arranged in stages (see pages 18–21). Some of these records can be accessed online and website addresses have been supplied where relevant. Each chapter provides examples of the various types of documents that record criminals and/or early settlers.

Since the publication of the first edition of this book, more documentary material has been uncovered relating to convicts and early settlers in Australia. Of particular interest was the discovery of a victualling list for the First Fleet at Tenerife, Rio de Janeiro and the Cape of Good Hope (see Chapter 1). The images on page 238 show samples of materials used for blankets, trousers and other items for the convicts in Australia. The discovery of records of forgers in the Bank of England Archives was indeed a major find. These records include those found guilty of forgery who were given a transportation sentence (see Chapter 3).

It was of particular interest to discover an application in 1838 for a land grant from Joseph Augustus Manton, the son of Joseph Manton. Joseph Manton was an inventor who developed the percussion cap used in pistols and guns. His design used mercury fulminate, which, when impacted, instantly exploded. Manton's invention resulted in a major change in the design of pistols and guns (see Chapter 12).

The Hatton Collection at The National Archives includes records of many criminals. There are petitions on behalf of convicts, some of whom were given a transportation sentence (see Chapter 20 and Appendix 22).

A search through the Treasury Board Papers at The National Archives (document class T1) for the whole of the Australian transportation period has been carried out and all references to prison hulks have been recorded. Appendix 7 lists these records, giving the name of each hulk with covering dates and relevant document piece numbers.

CONTENT OF CHAPTERS AND APPENDICES

1   Victualling Lists for those who sailed in the First Fleet to Australia.
2   Criminal registers dating from 1791.
3   Records in the Bank of England Archives relating to people involved in the forging of and dealing in banknotes and coins. Many of those found guilty of this crime were transported to Australia. Letters from convicted forgers have been published in *Prisoners' Letters to the Bank of England* 1781 to 1827, edited by Deidre Palk (vol. XLII, London Record Society, 2007).

Sydney from the west side of the cove. From the watercolour by J. Eyre, c. 1806, in the Dixson Galleries. (Library of New South Wales)

4   Prison and prison hulk records in which convicts are named.
5   Petitions from convicts and their families pleading for clemency. Details of a number of these have been published by the List and Index Society (see Bibliography).
6   Some convicts, although given a transportation sentence, were not actually transported. Those who received a seven-year sentence (or less) were often held on board a prison hulk in England and eventually released, never having left their homeland. Many other convicts were found to be too old or infirm to endure the voyage to Australia and were held in a prison or on a prison hulk in England. Examples of these convicts' records are provided in this chapter.
7   Military criminals from Canada who were transported to Australia.
8   Merchant Navy vessels were used to transport convicts and early settlers to Australia. Some crewmembers settled in the colony and did not return to England. Details can be found in the seamen's records.
9   Ships' logs recorded all sorts of details about the voyage to Australia. If a person became sick, whether convict or free settler, military guard or seaman, they may have been recorded in a surgeon's journal. These journals give details of the medical treatment to the sick. If a person died on the voyage a record was kept of their illness and the date of death given.
10   Most of the guards on convict ships, who later became guards in New South Wales, were men who had retired from the army in Britain. Their records are described in this chapter.
11   Records of the convicts held on Robben Island at the Cape of Good Hope who were sent to New South Wales.
12   Colonial Office records at TNA include a large variety of information about early settlers, examples of which are given in this chapter.

13   Colonial Office records relating to convicts in New South Wales.
14   Many families of male convicts were given a free passage to Australia to join them. Details of some of these families, usually naming each family member, are given in this chapter. A number of working-class families were offered a free passage.
15   Inevitably, crimes were committed in the colony. Examples of the records of these, naming the culprits and giving details of their crimes and punishments, are provided.
16   Norfolk Island, to the east of Australia, was occupied by both convicts and settlers. Some records, including early musters of the whole population, are given in this chapter.
17   From early times a police force was set up in New South Wales, records of which are to be found in Colonial Office correspondence. Some examples, naming the men, are given in this chapter. It is perhaps surprising, given opinions at the time, to find that some Aborigines were recruited as policemen.
18   A number of people, including free settlers, particularly seamen, soldiers and government officials, returned to England after a term in Australia. Occasionally a record can be found of a convict returning home after completing their term of transportation. Details of such records are given in this chapter.
19   A case study of John Hawkins reveals, in sequence, his story from his trial to his life on a prison hulk and transfer to a transportation ship. Details about the voyage are provided, together with records relating to his life in New South Wales.
20   Some abstracts are given of documents from the Hatton Collection that relate to crime.

Appendix 1   A full transcript of the Act of Parliament that resulted in the transportation of convicts to Australia.
Appendix 2   An early circular encouraging people to immigrate to Australia.
Appendix 3   Regulations regarding applications for the various types of pardons.

The remainder of the appendices give details of the various types of documents with their location and relevant document references.

It should be noted that the many pages of facsimile documents in the first edition of this book have been omitted to allow space for the additional material included in this edition.

LIST OF ABBREVIATIONS

BECLS	Bank of England Committee for Law Suits
BoE	Bank of England
Berks RO	Berkshire Record Office, Reading, Berkshire
BL/NL	British Library Newspaper Library
Dor RO	Dorset Record Office, Dorchester, Dorset
Hants RO	Hampshire Record Office, Winchester, Hampshire
Lancs RO	Lancashire Record Office, Preston, Lancashire
LMA	London Metropolitan Archives
NLW	National Library of Wales, Aberystwyth
NMM	National Maritime Museum, Greenwich, London
NSW	New South Wales
Ports RO	Portsmouth Record Office, Portsmouth, Hampshire
PRO	Public Record Office (now The National Archives), London
QS	Quarter Sessions
Som HC	Somerset Heritage Centre
SRANSW	State Records Authority of New South Wales
Sur HC	Surrey History Centre
TNA	The National Archives, London
VDL	Van Diemen's Land (Tasmania)
W Aust	Western Australia
W Dev RO	West Devon Record Office, Plymouth, Devon

THE NATIONAL ARCHIVES CLASS LIST ABBREVIATIONS

ADM	Admiralty		HCA	High Court of Admiralty
AO	Audit Office (Exchequer and Audit Department)		HO	Home Office
			J	Supreme Court of Judicature
ASSI	Assizes		MT	Ministry of Transport
BT	Board of Trade		PC	Privy Council Office
CHES	Palatinate of Chester		PCOM	Prison Commissioners
CO	Colonial Office		PL	Palatinate of Lancaster
DURH	Palatinate of Durham		T	Treasury
E	Exchequer		TS	Treasury Solicitor's Department
FO	Foreign Office		WO	War Office

SEQUENCE OF DOCUMENTS TO BE SEARCHED TO TRACE A TRANSPORTED CONVICT

The following list sets out in sequence the documents to be searched in order to trace the movements of a convict from conviction in England or Wales to their life in Australia. It should be noted that criminal registers for Middlesex and the Old Bailey commenced in 1791 and criminal registers for the rest of England and Wales do not start until 1805. To find records of convicts who were convicted before these dates it is necessary to begin the search in the respective Calendars of Prisoners at Stage 2.

TNA	The National Archives (TNA document class references are shown in italics)
C&BROs	County and Borough Record Offices
LMA	London Metropolitan Archives

STAGE 1 **Criminal registers** (see Chapter 2 and Appendix 4)
a. Series I – Middlesex and Old Bailey
TNA: *HO 26* These registers cover the years 1791 to 1849 and give the date of trial, a summary of the crime, whether guilty or not. A physical description of the accused is also given together with the sentence of the court.
For Old Bailey Court proceedings, see www.oldbaileyonline.org
b. Series II – All counties in England and Wales
TNA: *HO 27* These registers cover the years 1805 to 1892 (Middlesex begins in 1850, continuing from *HO 26*). They give a summary of the crime, date of trial and whether guilty or not, and the sentence of the court.
For all criminal registers (*HO 26* and *HO 27*), see www.ancestry.co.uk

STAGE 2 **Calendars of Prisoners** (see Chapter 2 and Appendix 5)
TNA: *HO 16, HO 77, HO 130, HO 140, PCOM 2* and at C&BROs
From the beginning of the nineteenth century the calendars are generally in printed format. Each prisoner's name is given and usually their age. A summary of the crime is provided, together with the name(s) of the person(s) who have brought the charge.

STAGE 3 **Legal proceedings** (see Appendix 8)
These usually include depositions of the witnesses.

a. Assizes TNA: *ASSI 1–73*
These cover all English counties except Durham, Lancashire and Cheshire. See d. below.
b. County Quarter Sessions and Borough Sessions (England and Wales)
c. Old Bailey and the Central Criminal Court (London)
The proceedings of these courts are printed in bound volumes, giving a detailed account of each trial with the verdict of the court. A full set is held by London Metropolitan Archives (LMA). Some Old Bailey proceedings are also held at The National Archives (see Appendix 8). The indictments relating to the proceedings are held at the London Metropolitan Archives (LMA). They are handwritten on parchment.
For Old Bailey court proceedings for the whole of the transportation period, see www.oldbaileyonline.org
d. Palatinate Courts
These courts are the equivalent of the English Assizes for the counties of Cheshire (up to 1830), Durham and Lancashire (up to 1876).
TNA: *CHES 24, DURH 16–18, PL 25–27*
e. Courts of Great Sessions of Wales
These courts cover the whole of Wales and are the Welsh equivalent of the English Assizes. The records are held at the National Library of Wales, Aberystwyth (Wales also held Quarter Sessions in each county).

STAGE 4   **Sheriffs' assize vouchers** (see Appendix 11)
TNA: *E 370*
The vouchers are in bound volumes arranged by county. They give the names of each criminal, a summary of the crime and the place and date of the trial.

STAGE 5   **Prison registers** (see Chapter 4 and Appendix 6)
TNA: *HO 8, HO 23, HO 24, KB 32, PCOM 2, WO 25* and at C&BROs
The registers give the name of the prisoner with their date of admission to the prison. The date and place of trial is usually provided. The date of release or transfer to another prison is also given. A physical description of each prisoner is sometimes recorded in these registers.

STAGE 6   **British newspapers**
British Library, C&BROs and local history libraries
Newspapers invariably reported local crimes and give names of criminals and details of the offence. Local newspapers are usually available at local reference libraries as well as the British Library Newspaper Library.

STAGE 7   **Petitions** (see Chapter 5 and Appendices 9 and 22)
TNA: *HO 17–19, HO 47–49, HO 54, HO 56, PC 1* (some *HO 47* published by the List and Index Society, see Bibliography)
Petitions were sent by relatives and friends of convicts to the authorities asking for clemency. There is little evidence to show that any of these were effective in gaining a prisoner's release, though sometimes a reduced sentence was forthcoming.

STAGE 8   **Home Office Warrants** – pardons, reprieves and related correspondence (see Appendices 10 and 22)

TNA: *HO 13, HO 15, HO 47* (Some *HO 47* published by the List and Index Society, see Bibliography)

STAGE 9   **Transportation order books** (see Appendix 8)
TNA: *ASSI 24*
The transportation order books are to be found for the Western Circuit of Assizes only, which include: Cornwall, Devon, Dorset, Somerset, Hampshire (often recorded as Southampton), and Wiltshire. They list everyone who was given a transportation sentence.

STAGE 10   **Sheriffs' cravings** (see Appendix 11)
TNA: *E 370*
These are requests by county sheriffs for payment by the Treasury for the expenses incurred in maintaining criminals in gaol and for conveying convicts who had been sentenced to a term of transportation from gaols to prison hulks. They usually name the convicts and the prison hulk to which they were being sent.

STAGE 11   **Books of sheriffs' payments** (see Appendix 11)
TNA: *T 90*
The books list payments made to county sheriffs by the Treasury and expenses for judges and gaolers.

STAGE 12   **Treasury warrants** (see Appendix 11)
TNA: *T 53*
The warrants include sheriffs' conviction money, which was paid out to people involved in apprehending and convicting criminals.

STAGE 13   **Prison hulk records** (see Chapter 4 and Appendix 7)
TNA: *ADM 6, AO 3, HCA 1, HO 6, HO 7, HO8, HO 9, HO 47, PC 1, PC 2, PCOM 2, T1, T38*
These records include details of the convicts held on prison hulks. They usually give the name and age of each convict, the date and place of their trial and the sentence of the court. They also provide the date of a convict's transfer to a transportation ship. The name of the ship is often given, together with its destination.

STAGE 14   **Convict transportation records arranged by ships** (see Appendix 14 and 17)
TNA: *HO 11, AO 3, ADM 108, ADM 102, PC 1, TS 18*
a. *HO 11*: Home Office lists of convicts on board transportation ships name each convict with the date and place of trial and the term of sentence.
b. *AO 3*: Audit Department records give the costs incurred by private contractors who undertook the transportation of convicts. The records include the names of convicts and the ships.
c. *TS 18*: Treasury Solicitors' records include contracts for the transportation of convicts, giving the names of the convicts, date and place of trial and the sentence.
d. *PC 1*: Privy Council correspondence includes lists of convicts and the names of the transportation ships.
e. *ADM 108*: Admiralty records give the names of transportation ships and

list the convicts on board, together with guards, the wives and children of the guards, and the ship's company.

f. *ADM 102*: Admiralty hospital musters are monthly musters of seamen and marines and occasionally include references to sick convicts from transportation ships.

STAGE 15   Ships' records
TNA: *CO 201, AO 3, ADM 108, ADM 102, ADM 153, TS 18*
Colonial Office correspondence includes reports by ships' masters and medical officers of irregular and unusual events at sea.
Admiralty correspondence *(ADM 1)* includes correspondence from naval captains. (*ADM 1* is accessed by the use of the digests and indices in *ADM 12*.)

STAGE 16   Ships' captains' logs (see Appendix 19)
TNA: *ADM 51*

STAGE 17   Ships masters' logs (see Appendix 19)
TNA: *ADM 52, ADM 54*

STAGE 18   Ships' lieutenants' logs (see Appendix 19)
National Maritime Museum (arranged under the name of the lieutenant and *not* the name of the ship).

STAGE 19   Ships' surgeons' journals and Admiralty hospital musters (see Appendix 19)
TNA: *ADM 101, ADM 102, MT 32*

STAGE 20   Foreign Office correspondence from the Canary Islands
TNA: *FO 772*: British Foreign Office correspondence from Tenerife, Canary Islands, sometimes gives details of British ships entering and leaving Tenerife.

STAGE 21   Port records at the Cape Archives (South Africa)
These record the name of each ship and the date it entered and departed from The Cape. The ship's captain's name is given, together with type of cargo.

STAGE 22   Australian newspapers – *Sydney Gazette*, etc.
TNA: *CO 201* and British Library

STAGE 23   Convict muster rolls for New South Wales and Tasmania (see Appendix 15)
TNA: *HO 10* (Some convict muster rolls have been published, see Bibliography.)

STAGE 24   Census of New South Wales, 1828 (see Appendix 16)
TNA: *HO 10* (this has been published in full, see Bibliography)

STAGE 25   Pardons and tickets of leave (see Appendix 18)
TNA: *CO 201*

STAGE 26   Miscellaneous convict records (see Appendix 18)
TNA: *CO 201, CO 207, CO 386*

CHAPTER 1

THE FIRST FLEET TO NEW SOUTH WALES

The First Fleet to New South Wales left Portsmouth on 13 May 1787, sailing via Tenerife (Canary Islands), Rio de Janeiro (Brazil) and Cape of Good Hope (South Africa), arriving at Sydney Cove on 26 January 1788. The cost of feeding everyone on board the ships was paid for by the Treasury. Victualling lists for the convicts, both male and female, and their children, and marine guards and their wives and children, have been discovered at The National Archives, London. All the convicts and marines and their families are named. The lists include the names of children born on the voyage and also the names of those who died.

TNA ref T 46/22 A List of People Victualled at Teneriffe, Rio Janeiro and the Cape of Good Hope bound for New South Wales

There then follow lists giving the names of men, women and children. The lists include Royal Marines but not government officials or Royal Navy personnel. There is a list of children born on the voyage and also a list of those who died.

Table 1.1: A List of Officers and Men with their Wives and Children belonging to the Garrison intended for this Settlement at New South Wales that were Victualled by order of His Excellency the Governor at the following Places: At Teneriffe from 5th to 10th June 1787 both days included – 6 days; Rio Janeiro from 8th August to 2nd Sept. 1787 both days included – 26 days; Cape of Good Hope from 15th October to 11th November both days included – 28 days. (TNA: T 46/22)

No.	Names	Quality
1	James Campbell	Captain Marines
	John Shea	"
	Jas. Meredith	Captain Lieut
	Watkin Tench	"
5	Jam. Maxwell	First Lieut
	Geo. Johnstone	"
	John Creswell	"
	Robt. Kellow	"
	John Poulden	"
10	John Johnstone	"
	Jas. Mat. Sharp	"

	Thos. Davey	"
	Thos. Timins	"
	Ralph Clarke	Second Lieut
	etc.	
	—	
138	Richd Asky	Private
	Thos. Bulmore	"
140	Thos. Spencer	"
	Abraham Hand	"
	Jas. Healey	"
	John Eastey	"
	Jno Brown	"
145	Jno Gannon	"
	Fras Mee	"
	Jno Escott	"
	Richd Dukes	"
	Thos. Swinerton	"
150	Jas Kirby	"
	Chas. Green	"
	John Woods	"
	Alexr Mc Donald	"
	Wm Dew	"
155	Jno Clayton	"
	etc.	

Table 1.2: A List of Convicts, Men, Women and Children that were Victualled by Order of His Excellency the Governor at the following Places: Teneriffe – 6 days; Rio Janeiro – 26 days; Cape of Good Hope – 28 days. (TNA: T 46/22)

No.	Names
1	Nathl Lucas
	John Fuller
	Richd Lyne
	Jno Williams (1st)
5	Jno Williams (2nd)
	Jno Mosley
	Thos. Josephs
	Wm Reed
	Jno Carney
10	Geo. Fry
	Jas. Campbell
	Wm Wordsall

	Wm Johnson
	Jas. Morrisby
15	Wm Bell
	Edwd Humphry
	Wm Hubbard (1st)
	Nichs Todd
	Saml Mobbs
20	Robt Morgan
	Wm Snailham
	Jno Rowe
	Edw Miles
	Wm Rowe
25	Stepn Johns
	Jno Richards
	Edwd Willen
	Jno Mullers
	Jno Ruffler
30	Corn^s Teague
	Jas Ruse
	Wm Cockow
	Wm Philimore
	Josh Wright
35	Josh Hatten
	Dav^d Kelpack
	Thos Eccles
	Jno Thomas
	Jas Thompson
40	Henry Vincent
	James Wallbourne
	Jno Welsh
	Chas Williams
	Wm Connelly
45	Jacob Norrish
	Jno Lawrell
	Richd Middleton
	Chas Peal
	Richd Percivill
50	Jno Rougless
	James Smith
	Robt Williams
	Wm Cole
	Jas Clark
	etc.

These are to Certify the Right Hon'ble the Lord Commissioners of His Majesty's Treasury – That the Convicts, men and women with their children as named in the foregoing list were actually Victualled by the Commissary on board the different Transports at the following places, the number of days as against each of their names Expressed according to the following Rations. Viz.

At Teneriffe

Marines	One pound of Bread, one pound of Beef, one pint of Wine each per day, and four ounces of Butter each on the two serving days.
Women	Half a pound of Bread, half a pound of Beef, half a pint of Wine each per day, and two ounces of Butter each on the two serving days.
Children	One quarter of a pound of Bread, one quarter of a pound of Beef each per day and one ounce of Butter each on the two serving days.

At Rio de Janeiro

Marines	One pound of Rice, one pound & a quarter of Beef and half a pint of Rum each day.
Women	One pound of Rice, one pound & a quarter of Beef and one quarter of a pint of Rum each per day.
Children	One pound of Rice, and three quarters of a pound of Beef each per day.

At the Cape of Good Hope

By Contract with Messrs Petrus Johannes De Witt & Jan Fredk. Kirsten at the following Rations.

Marines	One pound of Beef or Mutton, one pound & a half of Soft Bread & one pint of Wine per day, with nine ounces of Butter each per week.
Women	One pound or Beef or Mutton, one pound & a half of Soft Bread with half a pint of Wine per day & five ounces of Butter each per week.

At Teneriffe

Convict Men & Women	Three quarters of a pound of Bread, three quarters of a pound of Beef each per day & three ounces of Butter each on the two serving days
Children	One quarter of a pound of Bread, one quarter of a pound of Beef each per day & one ounce of Butter each on the two serving days.

At Rio de Janeiro

Convict Men & Women	One pound of Rice and one pound and a quarter of Beef each per day.
Children	One pound of Rice & three quarters of a pound of Beef each per day.

At the Cape of Good Hope

By Contract with Messrs Petrus Johannes De Witt & Jan Fredreick Kersten at the following Rations. Viz.

Convict Men & Women — One pound of Beef or Mutton and one pound & a half of Soft Bread each per day.

Children — Three quarters of a pound of Beef or Mutton & one pound & a half of Soft Bread each per day.

Given under my hand on board His Majesty's Ship *Sirius* in Table Bay, Cape of

Good Hope, November 12th 1787.

A. Phillip

Table 1.3: Births and Deaths were recorded. *(TNA: T 46/22)*

Mary Cook	marine's wife	died 17th Oct.
Jane Davis, born 9th May 1787	marine's child	died 12th July
Daniel Dougherty	marine's child	born 10th July 1787
Elizabeth Scott	marine's child	born 29th August 1787
Samuel Richards	marine's child	born 9th October 1787
Elizabeth Wright	marine's child	born 17th October 1787
Mary Spencer	convict's child	born 1st July 1787
Charlotte Braud	convict's child	born 8th September 1787
John Hart	convict's child	born 6th October 1787
Henrietta Langley	convict's child	born 21st October 1787
Thomas Smith (2nd)	convict	died 4th July
George Sharp	convict	died 24th September
Jno Ward	convict	died 29th June
Isaac Rogers	convict	died 21st July
Josh Longsheet	convict	died 19th July
Jno Hartley	convict	died 5th August
Patk Delaney	convict	died 23rd June
William Brown	convict	died 19th September
Jno Clark	convict	died 6th June
Elizabeth Beckford	woman convict	died 11th July
Jane Bonnor	woman convict	died 30th July
Thomas Mason	convict's child	died 29th September

The following summarises the number of men, women and children in the First Fleet, but these figures do not include the government officials and naval personnel:

Marine Officers and Men	212
Marines' wives	30
Marines' children	22
Male Convicts	559
Female Convicts	192
Convicts' Children	17

In addition to these figures there were 15 children born on the voyage one of which died. Other Deaths on the Voyage: 9 male convicts; 2 female convicts; 1 male child of a convict.

CHAPTER 2

CRIMINAL REGISTERS, CALENDARS OF PRISONERS AND COURT LEGAL PROCEEDINGS

(See Appendices 4, 5 and 8)

CRIMINAL REGISTERS

Among the Home Office records at The National Archives is a series of bound volumes known as Criminal Registers (see Appendix 4). Those for the Old Bailey (Middlesex) are recorded as *Series I; TNA document class HO 26*. They date from 1791 and continue in this series to 1849. Volumes for all other counties in England and Wales are in *Series II; TNA documents class HO 27*. They commence in 1805 and continue to 1892. Middlesex, from 1850, continues with the rest of the country in Series II. Series II often has several volumes for one year, and each year is arranged alphabetically by county, and within each county chronologically by date of court hearing. Occasionally some counties, and some courts within counties, are bound out of order and the researcher is advised to search the whole of each volume to ensure that part of a county has not been overlooked. It should also be noted that the county of Hampshire is entered as 'Hampshire' from 1805 to 1837 and as 'Southampton' from 1838 to 1891. Shropshire is entered as 'Shropshire' from 1805 to 1808 and as 'Salop' from 1809 to 1891. Welsh counties from 1805 to 1814 are entered after English counties; that is after Yorkshire. From 1815 to 1845 Welsh counties are listed alphabetically with English counties, and from 1855 are again listed after the English counties. This series does not include Scotland or Ireland.

The Criminal Registers list all persons in England and Wales who have been committed for trial for indictable offences whether found guilty or not. They give the date and place of trial, whether at Borough Sessions, Quarter Sessions, or Assizes. A very brief note of the crime is given, together with the sentence of the court. From 1834 to 1848 the age of the accused is usually given together with the Degree of Literacy (whether the accused could read and write). Some examples of entries of those sentenced to a term of transportation are tabulated on pages 30 and 31.

The Middlesex Criminal Registers (1791–1849) often provide additional information, such as physical description of the prisoner – height, colour of hair, eyes and complexion – as well as their age and trade. The place of residence of the accused is often given and occasionally their place of birth. In the case of a transportation sentence, the name of the prison hulk to which the convict was transferred is also recorded. Sometimes the name of the transportation vessel on which the convict was to sail to Australia is given. Persons awaiting trial at the Old Bailey were usually held at Newgate Gaol.

Both series of Criminal Registers are accessible via www.ancestry.co.uk

The following is an example of an entry from a Middlesex Register, resulting in a transportation sentence:

Criminal Registers, Series I

TNA ref HO 26/56

Date when brought to Newgate	22 October 1791
Name	Thomas Eagleton
Age	22
Height	5 feet 2 inches
Hair	Brown
Eyes	Grey
Complexion	Pale
Born	Saint Albans [Herfordshire]
Trade	Baker
To what place committed	Newgate
By whom	Court of King's Bench
Crime	Petit Larceny
When and where tried	22 October 1791, Sessions Place
Before whom	Mainwaring
Sentence	Transported 7 years
If capitally convicted, when and where executed	—
If transported, when	6 March 1793, see order page 47[1]
On board what hulk	*Lyon* Hulk
At what place	Portsmouth Harbour
To whose care	James Bradley

1. Page 47 states: 'Order for Transportation of 30 Convicts to the charge of James Bradley Esq. Overseer of Convicts on board the Hulk at Portsmouth.'

Criminal Registers, Series II

Table 2.1: Examples from Criminal Registers, Series II (*HO 27*), which for the period 1834–48 gives the degree of literacy and age of the accused.

Name	Degree of Literacy	Age	Sentenced		Offence	Sentence
			Place	Date		
Robert Simpson	Well	23	Cumberland County Assizes	30/7/1836	Cattle Stealing	Life Trans.
Charles Bayford	No	27	Essex, County Assizes	11/7/36	Burglary	Death, commuted to Life Trans.
John Cliridge alias Pratley	Imperfect	26	Gloucester, County Assizes	29/3/1836	Feloniously stealing a Deer	7 yrs. Trans.
Joseph Abel	Well	57	Hereford County Assizes	2/8/1836	Forgery of a deed	Life Trans.
Edwin Coulter	No	17	Kent, Maidstone	30/6/1836	Stealing a fixture	7 yrs. Trans.
James Kershaw	No	19	Lancaster Co. Sess. Salford	4/7/1836	Larceny before convicted of Felony	7 yrs. Trans.
William Brown	Imperfect	54	Lincoln, County Assizes	16/7/1836	Maliciously stabbing with intent	Death commuted to Life Trans.
James Paul	Read	28	Norfolk, County Assizes	28/3/1836	Night Poaching	14 yrs. Trans.
Daniel Ball	Read	18	Stafford	29/2/1836	Larceny, two convictions and fined 6d	7 yrs. Trans.
William Bonill	R & W	68	Surrey	21/10/1836	Sodomy, an accessory before the fact	14 yrs. Trans.
Charles Price	R & W	21	Worcester	10/3/1836	Maliciously attempting to shoot a person with intent to murder	Death commuted to Life Trans.
Thomas Gogley	R & W	19	York Leeds Boro. Sess.	20/4/1836	Larceny	7 yrs. Trans.

Table 2.2: For the period 1805–33, and 1849 onwards, Criminal Registers, Series II, do not give the degree of literacy or age of each of the accused.

Name	Sentenced		Offence	Sentence
	Place	Date		
Joseph Blewett and Edward Harwood and William Richards	Devon, Midsummer Q.S.	1850	Ripping & stealing lead from a dwelling h'se. Their sentence was afterwards remitted on their severally offering to serve in the navy, they were delivered accordingly	7 yrs. Trans.
Frederick Fowler	Bedford Q.S.	13/10/1850	Breaking and stealing from a building within the curtilage, before convicted of felony	7 yrs. Trans.
Charles Stroud	Berkshire, Epi.Sess. at Abingdon	31/12/1849	Sheep Stealing, before convicted of felony	15 yrs. Trans.
James Millard	Brecknock, Assizes at Brecon	22/3/1850	Wounding with intent to do G.B.H.	7 yrs. Trans.
Dennis White alias Lodge	Chester, at Chester Assizes	30/3/1850	Feloniously uttering counterfeit coin having been before convicted of uttering	7 yrs. Trans.
George May	Devon Q.S. at the Castle, Exeter	26/2/1850	Larceny by a servant, two convictions	2 months pris. 1st conviction. 10 yrs.Trans. 2nd conviction
Robert Pringle	Durham, Assizes at Durham	24/7/1850	Rape on an Infant.	Life Trans.
Thomas Hookey	Southampton, Assizes, The Castle, Winchester	28/2/1850	Embezzlement by servant in Post Office	10 yrs. Trans.
John Turner	Stafford, Assizes at Stafford	13/3/1850	Night Poaching to the number of 3	10 yrs. Trans.
Stephen Boxall	Surrey, Central Criminal Court	1850	Manslaughter	Life Trans.
William Bennett	Gloucester, Assizes at Gloucester	30/3/1850	Maliciously wounding to maim	7 yrs. Trans.
Elijah Herbert	Hereford, Assizes at Hereford	23/3/1850	Burglary	20 yrs. Trans.
Mary Jennings	Somerset, Assizes at Taunton	28/3/1855	Feloniously attempting to suffocate her child in a cesspool	Life Trans.

A list of men and women convicted at Surrey Lent Assizes in 1802, including those given a transportation sentence. (Surrey History Centre)

CALENDARS OF PRISONERS

(See Appendix 5)

Pre-trial Calendars

These are to be found in County Record Offices and at The National Archives. They supplement the information given in the Criminal Registers. They record the name(s) of the person(s) bringing the charge and usually give the age of the accused, and the crime with which they have been accused.

Pre-trial Calendars of Prisoners were drawn up and circulated before the court sat so that the magistrates or judges and other court officials, and the jury (where appropriate), had advance notice of the cases to be tried. They were printed in most counties from the late eighteenth century and usually have an index of surnames of the accused on the front page giving the case number of each. Before the printed versions were produced they were handwritten in various formats.

Post-trial Calendars

These are similar in format to the Pre-trial Calendars and, in addition, include details of any previous convictions, with a record of the sentences given out by the court for the current crime if found guilty. They also have a note of Degree of Instruction as to whether the accused is able to read and write. This is answered as 'R & W' (can read and write), or 'Yes' or 'No', 'Well' or 'Imperfect'.

A

KALENDAR

OF THE

Prisoners

IN THE CUSTODY OF THE KEEPER OF

HIS MAJESTY'S GAOL,

IN AND FOR THE COUNTY OF

SURREY

AND THE

House of Correction,

AT NEWINGTON,

FOR THE

General Quarter Session

OF THE PEACE,

OF OUR SOVEREIGN LORD THE KING,

TO BE HOLDEN

(BY ADJOURNMENT)

At Newington,

IN AND FOR THE SAID COUNTY,

On MONDAY, 24th of OCTOBER, 1814.

RICHARD BISH ESQ.

Barnes and Robins (late Grant) Printers, No. 3, Kent Street, Borough.

The first page of the Calendar of Prisoners for the Adjourned Quarter Sessions for Surrey, 24 October 1814. (SURREY R.O. ref QS 2/6/1814 Michaelmas)

COURT LEGAL PROCEEDINGS

(See Appendix 8)

The following is a selection of Quarter Sessions cases in which each defendant was found guilty and sentenced to a term of transportation.

Berks RO ref Q/SR 336, Sessions Rolls

Berkshire Epiphany Sessions, 13th January 1818, at Reading
The King v Richard Eagle and James Tocock

The examination of John Cotterell of East Hampstead, broom maker on oath says that on Wednesday evening last at nine o'clock he saw his black spotted pig in the stye at Easthampstead that soon as it was light on Thursday morning he missed his pig. That he tracked the pig from the stye for near six miles to Frimley that he went up to the house of George Crozier a pig killer to which house door he traced the pig that he saw the pig hanging up just killed which he is positive was his pig. That Crozier was willing to shew the pig, that Crozier said he had bought it of two men. The pig is worth about three pounds.

X The mark of John Cotterell

Henry Cotterell cousin and living close to John Cotterell of Easthampstead went with John Cotterell in search of the pig and confirms on oath the above statement of John Cotterell.

X The mark of Henry Cotterell

Part of the list of convicts under sentence of transportation held at the House of Correction, Cold Bath Fields, 18 September 1818. (TNA ref PCI/69)

George Crozier on oath says that on Tuesday last two men came to him at Frimley and asked if he would buy a pig. Crozier said he must see it first. They said they would bring one on Monday morning. They did bring it and he gave three pounds for it and scalded and hung it up when Henry and John Cotterell claim it.

X The mark of George Crozier

Richard Eagle and James Tocock state that they have nothing to say to the charge made against them by Henry Cotterell of Easthampstead, Berkshire of stealing a pig on Wednesday last.

Berks RO ref Q/SO 11

Quarter Sessions Order Book

Ordered by the Court that Richard Eagle and James Tocock convicted of stealing on 12th day of November last in the parish of Easthampstead one pig of the price and value of ten pounds of the goods and chattels of one John Cotterell the said Richard Eagle to be transported for the term of 7 years and the said James Tocock to be confined for two years hard labour in the House of Correction at Reading.

Berks RO ref Q/SR 339, Sessions Rolls

Berkshire Michaelmas Sessions, 20th October 1818, at Reading
The King v Francis Smith and Hannah the wife of Francis Smith

The examination of Mary Anne Cowderoy of Bucklebury in the county of Berks, spinster, taken on oath this 2nd day of October 1818.

Who saith that during the last two years up to the month of June last a great number of pigeons young and old to the amount of ten or twelve dozen at least, the property of her mother Sarah Cowderoy widow, have been stolen out of her dovecote at Bucklebury aforesaid. Also about a year and a quarter ago ten or twelve chickens, a duck, and gallini out of a peat house. Also about twelve months ago a considerable number of chickens at various times out of a hen house and peat house. Also about Christmas last about eight or ten turkeys from the turkey house. Also at various times lately a considerable number of depredations have been committed in her mother's garden and vegetables and fruit stolen therefrom and particularly about the month of May last on a Saturday night about thirty cabbages were stolen from her mother's garden and the next morning this examinant observed near where they grew the print of a child's shoe, tipped and nailed, on the ground and about a month afterwards some more cabbages were stolen and about five weeks ago half a bushel of onions were stolen from the greenhouse. That she also verily believes from the small quantity of milk produced from her mother's cows the same had been from time to time previously milked and the milk taken away. That about Christmas last at several times about seven knives and forks were stolen and since two silver tea spoons and a salt spoon and some iron spoons, also soap and candles, knife and glass cloths, towels, about six women's white cotton stockings, a tin, bucket, belts, baskets and other articles and things the property of her said mother have been stolen at the parish of Bucklebury aforesaid with some babe's linen the property of Mr Thomas Wartons. And this examinant further saith that on Friday the twenty first day of August last this examinant went into her mother's barn with her servant Harriet Lawrence in order to feed some rabbits in an adjoining rabbit house, she then observed the wheat which had been thrashed was placed in one heap and pressed down smooth, and the servant locked the barn door in her presence and the key was brought into the house. On the following morning this examinant accompanied the servant a second time to the said barn and discovered on entering therein that the opposite doors which opened into the Lane were not in their usual state of security but appeared to have been strained as the one door from the bottom to the lock was separated at least three inches from the other. (A few days before this examinant and her cousin had been in the barn to get some straw for a bonnet and they examined the door in order to discover whether persons in the lane could see them and saw no aperture but the small crevices between the planks of which the door was composed and the same door was quite close in other respects.) That this examinant observed that the wheat was not in the same state as it had been left when she was last in the barn, the marks of the rake were erased and heaps were in rough state. This examinant noticed it to the servant and said she was afraid she had let the fowls in, which the servant denied. That the thresher first threshed three days and left the heap as before stated and on his return to finish the threshing this examinant said to him James are you sure the barn is secure as the wheat does not appear in the state in which you left it. To which he replied he did not know how anyone could get into the barn as the doors were locked, but that when he winnowed it he should know how much he ought to have. That the prisoner Francis Smith on the morning of Wednesday the twenty sixth day of August last offered his services to assist in winnowing and was employed for that purpose. And in the evening of Saturday the twenty ninth of the same month this examinant missed about half a bushel of onions out of the greenhouse which she had seen a day before in their usual state and quantity, and the next day one of the cows was found to have been milked dry and on the Monday this examinant suspecting George Smith the boy (in consequence of his having before taken milk) questioned him when he acknowledged having stolen the milk. That the said boy George Smith has worked for this examinant's said mother for about two years on and off. That the prisoner Francis Smith has also occasionally worked for her mother and that at the time the gallini was taken the prisoner was mowing for her and she believes Smith also Thomas Alisbury. That the pair of stockings now produced by her servant Sophia Stacey and also the two knives and house cloths also produced by her are severally the property of her said mother and part of what has been stolen as aforesaid.

signed Mary Anne Cowderoy

The Examination of Sarah Cowderoy of Bucklelbury in the county of Berks, widow, taken on oath this 2nd day of October 1818.
Who saith that about a month ago she observed some onions her property had been stolen from the Grass Walk in the garden. And that a little before last midsummer in the night she was awoke by a violent ringing of the bell in her daughter's room which she answered by her own and went herself to her daughter's room. That she called the servants up who struck a light she sent one of them down stairs who returned and said that everything was safe. The examinant has other times been alarmed by the hearing of noises and has in consequence been obliged to procure men to sleep in the house as a protection one time in particular the whole family sat up till 3 or 4 o'clock in the morning in consequence of noises which had alarmed them.

signed Sarah Cowderoy

The Examination of James Brown of the parish of Brimpton in the county of Berks, labourer, taken on oath this 2nd day of October 1818.

Who saith that he has worked at Brimpton for Sarah Cowderoy and her late husband for 30 years and since the said Sarah Cowderoy has resided at Bucklebury in the said county he has occasionally been employed there. And that since last harvest he has worked at Bucklebury in threshing wheat, after threshing part thereof he stayed away and worked for Mr Shaw of Brimpton and he left the heap of wheat in the barn of the said Sarah Cowderoy tight and patted with a rake in his usual way and on his return to finish threshing it he found the heap had been disturbed at one end and appeared to be smaller than he had left it. He asked the servant maid when she came to feed the poultry who had been in the barn for the heap seemed to have been disturbed. She told him she knew nothing about it, he finished threshing and on Wednesday the twenty sixth of August, he winnowed the wheat and was surprized to find a deficiency of seven bushels according to his former calculation. He has been a thresher for ten years past and the barn doors of the said Sarah Cowderoy in the Lane are never open but when her men or servants are winnowing therein.

X James Brown his mark

The Examination of Sophia Stacey servant to Mrs Cowderoy of Bucklebury in the county of Berks, taken on oath this 2nd day of October 1818.

Who saith that for about two years past she has lived in the service of the said Sarah Cowderoy at Bucklebury and that in the course of that time numerous articles and things, the property of the said Sarah Cowderoy, have at various times been stolen from her house there and among them towels, knife cloths, white cotton stockings, silver tea spoons, salt spoons and many other depredations have been at different times committed upon the premises of the said Sarah Cowderoy. And that on Tuesday the twenty second day of September last she went to the house of the prisoner Francis Smith about half a mile by the desire of her mistress to desire his children to come down to her house and this Examinant there saw the pair of white cotton stockings now produced by her mark C lying on the kitchen table and seeing Hannah Smith one of the children has a pair of worstead stockings which did not match with her frock asked her why she did not put those stockings on (meaning the said cotton ones) and the girl replied they were dirty and this Examinant on taking them up discovered they were her mistresses but desired the said Hannah Smith to pull off the worstead stockings and put on the cotton ones, which she did and then wore them down to the said Sarah Cowderoy's to whom this Examinant named the circumstances of her finding the stockings and in the evening this Examinant desired the said Hannah Smith to pull off the said cotton stockings which she did and they have ever since been in this Examinant's possession. And that the next day having missed an apron of hers she went to the house of the said Francis Smith to enquire for it and found the said Hannah Smith upstairs making a bed, and turning the bed over this Examinant discovered the knife cloth produced by her and marked with the number 6 and letter C which she is positive is the property of the said Sarah Cowderoy and one of those stolen as aforesaid and that at the time of such discovery this Examinant asked the said Hannah Smith if she knew what cloth it was to which she replied 'No', and turning round to her sister Mary said 'Do you know Mary' and she said 'No' and in almost the same breath in a fearful manner said Oh! our Hannah and they both appeared confused and said no more about it. And that on the twenty eighth day of September last (Monday) still suspecting her apron was at Smith's house she went there and saw the said Mary Smith whom she told she would give some halfpence if she would give her her apron and she said the apron was not there but she could find something of Mrs Cowderoy's and went up stairs immediately and brought down the cloth now produced and marked R3 J.M. and gave to Miss Mary Anne Cowderoy and she gave her a penny and the next day she said George, meaning her brother, had brought it there.

X Sophia Stacey her mark

Berks RO ref Q/SO 12

Quarter Sessions Order Book

Ordered by the Court that Francis Smith convicted of Stealing on 2nd October 1818 in the parish of Bucklebury seven bushels of Wheat in the chaff, of the value of ten pence, the goods and chattels of one Sarah Cowderoy widow, be transported for the term of seven years.

Ordered by the Court that Hannah the wife of Francis Smith convicted of receiving four knives of the value of one penny, three forks of the value of one penny, six pairs of woman's cotton stockings of the value of two pence, two knife cloths of the value of one penny, two glass cloths of the value of one penny, and two towels of the value of one penny the goods and chattels of Sarah Cowderoy, widow, to be confined in the House of Correction at Reading for one year.

Dor RO Quarter Sessions Rolls

Dorset Michaelmas Sessions, 19th October 1824 at Bridport

Mary Sample, aged 20, of Ringwood [Gaol Book says of Ringwood but indictment says of Blandford Forum], Hampshire, hawker, single woman, and Susannah Jefferies, aged 26 of Blandford Forum, charged with stealing banknotes of the value of £26 the property of William Lambert of Blandford St. Mary.

The deposition of William Lambert of Blandford St. Mary, Dorset, yeoman, taken 17th September 1824. Who saith that as he was passing down Salisbury Street in the town of Blandford about 9 o'clock last evening (the 16th) he was accosted by a party of men & women two of whom laid hold of his arms and asked him to give them something to drink, & another of the party, a man with a dark coat took hold of him, he then missed his money when supposing some of them to have taken it, he accused the women of it, that one of the women fell down on the arrival of the constable. That the money he lost consisted of sixteen one pound bills or notes of different banks (to wit Southampton, Blandford & Wimborne) and two five pound notes one of them of the Sturminster & the other of the Blandford Bank. That he had seen the said notes & put them into his pocket at the house of Mr Wm. Newman which he last left; after the scuffle he saw the said two five pound notes which Mr Simmonds of Blandford, builder, held in his hands. That the notes now produced by the constable namely the two five pound notes, one of Blandford and the other of the Sturminster Bank are the same he lost. That the two women now in custody who call themselves Mary Sample & Susannah Jefferies are two of the women who were present when the scuffle took place and the said two women were those who took hold of him & asked him for something to drink.

signed Wm. Lambert

The deposition of William Boucher, shoemaker, taken 17th September 1824. Who saith: That hearing a row about 10 o'clock in the evening of the 16th September he went to the place where he heard Mary Sample crying 'murder', and that on a light being brought out he saw Mary Sample fall down and throw her arms open as if throwing something from her. That James Jarrett joined him and they went with a light to the place where the scuffle had been and after searching, found about 6 yards from the head of Mary Sample, who was then laying down, two notes which he gave to Mr Simmonds who said they were two notes of £5 each. That James Garrett wished him to go to another place & he suspected by his manner that he was one of the party.

signed William Boucher

The deposition of Joseph Cantrill of Blandford Forum, cabinet maker, taken 17th September 1824. Who saith that having been sent for as constable of the Borough of Blandford he went to a place called the Plocks when he took into his custody Mary Sample and Susanna Jefferies by desire of Mr Simmonds. That Simmonds gave him two five pound notes now produced which he knows to be the same by a mark which he put upon them at the time. That he searched the prisoners and on the person of Mary Sample he found a purse containing a quantity of pawn broker's duplicates, and on the person of James Garrett a five pound note purporting to be of the Weald of Kent Bank, and nine shillings & sixpence in silver and two duplicates.

signed J. Cantrill

The deposition of John Simmonds of Blandford, builder, taken 17th September 1824. Who saith that between the hours of nine and ten last evening (the 16th inst.) hearing a screaming near his house he went out to the place from where it proceeded & saw Mr Wm. Lambert of Blandford St. Mary there with two women, Mary Sample & Susanna Jefferies in his hands. This deponent then sent for the constable, that Mary Sample fell down & struggled and threw her arms open and this deponent suspecting that she might have thrown away something called for a light and desired some of the bystanders to look round. That shortly afterwards William Butcher of Blandford said 'Here are two of the notes.' That this deponent took them of the said William Butcher and opening them by the aid of a candle found them to be five pounds, one of the Blandford and one of the Sturminster Bank. That William Butcher said to this deponent, 'That man (pointing to one of the prisoners) who calls himself James Garrett appears to know something about it.' upon which he gave James Garrett in charge to the constable, having ascertained from Susannah Jefferies that the said James Garrett was connected with her husband's party at the *Cricketers*. That this deponent said to Susannah Jefferies 'If you know anything of the money tell us all about it.' She said 'I know nothing of it, you may search me if you please, search the little one' meaning Mary Sample. That he attended the search of the said James Garrett. That the notes now produced are the same that William Butcher gave him last night and which he afterwards delivered to the constable.

signed John Simmonds

Mary Sample and Susannah Jefferies, both Guilty – 7 years Transportation and in the mean time to be kept in hard labor.

Dor RO Quarter Sessions Rolls

Dorset Epiphany Sessions, 6th January 1835 at Dorchester

Hannah Swayne, aged 43, of Tyneham, Purbeck, charged with stealing from Grace Mowlam one table cloth, one white petticoat, one black cloth shawl, one white calico apron marked GM and divers other articles.

The information and deposition of Grace Mowlam of Warbarrow, Dorset, taken 18th December 1834. Who on her oath saith: 'I live at Worbarrow, Purbeck. I am the widow of George Mowlam deceased. Between the hours of five and eleven o'clock in the morning of the 15th inst. (Monday) some person broke open a box locked in my dwelling house by the bottom of the box being forced off and five sovereigns & two guineas taken there from, also I missed from another box not locked a black cloth shawl, a pair of black stockings and from another I missed two dowless calico shifts, two calico pillow cases, two calico (white) aprons & a white striped petticoat. I also missed from a brunet box a flowered net cap with French white ribbon and tied with white strings. The white apron was marked GM. The stockings marked GM, one pillow case marked the same, and half cross bordered I also missed from a clothe basket. I also missed a large diaper table cloth, a pocket handkerchief marked GM, a pair of speckled gloves, a flannel petticoat, a thick cross bordered cap, one night cap, a book and a drawing or painting which I should know if I see it again. I perhaps might have lost other articles. The black shawl produced is my property, also the following articles are my property. 1 calico shift, 1 piece of calico not made up, 1 white calico apron marked GM, 1 pair of black worsted stockings marked GM, 1 colored pocket handkerchief marked GM, two white cross bordered muslin caps, 1 Holland apron, 1 worked net dress cap with French drawing ribbon and net strings, 1 cross bordered half handkerchief, 1 pair of worsted gloves, 1 book titled "The Great Importance of a Religious Life" with my name and my daughter Grace Hannah's name written therein, 1 piece of diaper, a book titled "Serious Advice to the Persons Who Have Been Sick," 1 shoe brush and the painting or drawing. The trunk and box from which all the above articles were taken belong to the Prisoner Hannah Swayne they have been in my house a considerable time, the prisoner Hannah Swayne lived in my house which she left on Tuesday and have not seen since till this day she being in custody at Wareham on a charge of stealing the above articles.'

The mark of X Grace Mowlam

The information and deposition of Henry Hellier of Tyneham, Dorset, taken 18th December 1834. Who saith: 'I am the Tythingman in Purbeck, on Tuesday evening last the 16th inst. a warrant was placed into my hands to apprehend Hannah Swayne on a charge of stealing diverse articles from Grace Mowlam at Worbarrow. I went to Weymouth the following morning the 17th inst. I apprehended her at the George Inn where I heard she was going to Guernsey. She had the trunks or boxes now produced with her. I did not search her. I brought her to Wareham and also the boxes. I delivered her and the boxes to the care of Mr Charley Card one of the constables when I got there.'

signed Henry Hellier

The information of Charles Henry Card of Wareham, Dorset, taken 18th December 1834. Who saith: 'I am one of the constables of Wareham. Last evening about

6 o'clock the prisoner Hannah Swayne was delivered into my custody, she was tipsy, the two boxes were also delivered into my care and have been so ever since. I told her she was to be searched when she delivered up a large purse containing £3-13-6 in silver and 9 pence halfpenny in coppers, also a smaller, a steel, purse containing four sovereigns and a half. She also delivered up a knife and keys of the two boxes. This morning the two boxes were also searched and the articles mentioned in the schedule were found which Grace Mowlam claimed as her property.'

signed Charles Henry Card

The information and deposition of Thomas Roe of West Lulworth, Dorset, taken 18th December 1834. Who saith: 'I am by trade a cordwainer. I know the prisoner Hannah Swayne. On Monday sometime in the day before I went to dinner the prisoner came to my house and bought a pocket handkerchief for 7d and 6 oranges, she asked me if I could change a sovereign if not a guinea. She gave my wife a guinea in my presence, my wife gave (in my presence) the prisoner the change, deducting what she had bought, the guinea produced is the same received from her. The same time the prisoner ordered a pair of shoes of me to be got ready by the next morning. The following morning Tuesday between 7 and 8 o'clock she came had her shoes and paid 5/6 for them. She said she was going to Weymouth, she had a small bundle with her.'

signed Thos. Roe

Hannah Swayne the prisoner in her defence says 'I claim the things. I never stole any thing from any one, the things I got I worked hard for and as to the money I sold my things and that's how I came by it. The black stockings Grace Mowlam gave me.'

[not signed]

Hannah Swayne, guilty – 7 years Transportation

Som HC ref QSR No. 406, Quarter Sessions Roll

Somerset Michaelmas Sessions, 13th October 1817, at Taunton

John Parsons, aged 15, labourer of Frome Selwood, Somerset. Charged with stealing a smock frock the property of James Coward.

The information of James Coward, shopkeeper, and Mary Vigor, spinster, both of Frome Selwood in the said County, taken upon oath before me Thomas Suginmer Champreys Esquire one of His Majesty's Justices of the Peace for the said County this second day of October 1817.
The said James Coward on his oath saith that this morning about ten o'clock one James Parsons came to his shop in which various articles were exposed for sale, at the time he the said James Coward was engaged in delivering some articles to a child, and enquired if he wanted any coal, immediately after which the child having quitted the shop returned back again and said the man had gone off with a smock frock.

The said Mary Vigor on her oath saith that this morning about half past ten o'clock as she was passing the shop of the said James Coward she saw John Parsons take from a hook on the outside of the shop door of the said James Coward a new smock frock and carry it away with him.

The said James Coward further states that on being informed of the taking away the smock frock by John Parsons he immediately followed him and overtook him at about thirty yards distance from his shop and upon taking in the said John Parsons into custody he discovered the smock frock concealed under his clothes after the which being now produced is proved to be his the said James Coward's property.

signed James Coward

the mark of X Mary Vigor

John Parsons, guilty – 7 years transportation.

Som HC ref QSR No. 600, Quarter Sessions Roll

Somerset Midsummer Sessions, 28th June 1853, at Bridgwater

William Snook, aged 22, groom of Kilmersdon, Somerset. Charged with stealing at Writhlington on 15th Dec. 1851, a horse the property of Henry Britten, of the value of £16.

The examination of Henry Britten of Writhlington in the County of Somerset, yeoman, Joseph Crutcher of Salisbury in the County of Wilts, horse dealer, and Edward Newport of the parish of Frome in the County of Somerset, Parish Constable. Taken upon Oath this first day of June, 1853 at Frome before Thomas Sunderland Harrison Esquire, one of Her Majesty's Justices of the Peace for the said County.

Henry Britten on his Oath saith, 'I am a farmer in Writhlington. In December 1851 I had a horse, my property on my premises which was missed on the 16th of that month. I saw the horse in my farm yard at 8 o'clock in the evening of the 15th December. There is a gate leading into the yard which is fastened by a hasp but not locked. I missed the horse from the yard on the morning of the 16th December at about 6 o'clock. I traced the horse to Salisbury and found him in the possession of Joseph Crutcher the younger, horse dealer at Salisbury on the 16th December. Mr Crutcher told me he had bought the horse in the market. I obtained possession of the horse at Salisbury on the 22nd Dec. The Prisoner had been in my employment up to the week before I lost the horse. I have never seen the Prisoner since until he was brought to Kilmersdon last Monday.'

signed Henry Britten

Joseph Crutcher on his Oath saith: 'I am a horse dealer living at Salisbury and I was living there in December 1851. On Tuesday the 16th Dec. 1851 I saw a horse in the market at Salisbury which a man was leading, and on my asking whose it was the man pointed out the prisoner. I then asked the Prisoner the price of the horse and who it belonged to. He said it belonged to his father, and the price was £16. He said his father was a farmer and wanted the money. I bought the horse of the Prisoner for £12 and paid him the money. I took from the Prisoner at the same time the warranty now produced which I saw him write.'

signed Joseph Crutcher

Edward Newport on his Oath saith: 'I am a Constable of Frome. From information I received I went to Southampton in search of the Prisoner, and I took him into custody there last Saturday evening. On Monday last the Prisoner told me that he got tipsy at Buckland Bell, or he should not have done it, and that he took the horse and went directly to Salisbury.'

signed Edward Newport

The foregoing depositions of Henry Britten, Joseph Crutcher Junr., and Edward Newport were duly taken before me this first day of June 1853.

signed Thos. Harrison

William Snook, guilty – 10 years Transportation

Sur HC ref QS 2/6/1814, Epiphany Sessions Papers and QS 3/5/12, Process Book

Surrey Epiphany Sessions, 11th January 1814, at Newington

Benjamin Ratty of Merton, labourer, committed 27th October 1813 by T. Evance, esq., charged on the oath of Anne Hudson with feloniously stealing at Merton three pairs of stockings and other articles, the property of Thomas Hudson.

Anne the wife of Thomas Hudson of Merton, printer, on her oath says, 'the three pair of stockings and shawl and two handkerchiefs now produced are the property of my husband and I hung them up to dry in my garden on Tuesday the 12th instant.'

Ann X Hudson her mark

Edy Cooper daughter of John Cooper of Merton aforesaid on her oath says, 'on that day I saw Benjamin Ratty get over the pales of Mrs Hudson's garden and take the said things off the line and go away with them across the fields.'

Edy X Cooper her mark

James Theobalds a constable of Tooting on his oath says, 'hearing of the robbery I went with others in pursuit of the prisoner and assisted in apprehending him and the articles now produced were found in a hedge where the prisoner had ran by and were delivered to me. I searched the prisoner and found upon him the two picklock keys now produced.'

signed James Theobalds

George Elliot of Fothergay Buildings, Clapham Common on his oath says, 'I assisted in pursuit of the prisoner and stopped him.'

signed George Ellyett

Amos Jackson son of Bartholomew Jackson of Putney within the said County on his oath says, 'I also assisted in pursuing the prisoner and picked up the articles produced in a hedge and delivered them to Theobald the constable.'

signed Amos Jackson

Sworn before me, 20th October 1813, T. Evance
Benjamin Ratty, guilty – 7 years Transportation.

Sur HC ref. QS 2/6/1830, Epiphany Sessions Papers and QS 3/5/14, Process Book

Surrey Epiphany Sessions, 12th January 1830, at Newington

George Curtis of Lambeth, labourer and Robert Kemp, labourer, committed 11th January 1830 by R.J. Chambers, esq., charged on the oath of James Palmer and others with feloniously stealing at Camberwell, cheese, his property.

The information of John Palmer of the Camberwell New Road in the parish of Saint Giles, Camberwell in the County of Surrey, cheesemonger, of William Clark, servant to

Jonathan Hawkins of the Sign of the *Duke of York* in the same Road, and of Thomas Currant, night constable of the Camberwell New Road Trust. Taken on oath this eleventh day of January in the Year of our Lord one thousand eight hundred and thirty before me Robert Joseph Chambers, esq., one of His Majesty's Justices of the Peace in and for the County of Surrey, at the Police Office, Union Hall, in the parish of Saint Saviour, in the said County of Surrey, upon the examination and in the presence and hearing of George Curtis and Robert Kemp then and there brought before me and charged with Felony.

And first the said John Palmer on oath saith, 'during the time I was getting my dinner on Saturday last I saw the two Prisoners standing by my shop window and a few minutes afterwards I saw one of them step into my shop and take the cheese now produced from out of the window they then both run away. I followed after them immediately and saw the prisoners both running together, the prisoner Curtis was carrying the cheese which I saw drop as I was pursuing him. I cried out "Stop Thief" but they both run down a turning and I lost sight of them. About five minutes afterwards the two prisoners were brought to me by the witness and I gave them into the custody of the witness Currant.'

signed John Palmer

The said William Clark on his oath says, 'at about 2 o'clock on Saturday afternoon last I heard the cry "stop thief" I immediately pursued the two prisoners across several fields when they both stopped and the prisoner Curtis took a knife, the same now produced, from out of his pocket and said if I attempted to stop him he would run me through. I secured them with the assistance of another man.'

X Wm. Clark his mark

The said Thomas Currant on his oath says, 'I received the prisoners on Saturday last from the prosecutor. I searched them and found the knife now produced in the prisoner Curtis's pocket.'

signed Thomas Currant

George Curtis – Guilty Transportation for Life
Robert Kemp – Guilty – Transportation for 7 years

INDICTMENT ROLLS

Sessions Rolls, which include depositions (sworn statements made by witnesses and defendants) as shown in the examples above do not survive for all counties for the transportation period. In such counties Calendars of Prisoners or Indictment Rolls may be the only record of Sessions cases. The Indictment Rolls give the place of residence of the accused with a summary of the crime. Calendars of Prisoners invariably give the age of the accused, with a summary of the crime. The following are examples.

Lancs RO ref QJI/1/188, Indictment Roll

Lancashire Epiphany Sessions, 19th January, at Salford

The Jurors of our Lord upon their Oaths present that Thomas Jones late of the Township of Great Bolton in the County of Lancashire, labourer, on the 4th day of January in the fifty fourth year of the Reign of our Sovereign Lord George the Third, at Great Bolton in the County aforesaid, one shawl of the value of one penny, one

handkerchief of the value on one penny and one brush of the value of one penny, of the goods and chattels of John Glassbrook then and there found and being, by force of Arms, feloniously did steal, take and carry away against the Peace of our said Lord King, his Crown and Dignity.
Witnesses: Thomas Barrett, Alice Glassbrook
Guilty – 7 years Transportation

Ports RO ref. S8/15

Portsmouth Borough Sessions for 23 July 1851 – Indictment

At the Sessions for the Borough of Portsmouth on 11th April 1851 John Williams was convicted of Felony. John Williams charged with having on 25th June 1851, at the parish of Portsea, feloniously stolen from the person of Elizabeth Nicholson, one shilling and two penny pieces, her monies.
Witnesses: Elizabeth Nicholson, Maria Windsor, William Windsor, Charles German.
Guilty – 10 years Transportation

Ports RO ref S7/1

The Calendar of Prisoners for 11 April 1851

John Williams, aged 19, mariner, charged with stealing a drinking glass [with William Brown, aged 19, mariner] the property of Joseph Adams. Williams and Brown were each sentenced to 2 months' imprisonment with hard labour.

CHAPTER 3

FORGERS OF BANKNOTES AND COINS

The directors of the Bank of England were naturally concerned about the forging of banknotes and coins, and paid agents and informers to report on any person involved in, or suspected of such practices. The archives of Freshfield, the solicitors who acted for the Bank of England, contain much about the forgers and their accomplices and include some correspondence from the criminals themselves after their apprehension and conviction.

Many convicts who had been given a transportation sentence were not transported, but served out their full sentence in prison or on a prison hulk. It is surprising to discover records which show that the Bank of England sometimes gave financial aid to prisoners who had no means of supporting themselves while in prison. These payments are found recorded in the minutes of the Bank of England Committee for Law Suits (BECLS).

The following examples are of forgers who were given a transportation sentence. The related Old Bailey trials have been included (Old Bailey proceedings can be accessed online at www.oldbaileyonline.org).

Old Bailey Proceedings, 9 September 1818

Sarah Ward was indicted for that she, on the 5th June at St. James, Clerkenwell, feloniously did dispose of, and put away a certain forged and counterfeit banknote (setting it forth, no. 12,075, £1, March 6, 1818, signed R. Clough), with intent to defraud the Government and Company of the Bank of England, she knowing it to be forged and counterfeit; against the statute.

Second Count, for feloniously offering to John Terry a like forged note, with like intent.

Third and Fourth Counts, the same only calling the forged instrument a promissory note for the payment of money instead of a banknote.

Four Other Counts, the same only stating the prisoner's intent to be to defraud the said John Terry.

John Terry. 'I keep the Plough public house at Hoxton. On the 5th June the prisoner came into my house about twelve o'clock in the morning and had a quartern of gin, which came to fourpence. She tendered me a £1 bank note. I took it. Mr Lewis who was sitting near me told me to be cautious as I had only been in the house three days; he requested to look at the note, which he did, and said it was a bad one. She heard it. She had a child in her arms. I asked her by what means she got the note? She said a man at the corner had given her the bottle and the note to get changed. I, Lewis and the prisoner all went out to look for him. She led us to the corner which was twenty or thirty yards off. We saw no-one there. She said she did not know the man. We told her we must detain her. She said she hoped we would not, for we might keep the note if we liked. I went for a constable. Lewis had the note. He did not return it to me.'

Cross-examined by Mr Adolphus.
Question: 'How long was it from the time she came until she went out?'
Answer: 'The whole did not last above ten minutes. It took up no more time than merely helping her to gin and giving change, which would not take a minute. I detained her long enough to alarm a person who was waiting outside.'

Mr Reynolds
Question: 'How long was she in the house before you went to look for the man?'
Answer: 'Not more than five or six minutes.'

William Lewis: 'I am clerk to Mr Davis who is a distiller and lives in Old Street. I live in Bartholomew Square. On the 5th June I was at Terry's house, saw the prisoner come in with a bottle for some gin and tender a £1 note. Mr Terry handed it to me. I looked at it and immediately said, in her hearing, it was a bad one.'
Question: 'Did you ask her how she came by it.'
Answer: 'Terry asked her. She said a man gave her the bottle and note at the corner of the street to get some gin. He was a stranger. We all three went out to look for him. We went to the corner but found no person there. She said he was gone.'
Question: 'During this time what was done with the note?'
Answer: 'I put it in my breeches pocket and held it in my hand. The prisoner requested me to let her go and seemed a great deal agitated. I took her into custody. While Terry was gone for an officer a crowd came round. I walked through Hoxton with her, put her into a coach and took her to the office. I asked her in the coach what her real name was. She said it was Sarah Ward and that she lived at no. 5 John's Row, City Road. I kept the note in my pocket, holding it in my hand. When we got to Worship Street I gave the note into the hands of Mr Yardley the clerk of the office. I took it from him again before he left my presence and took it to the Investigator's Office at the Bank and wrote my name on it before I parted with it (looking at it). This is it.'
Question: 'Did you make enquiry at John Row?'
Answer: 'The day after she was taken I went and made a diligent inquiry in John Row. I found two houses of no. 5. I inquired at both of them and all the houses of that number in the neighbourhood leading from John Row, but could hear no account of her.'
Cross-examined by Mr Adolphus: 'Where did she give her address?'
Answer: 'Turner asked her address at Worship Street. I took down what she said.'
Question: 'Did she not say it was Little West Place, St John's Row?'
Answer: 'She did not; two persons attended at her third examination by her desire. I do not remember West Place, John's Row. I went to all the streets about there.'

Edward Bishop: 'I live at no. 5 John's Row in the parish of St. Luke. I have lived there fifteen years. The prisoner never lived there. I never had any lodgers.'
Cross-examined: 'Is there such a place as Little West Place, leading into John's Row?'
Answer: 'There is a place they call West Place, leading into John's Row. John's Row is a public place."

Eliza Rawlings: 'I live at no. 5 John's Row, City Road. There are two nos. 5 on the same side of the way. I have lived there eighteen months; the prisoner did not live there. I do not know her.'

Thomas Smith: 'I am a feather manufacturer and live in Union Street, Hackney Road. On the 11th February the prisoner came to my shop and bought a feather which came to 1s-4d. She gave me a £1 note. I asked her name and address. She said her name was Sharp, residing in Bell Alley, Whitecross Street which I wrote on the note with my own name. (Looks at a note). This is it.
Cross-examined. 'I never saw her before until the 9th June.'
Question: 'Do you remember anything particular of her?'
Answer: 'I had an opportunity of taking particular notice of her and am not afraid to swear to her; she appeared very much swollen, as if she had a cold. She did not appear pregnant. The note is not signed, which I did not notice at the time. She was five or ten minutes with me.'

Charles Christmas: 'I am an inspector of the bank notes (looks at the notes). That uttered to Terry is forged in paper, plate and signature. The other is also forged and has no signature. They are both off one plate.'
Cross-examined: 'Is it not a note that a woman might take without noticing it.'
Answer: 'It would impose on many persons.'

Roger Clough: 'I am signing clerk at the bank; the note has not my signature.'

Prisoner's Defence: 'I solemnly declare I did not know it was forged. I was going to Hoxton to seek for lodgings, a decent man gave it to me with a bottle, and asked me to fetch half a pint of gin. I asked him his name, he said he lived in Turner Square. I told him my name was Ward and I lived in West Place, John's Row. I have four small children.'

Verdict: GUILTY
Sentence: DEATH   Recommended to Mercy

BoE ref F26/6 no. 5

Newgate
Wednesday Morning, Octr 6th 1819
Honored Gentlemen
In consequence of receiving orders to hold myself and family in readiness to embark on Friday morning for New South Wales, I consider myself in duty bound to return my most grateful acknowledgements for all the unmerited favours conferred upon me during my confinement here and,
Remain with the Most Profound Respect
Your Most Humble and Devoted Servt
Sarah Ward

To Mr Hooker
No.2 Bank Buildings
Not known as directed in Old or New Bank Building as she addressed it to
Mr Hooker, rather than Rooker, clerk to solicitors.

The General Muster of New South Wales for 1822 records Sarah Ward as living in Sydney having received a sentence of Transportation for Life. She was then recorded as the wife of Thomas Porter. She had sailed in the ship *Janus* which arrived on 3 May 1820.

Elizabeth Bamford, Rebecca Bamford, Mary Bradney, Amelia Hines and Anne Dickens were convicted at the Warwick, Lent Assizes, 1818.

Note: Warwick Assizes was in the Midland Assize Circuit. The records of this Circuit do not survive but the following was found in the *Warwick Advertiser* dated 4 April 1818:

Wednesday April 1st

Joseph Bradney was first placed at the Bar. He stood indicted for uttering a £1 Bank of England note, purporting to be a note of the Governor and Company of the Bank of England, he well knowing the same to be forged and counterfeit, to which indictment he pleaded *Guilty*.

Mr Baron Garrow, with the characteristic humanity of a British Judge told him that the offence with which he was charged was a capital one, and would affect his life, and requested him to consider the subject and put himself upon his trial. The Prisoner replied that he was guilty, and that it would be only adding to his crime to plead not guilty. The learned Judge said that the Court would wait awhile and give him time to consider of the subject before his plea of guilty was recorded. His Lordship, some time after, asked him if he had considered the advice which had been given to him, to retract his plea, and if he knew the consequences of it. He replied, he had and still wished to plead guilty. His Lordship then directed that the indictment should be again read over, and the prisoner formally asked if he pleaded *Guilty* which plea was then recorded and the Judge immediately passed sentence of Death upon him.

Mary Bradney (wife to the last mentioned Prisoner), **Rebecca Bamford**, **Elizabeth Bamford**, **Amelia Hines** and **Benjamin Hines** were also capitally indicted for uttering forged Bank of England notes, well knowing at the time of uttering, that they were forged and counterfeit. They pleaded *Guilty* and his Lordship immediately passed sentence of Death upon them, but stated that as there were favourable circumstances in their cases he should be induced to recommend them as fit objects for the Royal mercy, and held out a hope to them that their lives might be spared.

Richard Hancox, **John Poultney** and **John Jones** severally pleaded *Guilty* to an indictment for having forged Bank of England notes in their possession.

Mr Sergeant Vaughan stated to the Jury that he was instructed by the Bank not to produce any evidence against the Prisoners on another indictment, which was of a capital nature for uttering forged notes. The offence to which the Prisoners pleaded guilty exposed them to 14 years transportation, and the Bank hoped that this punishment, and the dreadful example which was in contemplation, would be sufficient to answer all the ends of public justice.

The Prisoners pleaded *Not Guilty* to the capital indictment on which they were *pro forma* arraigned and no evidence being adduced, they were of course acquitted of that branch of the charge.

The Court immediately sentenced them to *Fourteen Years Transportation* for the minor offence.

BoE ref F25/8 no.3

To the Governor and Company of the Bank of England.
The Humble Petition of **Elizabeth Bamford, Rebecca Bamford, Mary Bradney, Amelia Hines** and **Anne Dickens**. Sheweth that your Petitioners are on the eve of going out to New South Wales, in the *Lord Wellington* convict ship. That they were convicted at Warwick Assizes in April 1818 and pleaded Guilty to the minor offence of having forged notes in their possession for sale. That your poor Petitioning Prisoners were

seventeen months in Warwick Jail and utterly destitute not having one farthing in the world. Under their deplorable circumstances they humbly hope the Govr and Company of the Bank of England will take their case into consideration and order them to be paid the five pounds each as they have been good enough to pay some of their fellow Prisoners under similar circumstances.

And your Petitioners will be in duty bound to Pray.

The X of Elizabeth Bamford
The X of Rebecca Bamford
The X of Mary Bradney
The X of Amelia Hines
The X of Anne Dickens

Lord Wellington convict ship, Woolwich, May 21st 1819
I do hereby certify that the above named women are prisoners under my charge on board the *Lord Wellington* female convict ship and have during the time they have been on board conducted themselves with propriety; and I do certify that they are in extreme poverty.

E.J. Bromley, Surgeon and Superintendent.

BECLS 19 May 1819

Considered payments to prisoners on *Lord Wellington;* refused all the above since they were very notorious wholesale dealers and vendors of forged notes and unworthy of the liberty of the Bank.

Note: The *Lord Wellington* arrived at New South Wales on 20 January 1820. The 1822 General Muster of New South Wales records the following: 'Elizabeth Bamford, a government servant employed by Major Druitt at Parramatta. Mary Ann Bradney, wife of J. Bradney.' Both of these were recorded as having arrived by the ship *Lord Wellington*. Neither Amelia Hines nor Anne Dickens are recorded in the 1822 Muster.

Old Bailey Proceedings, 9 September 1818

Thomas Owen (together with Jane Williams, Mary Pendleton, William Wilks, Maria Wilks, William Chalker, Charles Hanscombe, John Anderson, Sarah Ireland, Hannah Gilbert, Timothy Lane, James Yeoell, James Dalas, John Dunn, John Watson, Benjamin Tathan Willis, Henry Way, Joseph Turner, Thomas Seeney, William Quin, James Woole, Edward New, and Joseph Longwood), were severally and separately indicted for feloniously and unlawfully having in their custody and possession forged bank notes, they well knowing them to be forged.
To which indictments they severally pleaded Guilty.
Sentence: Transportation for Fourteen Years.

BoE ref F25/6 no. 4

To Henry Hase, Esqr Bank of England

Honored Sir,
I hope you will not think me predominant by taking the liberty of addressing myself to you it is to inform you I was convicted at this present Sessions 1819 for uttering

a forged one pound Note and was by the Humanity of the Bank allowed to plead Guilty which Sentenced me to fourteen years Transportation. I beg to state to you that having a large family and no one to assist me in any way whatever induces me to solicit you to render me some small assistance to provide myself with a few necessaries to help to assist me on my voyage to my place of destination. Honored Sir, hearing of your humanity on all former occasions induces me to address myself to you hoping you will take my unfortunate case into your kind consideration and you may depend my prayers shall always be offered up for you and yours. It may be recollected before I was committed I named to Mr Christmas the Inspector I would do every thing in my power to place the man in your hands I had the notes off at that time. I thought it would be of very essential service which I would have done but very likely you could not place that confidence in me it was a man that I am sure from what I have collected in the prison and out doors, he is the principle vender of them diabolical things were so many poor creatures are torn from the comforts of their wife and family wich is my unfortunate situation but I hope providence will smile on me in another part of the World; there is a man which at certain times in the week attends regularly at the Crown & Sceptre near Golden Lane and disposes of them to people at this time not the man himself that I named to Mr Christmas but a man from the same party you may depend I am not informing you wrong as I am sure of leaving this Country but I do it for the good of mankind. I am sure and certain he is the principal man in them and if I had been allowed at the time I would have put him into your hands. I hope you will excuse the liberty I am taking in writing to you in such plain terms the bearer of this is my wife and she will be left with three small children wich I hope and trust you will take into your kind consideration.

I remain with due submission
Your Obedient and Humble Servant
Thomas Owen
Middle Yard, Newgate.
Monday morning

NB I hope you will not communicate this to any one but whom it may concern or else I may be very much ill treated in this place.

Mr Rooker
Solicitor of The Bank

Newgate
Septr 28th 1819

Sir
Hearing of your humanity on all former occasions induces me to Solicit you at this present time I beg to state to you that I have been Convicted at this present Sessions which is now sitting for putting off a forged one pound note and through the humanity of the Bank of England I was allowed to plead Guilty which Sentenced me to fourteen years Transportation. I beg further to state to you I have a wife and a large family which induced me to write to Mr Hase the Governor of the Bank of England to send me some small assistance to get me a few necessaries to assist me on my voyage to my place of destination. My wife was the person that took the letter to Mr Hase and he told her it rested with you and she might depend he would lay the letter before you. I further beg to state to you that I have not a friend in the world to assist me and if you will have the Goodness to use your interest for me it shall never be erased from my breast but my prayers shall always be offerd up to the almighty for you and yours. I further beg to state to you I have gave in my letter to Mr Hase every

Information respecting the Party I had the note off and a correspondence in which is now carried on by the Party at the Crown and Sceptre near Golden Lane. I will give you the description of the person that attends there to dispose of them. I put Mr Christmas in possession of a part of this.

I remain Sir

Your Obedient & Humble Servant

Thomas Owen

BECLS: 30 September 1819: Request refused.

Oct. 4. 1819

Sir

According to your request I have called for an answer to the letter I brought you the beginning of last week from my husband who is now in Newgate for passing a forged one pound note stating to you he had wrote to Mr Hase and he promised he would lay the letter before you for it was entirely at your option. I hope Sir, if you can have the goodness to remit me a trifle it will be of great service to him as he has not a friend in the world to give him a trifle to purchase him a few necessaries to his place of destination. I am sure it is quite out of my power, as myself and family must apply to his Parish. I hope Sir, you will take my husbands case into your consideration.

I am Sir Your Obedt Sevt

Elizabeth Owen

Note: The General Muster of New South Wales for 1822 records Thomas Owen, a convict (who was sentenced to fourteen years) living at Emu Plains. He came by the ship *Asia*. This ship arrived at New South Wales on 28 December 1820 having sailed on 3 September 1820.

Old Bailey Proceedings, 30 October 1818

Mary Hartnell (with James Turner, James Close, John Carpenter, William Jasper, John Egan, George Baker, David Crawley and Thomas Kirby) were severally and separately indicted for feloniously and knowingly having forged notes in their possession.
To which indictments the prisoners severally pleaded Guilty
Sentence: Transportation for Fourteen Years.

The above persons, except Thomas Kirby, but with George Velton, were also, on 3 November 1818, 'Indicted for forgery'. 'Mr Reynolds on the part of the Governor and Company of the Bank of England, declined offering any evidence.' They were found 'Not guilty'.

BoE ref F25/7 no. 17

Newgate

January the 6th 1819

Honored Sir

Pardon the Liberty of my intruding on you begging of you to take into your kind consideration my distressed situation and hopes you will have the Goodness to lay my Petition before the Honorable Governor and Company of the Bank and hoping thro' your kind interest to have a little of their Charity extended towards myselfe and children we being in a most distressed state and humble hoping the liberty will be excused I beg leave to subscribe myselfe with every respect your very Humble Servant and Prisoner.

Mary Hartnell

BECLS: 1 January 1819, granted her 7s 6d a week.

Note: The General Muster of New South Wales for 1822 shows a Mary Hartnell (with a child) who was employed by Mrs Jenkins at Appin. Mary Hartnell is recorded as having come by the ship *Lord Wellington*, which sailed to New South Wales, arriving on the 20 January 1820. It is also noted that a Mary Hartnell alias Lewis was convicted at the Old Bailey on 15 June 1837 for feloniously uttering a counterfeit half-crown to Emanual Passmore, 'she having been previously convicted as a common utterer' to which she pleaded guilty. She was sentenced to transportation for seven years.

This may be the same woman who was convicted in 1818. If so she must have returned to England from New South Wales after the expiration of her first sentence.

Old Bailey Proceedings, 13 January Sessions, 1819

Hannah Currell, aged 50 Was indicted for unlawfully procuring four pieces of counterfeit money of the likeness and similitude of good shillings, with intent to utter the same.

The following gave evidence:

Christian Davis: 'I live with Mr Sinclair who is a pastry cook and lives in Gracechurch Street. On the 23rd December the prisoner came to the shop about five o'clock in the afternoon, threw down 1 shilling and took up two one penny buns. I gave her change and put the shilling with five or six others in the till. The one she paid me was quite new, the rest were all dirty. Stephens came in and I gave him the same shilling.'

John Stevens: 'I am constable of Bishopsgate. I saw the prisoner and Mary Ann Brown between Sinclair's shop and a chymist's; something passed from one to the other. The prisoner then went into Sinclair's shop. I went in and Davis gave me the shilling. I saw Mr Brown at his door; we followed them. I took Mary Ann Brown and he took the prisoner. I searched them. Before that one of them dropped a bad shilling; we found four bad shillings in an area in a piece of paper. The prisoner had two good shillings and 6d in copper about her.'

James Brown: 'I am a fishmonger. I took the prisoner and heard something drop from her as we went over grating. Nobody was near enough to drop it but her. We afterwards went and found it was four counterfeit shillings in a piece of paper.'

Mr Caleb Edward Powell: 'I am an assistant to the Solicitor of the Mint. The shilling found at Sinclair's and the four found in the area are all counterfeit and of the same dye.'

Prisoner's Defence: 'I took the shillings for good.'

Sentence: GUILTY

Confined one year

BoE ref F25/6 no. 45

The following two letters are addressed to Mr Marsh, No 18 Claverton Street, Witcomb, Bath. Both are signed H.Cr. It is assumed that they were written by Hannah Currell who was convicted at the Old Bailey January Sessions, 1819.

London, July 26th 1819

Dear Mother,

I received your letter and am glad to hear you are all well. I am but very indifferent, the poor children are all tolerable well thank God. I am very happy to hear poor Peggy is comfortable and has got a good husband. I hope God will give them both a Blessing. I am surprised at your not mentioning any thing about Kitty or Mary. Don't omit it in your next and let me know all particulars of every thing. You need not be uneasy about the things in the bed, they are all safe, they are only pert down in the Ticket that way for shortness. Tom Porter and his woman are both don for fourteen years and expect to sail for the Bay in course of 5 or 6 weeks at furthest. There is a women's ship going and God only knows but it may be my fate to go if it should I must resign myself to the will of the Allmighty God who I hope will protect me by Sea as well as by Land but I have one Great consolation that is that I can take my children with me. John now does what he can for me and says if I go he will com up to Bristol and sell his share of the Property coming to him and will go with me. I hear Jim Hall is doing very well there. Durham is married to a settlers daughter and does well, also I can give no answer about sending Mary to you until I find how things will turn out with me. Should I remain here I will send her to you if not she must go with me. She is grown a fine girl. Poor little Margaret is sent out 5 miles in the Country with some more little children to nurse. Poor John and Mary is both together in the house I have the youngest with me. I mean to send a Petition to the Secretary of State but God only knows what Effect it may have however I will be able to let you know more in my next. Let me hear from you as soon as possible and if it should be in your power to send and has got a good husband. I hope God will give them both a blessing. I am surprised at your not mentioning any thing about Kitty or Mary, don't omit it in your next and let me know if Mary is married and let me know all the pirticulors of every thing. You need not be uneasy about the things in the bed they are all safe they are only pert do may have however I will be able to let you know more in my next. Let me hear from you as soon as possible and if it should be in your power to send me a trifle (but don't distress yourself) you may send it to Smiths. John still lodges with them it wont do to send it to me. Every thing is opend here. If you could send me a bit of muslin to make a cap or two I should be thankfull for it. Keep my unhappy situation as secret as possible and don't say any thing about it to Carpenter. John has now got nothing to do, his busing[sic] is all over until Christmas again. John and the children joins in Love with me to you all and may God Bless and Protect ye all are the constant Prayers of your Unhappy and Dutifull Daughter,

Till Death

H – Cr

P.S. Don't omit writing to me as soon as possible and let me know all you can and direct as before, then John will get it and bring it to me. It was a travelling woman that told me she saw Peggy at Cheltenh[am] [torn away].

London
August 22, 1819

My Dear Friends

I now embrace this oppertunity of writing to you in consequence of not having an answer to my last letter and am very uneasy at not hearing from you. I hope all is well with you and let me beg of you to answer this as soon as it comes to hand. I have not heard any thing as yet respecting a mitigation of my sentence but there are mitigations expected down every day and likewise orders for those that are to go to

Botany Bay but I trust in god it will not be my fate to be sent away. Tell Kitty, Leeson is in London. John often sees him he says he has been to sea and wanted to know where ye are as he should like to see Kitty more but John did not tell him where ye lived. I expect John will be obligated to go to Bristol in the course of a few days to see if his father will assist him for he has nothing to do here and of course he cant live on the air, he will call on ye on his way to Bristol, don't omit writing by return of Post and let me know all pirticulors. Should I be Mitigated I may be sent away to another Prison from here. I have no more to add but hope you are all in good health and conclude with my Love and Sincere Wishes for your Welfare and Remain,

Yours Affectionately
H. Cr.

In the letter above to her mother, Hannah Currell is concerned that she will be transported. At this time a sentence of seven years implied a transportation sentence to Australia, although many such convicts served out their full sentence on a prison hulk in Britain. No record of Hannah Currell has been found in New South Wales.

Old Bailey Proceedings, 26 May 1819

David Sharpe (together with Hamilton Ross, James Shaw, Michael Mullen, George Young, John Moore, Lydia Hogan and John Martin) – were severally and separately indicted 'For having in their custody forged bank notes, they well knowing them to be forged.'
To which indictments the prisoners pleaded Guilty.
Sentence: Transported for Fourteen Years.

BoE ref F25/8 no. 1

To: The Governor and Company of the Bank of England
The Humble Petition of David Sharpe a Prisoner in Newgate
Sheweth
That your Petitioner was convicted at the Old Bailey Sessions of Having a forged note purporting to be of the Governor and Company of the Bank of England, and was sentenced to be Transported fourteen years for the same.
That your Petitioner having been informed that in many instances you have made an allowance of a small sum of money to such as were considered not altogether unworthy of it, prior to their leaving their Native Land in order to furnish themselves with a few articles necessary to take during so long a voyage, most humbly beg leave to inform you that his friends are utterly incapable of rendering him the smallest pecuniary assistance, this compels him to solicit your benevolence not only in consideration of his distressed situation, but also on account of his having become a dupe to more artful and designing men who made him subservient to their advantage.
Your Petitioner therefore most humbly Prays you to grant him some allowance as has been before given to others in a similar unfortunate situation

And Your Petitioner as in duty bound will ever Pray.
David Sharp

The General Muster of New South Wales for 1822 records David Sharpe working in a Clearing Party at Liverpool.

Old Bailey Proceedings, 30 June 1820

James Downes (together with Joseph Greenop, Benjamin Glover, Thomas Matthews, William Shribs, Charles McKay, Sarah Hewster, Harriet Freeman, Sarah Carter, Philip Johnson, Daniel Cummings and James Hinnegan) were severally and separately indicted for having in their custody and possession forged Bank notes knowing them to be forged.

To which indictment the prisoners pleaded Guilty.

Sentence: Transported for Fourteen Years

The same prisoners, except James Hinnegan, were again indicted for disposing of and putting away forged Bank notes, with the intent to defraud the governor and Company of the Bank of England.

Mr Reynolds, on behalf of the prosecution, declined offering any evidence.

Sentence: Not Guilty

BoE ref F25/8 no. 38

To Bank from James Downes
Rooker Esqr , Solicitor, Bank Buildings

Newgate
June 19th 1820

Sir

As I have been made the fool of a designing party and been innocently, on my part, drawn into this dreadful situation, I am therefore fully determined for my own sake and for the happiness of my wife and family; (provided I can obtain my discharge), to inform you of a man that passed together with the person they were had of, should you Sir think this worth your attention you will find that I have been the dupe of these people and that I have a claim to be exonerated from the base treatment I have experienced.

I am Sir,
With great respect,
Your very obedient Servant
James Downes

Old Bailey Proceedings, 2 December 1818

William Davis – (together with William Sutton, John Morris, James Mullens and Richard Broderick) were severally and separately indicted for feloniously having forged notes in their possession, knowing them to be forged; to which they severally pleaded Guilty.

Sentence: Transported for Fourteen Years.

BoE ref F25/6 no. 29

For the Bank in Spector [sic]

London March 1st 1820

To the Bank inspector saying that the man of wom I had the nots is name is Samuel McCloud and is I believe is now in Horse Monger Lane for a resque. But I do not now of any one elce for I have not been aquainted with them. Not in a fortknight so that I doo not now but verey littell about them for wen hee gave mee the nots it was in a publick house that whe used and I paid 5s a note.

Wm Davies [sic] by the Name of Wm Young,
Clerkenwell New Prison

Old Bailey Proceedings, 15 April 1820

Elizabeth McBride was indicted for having in her custody and possession a forged £1 Bank of England note, she well knowing it to be forged.

John Garden Ross: 'I live with Mr Thomas Somerville, who is a grocer and lives in Clare Street. On the 8th of February, about seven o'clock in the evening the prisoner came to our shop and bought two ounces of tea and a pound of sugar. She gave me a £1 note; I suspected it to be bad and asked her address. She gave me "Elizabeth M'Bride, No. 6 King Street, Drury Lane" which I wrote on it – (looks at one) – this is it. I asked her where she got it? She said she had it from a gentleman that day, she did not know where. I sent for a constable and gave her in charge.'

James Brandon: 'I am a constable of St. Clement's. I took the prisoner in charge. Next day I found she lived at No. 14 King Street, and not at No. 6.'

Thomas Collins: 'I am a grocer and live in Drury Lane. On the 29th of January; in the evening the prisoner came into the shop and bought two ounces of tea and a pound of sugar; she tendered me a £1 note. I asked her where she lived? She said at No. 6 King Street, Drury Lane, and that her name was M'Bride. I suspected it was bad and sent it out by Lee; he brought it back. I did not mark it. I then asked her who she took it of? She said of a gentleman, she did not know who. She said a woman of her description might take a note and not know from whom. I said it was bad and if she would leave it I would send it to the Bank on Monday and if it was good or bad she should have it again. She said, "Very Well" and left the house. I locked the note up in my desk by itself and on Monday sent Lee with it to the Bank. He marked it in my presence before he took it away (looking at it). This is it. She did not call for it.'

George Lee: 'I am a shopman to Mr Collins. When the prisoner came to the shop Mr Collins gave me the note. I took it to Mr Bealby and brought it back. I am sure she is the woman. On Monday I took it to the Bank and found it was forged.'

Thomas Brown: 'I am a linen draper and live in High Holborn. On Saturday night the 5th of February, between seven and nine o'clock, the prisoner came and bought goods to the amount of 5s 2d. She tendered me a £1 note. I asked her where she had received it? She said she had just got it from a gentleman down Holborn. I asked her name and address, she said "Elizabeth M'Bride, no. 13 King Street, Drury Lane' – (looks at one); this is it. I told her I intended to send it to the Bank on Monday as it was forged. I told her to call on Monday morning to ascertain if it was good. She did not come. I went out soon after she left.'

George Price Griffiths: 'I am a shopman to Mr Brown. I saw the prisoner in the shop. Mr Brown's account is correct. The prisoner returned in about an hour and a half my master was then out. She said she came to pay for the goods, she had not sufficient money, but she would pay for what was cut off and have the note back. I told her Mr Brown had not got the note and if she called about twelve o'clock on Monday she might know about it; she said she would but did not. I went on Tuesday to no. 13 King Street, but could not find her there. I met her in the street and she returned with me to no. 13. She said she was in a hurry but would call in the evening and pay for the goods. I believe she lived at no. 13.'

Mr Glover: 'The three notes are all forged in every respect and appear to be impressed from the same plate.'

James Vautin: 'I am a signing clerk. The signature to the notes is not my writing.'

Verdict: GUILTY – aged 19.
Sentence: Transported for Fourteen Years.

BoE ref F25/8 no. 26 17 May 1820

To the Honble Company of the Bank of England.

Gentlemen
Pardon the liberty I have taken in writing to you humbly soliciting you to afford me a temporary relief for I am in absolute distress or I would not have done to trouble you I was a long time in confinement before trial and having no friends to assist me I was oblidged to sell and pledge my cloaths to procure some necessaries so that I have not a change of apparel neither will the ladies allow me any one in such a case as mine even be they was so distressed a course garb which I have them washed I have on. I have not had assistance from my own whatever since I have been in confinement & therefore intrust you to take my case into your consideration and hope and trust you will afford me relief be it even so trifling it will be truly eventable for I have a long time to remain in confinement before I leave my own Country and if in that time my health will be greatly impaired not having tea and sugar which wont be my chief support so that if you gentlemen refuse me relief I shall be a wretched spectacle by the time the Ship goes I therefore most earnestly beg of you to relieve my distress and your Honorable Petitioner will be very grateful for your kindness.

Your Humble Servant
Elizth Mc Bride

2th July 1820 Bank to Mrs Gray   Newgate
Rex v Eliz. McBride   July 12

Sir,
I am sorry I omitted when I saw you in the morning to mension Eliz. McBride's case to you. But thank you to present it to the Board as she have no friends on Earth to do any thing for her. She is a very deserving quiet young woman & I believe did not know any thing of the notes till she was unfortunately drawn into them by Voss that sufferd here.
     If Sir you will have the goodness to think of her she will ever pray. & you will confer a favour on my self.

Most Respectfully.
M. Gray   Matron

Mr Glover
Investigation Office
Bank

Note: No further information has been found about Elizabeth McBride.

CHAPTER 4

PRISON AND PRISON HULK RECORDS

(See Appendices 6, 7 and 22)

The registers of many prisons are held at The National Archives, London. They list inmates, usually giving the date and place of conviction of each convict and the number of years meted out by the court. Sometimes the physical description of the prisoners is also recorded. It is usual to find, in the case of a transfer to or from another prison, a record of *Removed To*, or *Received From*. Some of these registers have name indices.

Similar registers survive for many of the prison hulks, which were moored at various ports around the south coast of England. The cost of maintaining convicts on the hulks has been recorded by the Treasury (TNA document class T1). The Treasury records also include lists of convicts and the date of death of any convict who died while on board. Sometimes coroners' reports are filed with these papers.

The records of the High Court of Admiralty include details of seamen and workers who died on board various ships while in dock, including convicts on board prison hulks (TNA document class HCA 1).

Prison hulks were also established at Bermuda and Gibraltar, where convicts were sent as an alterative to Australia. Records of prisons and prison hulks are listed in Appendix 6 and Appendix 7.

Originally, prison hulks were to be used as 'a place of temporary confinement' for convicts awaiting transportation, as is shown in the following documents:

TNA ref T1/619

Mincing Lane
5th March 1785

Dear Sir,
Yesterday I had the Honor of receiving your letter of the 4th Inst. wherein you are pleased to inform me that the Plan of sending the convicts ordered for Transportation to Africa cannot be put to execution till the month of Septr next stating to me likewise the necessity there is for an immediate removal of those Convicts from the sundry Gaols into a temporary Place of Security & Confinement, till that period arrives, & desiring to know whether I can provide a vessel for the reception & security of 250 convicts, & upon what Terms.

In answer to which I beg leave to inform you that I have at present no spare Hulks but I can nevertheless provide such a vessel as is fit for the purpose in a few days,

& I think I can be able to get her ready to receive the number of Male convicts you mention in a fortnight after. As to the Terms; If these people are meant only for a temporary confinement & not to be put to labour, I will provide them upon the same Terms as has hitherto been allowed me for those on board the *Censor* Hulk vizt one shilling each man per diem, & 10/- a head for cloathing to be paid quarterly. As I must incur a very large expense in buying & fitting with anchors, cables &c a vessel for this service vizt 700 tons burthen & for so short a period, the monthly hire of such a vessel with boats, proper officers & guards, & ship's company, will not, I trust, be thought unreasonable at £175 per month for the first six months; if kept after that time to be reduced to £150 per month. The ship hire to commence on making the agreement but if it is meant to put the Convicts in question to Labour, in that case the furnishing Lighters &c will increase the expense. On this head I had the honor of submitting by Letter to Lord Sydney dated 12th Jany my expectation of an increase of allowance for the Convicts now on board the *Censor* Hulk. In consideration of having received His Majesty's Instructions to put them to Labor & under the same Regulations as those sentenced to hard labor on the River Thames, to this letter or to one on the same subject of an earlier date which I wrote to Mr Rose with my proposals & which I understand were referred to the Navy Board, I have not as yet received any answer. When opportunity offers I pray you, Sir, to remind His Lordship & Mr Rose that this matter is still depending.

I have the honor to be &c
Dun. Campbell

TNA ref T1/619

Whitehall
20th March 1785

My Lords,
The season of the year having so far advanced, it has been judged advisable that the Transportation of the Felons to the coast of Africa, who are now confined in the several Gaols in this country should be deferred until such time as the rainy sickly season upon the coast shall be over, but as the Gaols are in so crowded a state, that infectious distempers are daily expected to break out, His Majesty has thought fit that some place of temporary confinement should be appointed for the reception of such of the said convicts as are under sentence or order of Transportation.

    The *Censor* Hulk [at Woolwich] which has already been hired for that purpose has been found a proper place of security, and upon an application by my order to Mr Duncan Campbell, he has offered to supply another vessel. I transmit herewith a copy of his letter stating the terms he is ready to agree upon, and I must desire that Your Lordships will take the matter into your immediate consideration, and receive His Majesty's further Commands with respect to the hire of this vessel, or for preparing some other place of temporary confinement for the convicts above mentioned until the latter end of August or the beginning of September next, at which time the Season will arrive for carrying into execution the Plan transmitted to Your lordships in my letter of the 9th of February last.

I am,
Your Lordships most obedient humble Servant
Sydney

Many more prison hulks were soon to be located at various ports in England, including

Chatham, Woolwich, Sheerness, Portsmouth, Gosport, Devonport and Plymouth. The following are examples of entries from these records.

PRISON REGISTERS

Prison Commissioners' records
(TNA document group PCOM)

TNA ref PCOM 2/21

Prison Register, Millbank Prison, Westminster

No. 1331	James Hawkins
Age	42
Married or Single	Single
Read and Write	Both
Trade	Wheelwright
Convicted	2 Jan. 1844 Chelmsford Epi[phany] Sessions
Offence	Stealing 6 fowls
Sentence	7 years
Received From	25 Jan. 1844, Springfield Gaol
Character	Convicted before 14 times for bastardy
Removed To	*London* Convict Ship, 9th March 1844

TNA ref PCOM 2/354

Portland Prison: Prison Governors' Journals

Portland Prison – An entry from a day in the Governor's Journal

13th Septr 1849 Thursday

The Prisoners employed as usual, except 1 to 3 pm occupied in a general change of Hulks, &c.

Reported for irregularity and disposed of as in Report Book and Misconduct Book: Regr No. 753, 244, 299, 357. Also the following prisoners received here on the 11th instant, who were guilty of the following outrageous conduct:

Prisoner No. 893 T. Warburton finding that he was going to be reported by Principal Warder Steine for an offence, assaulted him and in the Deputy Governors ordering him to close confinement & several Prisoners who had been at the Hulks with the above named man, rushed in a violent manner to the Palisade of the yard and endeavoured to force it. On my being sent for I found these men very much excited and wanting to see me. Accordingly two of them, No. 897 T. Atkins and 895 M. Brittain were passed successfully through the door of the Palisade and having stated what they had to say (which merely amounted to a kind of intended justification of their previous violence) they were passed back and a third brought out who was immediately pointed out to be as one who had struck Asst Warder Bond in the face because he required him to perform more work (stone breaking) than he was doing. The Prisoner, No. 891 J. Gallavin said at once that he had struck the officer, and on my ordering him off to close confinement he hesitated and drew back. The two officers standing by him took hold of him to take him away when he appealed to me to desire them to take their hands off him and he would go quietly. To shew him that there was no wish to treat him harshly I said 'Very well then take your hands off him' and the moment they did

Female convicts at work during the 'silent hour' in Brixton prison.

so he struck at me but the blow only reached me lightly on the face. The two officers then secured him and immediately the other Prisoners inside the Palisade tried to force the wicket of it to come to his assistance. There being 65 men in this yard and only 5 officers present and the whole of the other prisoners being on this point of coming in from labour I sent for the Military Guard to assist in quelling the disturbance, and went to assist Principal Warders Bouverie and Warren who were struggling with the

Prisoners that were trying to force the wicket. Before it could be closed these officers were severely kicked and beaten by the Prisoners inside and the whole of those taking an active part in this violence being, as far as I could ascertain at the time, men who had formerly been at some of the Hulks and were removed to separate confinement for misconduct; their names are 892 T. Thorpe, 894 J. O'Neill, 895 M. Brittain, 896 S. Hayes, 897 T. Atkins, 898 S.J. Riggs and 899 F. Haynes. I could not ascertain that the other Prisoners in the yard (all of whom had arrived from Pentonville with these men on the 11th), had taken any part in the disturbance.

The Military Guard having promptly come up and been drawn up opposite the Palisade ready to act, I went into the yard with several officers (who had come in with the working parties) and sent all the Prisoners off to their cells by wards.

The two who had previously been sent to the separate cells as before mentioned appeared so much in the character of ringleaders that I judged it better not to send the others into their hearing and I according[ly] directed them to remain for the present, unless they were troublesome, in their own cells. The main body of Prisoners had come in from the works which these were going on but had gone off quietly to their different Halls; and the working Prisoners who had been stationed for different reasons in the separate cells were moved down to the Halls to be out of hearing of the mutinous and gross language shouted to each other by the men in close confinement. It was evident from this language that these Hulks men had come from Separate Confinement to a state of association with an intention of resisting the Prison authorities and discipline as they had done before at the Hulks, and that after the arrival of another lot of similar characters on the 14th from Pentonville they intended to renew their violence.

I greatly fear that the presence of these notoriously bad characters from the Hulks will prove most nefarious to the discipline of this Establishment, which has hitherto been so far successful as to render it practicable to take outside the Prison walls several hundred Convicts (even to a distance from the Prison) provided with having hammers and tools of all kinds (in ground most favourable for concealment and escape) under the charge of unarmed officers aided by a very few unsupported, to enforce from therein a fair amount of labour concluded generally in a cheerful manner, to move them to and from their distant ground with order and quickness and to send them back to their cells with little fear of their breaking any establishment rules or shewing disrespect to their Officers. All this is so different from the general conduct of Prisoners at the Hulks that it appears impossible to introduce into this prison a number of the notorious ringleaders from those establishments without the greatest risk or even certainty of contravention and injury to the discipline, especially as there is here in fact no sufficient means of separating such characters and at the same time making them labour on the Public Works. I have also to observe that one of these men has been convicted since 1842; his sentence being only for 10 years, and that his presence in this establishment is in opposition to the terms of the 'Notice' which specifies a Convicts detention in this Country to be only for one half the period of his sentence, a circumstance which will doubtless be made use of by these discontented men to throw doubt on the intention of carrying the terms of these 'Notices' into effect, and unsettle the minds of the Prisoners who are anxiously looking forward to going abroad with tickets of leave as a reward for good conduct.

I did not attend morning prayers today having been kept up till a late hour by office business last night.

Visited the Prison at 11 p.m. and found all correct except that there had been much talking and resentment among the Prisoners in the Cells in the Hulks.

The Associated Rooms fully occupied by Prisoners of the Class stated in Page 157, and 100 men thus accommodated in hammocks without crowding or inconvenience or any apparent likely injury to discipline, (the side windows afforded good means of overlooking the rooms from outside independent of the Officer from walking at night in each room).

PRISON REGISTERS

Home Office records

(TNA document group HO)

TNA ref HO 23/13 Somerset County Gaol [Taunton]

Registers of County Prisons

Register Number	690
Name	Charles Hurtley alias Joseph Giles or Henry Palmer or Thomas James
Age	34
Married or Single	Married
Number of Children	2
Read or Write	Both
Trade or Profession	Labourer
When and Where Convicted	5th September 1864, Surrey Sessions
Specific Description of Crime	Stealing a watch from the person after a previous conviction for felony
Sentence	10 years
When and Whence Received	27th September 1864, Horsemonger Lane Gaol
Information Received Respecting Prisoner	Before sentenced to be transported,
	1849, Jan 25th, stealing 4s, 1 month
	1849, Aug 17th, assault, 14 days or pay 10s
	1850, Aug 6th, stealing from the person, 3 months
	1851, Feb, Surrey Sessions. Stealing from the person, 4 months
	1853, July, Middx Sessions, Stealing from the person, 7 years Transportation
	1857, Jan, Surrey Sessions, Attempted to steal from the person, 12 months

PRISON REGISTERS AND RETURNS

TNA ref HO 24/1 Millbank, Westminster

7 Oct. 1848 from Oxford City Gaol

Register Number	527
Name	Samuel Hawkins
Age	35
Crime	Felony

Convicted	Oxford City Sessions, 2 Oct. 1843
Sentence	10 years
Married or Single	Widower
Read or Write	Read
Trade	Sweep
Substance of Gaoler's Report on	
Character	Character and connexions bad
Discharged	17 Jan. 1844
How disposed of	*Equestrian* [transportation ship] to Van Diemens Land

ARMY PRISON REGISTERS

War Office records

(TNA documents group WO)

Some army deserters were sentenced to a term of transportation.

TNA ref WO 25/2956 Savoy Prison, Westminster [for Army Deserters]

Date	26 Nov. 1805
Name	Bywater, Joseph
Regiment	3rd Lancashire Militia
Where Confined	Nottingham
Whom Reported	Mr. Coldham
Escort to Take to	Nottingham to Plymouth by Birmingham, Gloucester and Bristol

PRISON HULKS

Home Office records

(TNA document group HO)

TNA ref HO 8/107: Coromandel prison hulk at Bermuda, quarter ending 31 March 1851

Prison Hulk – Quarterly Returns

No. 2047

Name	Thomas Gillespie
Age	39
Offence	Stealing a Lamb
Where	Wicklow [Ireland]
When	19 Oct 1848
Sentence	10 years
Surgeon's Report	Invalid
Behaviour During the Quarter	Good

PRISON HULKS

Admiralty records

(TNA document group ADM)

TNA ref ADM 6/422 Dolphin *Prison Hulk [no dates are given in this volume]*

Although the location of this hulk is not given in this volume it is known that the *Dolphin* was located at Chatham from 1823 to 1830.

No. 670	James Blakeway
Height	5' 8½"
Complexion	Sallow
Make	Middling
Visage	Oval
Eyes	Hazel
Eyebrows	D. Brown
Hair	D. Brown
Where Born	Haystock, near Much Wenlock, Salop
Trade	Labourer
Married or Single	Single
Read or Write	No
Remarks	Late soldier in the 1st Dragoon Guards. Scar left side of mouth. Lower part of the face inclined to right. Large hole in the breast from a pistol ball. Scar on the right wrist. Several scars on the back of left hand.

Convicts returning to the prison hulk after their labour in Woolwich Arsenal.

PRISON HULKS

Privy Council records
(TNA document group PC)

List of convicts sentenced to transportation are to be found in the Privy Council registers, and occasionally the prison hulk on which they were held is also noted. These lists record convicts sentenced up to 14 years' transportation, but only very rarely are those sentenced to 'life' included in this series of records. The reason for this omission has not been established. The following table is an example of an entry.

Table 4.1: List of Convicts under Sentence of Transportation Beyond the Seas. In the *Stanislaus* hulk at Woolwich, 2 May 1792. *(TNA ref PC 2/137)*

Name	Age	Offence	Where convicted	When convicted	Sentence
John Lewis	33	Felony	Maidstone	16 March 1789	7
Thomas Noakes	20	do	do	do	7
Jeremiah Bryant	11	do	do	do	7
John Hunt	22	do	do	do	7
Thomas Buchanan	20	do	do	do	7
James Oliver	23	do	do	do	7
Thomas Minton	30	do	do	do	7
Obedia Paxman	19	Grand Larceny	Bury St. Edmunds	25 March 1789	7
John Richard	49	Stealing	Glamorgan	13 April1790	7
Thomas Rumbold	20	Felony	Hertford Q.S.	20 April 1789	7
Thomas Pateman	19	do	do	do	7
Richard Marsden	22	Petit Felony	Westminster	2 July 1789	7
Thomas Plummer	19	Felony	Maidstone	27 July 1789	7
John Hodges	27	do	do	do	7
William Brown	33	do	do	do	7
William Drayton	18	do	do	do	7
James Green	18	do	do	do	7
Stephen Lawless	18	Petit Larceny	Westminster	22 Oct 1789	7
William Ireland	29	do	Maidstone Q.S.	6 Oct 1789	7
George Beach	22	do	do	do	7
John Twaits [sic]	24	do	do	do	7
John Smith	18	do	Stafford Q.S.	14 Jan 1790	7
Thomas Dean	46	Recg. Stolen Goods	do	10 March 1790	14
James Stapleton	35	Grand Larceny	do	21 July 1790	7
John Fenton	32	do	do	do	7
Edward Ward	37	do	do	do	7
William Riley	47	Recg. Stolen Goods	do	do	14
John Pheasant	22	Petit Larceny	do	15 July 1790	14

Name	Age	Offence	Where convicted	When convicted	Sentence
Thomas Tailby[1]	23	Grand Larceny	Leicester	28 July 1790	7
Edward Toon	27	do	do	do	7
William Meredith	14	Felony	London	20 July 1791	7
Thomas Singleton	23	do	do	do	7
Samuel alias John Stanton	20	do	Middlesex	20 July 1791	7
Thomas Williams	40	do	do	do	7
Richard Lattimore	20	do	do	do	7
Owen McCarty	50	do	do	do	7
John Pocock	50	do	do	do	7
Samuel Vanner	–	Petit Larceny	Middlesex	22 July 1791	7
Humphrey Taylor	16	do	Westminster	15 July 1791	7
William Green	36	Grand Larceny	Coventry	20 Aug. 1791	7
Daniel McGregor	42	do	do	do	7

1. Thomas Tailby/Taleby, later became the husband of Elizabeth Smith, who afterwards married John Hawkins (see Chapter 19).

Occasionally the Privy Council registers also include lists of Scottish convicts.

Table 4.2: Lists of Convicts Sentenced to Transportation Beyond the Seas, 8th Jan. 1794. *(TNA ref PC 2/139)*

Name	When Convicted	Where Convicted	Sentence
John Henderson	18th April 1791	Glasgow	To be whipped through Glasgow & transported beyond Seas for 14 yrs.
Thomas Morrison	22nd Sept.1791	do	Trans. beyd Seas. Life, His Service for 7 years to Contractor
Donald Turner	22nd Sept.1792	do	Trans. beyond Seas for 7 years
Thomas Dick	do	do	To be whipped thro' Glasgow & Trans. beyd Seas for 14 years.
Jno Mackinzie als. Mackenzie	11th April 1793	do	Trans. beyd Seas for Life
John Cambell	11th Sept. 1793	do	Trans. beyd Seas for Life. His Service for 7 yrs to Contractor
William Carswell	9th June 1791	Edinburgh	Trans. beyd Seas for Life
John Grant	3rd June 1793	do	Trans. beyd Seas for Life
John Stirling	12th July 1793	do	Trans. beyd Seas for Life
James McKay	10th Aug. 1793	do	Death – afterwards resptd and sentence changed into Banishment for Life to such place as His Majesty in council should direct
James Beerhope als. Beerhup	14th Aug. 1793	do	Trans. beyd Seas for Life.
Thomas Muir	31st Aug. 1793	do	Trans. beyd Seas for 14 yrs.

Name	When Convicted	Where Convicted	Sentence
John McLean alias McIntyre	6th May 1786	Inverary	Banished to one or other of His Majesty's Colonies or Plantations abroad for Life. Contractor to have property in his service for 4 years from time of conviction. In case of return to Scotland to be whipped and again Trans.
Neil MacInnish als. McInnis als. Nafemin	6th April 1793	Inverary	Trans. beyd Seas to such place &c. for Life. Service to Contractor for 7 yrs or if not within 12 months removed for transportation in lieu thereof at expiration of 12 months to be whipped and set at Liberty in order to his going into Banishment & within 3 weeks banish himself forth of Scotland for his Life and in case of return to be again whipped and to Banish himself.
Malcolm MacLellon	do	do	Trans. beyd Seas to such place &c for Life. Service to Contractor for 7 yrs in case not within 12 months removed for Transportation then in lieu thereof at expiration of 12 months to be whipped and set at Liberty in order to his going into Banishment & within 3 weeks to banish himself forth of Scotland for Life and in such case of return to be again whipped and to Banish himself.
Thomas Fische Palmer	13th Sept. 1793	Perth	Trans. beyd Seas to such place &c. for 7 years

Correspondence relating to convicts on prison hulks will also be found in Privy Council records. The following are examples:

TNA ref PC 1/67, February 1819

> Foxearth, near Sudbury, Suffolk.
> Feb. 13th 1819

Will Gibbons, said to have been discharged, 8th July 1818
Gentlemen,
The person names in the margin having returned to this parish, from on board the *Laurel* hulk at Portsmouth, without any documents of his having been set at liberty by authority, than a Certificate, signed Alexr. Lamb, Captain, which certificate is incorrect with respect to the date of the conviction, and has led to a doubt, whether the certificate may not be a forgery. I have therefore to request, on behalf of the inhabitants of this parish, that you will be pleased to inform me whether such person has been discharged in consequence of His Majesty's Free Pardon as set forth in the certificate of Captain Lamb.

> I have the honour to be,
> Gentlemen,
> Your Obt. Servant,
> Benjn. G. Hurrell

To the Commissioners of
H. Majesty's Navy
Transport Department.

Table 4.3: List of Convicts under Sentence of Transportation in the Gaol at the House of Correction at Cold Bath Fields on the 18th Day of September 1818. *(TNA ref PC 1/67 continued)*

Name	Age	Crime	When and Where Tried	Original & Present Sentence	State of Health
Elizabeth Black	38	Felony	Sept. 1815 Old Bailey	7 years	
Eleanor Henrickson	34	"	Oct. 1816 Old Bailey	"	
Ann Fines	34	"	Sept. 1816 Old Bailey	"	
Sarah Reeson	38	"	Sept. 1816 Old Bailey	"	Very ill health. T.Webbe
Mary Smith	46	"	Dec. 1816 Old Bailey	"	
Elizabeth Carr	28	"	Dec. 1816 Old Bailey	"	
Elizabeth Carney	36	"	Dec. 1816 Old Bailey	14 years	
Rebecca Roberts	36	"	Jan. 1817 Old Bailey	7 years	Ill Health. T.Webbe
Sarah Howell	27	"	April 1817 Old Bailey	14 years	
Sarah Jones	28	"	April 1817 Old Bailey	7 years	
Harriett Molineux	27	"	July 1817 Old Bailey	"	Very ill from disease of the liver which she has had a length of time and during her confinement she has become dropsical. I am of opinion the only chance of her recovery would arise from her native air. Tho. Webbe, Surgeon

PRISON HULKS

Treasury records
(TNA document group T)

Expense accounts for feeding, maintaining and clothing convicts on prison hulks are to be found in the Treasury Board Papers TNA document class T1. These often include complete lists of all the convicts on board particular vessels. The following are examples:

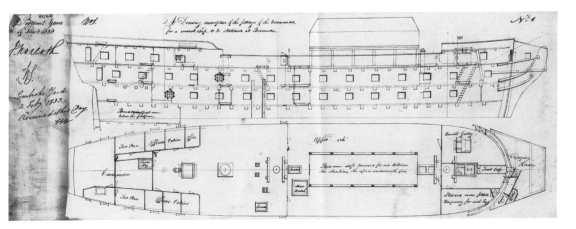

Plan of the *Coromandel* in use as a prison hulk in Bermuda. (National Maritime Museum)

Table 4.4: Account of the expenses of Keeping, Cloathing and Maintaining on board the *Prudentia* Hulk at Woolwich sundry Convicts under sentence of Transportation from 30 September to 31 December 1799 inclusive as per contract with the Lords of His Majesty's Treasury. *(TNA ref T1/835)*

No.	Expenses	Amount	Amount
259	Convicts being the Number on board at delivering last Account 30 September to the 31 December 1799 inclusive, 92 days @ 13½ per day	1340 6 6	
3	Convicts received from Surrey 15 October to the 31 December 1799. 78 days @ 13½ per day	13 3 3	
4	Convicts received from Reading 30 October to the 31 December 1799. 63 days @ 13½ per day	14 3 6	
1	Convict received from Reading 22 November to the 31 December 1799. 40 days @ 13½ per day	2 5 0	
8	Convicts received from Lancaster 6 December to the	11 14 0	
x	31 December 1799. 26 days @ 13½ per day	1381 12 3	
x	Deduct Maintenance of Convicts as per Account Annexed	48 5 3	£1333 7 0
	Due for an additional allowance of one penny per day for each Convict from the 30 September to the 31 December 1799 granted by Order of the Lords of His Majesty's Treasury Viz		
259	Convicts being the number on board the 30 September to the 31 December 1799 inclusive. 92 days @ 1d per day	99 5 8	
3	Convicts received from Surry 15 October to the 31 December 1799, 78 days @ 1d per day	19 6	
4	Convicts received from Reading 30 October to 31 December 1799. 63 days @ 1d per day	1 1 0	
1	Convict received from Reading 22 November to 31 December 1799, 40 days @ 1d per day	3 4	£101 9 6

TNA ref T1/521

Mr Duncan Campbell with Report of the Convicts received and discharged by Order of the Secretary of State. Only for information of the Treasury.
Received 14th March 1777

I had the honour of receiving your letter of the 9th instant, and in obedience to your commands I beg leave to hand to you a report of the convicts received and discharged by order of the Secretary of State, and the time each remained on board, which I humbly hope will be admitted as sufficient voucher to authenticate the charge for their maintenance, clothing &c. You will also be pleased to receive the particulars which constitute the charge for fees to Clerks of Assize, Keepers of the sundry Gaols and the expenses attending the conveying the convicts from the same on board the Ship, for most of which articles it has never been usual for me to take receipts, yet if their Lordships have any doubts in that respect, a circumstance which would give me much pain, they can still be obtained. The charge for deduction at the Exchequer I had the Honour of explaining to you in person, and at the same time submitting the propriety of it, which I still beg leave to do, that, for the ship of 240 Tons was made known to the under Secretaries of State and admitted of by them when by their desire I undertook this Service, many times since the Vessel might have been lett to Government upon better terms. As to what you are pleased to direct for making proposals for the future maintenance of these Felons, Mr Eden having some time since intimated to me that all the Gaols being now cleared of the Felons for Transportation and that soon as the sickness was over which for some time past has prevailed on board, in a greater degree than I ever have known, there would be no further service for this ship, that this Business will be then finely closed, and as the few people remaining on board will I have no doubt in a few days be in a healthy state, it may be unnecessary for me to trouble their Lordships at this time with any further proposals on that score. You will please to permit me to observe that I have made no charge for my own trouble and attendance on this business, and I most humbly trust their Lordships will not upon the whole think the account I have delivered unreasonable.

I am with the Greatest Respect
Sir
Your most obedient and Most Humble Servant
Dun. Campbell
Mincing Lane, 11th December 1776

John Robinson, Esq.

Report

Convicts received on board the ship *Tayloe* by order of the Right Honble Earl of Suffolk

March 14th [1776] On board sixty-two ────────────────────

William Barber	John Pelboan	Aled Woollen
Peter Harris	Mary Bins	Edward Sharnley
Thomas Cook	Elenor Ogle	William Westwood
Sarah Guy	Mary Smith	George Wilson
Hyder Champion	Elizabeth Turner	William Woodley

Acton Greenville
Richard Holmes
Elizabeth Davis
Mary Stephens
James Harrison
William Davis
John Smith
Benjamin Perry
Mary Keith
Thomas Burdet
Matthew Bevan
George Childs
Archibald Girdwood
Joseph Harrison
John Jennings
Silas Shears

Ann Guy
Ann Green
Elizabeth Ives
John Harsdell
Ann Plumer
Sarah Roach
Ann Walker
James Charleton
William Dow
James Best
Joseph Harper
Elizabeth Godley
Daniel Porter
Edward Smee
Thomas Holder
James Price

James Smith
John Clark
John Moore
Hannah Saunders
Robert Smith
Sarah Lazarus
Charles McLauchin
Thomas Smith
John Salmon
Thomas Pitt
Archd Burridge
Thomas Burly
Benjamin Davis
Thomas Purvey
Minian Pushman

May 20th from New Gaol, eleven

Thomas Brown
John Goodwine
George Hall
Francis Lush

William Lister
John Westwood
James Finlay
John Hazill

John Winter
Thomas Williams
Charles Hughs

May 20th from Hertford, two

John Colley
William Colley

May 21st from Chelmsford, five

Thomas Deadman
John Ellis

Alexander Harris
John Winterburn

William Wilson

March 22nd from Sussex, one

John Atwell

May 21st from St. Albans, two

William Howard
William White

May 24th from Maidstone, five

Richard Cathron
Joseph Dalton

Timothy Gard
James Johnson

Peter Quarton

Sept. 12th from Ipswich, two

John Ling
Ralph Smith

Sept. 13th from Norwich, two

Richard Baggot
William Goodwine

Sept. 14th from Coventry, three

James Dennis	Joseph Sutcliffe	John Clark

Sept. 14th from Warwick, one

Jarvice Wallace

Sept. 21st from Newgate, twelve

James Smith	Joseph Nash	Thomas Floyd
John Langford	James Birch	Abraham Sutcliff
William Morris	Thomas Winsborough	William Riley
Richard Evelyn	Joseph Bassett	Susanah Hudson

Sept. 24th from Lincoln, two

Joseph Marshall
Thomas Hams

Convicts discharged by Order of the Right Honourable the Earl of Suffolk

Most of the men enlisted in His Majesty's Service

March 20th

John Moore	Benjamin Davis	Robert Smith
John Salmon	Ninian Pushman	Thomas Smith
James Man	John Smith	Thomas Pitt
Thomas Holden		

March 30th

Mary Smith

May 2nd

William Davis

May 21st

William Barber	Sarah Guy	Acton Greinville
Elizabeth Turner	James McIntosh	William Westwood
Alea Woolten	James Harrison	William Davis

May 28th

John Goodwin

June 6th

Richard Holmes	George Wilson	James Smith
Eleanor Ogle	Edwd Sharnley	Hyder Campion
Edward Smee	William Woodley	Thomas Purrey

June 8th

Mary Bins	Ann Guy	Peter Harris
Elizabeth Ives	Ann Green	

July 1st

Thomas Burley	Thomas Cook	Archibald Burridge
Joseph Harper	Charles McLauchlin	

July 2nd

Benjamin Perry	Elizabeth Davis	Ann Plumer
Mary Stevens	Sarah Roach	

July 3rd

Mary Keith	Elizabeth Godley	Hannah Saunders
Ann Walker	Sarah Lazarus	

August 6th

James Price	James Finlay	William Lister
John Pilbean	John Hazill	Thomas Deadman
John Winter		

Escaped the 6th October

George Childs	James Charlton	William White
Silas Shears	William Dow	John Ling
Thomas Burdet	Thomas Williams	John Clark
Thomas Floyd	George Hall	Javice Wallace
Thomas Winsbourough	John Westwood	William Goodwine
Samuel Smith	Francis Lysh	Thomas Hams
John Langford	William Colley	John Marshall
William Merrit	Daniel Porter	James Johnston
William Riley	John Ellis	Richard Cathron
Joseph Bassett	Alex^r Harris	Joseph Dalton
Joseph Nash	John Atwell	

I do humbly certify that the above is a true List with the dates of receipts & discharges of the Convicts received on board the *Tayloe* of which Ship I am Master

[signed] Finlay Gray

A prison hulk in Deptford, 1826, from *Lyson's Environs of London*, Vol. IV, Pt. II. (Guildhall Library)

TNA ref T1/658

Bounties paid to Convicts on the Prison Hulks at Woolwich who had Received Pardons

Table 4.5: State of Bounties & Cloathing given by Order of Duncan Campbell Esqr to the several Convicts discharged from the Hulks at Woolwich and Pardoned by Recommendation of the Court of Kings Bench. (*TNA ref T1/658*)

Date	Expenses	Amount	Amount
1787 July 31	Paid Bounties since the 12th Inst. to: James Bradshaw als John Stewart, Joseph Coombes, William Davenport and Richard Walls @ 2½ Guineas) each	18 - 7 - 6	
	do to William Bell, John Garner, Edward Davis @ 2 Guineas each)	6 - 6 - 0	24 - 13 - 6
Aug 31	Paid Bounties this month to: John Roose & Abner Broster @ 1½ Guineas each	3 - 3 - 0	
	do to John Tout & John Shakespeare @ 2½ Guineas each	5 - 5 - 0	8 - 8 - 0

Date	Expenses	Amount	Amount
Sepr 30	Paid Bounties this month to: John Horner, Isaac Matthews, James Read, Edward Edson & William Spong @ 2½ Guineas each		13 - 2 - 6
Octr 31	Paid Bounties this month to: Robert Robinson, Edward Watkins, John Gough, Joseph Sceens, William Merritt, als. Axford, Dennis Kellyhorn, Robert Strickland, John Reed, Joshua Kemp, Richard Berry, Thomas Murray & James Spurway @ 2 ½ Guineas each		31 - 10 - 0
Novr 30	Paid Bounties this month to: John Wishart & Andrew Jordan @ 2½ Guineas each		5 - 5 - 0
1788 Feby 29	Paid Bounties this month to: George Johnson als. Williamson & Richard Nicholson @ 57/6 each	5 - 15 - 0	
March 31	Paid Bounties this month to: Thomas Blaydes, John Calvert & John Johnson @ 2 Guineas each	6 - 6	
	do to Charles Clayton & William Ardington @ 2½ Guineas each	5 - 5	11 - 11 - 0
April 30	Paid Bounties this month to: James Benton	2 - 2	
	do to George Martin & James Baker @ 2½ Guineas each	5 - 5	7 - 7 - 0
	carried forward		£107 - 12 - 0
1788 June 30	Paid Bounties this month to: Charles Larford & Jonathan Temperley @ 2½ Guineas each		5 - 5 - 0
July 11	Amount of cloathing furnished the several convicts pardoned and discharged		54 - 0 - 10
			£166 - 17 - 10

Convicts at work on the Thames, viewed from the Butt at Woolwich 8 May 1777, *London Magazine*. (Greater London Council)

TNA ref T1/695

Convicts who Died on board a Prison Hulk
Convicts who died in this manner are often found listed in report of a Coroner's Inquest:

Table 4.6: James Bedford, one of the Coroners for Hampshire, his Bill for taking Inquests on Convicts who have died on board the *Hornet* Hospital Hulk lying in Langstone Harbour in Hampshire [near Portsmouth] aforesaid between the first day of July 1790 and the 30th day of June 1791. (*TNA ref T1/695*)

Dates	Nos	Names	What Ship	Amount
1790 1st Oct.	1	Inquest on John Haggar	Ceres	1 - 0 - 0
		Journey from Wickham 15 miles		11 - 3
1st Oct.	2	Inquest on Wm Green	Ceres	1 - 0 - 0
16th Oct.	3	Inquest on Richard Goodwin	Ceres	1 - 0 - 0
		Journey from Wickham		11 - 3
2nd Novr	4	Inquest on Wm Norley	Ceres	1 - 0 - 0
		Journey from Portsmouth Common		3 - 9
7th do	5	Inquest on Richd Clemson	Ceres	1 - 0 - 0
		Journey from Portsmouth Common		3 - 9
19th do	6	Inquest on Benjamin Penn	Ceres	1 - 0 - 0
		Journey from Portsmouth Common		3 - 9
22nd do	7	Inquest on John Morris	Ceres	1 - 0 - 0
		Journey from Portsmouth Common		3 - 9
4th Decr	8	Inquisition on John Porter	Ceres	1 - 0 - 0
		Journey from Portsmouth Common		3 - 9
1791 12th Jany	9	Inquest on Alexander McDonald	Fortuneé	1 - 0 - 0
		Journey from Portsmouth		3 - 9
14th do	10	Inquest on William Hook	Fortuneé	1 - 0 - 0
		Journey from Portsmouth Common		3 - 9
28th do	11	Inquest on Peter Smith	Ceres	1 - 0 - 9
		Journey from Portsmouth Common		3 - 9
1st Feby	12	Inquest on William Gilhespie	Fortuneé	1 - 0 - 9
		Journey from Portsmouth Common		3 - 9
16th do	13	Inquest on John Cocker	Fortuneé	1 - 0 - 0
		Journey from Portsmouth Common		3 - 9
21st do	14	Inquest on John Nix	Ceres	1 - 0 - 9
		Journey from Portsmouth Common		3 - 9
6th March	15	Inquest on Edward Bennett	Fortuneé	1 - 0 - 9
		Journey from Portsmouth Common		3 - 9
2nd April	16	Inquest on Robert Bence	Fortuneé	1 - 0 - 0
		Journey from Portsmouth Common		3 - 9
				£19 - 11 - 3

Note: All the above were recorded as Natural Death.

TNA ref T1/859

Expenses Paid to the Chaplain and Others who Attended the Prison Hulks

Table 4.7: An Account of the sundry expenses incurred by Andrew Hawes Bradley for Salaries to Chaplain, Coroners Inquests, Bounties & Cloathing to Convicts discharged at the expiration of their several sentences on board the *Fortuneé* Hulk in Langston Harbour, & the *Lion* Hulk in Portsmouth Harbour, during the year 1800. (*TNA ref T1/859*)

Date	Expenses	Amount
1800 July 1st	Paid the Revd John Jones, Chaplain to the Convicts on board the *Fortune* half a year's salary due the 30th June	£25 - 0 - 0
	Paid the Revd R.H. Cumyns, Chaplain to the Convicts on board the *Lion*, half a year's salary, due the 30th June	£17 - 0 - 10
Oct 1st	Paid Mr Groundwater his bill for expenses defrayed by him in conveying three Convicts to Winchester for the purpose of giving evidence in the prosecution of three other Convicts, charged with the murder of William Stovell a Convict on board the *Fortuneé*	£25 - 19 - 0
	Paid William Pollock Esqr the amount of Fees in passing, under the Great Seal, a special pardon to qualify the above mentioned Convicts to give evidence	£126 -19 - 4
31st	Paid Sergeant Thomas Evans, for apprehending James White, a Convict who escaped from the Public Works at Cumberland Fort	£2 - 2 - 0
	Paid the Revd John Jones, Chaplain to the Convicts on board the *Fortuneé*, half a year's salary due this day	£25 - 0 - 0
1801 Jany 1st	Paid the Revd R.H. Cumyns, Chaplain to the Convicts on board the *Lion* Hulk, half a year's salary due the 31st Dec.	£17 -10 - 0
29th	Paid Mr Grigg, one of the Coroners of Hampshire his Bill for Inquests taken on board the Hulks in Langston Harbour during the year 1800	£111 - 12 - 6
	Paid Juries on 94 Inquests taken on board the Hulks in Langston Harbour by Mr Grigg at 6s/8d each	£31 -12 - 10
	Paid Mr Barney, one of the Coroners of Hampshire, his Bill for Inquests taken on board the Hulks at Portsmouth Harbour during the year 1800	£17 - 13 - 4
	Paid Mr Bailey his Bill for the slops furnished, by order of His Grace the Duke of Portland, to 105 Convicts removed from the Hulks at Langston & Portsmouth Harbours, to the *Earl Cornwallis* Transport, to be sent to New South Wales	£154 - 7 - 6
1800 Decr 31st	Paid for Bounties & Cloathing to Convicts discharges from the *Fortunee* &c Hulks during the year 1800; vizt	
	From 1st January to 31st August, as per account attested by Captn Robt Burn £107 - 3 - 8	
	From 1st September to 31st December as per account attested by Captn W. Hartshorn £19 - 19 – 8	£127 - 3 - 4
	Paid for Bounties & Cloathing to Convicts discharged from the *Lion* & Hulks, as per account attested by Captn David Burn	£114 - 9 - 0
		£796 -12 - 8
	London, February 1801 (signed) A.H. Bradley	

HIGH COURT OF ADMIRALTY RECORDS
(TNA document group HCA)

Coroners' Inquisitions

Table 4.8: Convict Ship *Racoon* in Portsmouth Harbour. *(TNA ref HCA 1/ 105)*

Note: It is assumed that those men in the following tabulation, not recorded as convicts, were seamen.

No.	Name	Died	Cause
1	William West (convict)	13 Jan 1825	Typhus. Wm Charles Stedman, an assistant to Dr Porter the surgeon of His Majesty's Convict Ship *Racoon* in Portsmouth Harbour – attended the deceased. He died about 1 o'clock in the afternoon of 13 Jan. 1825. John Shorland, nurse on *Racoon*.
Inquest on *Havock* at Portsmouth			
3	William Cooper	14 January 1825	On board the *Three Crowns* at Portsmouth. Fell overboard – drowned
***Racoon* at Portsmouth**			
4	John Harvey (convict)	16 January 1825	Dropsy
5	John Hubbard (convict)	21 February 1825	Effusion of the lungs
6	Thomas Merrick (convict)	21 March 1825	Jammed between timber
7	Robert Moutell	9 April 1825	Pheumonia Typhoides
8	William Wardlown	15 May 1825	Inflamation of the larysang
9	George King (convict)	27 May 1825	Scruphula
10	William Playle (convict)	27 May 1825	Constipation of the bowels
11	Thomas Hills (convict)	2 June 1825	Typhus
12	James Pilgrim (convict)	2 June 1825	Inflamation of the lungs
***Magnificent* at Portsmouth**			
13	Isaac Bolton	6 June 1825	Drowned
***Racoon* at Portsmouth**			
14	Charles Bond (convict)	10 July 1825	Pleurisy
15	Joseph Knipe (convict)	2 July 1825	Consumption
16	Charles Whiting	24 July 1825	Typhus
17	Thomas Fetwell (convict)	28 July 1825	Drowned whilst bathing
18	James Powton (convict)	3 Sept. 1825	Chronic affection of the chest
19	John Scott (convict)	22 Oct. 1825	Pulmonary Consumption
20	William Gilligan (convict)	2 Oct. 1825	ditto
21	Walter Nunn (convict)	6 Nov. 1825	Typhus Fever
22	Henry Ford (convict)	6 Nov. 1825	Asthma
23	Robert Dawes	13 Nov. 1825	Inflammation of the Lungs
24	John Wilson (convict)	18 Nov. 1825	Mortification of the Foot

No.	Name	Died	Cause
25	James Jarvis (convict)	24 Nov. 1825	Diarrhoea
26	Francis Miller (convict)	28 Nov. 1825	Nervous Fever
27	Daniel White (convict)	10 Dec. 1825	Typhus Fever
28	John Densy (convict)	14 Dec. 1825	Palsy and Inflamation of the Lungs
29	John Newman (convict)	24 Dec. 1825	Dropsy
Victory at Portsmouth			
30	James Moatt	25 Dec. 1825	Excessive drinking
Racoon at Portsmouth			
31	John O'Neal (convict)	27 Dec. 1825	Inflamation of the Lungs
32	William Todd (convict)	28 Dec. 1825	Typhus

Investigation into the Escape of a Convict

The following is a rare example of the cost of the investigation and prosecution of an escaped convict, William Topper, from a prison hulk in 1802.

Table 4.9a: *Stanislaus* Prison Hulk at Woolwich. *(TNA ref T1/898)*

Kent   The King against William Topper   On the presentation of Thomas Nicholson for returning from Transportation

Summer Assizes 1802	
The prisoner having been committed for trial at these Assizes but having been found at large in the County of Middx he could not be tried for the same in Kent therefore drawing and Engrossing Affidavit of facts to apply to the Court to have him remanded for the next Old Bailey Sessions	0 - 6s - 8d
Attending Court to get same Sworn and Paid	0 - 4s - 4d
Motion Paper	0 - 2s - 6d
Fee to Mr Knowlys and Clerk	£1 - 3s - 6d
Attending him therewith	0 - 3s - 4d
Attending Court Motion granted and prisoner remanded to Newgate	0 - 6s - 8d
	£2 - 7s - 0d
	Sir, This is my Bill W. Teeckainph [?], Solicitor for the Prosecution Shadwell 26th January 1802 Stewart Erskine Esqr.

Table 4.9b: An Account of the expenses incurred by Mr John Leaford, Keeper of the Gaol at Ely in the prosecution of William Topper, a Convict who had escaped from the *Stanislaus* Hulk at Woolwich. *(TNA ref T1/898 continued)*

Date	Expenses	Amount	
1802 July 26	Paid for horse & gig, going from Ely to Wisbech & returning, two days, to get Certificate of Topper's conviction 16/- & Turnpikes 4/1	1 - 0 - 1	
Aug 1	Coach hire from Ely to Cambridge	5 - 0	
2	do from Cambridge to London	12 - 0	
3	do from London to Maidstone	10 - 6	
5	do from Maidstone to London	5 - 6	
6	do from London to Ely	13 - 0	
	Eight days allowance to a man for taking care of Gaol at Ely during my absence at 3/- per day	1 - 4 - 0	
	Eight days for my own expences going from Ely to Wisbech & to Maidstone & returning, @ 7/- per day	2 - 16 - 0	
	Extra charge for bed &c at Maidstone, 14 - 6	3 - 10 - 6	
Septr 9	Paid for horse & gig going from Ely to Wisbech & returning, to get Certificate of Topper's Conviction, the former one being lost at Mr Knapp's Office at Maidstone, 16/- & Turnpike 4/1	1 - 0 - 1	
	Two days allowance to man for taking care of Gaol @ 3/- & allowance for self 14/-	1 - 0 - 0	
	Paid Mr Gordlestone for Certificate of Topper's Conviction	7 - 0	
20	Seven days expences for self going to London to attend the prosecution of Topper & returning to Ely @ 7/- per day	2 - 9 - 0	
	Seven days allowance to man for taking care of Gaol during my absence	1 - 0 - 0	
		£13 -17 - 8[2]	

September 23rd   Accepted (signed) John Leaford

Aug 21	To amount of Mr William Telkampff's [sic] Account on removing the Court at Maidstone to remand William Topper to next Old Bailey Sessions, Topper being apprehended in Middlesex		£2 - 7 - 0
Sept 11	Paid Mr Knapp, discharging recognizance at Maidstone & taking recognizance to prosecute William Topper in Middx as per receipt		£1- 11 - 0
	Paid postage from Gaoler of Ely with Topper's Certificate		1 - 9
Octr 7	Paid Mr J. Leaford, Gaoler of Ely, his Account of Expences attending the prosecution of William Topper, a Convict who had escaped from the Hulk at Woolwich as per acct & receipt		£13 - 17 - 10[3]

Date	Expenses	Amount	
	Less expenses allowed by the Court at Maidstone	£2 - 18 - 4	
	do at the Old Bailey	6 -18 - 4	
	Charge on receipt [deducted]	8 - 0	
		£6 - 10 - 4	7 - 7 - 6
	Paid Mr Nicholson, one of my Officers, his expences attending the prosecution of William Topper twice at Maidstone & once at the Old Bailey as per receipt		£7 - 10
	Less expences allowed by the Court at Maidstone & Old Bailey	£6 - 7 - 0	
	Charge paid Mr Recorder's Clerk	6 - 0	
		£6 - 1 - 0	1 - 9 - 0

2. As appears in the original document.
3. As appears in the original document.

Old Bailey Proceedings – Seventh Session, Saturday, 18 September 1802

William Topper was indicted for being at large before the expiration of the term for which he had been ordered to be transported:

> John Leaford sworn: (Produces a copy of the record of conviction of the prisoner).
> Question   Where did you get that?
> Answer   I received it from Mr Girdlestone, clerk of Assize at Wisbeach.
>   (It was read)
> Question   Were you present at the trial?
> Answer   Yes, I conveyed him from Ely to Wisbeach, prior to the trial.
> Question   Is the prisoner at the bar the same person?
> Answer   Yes.
> Question   Are you sure of it?
> Answer   I am convinced of it; I saw him again at Maidstone Assizes, on the 5th of August last. I saw him in Maidstone jail, I went to identify his person.
>
> Mr Knowlys
> Question   When you saw him at Maidstone was he not highly recommended?
> Answer   Mr Watson told me he stood first upon the list, the best behaved person in the world.
>
> John Ray sworn
> Question   You are an officer?
> Answer   I belong to the Police Office, Worship Street. In consequence of information I apprehended the prisoner on the 8th of March last in the parish of St George, Middlesex, in a house.
>
> Mr Knowlys
> Question   Do you recollect whose house it was?
> Answer   No, I do not.
> Court   Was he at work there?

Answer	He had been at work as a smith; he behaved himself remarkably civil. I have made every enquiry I could and found that from the time of his being at large he has been constantly at work, up to the time of my apprehending him.
Question	And he was apprehended merely for being at large?
Answer	Only for being at large.

For the Prisoner
Samuel Parker sworn.

Question	You are a furnishing ironmonger and live in Duck Lane, St George's in the East?
Answer	Yes.
Question	I believe the prisoner was your servant when he was taken up by Ray?
Answer	Yes.
Question	When was it he first came into your service?
Answer	In October last.
Question	Had you ever an honester, or more faithful servant in your life?
Answer	Never; he was my porter and money receiver; he always settled my money accounts in the most punctual manner, out of doors.

GUILTY, *DEATH*, aged 25
The prisoner was recommended by the Jury, to His Majesty's mercy on account of his good behaviour.
Second Middlesex Jury, before Mr Justice Le Blanc.

The Times newspaper, 20 September 1802, records:
> William Topper was capitally indicted for being found at large, he having been found guilty of felony in August 1800, at the assizes for the County of Cambridge and sentenced to seven years transportation. The record of the prisoner's conviction was put in and read. John Ray,[4] Police Officer apprehended the prisoner, for no other offence but being at large. Mr Parker, a Furnishing Ironmonger in St. George's in the East, gave the prisoner a most excellent character. He had entrusted him at various times to collect money, and in general placed the most implicit confidence in his integrity. The Jury found him Guilty, but recommended him to mercy on account of his good behaviour since he has been at large.

RECORDS OF PRISON ESCAPES

Sometimes a convict attempted to escape custody before transportation, and occasionally references to such occurrences can be found in prison records. The following example is taken from the records of Ilchester Gaol, Somerset.

Som.H.C. ref Q/AG(I) 16/4

> The statement of William Griffiths one of the Prisoners who attempted to make his escape from Van when being conveyed from Ilchester Gaol to the Hulks at Portsmouth. 'When I was taken into custody and conveyed to Yate's Lockup House at Bedminster two spring saws conveyed to me by a friend which I concealed in the collar of my

coat, previous to leaving the Gaol at Ilchester, I cut my own irons about half the way through, these were the only irons that were cut in the Prison, the irons of James Rose, Charles Lucas, Charles Lewis, were cut in the Van by the same saw, and no knife was used for that purpose, the bottom of the Van was also cut with the same instrument, and everything was accomplished for effecting the escape by the time we reached Salisbury, the only persons that knew of my being in possession of the saw were the three prisoners above named, who effected their escape. I have only to add that the saw was thrown away by me when I was taken in running away from the van.'

William Griffiths
X his mark

Witness to the statement and signature of William Griffiths
   Robt Kellick, Overseer
   J. Newman, Chief Mate
Leviathan, Convict Hulk
Portsmouth
21st May 1835

To: Mr Hardy, Keeper of Ilchester Gaol

CHAPTER 5

PETITIONS BY AND ON BEHALF OF CONVICTS

(See Appendices 9 and 22)

Numerous petitions were received by the Home Office from the wives, husbands and dependants of convicted criminals, pleading for clemency. They appear in several departmental classes of documents at The National Archives. It is possible that some petitions found in one series of documents are duplicated in another series, though to date no evidence to support this suggestion has been found. There are tens of thousands of petitions at TNA relating to criminals. There are also indices to some document classes that contain petitions. These documents often give further details of a crime and may refer to the dependants and the personal circumstances of a convict's family.

The official procedure (if there was a single procedure) is unclear, but it is apparent that a lot of these appeals were ineffective. It is not unusual to find no further reference to a petition. It is probable that many of them were ignored and filed away. Some petitions were successful, as can be seen from the Criminal Registers at TNA (document classes HO 26 and HO 27, see Chapter 2) where a reduction in a sentence, or a full pardon is recorded. Reprieves are also to be found recorded among Home Office Warrants (see Appendix 10). It is worthwhile searching through the Home Office Warrants to establish whether or not a reduced sentence was granted and then searching through the files of pardons around the appropriate date.

These respites and pardons were, in many cases, the direct result of petitions from convicts' families and occasionally from the convicts themselves. It should be noted that at the beginning of the nineteenth century there were more than 100 crimes for which the death sentence could be imposed. It is clear that justices, while obliged by law to apply this sentence, in a number of cases automatically followed it by granting a reprieve through the auspices of the Home Office. This would account for the large number of death sentences that were reduced to a term of transportation, or service in the army or navy. In such cases petitions rarely exist.

The Colonial Office correspondence is listed in CO 714/118 and acts as an index to this correspondence. Petitions and pardons are included in these records.

Not all petitions were straightforward appeals for mercy: see, for example, those from the Colonial Office records.

The following are examples of the detailed and pathetic appeals to be found among Home Office documents.

TNA ref HO 47/34 Judges Reports [undated, c.1808]

A Petition for a Pardon for Daniel Allen

To the Right Honourable Earl of Liverpool, Principal Secretary of State for the Home Department.

The humble petition of the aged and miserable parents of Daniel Allen who is on board the *Retribution* hulk at Woolwich under sentence of 7 years transportation.

Bows and prays with humble submission depending on your Lordships clemency and charity to restore unto them their unfortunate son he being the only one they have living out of eleven, by your Lordship give him a pardon whereby he may give his aged parents consolation for their tears and be a comfort to them and himself the remainder of his life. Which he and them pray that you and yours may ever flourish like the green bay tree that grows by the waters edge and is ever green or like Aarons rod which budded and brought forth fruit; praying may the blessings of Almighty God ever attend you and your posterity, may the Sun of Glory shine around your head, may the Gates of plenty honor and happiness ever be opened to you and yours, may no sorrows distress your days and may no grief disturb your nights. May the Pillow of Peace kiss your cheek and may the pleasure of imagination attend your dreams and when the light of time makes you tired of earthly joys and Curtains of Death closeth the last sleep of human existence may the Angel of God attend you and take care that the expiring lamp of Life receives one rude blast to hasten its existence. Which will be the prayers of your Lordship's sorrowful petitioners and as in duty bound will ever pray.

Robert and Ann Allen

N.B. We recommend the petitioners to your Lordship's compassion:

Wm. Hobson	Wm. Trip, M. Genl., 2nd Co. of Royal Engineers
Jos. Batho	W. Congreve, Lieut. General
Sawyer Thos. Spence	C. Neb. Mitchinor
William Green	Chas. Weaver, Woolwich
T.P. Weaver, Clerk of Works, Woolwich	

I believe the petitioner to be a subject worthy of consideration.

Wm. Bagwale, M.P.

Note: Despite this appeal, the *Retribution*'s register *(TNA ref HO 9/4)* shows that Daniel Allen (aged 22 at his conviction at Middlesex Sessions on 1 June 1808) was transported on 27 February 1811. He sailed in the *Admiral Gambier (TNA ref HO 11/2)*.

TNA ref HO 17/1 (part 1)

A Petition for a Pardon for James Taylor

Margate, June 30th, 1824

At a very Numerous and highly Respectable Meeting of inhabitants convened by the Deputy, and held this day at the Town Hall, at Twelve o'clock, for the purpose of laying before them the Measures which have been adopted with the view of obtaining the Pardon of JAMES TAYLOR, now at Botany Bay, under a commuted sentence of Transportation for Life, but who it is believed, is guiltless of the Crime, for which he was transported, and to adopt such further means in the Case, as shall be deemed most advisable.

FRANCIS COBB. Esq., Deputy,
In the Chair

This Meeting having fully considered the Case of James Taylor, who, with eighteen others, were tried before the Honourable Baron Wood, at the Spring Assizes for the County of Kent, held at Maidstone, in the Year One Thousand Eight Hundred and Twenty Two, under the Statute Fifty-Second George the Third, upon a charge of having on the Second Day of September, One Thousand Eight Hundred and Twenty-One, feloniously assembled together with Fire Arms, and other offensive Weapons, at, or near Marsh Bay, in the Parish of Saint John the Baptist, in this County, for the purpose of removing Smuggled Goods. It appears that upon the Trial of the said Indictment, Thomas Cooke, James Justice, Samuel Kerby Meredith and Thomas Mears, were examined, on the part of the Crown, not one of whom (except Cooke) charged the said James Taylor with being in the affray which was the subject of the Indictment; that Cooke, upon Cross Examination, admitted that there was much confusion and noise, that he himself was in a state of considerable alarm, and that morning was dark and hazy at the time at which it appeared to him that he saw and heard Taylor in the Affray; that it is evident that if Taylor was in the Affray his presence there must have been known to Justice, Meredith and Mears, in as much as they were Accomplices in the Offence with which Taylor was charged; that on the part of Taylor, Three Witnesses, Robert Harman, Charles Winch and James Saunders were separately examined; all of whom proved most clearly and distinctly that Taylor was engaged with them, from Twelve to Three o'Clock in the morning, in another transaction at one of the Bathing Houses at Margate, a distance of nearly Two Miles from the place at which the Affray happened, for which Taylor stood indicted; that although the Transaction in which Taylor was so engaged, was one of an illicit nature, yet it amounted however, only to a Misdemeanour, and was totally unconnected with the Affair which took place at Marsh Bay, as is fully proved by the Affidavits of the said Robert Harman, John Saunders, Charles Winch, and one John Jones; that Taylor being naturally anxious, not only on his own account, but for the protection of the persons concerned with him in the illicit Transaction at Margate, was induced on his first Examination, to suppress that fact, and consequently, to give an unfaithful account of what he was doing during the time of the Affray at Marsh Bay; the minds of the Jury being unduly impressed with this Circumstance, found Taylor, together with the other Eighteen Persons who were indicted with him, guilty of the capital Felony with which they were charged; it appears also that Mr Adolphus who had been retained as Counsel for Taylor, handed over his brief to Mr Walford, and he left it to Mr Ryland, who had not read one word of it.

And also, that the Learned Judge, who presided at the Trial, being convinced that Cooke was mistaken as to the identity of Taylor, and being therefore dissatisfied with the Verdict of the Jury, recommend Taylor to His Majesty for a Free Pardon. That notwithstanding this recommendation, Taylor has been Transported for Life, contrary to what has been uniformly the benign course pursued, in similar cases, by His Majesty's illustrious Family, since their Accession to the Throne of these Realms.

It is acknowledged by the Secretary of State, that Mr Baron Wood did recommend Taylor for Pardon, but it is stated the Judge altered his opinion after he had received further information from Mr Peel; from whence he obtained it, or how he could ascertain its truth is very difficult to understand.

AND FARTHER, that in addition to the Case made by Taylor at his Trial, farther proofs of his innocence are to be found in the dying Depositions of Four Persons, who were executed for the Offence upon Taylor, all negativing Taylor's presence at or participation in, the Crime for which they suffered; and also in Stephen Laurence, who employed all the Persons who were engaged in the said Affray, at Marsh Bay, declaring to several Persons of the most Respectable Rank and Character at Margate, that Taylor was wholly innocent of the Charge brought against him, and that he (Laurence) was the Person who spoke the words, and did the acts, attributed by Cooke to Taylor.

THAT THEREFORE, whether regard be had to the Evidence given at the Trial, or that which has been subsequently obtained, but more especially when both are taken together into consideration, there is abundant proof of Taylor's Innocence; for it is clear that of the Four Witnesses who were produced on the part of the Prosecution, One only affected to identify Taylor; and that Witness admitted that he was at the time to which his Testimony referred, placed in such circumstances as necessarily to induce much suspicion as to the possibility of his accuracy; for there was great noise and confusion then prevailing, and he was in a state of much personal alarm, and the night was dark and hazy; and moreover if such testimony stood alone, it ought to be deemed to ground a Judgement of Guilty upon; but Taylor's defence is fortified by the negative Testimony of Three of the Witnesses produced on the part of the Crown, by the direct and positive Evidence of Three consistent Witnesses produced by the Prisoner, who could not be mistaken as to the Fact to which they deposed, by the dying Depositions of Four Convicts who were Executed, and by the declaration of Laurence, who admitted himself to be the Person whom Cooke mistook for Taylor; so that the Charge against Taylor is sustained by the Testimony of One Witness only, who was placed in circumstances which furnish strong ground to conclude that he was mistaken; while his innocence is attested by Eleven Witnesses, neither of whom could be under any mistake or delusion as to the Prisoner's Identity.

And again it appears, that upon a late application to the Honourable House of Commons, in behalf of James Taylor, Mr Peel stated his wish 'To do justice to the Man, and had been so careful, that when one individual has described himself to have heard words spoken while in his own house at the time of the affray, which made in favour of Taylor, that he had caused the distance between that House and the Spot to be measured; the consequence was, the House was found to be fifteen roods, more than half a mile from the Place where the words were said to be spoken.' Now it appears from direct evidence of several persons at this Meeting, that in the Evening of Tuesday the twenty second instant, the experiment was tried; when only four sentences were spoken by Mr Jarvis, at Mr Cramp's House and every word was distinctly heard at the place of the outrage.

This Meeting therefore Unanimously Resolve that they consider James Taylor innocent of the Crime for which he is punished; and earnestly entreat the Committee to take such further steps in the Case, as shall appear to them most advisable.

Resolved Unanimously – That a Subscription be forthwith entered into to relieve the immediate necessities of Taylor's Wife and Children; and that it be appropriated under direction of the Gentlemen who signed the Requisition for this Meeting.

Resolved Unanimously – That we shall always consider ourselves most highly indebted to J.P. Powell, Esq., the late High Sheriff of the County, for the very manly and kind part he has taken in favor of Taylor and his family.

Resolved Unanimously – That our sincere expression of Thanks be offered to R. Martin, Esq., M.P., for the very humane and active part he hath taken, in behalf of James Taylor.

Resolved Unanimously – That the Cordial Thanks of this Meeting are especially due to the Inhabitants who signed the Requisition to the Deputy, particularly to Daniel Jarvis, whose unwearied exertions in developing the intricacies of the Case, are most highly creditable to his Head and Heart.

Resolved Unanimously – That the Thanks of this Meeting are due to our Deputy, F. Cobb, Esq., for his able conduct in the Chair.

Resolved Unanimously – That these Resolutions be printed, and published in the London, and also in the Kentish papers.

Francis Cobb, signed,
Chairman.

[The following note has been added:]
'3 approven swore that James Taylor was not there – if he had had aid of Counsel!'

To the Knights, Citizens and Burgesses in Parliament assembled.

The HUMBLE PETITION of MARIA TAYLOR. Wife of James Taylor, late of Margate, Bricklayer, but now a Convict in New South Wales, under a Commuted Sentence of Transportation for Life.

[This petition repeats word-for-word the story as given in the last document and concludes as follows:]

That your Petitioner, relying upon the circumstances of the Case, upon the learned Judge's Recommendation, and, above all, upon the unbounded Benevolence of the Royal Breast, preferred a Petition to His Most Gracious Majesty, through the Right Honourable the Secretary of State for the Home Department, stating the Facts herein before mentioned, and praying that His Majesty might be graciously pleased to grant to the said James Taylor, His Majesty's Free Pardon, and to restore him to his disconsolate Wife, and three Infant Children.

That shortly afterwards, the Secretary of State returned to your Petitioner's Application, stating that he could not recommend the said Convict for any further extension of the Royal Mercy.

That under the foregoing circumstances, your Petitioner submits the Case of the said James Taylor to the Justice of this Honourable House, and prays such Relief as to them in their Wisdom shall seem meet.

And your Petitioner shall ever pray,

Maria Taylor

[undated]

[The final outcome of this case is not recorded here.]

TNA ref HO 47/35

A Petition from James Gilling, a Convict

To the King's Most Excellent Majesty,

The Humble Petition of James Gilling convicted of Bigamy at the Old Bailey in December Sessions 1804 and Sentenced to 7 years Transportation

SHEWETH

That your Petitioner having been thought deserving the punishment inflicted, Humbly implores your Most Gracious mercy extended in his behalf, and deplores with the most heartfelt remorse, and contrition having been guilty of the same, and that at the time he contracted Marriage, He had every reason to believe his former Wife had departed this Life having been separated from her a considerable length of time. That after the marriage took place between your Petitioner and his present Wife the Prosecutrix much uneasiness took place from the bad dispositions she possess'd, and the evil influence of her friends against your Petitioner, tho no just case was ever Assign'd as your Petitioner was not actuated by any motives of Interest in the marriage, but from those feelings of Affection which constituted his regard.

YOUR PETITIONER with the utmost humility presumed to intrude on Your Majesty's humane consideration, his ever having supported an unblemished character, until this unfortunate circumstance, and from the consequences of which, He has involved himself and family, in misery, and distress of mind, and all the horrors of poverty and want is such ultimately will entail his ruin. [sic]

YOUR PETITIONER therefore most humbly implores your Majesty's most Gracious mercy may be extended in permitting your Petitioner to enter into the East London Regiment of Militia, commanded by Colonel Sir John Eamer, Sir John having signified his willingness to accept your Petitioner's services in that capacity, that by a future conduct he may certify the just sense he shall ever retain of that mercy bestowed.

AND YOUR PETITIONER as in duty bound will pray.

James Gilling

We the undersigned presume to recommend to your Majesty the above Petitioner James Gilling as truly Loyal and well Affected to your Majesty's person and Government and as an object deserving the extension of your Royal Mercy having served as Volunteer in the Loyal Southwark Regiment.

John Alcock Lieut. Col. Commandant L.S.V. [Loyal Southwark Volunteers]
Soloman Davies Liet. Col. L.S.V.
J. Jones Captain 2 Compy. L.S.V.
Henery Warecamp
John Fox, Borough High St.
John Gray, Borough
George Ford, Boro
John Turrell, Boro

[Attached to this petition, unusually, there is a document showing that the case was investigated.]

Chancery Lane, April 13th 1805

My Lord,

In obedience to His Majesty's Command, which your Lordship has done me the Honor to signify, I have taken into consideration the Case of James Robert Gillan, otherwise James Gilling, who was indicted, for that he on the 4th of July 1791, at the Parish of Saint Ann, Westminster, did take to wife Ann Smith, and to her was married; and that he afterwards on the 3rd of November 1801, at the Parish of Saint Martin in the Fields, did take to wife one Olive Adams, his former Wife being then living.

Jane Thompson swore that she knew the Prisoner; she also knew a person of the name of Ann Smith; the Prisoner and Ann Smith were married in the year 1791, at Saint Ann's Westminster; she had seen Ann Smith only a minute or two before her Trial, she was sure the Prisoner was the Person.

Olive Adams swore that she knew the Prisoner; she was married to the Prisoner in November 1801, at Saint Martin in the Fields; she was sure the Prisoner was the Man.

GUILTY To be Transported for Seven Years.

As it does not appear that this Case has been attended with any material circumstances of aggravation, and considering the previous good Character of the Prisoner, together with the strong recommendation now in his favour, I think that Public Justice will not suffer if His Majesty should be graciously pleased to grant the Prayer of his Petition; All which I submit to His Majesty's Wisdom.

I am with Respect, My Lord,

Your Lordship's Most Obedient, Humble Servant,

John Silvester

The Right Honble Lord Hawkesbury

Note: The Middlesex Criminal Registers (HO 26/10 and HO 26/11) show that James Robert Gillan alias James Gilling (aged 38, from Bristol) was pardoned on 15 April 1805 and was to serve in the army. Further details of this pardon are given in a Home Office Warrant in HO 13/16, page 392:

Wheras James Gilling was at a Session holden at the Old Bailey in December last tried and convicted of Bigamy and was sentenced to be Transported seven years for the same. We in consideration of some favourable circumstances humbly represented unto us in his behalf are graciously pleased to extend our Grace and Mercy unto him and to grant him our Pardon for the said Crime on condition of his enlisting and continuing to serve us in our East London Regiment of Militia until duly discharged therefrom. Our Will and Pleasure therefore is that upon his enlisting to serve in the said Regiment of Militia you cause him the said James Gilling to be delivered unto such person as shall be duly authorized to receive for that purpose and that he be inserted for his said Crime on the said Condition in Our first and next General Pardons that shall come out for the poor convicts in Newgate. And for so doing this shall be your Warrant, Given at our Court in St. James' this 15 day of April 1805 in the forty fifth year of Our Reign.

By His Majesty's Command

Hawkesbury

TNA ref HO 17/64

A Petition from Alexander Wood On Behalf of his Wife Susan Wood

Susan Wood, 32, Kent Quarter Sessions, Maidstone, July 1833
Stealing shoes – 7 years transportation
Gaoler's Report – Married, 4 Children

Petition of Alexander Wood
In behalf of his Wife Susan Wood, convicted at the last July Sessions at Maidstone in the County of Kent
To the Right Honorable the Secretary of State for the Home Department

Your Petitioner having been plunged into the deepest affliction from a crime committed by his wife Susan Wood, now a convict in Maidstone Gaol against the Laws of her Country for having pawned goods entrusted for your Petitioner's care in the moment of extreme distress when a Family of 4 small children aged 2 years, 4 years, 6 years & 8 years was in a state of absolute starvation and your Petitioner labouring under severe illness these circumstances drove your Petitioner's wife Susan Wood (now far advanced in pregnancy) in an unguarded moment to commit the act to supply food for her starving and destitute Family and for which she deeply and sincerely repents and which has subjected her to the severest suffering of her being torn from her Infant Family to undergo the penalty of 7 years Transportation.

Your Petitioner most humbly submits his distressing case to Your Lordship's most merciful consideration to be pleased to mitigate the Term of imprisonment and to restore your petitioner's wife Susan Wood to her distressed Family and disconsolate Husband. Your Petitioner trusting that this being her first offence and committed under such peculiar and distressing circumstances. Your Lordship may deem her case one entitled to your Lordship's feeling and merciful recommendation and restore a Wife and Mother to her lost unhappy and destitute Family and your Petitioner will in duty bound ever pray.

County Gaol
Maidstone
29th Oct. 1833

Sir,
I beg to acknowledge the receipt of the Order for the removal of Susan Wood a Convict under Sentence of Transportation for seven years to the Penitentiary at Millbank. Since the return was forwarded Viz. on the 10th of September last she was delivered of a Male Child which is still alive.

I shall therefore feel obliged by your informing me if it is requested that the Order should direct the admission of the Child also as it must of necessity accompany the Prisoner its Mother for nurture.

I have the honor to be,
Sir
Your most obedient humble servant
Thomas Agar

Keeper
J.H.Capper Esq.

County Gaol, Maidstone
6th August 1836

My Lord
I beg to state to your Lordship that Susan Wood a Convict now in this Gaol was tried at the Midsummer Sessions 1833, and sentenced to Transportation for Seven Years, and on the 26th of October following an Order was received to remove her to the Penitentiary at Millbank, but she having been delivered of a child in the Gaol, a subsequent Order was received not to remove her till the child was disposed of, the Prisoner having had no means of disposing of the Child is consequently remaining in the Gaol. Should your Lordship think proper to recommend her to the Royal Mercy. I further beg to add, the Chaplain and Governor of the Prison represent that she has conducted herself with strict propriety during the whole period of her imprisonment.

I have the honor to be
My Lord
Your most ob^t & humble Servt
Manham Vinting, Justice

To the Right Hon'ble
The Secretary of State
Home Department

Further petitions are recorded in the Colonial Office correspondence. The following are examples:

TNA ref CO 201/199, f 260

A Petition from John Hurst, a Convict

Bolton le Moors, 29th November 1828

To the Rt. Hon. The President and Transport Board
Sheweth,
That your humble petitioner was convicted at a Special Commission held at Lancaster on 23rd May 1812 to seven years Transportation for being present at the Taken unlawful oaths, was sent with others to New South Wales.

That your petitioner's conduct was such that he was chosen to act as Constable for the District and did act as such for 3 years in various important cases, as the Governors, if alive, will prove, after which he was made the Chief Constable but one, and had the Command of all the officers in the absence or indisposition of the Chief, in which office he did his Duty to the satisfaction of the authorities full two years, at the end of which he came home to his native land leaving some property in the Country.

That in consequence of your petitioner having lost all that set value upon this Country [sic], and having some property in the one which he lived so many years, being besides well skilled in agriculture, it is his wish to go thither once more as a free settler and if it please the Honourable Board he wishes to have a Grant of Land there that so he may, not only cultivate that but recover his former property which he has reason to fear is either misapplied or is in improper Hands, and that he prays such information as will be necessary on the said subject

Your Humble Petitioner there prays that he may have an order for such quantity of land as shall be thought proper when he arrives at New South Wales. That in return he may be informed when a ship will sail thither, and from wherever with every other matter necessary and if he has made an improper application he requests that this petition may be refferred [sic] to the Proper Office, and he be instituted to whence it is referred, Directed to 26 Spring Gardens, Bolten le Moors, Lancashire.

and your petitioner as in Duty Bound will ever pray,
John Hurst.

That annexed is a copy of petitioner's emancipation No. on Indent (His Majesty's Arms). No. Twenty One.
These are to certify that the bearer hereof, John Hurst, who was tried at Lancaster May 23rd 1812, and who came to this colony in the ship *Fortune 2nd,* Walker master, in the year 1813, under sentence of transportation for seven years and whose description [not entered with the document] is hereunto annexed, hath duly served the period for which he had been transported and is henceforth restored to freedom.

Given under my hand at the
Secretary's Office, Hobart Town,
Van Diemens Land this 25th May 1819
Wm. Sowell
Lt. Governor

Registered in the Secretary's Office,
May 25th 1819
T. Wells, P.Clk.

TNA ref CO 201/73

A Petition on behalf of Thomas Alford, a Convict

Sydney, N.S. Wales
17th May 1814

Sir,

1. Thomas Alford an old and very faithful Servant to Government, and who has been for upwards of twenty five years in the Colony, the greater part of which time he has served as Head Government Gardener, to the entire satisfaction of every successive Governor; having determined to pass the remainder of his days in this Country, is particularly desirous to have his wife (who is still alive in England) and any of his Family who may be willing to accompany her, sent out to join him, providing it could be done without any expense, which he is unable to defray.

2. I have therefore to request you will be so good as to move Lord Bathurst to have the goodness to order a passage to be found for Thomas Alford's wife, and such of her family as may wish to accompany her, at the expense of Government on board of one of the first Convict Ships from England to this Colony.

3. The following is Mrs Alford's address, vizt Mary Alford, Curry Rivel, near Taunton, Somersetshire, England. I also enclose a letter from her husband for her, which I take the liberty to request you will have the goodness to forward, and shall esteem it a favor if you will be so good as to give the necessary facility to the request contained in the letter being complied with,

I have the honor to be,
Sir, Your Most Obedient
Humble Servant
L. Macquarie

Henry Goulburn Esq.,
Under Secretary of State
Downing Street
London

Curry Rivell
Nov[r] 14 – 1814

Sir,

In behalf of Mary Alford, wife of Thomas Alford of Sydney, New South Wales, I beg to make the following reply to your letter of the 9th instant. Mary Alford is impressed with gratitude at the kind offer of a passage to Port Jackson at the public expense, but as she is far advanced in years she considers the voyage would be an undertaking beyond her strength to accomplish, and therefore she is compelled to decline the opportunity now offered her of visiting her husband. Her family are grown up and married and consequently settled. She imagines that her eldest son would probably like, if possible, to go to his father with his wife and child but as he lives at a distance of many miles she cannot have immediate communication with him, nor does it seem necessary as the present vessel would not take him being above the age specified. Should he be willing to go to his father with his wife and child could he be permitted to go at the public expense by some future ship, if so could you be kind enough to inform her of the circumstance and opportunity? Mary Alford will feel much obliged if the inclosed letter to her husband could be conveyed by you inclosed in the dispatches to New South Wales. Owing to the death of a relation a sum of money between £70 and £80 falls to Thomas Alford. This money would add much to the comfort of his wife in her old age to the families of her children, but the Exor [executor] refuses to pay it unless she can produce an order from her husband to that effect. This she has written to her husband for but received no answer and as her letter from him inclosed in yours made no mention of the subject she conceives her letters must have miscarried. She has a conviction however that the inclosed letter if forwarded from the Secretary of State's Office, would both reach her husband and obtain the order for the money. She hopes therefore this representation will apologise for the liberty she takes in requesting her letter may be sent to Sydney through your conveyance.

Your humble Servant
Samuel Alford
Heale House
near Langport
Novr 14 – 1814

Note: Thomas Alford probably returned home in 1817 (see Chapter 18).

TNA ref CO 201/281

The Case of John Watts and his Wife and Eight Children

John Watts of Tusmore in the County of Oxford, labourer, was convicted of sheep stealing and was sent to Sydney by the Ship *Stratfieldsay* which arrived in the Colony in June 1836. He left behind him a wife and 8 children viz:

Elizabeth Watts	- the wife now aged 35
John Watts	- the eldest son 15
Sarah Watts	- the eldest daughter 14
George Watts	- the 2nd son 13
James Watts	- the 3rd son 11
Charlotte Watts	- the 2nd daughter 9
Catherine Watts	- the 3rd daughter 7
Jane Watts	- the 4th Daughter 5
Elizabeth Watts	- the 5th daughter 3

John Watts before his trial bore an excellent character and the woman on whose evidence he was convicted has since been shewn to be utterly unworthy of belief and all the Gentlemen in the neighbourhood are satisfied that in point of fact he was innocent. On his arrival in the Colony he was assigned to a Mr G.F. Davidson who on the 9th of May 1838 addressed a Letter to Mr Mitchell of Hithe House near Bicester who had taken an interest in this unfortunate Family speaking in the highest terms of Watts conduct & Mr Davidson's letter proceeds as follows:

   'The Government of this Colony will do nothing towards getting Watts' wife and family out until he has served the regular term of eight years from the day of his assignment to me. However if you or any other party interested in the family's welfare can thro' the medium of Subscription or by assistance from the parish, raise means sufficient to pay half the expense of sending them to this Country I hereby bind myself to pay the other half on their arrival in Sydney. The family must be a burthen to the parish at home whereas in this Country they could easily earn a comfortable living. Indeed I would gladly employ them on my own farm where they could live with their Husband & father. There are numerous emigrant ships leaving London for this Colony almost every month so that there would be no difficulty in providing them a passage on moderate terms & Commander of the vessel can be referred to my Agent Mr S.A. Donaldson of Pitt Street, Sydney who will see every thing done on their arrival.'

The most satisfactory testimonials can be given of the character & conduct of Elizabeth Watts & all her children. The three boys have been accustomed to plough, reap & attend Cart Horses. The 4 eldest girls can read & can make lace, sew, hem, &c.

The object of the present application is to obtain a passage for the wife & children to Sydney either free or at the smallest possible expense, and any communication on the subject will be thankfully received by

Mr Michael Clayton
New Square
Lincolns Inn

TNA ref J 76/8/6 part 2

A Petition from John Pearce, Ex-soldier

The following is a rare example of a petition from John Pearce, an ex-soldier (and later a convict in New South Wales), to his commanding officer. There is also a petition on his behalf from his commanding officer Lieutenant Colonel Gideon Gorrequer whose papers are deposited at The National Archives in the records of the Supreme Court of Judicature, document class J 76.

To Lt. Col. Gorrequer

9th October 1829

Sir,
I am induced from personal knowledge of your humanity to solicit fair interception in my behalf with the Secretary of State or some other State Officer by obtaining a pardon, or emancipation for me. I at present hold a ticket of leave. I have, with many others, a petition signed for freedom by G. Sir Thos. Brisbane we have not received any. Col. Dumarey directs this letter for me whose good graces I have always merited with his brother likewise Major Marley, 3rd Regt or Buffs tho I believe is now in Chester for any reference on my account he would cross the Kingdom to save me. I am overseer of Plastins gang since 1814 by appointment of Govr Macquarie. I still continue as such in the Engineers Department which is always conducted by a military officer man of great merit whose good will I have always merited. Gnl Darling will give no pardon unless an order from home. The information of Col. Dumarey to me of your being in London causes me to beg your favor in obtaining my liberty for me.

I was transported for life from Gloster [sic] City in March 1810 from the 18th or R[oyal] I[rish] Rgt of Foot which you commanded at that period. I have been here 19 years in the actual employ of Government with the firmness of a man without the least blemish attached to my character. Major Marly or Lieut Hesting [?] Sir Thos's Adjt will inform you of the same therefore I am done & beg pardon for this long epistle & live in hopes that I do not merit your displeasure I look to you only for my liberty.

Sir with full of respect
I am your most humble & obedient memorialist
John Pearce

Sir Please to direct to Col. Dunning for me.

The Adjt General of the Forces
c/o Horseguards A.S. Club
15 April 1830

Sir,

I take the liberty of bringing under your consideration the enclosed letter addressed to me by a convict at New South Wales who formerly served under my command as a private soldier in the 18th Rgt of Foot and as his case presents circumstances of a peculiar and interesting nature which may tend to produce mitigation of his doom I have not hesitated soliciting your humane interception with H.M's Govt on his behalf should the following explanation of those circumstances superadded to 20 years prisoner exile appear to render him a fit subject for your favourable intervention.

John Pearce was inlisted in the 18th Rl Irish Regt in the year 1809 and some time after was apprehended for a robbery the particulars of which were as follows:

In the evening of a market or fair day at Glocester [sic] Pearce went to a public house in that city to which soldiers were in the habit of resorting and was there treated to some drink by a farmer who on paying the reckoning exhibited a purse which contained some bank notes and cash. Pearce left the public house. The farmer retired to his room locking the door of the room and placed his small clothes, which contained the purse, under his pillow for security, and having drunk freely he was not disturbed during the night. On his arising from his bed the following day he found his small clothes on the floor; the purse missing; the window open and the muddy track of a man's feet traceable from the inn yard through the window into the room.

Pearce was naturally suspected of the robbery but the magistrates before whom he was brought and examined not considering the circumstances above were sufficient by them to authorize his committal. He continued at large without ever shewing any symptoms of an intention to abscond from his Corps though his escape could have been certainly effected. He was after however taken up and committed to gaol for trial upon the deposition of one of his comrades, a soldier of the same Regt who then swore that Pearce had confessed to him he was the person who had stolen the farmer's purse and money.

As the soldier who thus accused Pearce before the magistrates, had never reported the circumstances either to his Com'g Officer which was his duty in the first instance to have done, or to any other officer & that thus he had given this information against Pearce immediately after having a quarrel with him though some time had elapsed since the alleged confession as he further stated that though Pearce had taken him there he deduced the money had been concealed by him it could not be found. I felt surely disturbed at his dismay and determined to be in attendance at the trial at the following Assizes to offer such evidence as I concluded could be advantageous to him and which from his good conduct in other respects since his enlistment would I have every reason to hope have had considerable weight with the Court and Jury.

It however unfortunately occurred that on the last day of the Assizes the Judge who sat on the Civil Bench having gone through his list before the termination of the criminal court took several of the remaining cases to himself to judge among others that of Pearce but as these trials were transferred to the other extremity of a remarkably large Town Hall and that his prime witness was not made aware of it but remained in attendance at the criminal side. Pearce thus lost the advantage of this deposition and was convicted of the robbery and sentenced to death on no other proof than his own alleged confession. The suspicious circumstances I have before mentioned and when the witness appeared at this trial which had occupied but a very short space of time was disposed of on the termination of the Assizes however the Judges were induced by the representation I submitted to them to reprieve Pearce and his sentence was commuted to Transportation for Life.

The awful plite of this man under the circumstances I have related could not fail causing me great anxiety and the interest I felt on his part has to this day remained undiminished and though I was unsuccessful and failed to precure mitigation of his sentence I trust through your kind offices that the term of his transportation will soon cease particularly if his conduct at New South Wales has, as he reports in his letter been favourably signified by the authorities at that settlement.

Should any further details be required from me I shall be most happy as far as my recollections may be at this distant time are in my possession to give them.

Whitehall
April 23rd 1830

Sir
Having laid before Mr Secretary Peel your letter of the 16th Instant, transmitting one from Lt Col. Gorrequer, with its enclosure, in favor of John Pearce a convict in New South Wales, I am directed to acquaint you, for the information of The General Commanding in Chief, that Mr Peel has felt himself warranted in recommending this man for a Free Pardon, provided that his conduct in the colony may merit such an extension of Mercy.

I am &c
S.M. Phillipps
Lt General Sir Herbert Taylor, GCH

Privy Council records contain all manner of requests. These include petitions from convicts. The following is an example:

TNA ref PC 1/67 (Oct 1819)

A Petition for Free Pardon from John McCoy

Hobart Town,
Van Diemens Land,
November 17th, 1818

To the Right Honourable Lord Fitzgerald

My Lord,
I here take the liberty of troubling your Lordship with a letter to inform you that my conduct since I have been in this Colony has enabled me to obtain a Conditional Pardon, I was promised a free pardon but I fear it will be a considerable time before I shall be able to obtain it and as your Lordship was so kind to me before I left England I hope I may beg to intrude upon your goodness once more to procure me a free

pardon in hopes that I may once more be enabled to see my native land and to prove my gratitude for your kindness. I wrote two letters to your Lordship before but as I heard nothing from you I was fearful my letters never came to your hands. I return your Lordships many thanks for the letters of recommendations you gave me to bring to this Colony, they were very serviceable to me and family. I gave them to Lieut. Governor Col. Davey but he never return them to me again. I hope this will find your Lordship and all your good family in good health and I remain your Lordships most humble and grateful servant.

John McCoy

I gott my Conditional pardon for discovering lime stone and I burnt a great quantity of lime for government and was promised a free but only got a conditional pardon.

Paris
October 5th 1819

My Lord,

I once took the liberty some years ago of troubling your Lordship respecting the unfortunate man the writer of the enclosed letter who stated to your Lordship was a person well known to me, and of an exceeding good character until in a drunken frolic he fell a victim and became the Dupe of the worst of characters.

Yours Lordship, when he was condemned to transportation very kindly allowed him the indulgence of taking his wife and child with him, if not in the same vessel at least in the same Fleet. If your Lordship would extend your goodness to him so far as to make enquiry whether his statements are true and whether he continues a deserving person and finding them correct would grant the Prayer of his Petition, I firmly believe you could not find an object on whom Pardon could be better bestowed. I have the Honor to remain your Lordship's most obedient and very humble Servant.

Henry Fiztgerald

CHAPTER 6

CONVICTS WHO WERE NOT TRANSPORTED

The Colonial Office, Home Office and Privy Council records at The National Archives contain much detailed information about convicts who had been given a transportation sentence but were not transported. Some convicts were not transported because they were too ill to suffer the voyage or were considered too old. Very occasionally documents recording those who were not transported may also be found in county or borough record offices. Records of convicted men who were given the option to join the army or navy as an alternative to transportation may be found in War Office and Admiralty records. The following are some examples:

TNA ref HO 47/35

A Man who Cannot be Transported due to Ill-health

Old Bailey – July Sessions, 1802

Thomas Jones was convicted of picking a pocket and sentenced to transportation for seven years. Being then in his 59th year, he was thought to be (as represented as such by Mr Kirby) too old for transportation, and too infirm for labouring at the Hulks. For these reasons he was permitted to remain in Newgate till June last: (that is to say, 2 years) when, by an unexpected order he was sent on board the *Captivity* Hulk at Portsea. Whether or not he was guilty of the crime for which he was convicted, I do not presume to assert, though I had then strong doubts about it, be that, however, as it may, I can vouch from my own knowledge, that, if the offence had been of much greater magnitude than it was, he was punished sufficiently during his continuance in Newgate, to make a complete expiation of his transgression.

Poor Jones's former situation in life was truly respectable. He had been a very eminent Manufacturer at Manchester, before and through the continuance of the American War on the conclusion of which, by his losses in his connexion with that country, he became a bankrupt. Necessity then brought him to London and he opened a shop in St. Martins Lane in which he was doing pretty well (having respectably filled some of the Parish Offices), when the foregoing unfortunate transaction took place, and of which I have since had (unless I am very much deceived indeed), almost incontestable proof that he was not guilty. His education has been superior to the generality of tradesmen, and his conduct in the prison was so uniformly correct as to draw upon him the indignation of the other Criminals because he would not herd with them, nor enter into their parties of drinking, gambling, &c, insomuch that they were constantly insulting him with every indignity, as well as personal injury which they could inflict, and which they seemed disposed to pursue, even to the finishing his existence. I seldom met him in the Chapel (of which, from his good behaviour I had appointed him Clerk) without his having a black eye, or a cut face. Five of his teeth were beaten out within the last six months of his confinement and I have been in daily expectation of hearing that he had been murdered; as several of the identical villains, who had so cruelly maltreated him when in Newgate, were taken along with him to the same Hulk.

As Jones is now in his 61st year, infirm and debilitated; nearly blind of an eye and very few teeth; his intellect weakened by trouble and poor living, it can answer no profitable end to Government to transport him, or to keep him idling in the Hulk; as, by the certificate of the Doctor, he is exempt from every species of labour by reason of his infirmities. I may safely add, if Jones were to be indulged with a free pardon, no temptation whatsoever would induce him to venture the risk of a second imprisonment, having so severely suffered for his first and only offence.

To the Rt. Hon. the Earl of Spencer, the case of Thomas Jones is most humbly presented for a free pardon, from a strong opinion of his innocence of the crime of which he was convicted, and from a conviction that his crime, had it been clearly proved, has been sufficiently punished by two years imprisonment in Newgate, and almost two years in the Hulk, by his Lordships most dutiful and obedient Servant.

Brownlow Forde, Ordinary of Newgate
No.1 Newgate Street
May 1st 1806

Thomas Jones, aged 59, was convicted of picking the pocket of Peter Martin, July Sessions, 1802, in the sixth Sessions of the Mayoralty of Sr. Jn. Eamer. (*Vide* Sess. Paper, page 382, trial no. 563).

Jones was sent to the *Captivity* Hulk at Portsmouth, Capt. Thos. Thompson, 13th June 1804. Having lost an eye, being nearly blind of the other, scarcely any teeth, and too old and infirm to send abroad or to work at home, he is earnestly recommended for a pardon.

Dr. Forde's reasons for the pardon of Thos. Jones, now on board the *Captivity* Hulk at Portsmouth:

1. If the crime had been committed by Jones it was in the midst of a drunken party, at a Tavern, and fully as likely to be done by the Landlord (who was one of the party and a notorious character) as it was by Jones.
2. If Jones had committed the theft, and had gone home to conceal the property, it was not likely that he would return to the same party with one of the stolen notes in his coat pocket. Rather am I convinced that the Landlord put a small Note into Jones's pocket to save himself.
3. If Jones (as it was stated) had kept £300 of the stolen property, it was not to be suppose that he would have remained two years in Newgate in a starving condition, having nothing except the prison allowance during that period, except a little relief now and then, from the Keeper & the Ordinary, each of whom had known him for years, his former situation in life being truly respectable till, by the American War, he became insolvent.
4. During Jones's continuance in Newgate he was appointed Clerk to the Chapel, owing to his uniformly good conduct in the Prison, and for which duty (as the only remuneration, the Keeper has it in his power to bestow) he was rewarded with double allowance of Bread.

Despite this appeal Thomas Jones served out his full sentence. He remained on the *Captivity* until his discharge on 14th July 1809. He was recorded as being sick for much of the time. *(TNA ref T 38/314)*

W Dev RO ref 1/682/18

A Woman who Cannot be Transported because she is too Old and Unfit

Whitehall, 7th August 1816

Sir,
The Commissioners for the Transport Service having transmitted to Lord Sidmouth a Report from the Surgeon of the *Lord Melville* Convict Ship, that Sarah Dunn, a Prisoner lately removed from Plymouth to that vessel, for the purpose of being Transported to New South Wales, is not only old and infirm, but is stated to be unfit from an inward complaint, to proceed on the voyage. I am directed by Lord Sidmouth to communicate the same to you in order that you may direct the person who will convey the male convict named in the inclosed letter to Woolwich to take charge of Sarah Dunn (who is now on board the Hospital Ship at that place) and carry her back to the Gaol at Plymouth.

I have the Honor to be The Mayor of Plymouth
Sir
Your most obedient Humble Servant
J. Becket

Mr Secretary Beckett. That Sarah Dunn, a Convict,
was too old and unfit to be removed to New South Wales.

W Dev RO ref 1/682/21 (Sarah Dunn contd.)
Joseph Whitford, Esq.,
Deputy Town Clerk
Plymouth

Whitehall
26 Nov 1816

Sir
I am directed by Lord Sidmouth to acquaint you for the Information of the Mayor of Plymouth, in reply to your Letter of the 21st Instant that no Returns have of late been received from the Governor of New South Wales, of the names of persons pardoned by him in that Colony, but if the Document which is in the possession of George Keene, purporting to be a Free Pardon, is transmitted to this Office, it can be ascertained whether the Signature affixed to it is of the handwriting of Colonel McQuarie.

I am also directed by Lord Sidmouth to desire that you will call the attention of the Mayor of Plymouth to the Letter written by His Lordship's order on the 7th August last respecting Sarah Dunn, a convict under sentence of Transportation, whom it appears from a Report made by the Superintendent of Convicts, still remains on board the Hospital Ship at Woolwich, and is not likely from her age, and the nature of her complaint, ever to be in a fit state to undergo the voyage to New South Wales.

I am Sir
Yours most obedient
Humble Servant
J. Beckett

Secretary of State in Whitehall

Note: Sarah Dunn was the wife of William Dunn. Details of her offence are given in another document at West Devon Record Office, *ref 1/695/104*.

TNA ref PC 1/67 (May 1819)

A Convict is too Ill to be Transferred to a Prison Hulk

Sir, I beg to inclose a Certificate from our Surgeon for your satisfaction, concerning John Wise, whose case is Hydrothorax, and which I supposed would render him not fit to be received on board the Hulk in the weak state he is in arising from that disorder, and have left him at home until he is recovered sufficiently to undergo the sentence which is Transportation for Life.

And am Sir,

respectful & humble Servant,

Geo. Ernest Eaststaff

To: Henry Capper, Esq.

I certify that John Wise, a Capital Convict for Life, is not able to be summoned from our Gaol, as he has had for some time past, a Dropsical Complaint which renders him at intervals unable to move from his bed.

John Bulley

Surgeon to the Gaol, Reading

May 22nd 1819

To: John Henry Capper Esq., Superintendent of Convicts

TNA ref ADM 1/1080

A List of Forty-Four Convicts Petitioning to Join the Royal Navy

Royal William at Spithead – 18th April 1803

Sir,

The Inclosed Petition having been sent me from the Convicts confined on board the Hulk in Langstone Harbour, I beg you will be pleased to lay the same before the Lords Commissioners of the Admiralty for their consideration.

I have the honor to be

Sir

Your most obedient humble servant

Geo. Montop [?]

William Marsden, Esq.

Hon^d Sir,

The Humble Petition of the undermentioned persons, prisoners on board the *Portland* hulk, Langstone Harbour.

Most humbly sheweth that your petitioners are all of them young men and in perfect health and are from the age of 21 to 36 and many of them were in His Majesty's Service during the last war and from their sufferings they have already undergone are fully convinced of their errors and have repented for there past misconduct therefore hope Your Lordship will take our sad case into your kind consideration and be so kind as to interfere in our behalf so as we may be permitted to serve in His Majesty's Royal Navy and do most faithfully promise to become true and loyal subjects the remainder of our days.

And Your Petitioners as in Duty Bound

will Ever Most Gratefully Pray

Michael Brown	James White	Robt Carter
Robt Penn	Francis Williams	Henery Muggeridge
Joseph Vick	Thos Russell	Joseph Colebourne
John Freeman	Willm Bramble	John Summers
John Powell	Jasack James	Thos Cook
John Turner	Thos Wood	Mathew Jackson
James Walker	Robt Ince	Willm Robinson
Philip Luck	John Foster	Thos Robinson
James Ireland	Thos Aiton	Samuel Jinkins
Will Ivey	James Loyd	John Jinkins
John Durant	Thos Spencer	Willm Turnbull
Simon Tripp	Thos Westoby	Joseph Starkey
George Green	Willm Hobbs	James Wright
Joseph Verrity	Thos Moore	Willm Dunscomb
John Bishop	John Pounsforde	

TNA ref WO 1/627

Fit for Service in the Army

Horse Guards
13th March 1804

Sir,

Having had the Honor to lay before The Commander in Chief your letter of the 1st instant with its enclosures, I am directed by His Royal Highness to acquaint you for the Information of Lord Hobart that, in consequence of what is therein stated, an inspection has been made of the convicts on board the *Captivity* and *Portland* Hulks at Portsmouth, who are stated to be willing to enter His Majesty's Service in the Army, on condition of receiving a Pardon and it appearing from the report made that a considerable number of the said Convicts are fit for the Service, His Royal Highness is desirous that a certain number thereof may be placed in the 66th Regiment in order to make up the deficiency to complete that Regiment which cannot be supplied from the Army Depot, amounting to about 120 men, but the precise number can only be ascertained at Portsmouth. His Royal Highness requests that the necessary Official Order may be sent by this night's post (it being expected that the 66th will sail tomorrow) to deliver up to General Whitlocke such men as are willing, and are returned fit for service in the Returns before alluded to, and which have been transmitted by Lieut. General Howell to Major General Whitelocke to make His selection accordingly.

I have the Honor to be
Sir,
Your most obedient humble Servant
W.H. Clinton

TNA ref HO 47/35

Fit for Service in the Royal Navy

Captivity, Portsmouth
31st Jan. 1805

Sir,

Jacob Payne and James Knight are in good health and sound in body, they are only eighteen years of age and very short in stature, consequently are not fit for soldiers. If you are inclined to show them any favour they would answer very well for the Navy as they have been accustomed to work in barges.

William Cook from Newgate as [sic] behaved himself exceeding well ever since he has been at the Hulks.

I am Sir, Your most obedient, humble servant

Thos. Thompson

J. H. Capper, Esq. [Superintendent of Convicts]

Another letter says that Payne and Knight were convicted at Bedford Assizes on 9 March 1804 for stealing from the Compting House of Mr John Foster of Biggleswade, Bedfordshire, the sum of £7. The *Captivity* records show that Payne and Knight were discharged to the Navy on 6 February 1805 *(TNA ref T 38/312)*.

CHAPTER 7

CONVICTS TRANSPORTED FROM CANADA TO VAN DIEMEN'S LAND

The Colonial Office correspondence for Canada is to be found in TNA document class CO 42 and covers 1,045 volumes dating from 1700 to 1922.

This correspondence for the early nineteenth century includes much detail about the transportation of criminals convicted in Canada and who were transported to Van Diemen's Land (later named Tasmania). Many of these were, in fact, men from the USA who had been captured after invading Upper Canada. Some were given the death sentence, which was later commuted to transportation for life. The following are some examples:

TNA ref CO 42/461

Despatch from Lieutenant-Governor Sir George Arthur, K.C.H., to the Marquis of Normandy.

Government House
Toronto
29th July 1830

My Lord,
I have the honour to inform your Lordship that I have again gone through the whole of the cases of the prisoners under sentence and have selected eleven more for free pardon, under circumstances which I feel satisfied I can fully justify. This leaves 78 of the Prescott and Windsor brigands and four other convicts for transportation as soon as the *Buffalo* arrives or is ready to receive them.

I have the honour herewith to transmit to your Lordship the following documents:

1st   A certified list of all the convicts who are to be conveyed from Upper Canada to Van Diemen's Land.

2nd   Copies of two of the patents of pardon by which the capital sentences of the convicts were committed to transportation for life. (One of these documents applies to the case of British subjects and the other to that of aliens. Similar patents have been prepared for the whole of the 78 brigands).

3rd   Copy of the papers connected with the order for transportation of William Highland, tried and convicted before a Militia Court Martial for desertion.

4th   Copy of the Civil Secretary's letter to the Law Officers of the Crown, and of the answer of the Attorney General thereto. (In accordance with the suggestions contained in this answer I have caused an exemplification of the Provincial Statute, 1Vic.c.3 to be sent to the Governor of Van Diemen's Land).

5th   Copy of the Provincial Secretary's letter to the Colonial Secretary of Van Diemen's Land, transmitting a list of the brigands with particular observations on those cases which seem to present any grounds for a more favourable consideration.

6th   Copy of a warrant to the officer in command of the *Buffalo* to take charge of the convicts and convey them to their destination.

I have caused these several instruments to be prepared by the law officers of the Crown in this province. Great care and consideration have been used in their preparation and I hope they will be found to be correct and sufficient for the purpose intended.

As, however, the circumstances under which the proceeding has become necessary are new in this province, I thought it prudent to put your Lordship in full possession of all that has transpired on the subject as early as possible so that if it should happen that, unfortunately any error has crept into the proceedings Her Majesty's Government may be in a situation to take immediate steps either to remedy it, or to prevent any ill consequences ensuing by a communication to the colony to which the prisoners are destined.

Upon the case of William Highland, who, it will be perceived, has been tried for desertion before a Militia General Court Martial, I am anxious to remark that there have been several cases of desertion from the regiments of incorporated militia, the men taking off with them their arms, accoutrements and ammunition. It is of great importance that this disgraceful crime should be checked; and, as Highland's case is one of the worst inasmuch as he left his post to desert, I have selected him for severe punishment and trust the example may prove efficacious.

I have, &c
Geo. Arthur

Letter to Mr Justice Jones

Toronto
27th July 1839

Sir,

Whereas William Highland, a private in the third battalion of the incorporated militia of this province, (the said battalion being embodied for actual service) was by and at a militia general court martial held at Niagara in the district of Niagara and province aforesaid on the 29th day of April, in the year of our Lord 1839, duly convicted of deserting his post when sentry at Mississagua fort on the night of the 29th day of March in the same year, and of taking with him his arms, accoutrements and ammunition. And whereas the said Court did adjudge the said William Highland to be transported as a felon for the term of fourteen years, and which sentence of the said court martial her Majesty intends should be carried into execution. I am therefore, by the Queen's commands, to notify you the said sentence, together with her Majesty's pleasure that the same be carried into execution, and that the said offender be transported as a felon for the said term of fourteen years to the colony of Van Diemen's Land, that colony having been duly appointed as the place to which any offender convicted in this province, and under sentence of transportation, shall be transported. Which notification is hereby made to the intent that you may make such order for the transportation of the said William Highland as is by law required, and you may seem necessary.

I have, &c.

George Arthur

CORRESPONDENCE RELATIVE TO THE AFFAIRS OF CANADA

Province of Upper Canada

Table 7.1 Return of Convicts to be conveyed in Her Majesty's Ship *Buffalo* to Van Diemen's Land, and to remain there during the period of Transportation. *(TNA ref CO 42/462 contd.)*

No	Name of Convict	Crime	Date of Conviction	Sentence	Commuted Punishment
1	Edwin Merrit	murder	1st October 1838	Death	Trans. Life
2	Horace Cooley	burglary	26th Sept. 1838	ditto	ditto
3	Aaron Dresser, jun. [22]		3rd December 1838		
4	William Gates [23]		3rd "		
5	George T. Brown [22]		6th "		
6	John Cronkhite [30]		10th "		
7	James Pearce [22]		10th "		
8	Hiram Sharp [24]		19th "		
9	Calvin Mathers [24]		26th "		
10	Daniel Liscum [22]		28th "		
11	Jerry Griggs [22]		28th "		
12	Moses A. Dutcher [23]	Piratical invasion of Upper Canada	29th "		Transportation for Life
13	Alson Owen [24]		17th "		
14	Daniel D. Heustis [27]		17th "	Death	
15	David Allen [37]		19th "		
16	Stephen S. Wright [25]		22nd "		
17	Nathan Whiting [48]		22nd "		
18	Thomas Baker [47]		17th "		
19	John Gillman [38]		26th "		
20	Hiram Loop [26]		6th "		
21	Elon Fellowes [22]		6th "		
22	Orlan Blodgit [23]		6th "		
23	Reilly Whitney [25]		8th "		
24	John Thomas [26]		8th "		
25	Asa H. Richardson [23]		8th "		
26	Edward A. Wilson [23]		8th "		
27	Robert G. Collins [34]		8th "		
28	Thomas Stockton [29]		8th "		

No.	Name	Piratical invasion of Upper Canada	Date	Death	Transportation for Life
29	David Howth [24]		10th "		
30	Michael Fraer [23]		10th "		
31	Emanuel Garrison [22]		10th "		
32	Leonard Delino [25]		10th "		
33	Henry Shew/Show [23]		13th "		
34	Joseph Thompson [22]		13th "		
35	Jehiel H. Martin [31]		13th "		
36	Luther Darby [48]		13th "		
37	Joseph Stewart [25]		7th "		
38	Chauncey Bugbee [22]		17th "		
39	Andrew Leeper [42]		17th "		
40	John Berry [40]		17th "		
41	Owen W. Smith [26]		17th "		
42	Garret Hicks [27]		28th "		
43	John G. Swanberg [27]		22nd "		
44	Solomon Reynolds [33]		19th "		
45	Samuel Washburn [25]		19th "		
46	Gideon Goodrich [43]		19th "		
47	Chauncey Mathers [24]		26th "		
48	Jacob Paddock [17]		22nd "		
49	Beemis Woodbury [25]		22nd "		
50	Asa Priest [42]		22nd "		
51	Foster Martin [32]		26th "		
52	Ira Polly [23]		28th "		
53	Andrew Moore [26]		28th "		
54	Lysander Curtis [33]		28th "		
55	Nelson S. Griggs [28]		28th "		
56	William Reynolds [23]		28th "		
57	James Inglis [30]		11th "		
58	Hugh Calhoun[25]		11th "		
59	John Bradley [30]		27th "		
60	Patrick White [22]		27th "		
61	John Morrisette [22]		27th "		
62	Joseph Leforte [29]		27th "		
63	Samuel Snow [38]		28th "		
64	Elizar Stevens		28th "		
65	John S. [Seymour] Gutridge		7th January 1839		
66	John Sprague [28]		28th Dec. 1838		
67	Robert Marsh [26]		28th "		
68	Riley M. [Monson] Stewart [31]		28th "		

		Offence	Date		
69	Alvin B. [Burroughs] Sweet [22]	Piratical invasion of Upper Canada	28th "	Death	Transportation for Life
70	James P. [Peter] Williams [24]		28th "		
71	William Nottage		7th January 1839		
72	John Henry Simmons [23]		28th Dec. 1838		
73	Elijah C. [Croker] Woodman		7th January 1839		
74	Chauncey Sheldon [52]		28th Dec. 1838		
75	John C. [Chester] Williams		2nd January 1839		
76	James M. [Milne] Aitcheson		7th "		
77	John B. [Burwell] Tyrrell		3rd "		
78	Henry V. [Verrelon] Barnum [22]		28th Dec. 1838		
79	James De Witt Fero		7th January 1839		
80	Michael Morin [31]		28th Dec. 1838		
81	William Highland	desertion & taking arms	29th April 1839	Transn 14 years	Sentence confirmed
82	John McManigall	murder	22nd May 1839	Death	Trans. Life

Note: The added names in square brackets were found in other related documents. The number in square brackets is the age of the convict, which appeared in a second list.

I do hereby certify that the foregoing is a correct Return of the eighty two convicts now about to be conveyed to Van Diemen's Land, in Her Majesty's ship *Buffalo* and who are all subject to transportation under the condition of the pardons respectively granted to them, or in virtue of the sentence of a court of competent jurisdiction.

In testimony whereof I have hereunto set my hand and affixed my seal, at the city of Toronto in the province of Upper Canada, this 27th day of July in the year of our Lord 1839, and in the third year of Her Majesty's reign.

By his Excellency's command,
R.A. Tucker
Provincial Secretary

The following notes have been added to another list of the above convicts:

Of the 78 brigands included in this list, the cases of 17 appeared to the Executive Council, upon a careful investigation of various circumstances connected with them, as exhibiting somewhat stronger grounds for the extension of indulgence than presented themselves in the other cases. I shall accordingly consider those 17 as forming a distinct class, and shall prefix the letter A to the names of each of them as a general designation of that class, taking care to add with reference to particular individuals, such observations as seem to be peculiarly applicable to them.

Note: The number given against each name in the following is the number in the above tabulation.

18. (A) Thomas Baker. This man is acknowledged to be a drunkard, and is alleged that, without any previous connexion with the pseudo-patriots, he was tempted, whilst in a state of intoxication, to join in the expedition against Prescott.

3. (A) Aaron Dresser, jun. Several most respectable inhabitants of Kingston presented a petition in his favour. His father bears a good character, and his deep anxiety for his son, evidenced by his frequent and urgent solicitations in his behalf, rendered this case so particularly interesting, that a free pardon would probably have been granted Dresser if there had not been strong reason for believing that he acted a prominent part among the brigands, and was designed to bear an officer's commission among them.

4. (A) William Gates. Strong certificates of general good character, numerously signed, have been presented in his favour.

11. (A) Jerry Griggs. A touching application in behalf of him, and his brother, Nelson J. Griggs, backed by a recommendation from several persons, was received from the aged and bereaved parents.

14. (A) Daniel D. Heustis. This man's station in society appears to have been rather above that of the generality of the brigands and the applications in his favour have accordingly been from persons of higher influence; but his standing in his country has been considered as furnishing an argument against rather than in favour of, the grant of free pardon which has been solicited for him in many quarters.

32. (A) Leonard Delino. An order for the execution of this person was actually issued, and in his case was, of course at one time considered as one of the worst; but his conduct during his confinement has been exemplary and the Rev. Mr Cartwright, who has been most zealous in endeavouring to convey religious impressions to the minds of the brigands, conceives that his efforts have been particularly successful in the case of Delino and has interceded very strongly for him.

30. (A) Michael Fraer. Such strong recommendations of this man have been received, that he seems to be hardly, if at all, less entitled to indulgence than these included in the class of 17.

48. (A) Jacob Paddock. The very bad conduct of this individual prevented him from participating in the free pardon which was granted to all the other youths.

41. (A) Orin W. Smith. Strongly recommended by several respectable individuals.

37. (A) Joseph Stewart.   ditto

28. (A) Thomas Stockton.   ditto

24. (A) John Thomas.   ditto; and his conduct during his confinement very favourably spoken of both by the sheriff and Mr Cartwright.

23. (A) Reilly Whitney. A petition in his behalf, numerously signed, has been received and there is a strong certificate of his good conduct during the period of his incarceration.

The following eighteen brigands were captured at Windsor, in the Western District:

75. (A) John C. Williams is the only one of the Windsor brigands included in the list of 17; and he owes his station in that list entirely to the consideration which was felt for his brother, who is a very respectable inhabitant of this province.

63. (A) Samuel Snow. Strongly recommended.

64. (A) Elizar Stevens. Seven ministers of the gospel in the United States have recommended this man as having borne a good character.

69. (A) Alvin B. Sweet. The recommendations of this man are strong and from respectable quarters.

77. (A) John B. Tyrrell. The merits of Mr Burwell, the uncle of this man, may perhaps justify the extension of an indulgence to him, which he otherwise is not entitled to claim.

R.A. Tucker, Sec.
Office of the Provincial Secretary of Upper Canada
27th July 1839

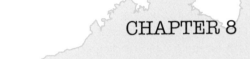

CHAPTER 8

CREW LISTS AND SHIPS' DETAILS

(See Appendices 20 and 21)

Some Australians may trace their ancestry back to someone who cannot be found recorded as either a convict or a free immigrant. In such a case it is possible that that ancestor arrived in Australia as a seaman in the Royal Navy or Merchant Service. In order to locate this lost ancestor, ships' crew lists should be investigated.

MERCHANT NAVY

Merchant seamen were usually contracted to sail for only one voyage at a time and some seamen, on arrival in Australia, were discharged from the ship's crew. Some transferred to another vessel, others decided to settle there, and some deserted. Lists of these men, with the ships' masters and other officers, are to be found in Merchant Navy crew lists. Occasionally with these lists are records of seamen committing crimes while in Australia and being detained in prison. Sometimes a ship's log may also be found filed with the crew lists. These often record only the serious events on board ship and the misbehaviour of the crew.

The following has been abstracted from two lists found for the *Mount Stewart Elphinstone*, which sailed to Australia in 1847 (see Table 8.1, p. 114, crew list; and Table 8.2, p. 116, seamen's diet):

TNA ref BT 98/1964 (part 2)

An agreement made in pursuant to the Directions of an Act of Parliament passed the 7th year of the Reign of Her Majesty Queen Victoria between Adolphus Holton the Master of the Ship *Mount Stewart Elphinstone* of the Port of London and of the Burthen of 611 10/94 tons and the several Persons whose names are subscribed hereto. It is agreed by and on board the said ship in the several capacities against their respective names expressed, on a voyage from the Port of London to Gibraltar thence to Hobart Town, Van Diemen's Land, [and] Sydney, New South Wales either or both and to any Port or Ports in the Globe during a period not exceeding two years eventually back to the Port of London. And the said crew further engage to conduct themselves in an orderly, faithful, honest, careful, and sober manner, and to be at all times diligent in their respective duties and stations, and be obedient to the lawful commands of the Master in every thing relating to the said Ship and the Materials,

Stores and Cargo thereof, whether on board such Ship, in Boats or on Shore. No spirits allowed. Wages to commence from date of joining the Ship.

In consideration of which Services, to be duly, honestly, carefully and faithfully performed, the said Master doth hereby promise and agree to pay the said Crew, by way of compensation or wages the amount against their names respectively expressed. And it is hereby agreed that any embezzlement or wilful negligent Loss or Destruction of any part of the Ship's Cargo or Stores shall be made good to the Owner out of the wages (so far as they will extend) of the seaman guilty of the same; and if any Seaman shall have entered himself as qualified for a Duty to which he shall prove to be not competent, he shall be subject to a Reduction of the Rate hereby agreed for,

Table 8.1: Extracts from the crew list for the *Mount Stewart Elphinstone*, which sailed to Australia in 1847.

Place & Time of Entry		Men's Names + Christian and Surnames	Age	Town or County where Born	Quality	Amount of Wages per Calendar Month £ s d		
Place	Day Month Year							
Deptford	16 Dec 1847	Adolphus Holton	47	London	Master			
Deptford	16 Dec 1847	Ralph Hobson Liddell	29	Gateshead	1st Mate	6	0	0
Deptford	16 Dec 1847	Charles Gear	26	Weymouth	2nd Mate	4	0	0
Deptford	16 Dec 1847	William Stinthers	21	Orkney	3rd Mate	2	0	0
Deptford	16 Dec 1847	Arthur Richardson	17	London	4th Mate	1	10	0
Deptford	24 Dec 1847	John William Smith	29	Norway	Carpenter	5	0	0
Deptford	26 Dec 1847	George Dymant	22	Edmonton	do's mate	0	15	0
Deptford	16 Dec 1847	Oliver Watts	28	Gloster	Steward	3	0	0
Deptford	18 Dec 1847	Arch. McPherson	41	Argyle	Cook	2	5	0
Deptford	21 Dec 1847	Sidney Smith	19	London	do's mate	10	0	0
Deptford	24 Dec 1847	William McCabe	36	Middx.	A. Seaman	2	0	0
Woolwich	21 Dec 1847	William Brown	28	Cape Gd. Hope	A. Seaman	2	0	0
Woolwich	21 Dec 1847	William Haynes[1]	26	Middx.	A. Seaman	2	0	0
Woolwich	23 Dec 1847	David Thomas	22	Kent	A. Seaman	2	0	0
Woolwich	23 Dec 1847	John Anderson	27	Hanover	A. Seaman	2	0	0
Woolwich	25 Dec 1847	George William Holiday[1]	18	Bristol	O. Seaman	1	0	0
Woolwich	23 Dec 1847	Samuel Robert Mackney	22	Deal	O. Seaman	1	5	0
Woolwich	23 Dec 1847	Henry Cray	21	Middx.	O. Seaman	1	5	0
Woolwich	23 Dec 1847	Daniel Warner	19	Rochester	O. Seaman			
Woolwich	23 Dec 1847	John Vuley	18	Lincoln	Apprentice			

1. A physical description of these men is given on page 117.

in proportion to his Incompetency. In witness whereof the said Parties have hereto subscribed their names on the Days against their respective signatures mentioned.

I hereby declare the truth of all the particulars set forth in this agreement delivered to the Collector of the Port of London this 17th day April 1849.
Agent's name: Thomas Barker
75 Cornhill

Reported this 6th day of April 1849:
signed R.R. Liddell, Mate
witness Thomas Barker

Amount of Wages Advanced at £ s d	Name of Ship in which last Served	Number of Registers Ticket	Time of Death or Leaving Ship	Place Where	How Disposed of	Date of Apprenticeship Indenture
	M.S. Elphinstone		April 1849			
12 0 0	Lady Bruce	24734	6 April 1849	London	Discharged	
8 0 0	Adelaide	4453	13 July 1848	Sydney	Discharged	
2 0 0	Stebonherth	324264	6 April 1849	London	Discharged	
1 10 0	M.S. Elphinstone	15409	6 April 1849	London	Discharged	
10 0 0	Marmion	foreigner	19 Jan. 1848	Portsmouth	Discharged	
15 0	Marmion	388859	19 June 1848	Sydney	Discharged	
3 0 0	London	344975	16 Sept. 1848	Calcutta	Discharged	
2 5 0	Mary Graham	173282	30 Oct. 1848	Calcutta	Discharged	
- - -	none	389876	19 June 1848	Sydney	Discharged	
2 0 0	Warlock	8296	25 June 1848	Sydney	Discharged	
2 0 0	Devonshire	325335	30 June 1848	Sydney	Discharged	
2 0 0	Hellen	389506	15 June 1848	Sydney	HMS Dido	
2 0 0	Royal Saxon	390013	8 July 1848	Sydney	Run	
2 0 0	New Liverpool	foreigner	10 July 1848	Sydney	Discharged	
1 0 0	Equestriane	324117	10 July 1848	Sydney	Run	
1 5 0	Bolton	204800	20 Sept. 1848	Calcutta	Discharged	
1 5 0	HMS Myrtle	389817	22 June 1848	Sydney	Run	
	Tartar	388854	19 June 1848	Sydney	Discharged	
	Java	324177	6 April 1849	London		17 June 1847

Table 8.2: The crew list for the *Mount Stewart Elphinstone*, which sailed to Australia in 1847, includes the details of the seamen's diet.

Days of the Week	Biscuits	Salt		Flour	Peas	Sugar	Tea	Water
		Beef	Pork					
Sunday	1	1½	-	½	-	2	½	3
Monday	1	-	1¼	-	⅓	2	½	3
Tuesday	1	1½	-	½	-	2	½	3
Wednesday	1	-	1¼	-	⅓	2	½	3
Thursday	1	1½	-	½	-	2	½	3
Friday	1	-	1¼	-	⅓	2	½	3
Saturday	1	1½	-	½	-	2	½	3

Lime Juice and Sugar as per Act.

Written on the back of the crew list is information relating to the discharge of some of the crew:

> In conformity with the Imperial Act 7 & 8 Vict. Cap.12 warrants have been taken out of this Office for the apprehension of Charles Birch, Henry Cray, D. Burgh, D. Thomas, Rd. Smith, John Anderson, Thomas Brokesby, Robert Machnay, G.W. Holliday, D. Jones, for desertion and up to the date neither of the said seamen have been apprehended and I further certify that John Fraser and William Sullivan, belonging to the said ship are left in Sydney under Colonial Sentence.
>   Water Police Office, Sydney
>
>   14th July 1848
>   H.H. Browne

Details are also recorded concerning the fate of several seamen on the *Mount Stewart Elphinstone*:

TNA ref BT 98/1007

> Island of Van Diemen's Land, To Wit
> In pursuance of the fifty fourth Section of the Police Act of the said Island, I hereby Certify that Thomas Carter, Alfred Wilson, Henry Clayton and John Robinson, articled Seamen, belonging to the Vessel *Mount Stewart Elphinstone*, now lying in the Port of Hobart were convicted before me, one of Her Majesty's Justices of the Peace for the Island of Van Diemen's Land of having in the Port of Hobart Town in the said Island refused to work on board the said vessel according to agreement, and sentenced to be committed to the House of Correction at Hobart Town, there to be kept to hard labour for the space of Two Calendar Months, which Sentence is still unexpired and unremitted, and that Mr Adolphus Holston [sic] Master of the said Vessel has rendered an account of Wages due to the said Thomas Carter, Alfred Wilson, Henry Clayton, and John Robinson and paid the same to them. Dated at the Police Office, Hobart Town this seventh day of July 1845.
>   John King
>   Police Magistrate

Personal details of merchant seamen are recorded in the Registers of Merchant Seamen's Tickets (TNA document class BT 113). They are arranged numerically by ticket number and reference to them is made by use of the alphabetical index (TNA document class BT 114). These entries include a physical description of each seaman. The following examples relate to seamen who sailed in the *Mount Stewart Elphinstone* in 1847, and who deserted or were discharged in Australia (see Table 8.1, pp. 114–15).

TNA ref BT 113/195

Number	389506
Name	William Haynes
Born	St. Marylebone, Middlesex, Sept. 1820
Capacity	Seaman
Age when Ticketed	26
Can Write	Yes
Height	5' 7"
Complexion	Fresh
Hair	Brown
Eyes	Blue
Marks	Anchor on Left Hand
First went to Sea as	Boy
In the Year	1836
Has Served in the Royal Navy	–
Has been on Foreign Service	–
When Unemployed Resides at	Marylebone
Issued At	London, 3 December 1847

Number	324117
Name	George William Holiday
Born	Bristol, 10 January 1830
Capacity	Apprentice
Age When Ticketed	15
Can Write	No
Height	Growing
Complexion	Dark
Hair	Brown
Eyes	Brown
Marks	None
First went to Sea as	Boy
In the Year	1844
Has Served in the Royal Navy	No
Has been on Foreign Service	No
When Unemployed Resides at	Commercial Road, London
Issued at	London, 6 October 1845

There are other Registers of Seamen in TNA document classes BT 112, BT 116 and BT 120, but these do not include physical descriptions.

Merchant Ships' Logs

Sometimes logs for merchant ships are to be found filed with the crew lists. The following are examples.

Table 8.3: List of Crew and Report of Character. Abstracts from the crew list and log of the *William Hammond*, which sailed from Plymouth on 5 January 1855 to Swan River, Western Australia, arriving 29 March 1856 *(TNA ref BT 98/4614)*.

Key: V.G. very good; G good; M middling; I indifferent
The Master may also insert particulars of ability or conduct; thus 'Helm good' or 'Sobriety indifferent'. If he declines giving any opinion he must state so opposite the man's name.

Christian and Surname of each Member of Crew	Capacity in which Engaged	Report of Character	
		For General Conduct	For Ability in Seamanship
Mr David Kid	1st Officer	Declines opinion	G
Mr Alexander Maclean	2nd Officer	G	M
Mr Gilbert Ingram	3rd Officer	G	M
Mr Charles Barconlet[?]	4th Officer	G	M
William Mathewson	Carpenter	G	G
William Hartwell	Steward	G	G
George Allen	Cook	G	G
Thomas Simonds	Boatswain	G	G
William Wingott	Carpenter	G	G
Calin Mill	Sailmaker	G	G
John Deady	Seaman	Declines opinion	G
Mauthirin Chinace	do	G	M
William Brown	do	G	G
Edward Paterson	do	G	G
Alfred Booth	do	G	G
Richard Lander	do	G	G
William Bullinara	Ord. Seaman	G	M
John Andrew	do	G	M
James Shirriff	do	G	M
Cornwall Jones	do	G	M
John Gollately	Seaman	G	G
James Adams	Ord. Seaman	G	M
John Soatley Spicer	Apprentice	G	M
Alfred Dennard	Chief Mate	G	G

The following abstracts from the log book of the *William Hammond* explain why the Master declined to give an opinion on the conduct of two of the men listed in Table 8.3:

TNA ref BT 98/4614 (continued)

December 24th [1855] off Portland
At 9 a.m. off Portland. Chief Mate sent five seamen out to bestow the jib when a seaman by the name of John Gollately fell overboard. We succeeded in picking him up with a rope on the starboard quarter. Just at the time the man was got on board a seaman by name of John Deady struck the Chief Mate a blow saying it was his fault the man fell overboard for sending them out to stow the jib. The Master interposed and stopped the man from striking the Mate again. The then mate made use of a great deal of talk saying he would be his bitter enemy for all the voyage. This all occurred on the poop causing great disorder in the ship many of the convicts being on deck at the time, that the Surgeon Superintendent thought it necessary to call out the guard. After a little time order was again made and the Master ordered hands out to stow the jib which was done without further trouble.

December 29th Plymouth
This day the above seaman [John Deady] was spoken to by the Master respecting the above assault when he said that he was no way sorry for what he had done. That he had done it in a passion, and that he would be able to show that the Mate was not a qualified person for Mate of the ship. This was read to the seamen in the presence of the Surgeon and Officers of the ship.

December 29th Plymouth
This day the six undermentioned seamen were examined by the Surgeon Superintendent and found unfit to proceed in the ship from several diseases and ruptures.

William Mathewson	carpenter	
Maturin Chanvirace	A.B.[2]	
Edward Paterson	do	December 31st 1855
Richard Lander	do	Sent in shore to be discharged
Alfred Booth	do	
James Adams	O.S.[3]	

2. Able Seaman.
3. Ordinary Seaman.

January 1st 1856 Plymouth
John Deady seaman was tried before a Magistrate and sentenced to 21 days imprisonment for an assault on the Chief Mate.

January 28th 1856
At 8 p.m. Master and Surgeon was taking their usual round to see all well. On going down the afte hold Master observed that afte store hatch was not locked, and on asking Third Mate or Storekeeper he was told that Mr Kid, Chief Mate, had been down there for business which did appear to him feasible as it was his watching. It was shortly afterward that Mr Kid, Chief Mate was intoxicated and quarrelsome about the deck. At 10.30 p.m. Master went in Poop and found him asleep on his watch on

deck, which caused the Master to step on deck until 12 o'clock, the Second and Third Mates was then called and on coming on deck the Chief Mate was still asleep. Their attention was called to the circumstances by the Master, he then went below leaving the Second Mate in charge with orders to call him again at 4 o'clock. On his coming up at 4 o'clock was informed by the Second Officer that Mr Kid had slept in same place until 2 o'clock and then got up and went to his bed without saying anything. He was called again at 4 o'clock and came on deck. A 6 he spoke to the Master and said he was sorry for what had occurred and promised it should not be the case again, but as the Master knew that it was not the first time it had occurred he could not look over it, requesting him to give up the key of the store room that he had charge of as it was quite clear it was the Government Stores he was making use of that he could go on with his duty but that he must leave the ship on her arrival at Swan River and that he was liable to severe punishment for such conduct and to have his Certificate of Competency taken from him. This was read by Mr Kid in the Cuddy.

Horatio Edward Master
A. Maclean 2nd Officer
Gilbert Ingram 3rd Officer

Transcripts and Transactions

The ships used to convey convicts and immigrants to Australia were privately owned merchant vessels. Some civilians sailed to Australia in Royal Naval ships. These people were presumably on official government business.

Details of merchant ships appear in Transcripts and Transactions, which record the ownership, and any subsequent transfer of ownership, of each vessel. The date of building, or capture as a prize, is given, with the port of registry and home port. The name of the surveying officer and nationality of building is also given, together with a brief description of the vessel. These records are arranged chronologically and by home port of the ship.

Below are some details taken from records of the *Fortune* and the *Alexander*.

TNA ref BT 107/18 p291

Fortune Registered 1805, London. Owner: Peter Everitt Mestaer of Rotherhithe, ship builder.
Length 120 feet 10 inches; breadth 35 feet 10 inches; 2 decks; 3 masts; 626 tons; Master: Henry Moor; a prize legally condemned and made free as appears by a Register No. 71 granted at London 25 August 1795 and delivered up and cancelled; Surveying Officers: Tho. Peters, T. Willimott, J. D. Hume; foreign built; Kind of vessel 'Square stern ship with poop and quarter decks'.
14 December 1805 Peter Everitt Mestaer 'sold and transferred one third part share of the ship or vessel mentioned in the within Certificate of Registry unto Henry Moor of Greenwich in the County of Kent, master mariner'.
Vessel sailed from New South Wales for China Sept. 1813 and not having been heard of it is feared she foundered. Lloyd's Reg. 28 Oct. 1814.

TNA ref BT 107/7 p254

Alexander Registered 6 Nov 1804, London; owner John Locke of America Square, merchant; Master: James Taylor;
'Built at Quebec in the year one thousand eight hundred and one as appears by a

Register No. 163 granted at London 21 April 1802 now delivered up and cancelled.'
Length 98 feet 6 inches; breadth 25 feet 11 inches; 2 decks; 3 masts; 278 tons;
Surveying Officers Thomas Peeters, T. Willimot, J.D. Hume, British Plantation built;
kind of vessel 75/94 square sterned ship with flush deck. Endorsed at Kingston
Jamaica 11 November 1805 to John Davis, ditto at London 18 November 1805 to
Richard Brooks; 26 June 1807 John Locke 'Have this day sold and transferred all my
right, share and interest in and to the ship or vessel *Alexander* mentioned in the within
Certificate of Registry unto Henry Wright of Wallbrook, merchant.'

Lloyd's Ship Survey Reports

Further details of merchant vessels are given in Lloyd's ship survey reports held at the
National Maritime Museum, Greenwich. The following has been abstracted from the survey
made on the *Corona*, which sailed to Western Australia, arriving on 22 December 1866
after a voyage of sixty-seven days.

**No. 3334 Survey held at Dundee, 25th July 1866 on the Ship *Corona*, Master
W.S. Croudace.**
Built at: Dundee
When built: 1864 to 1866
Launched: 14th June 1866
By whom built: A. Stephen & Son
Owners: A. Stephen & Son
Port belonging to: Dundee
Destined Voyage: India
If Surveyed while Building, Afloat, or in Dry Dock: Building & Afloat
Tonnage under tonnage deck: 1067.94
Gross Tonnage: 1199.17
Total Register Tonnage: 1197.17
The Floors consist of: Plate and Angle Iron
The Main piece of Rudder is British Oak
Windlass is of Cast Iron
The Keel is Canada Oak
The Main Keelson is Iron
The Stern and Stern Post of British Oak and Teak
The Transoms, Knight Head, Hawes Timbers and Aprons of British Oak and Iron Bars
The Deck and Hold Beams of Bulb Iron
The Breasthooks of Iron

Planking Outside
From the Keel to the Height defined is American Elm and Teak
From the above named Height to the Light Water Mark, Teak
From the Light Water Mark to the Wales Teak
The Wales and Black-strakes are Teak
The Topsides and Sheerstrakes, Teak
The Spirketting and Planksheers, Teak
The Water-ways Upper Deck, Teak
The Decks: Yellow Pine; State of: Good
How Fastened to Beams: Screw pointed bolts & nuts
The Shifts of the Planking are not less than 6 feet

Planking Inside

The Ceiling is flat

The Ceiling, Lower Hold and between Decks: American Red Pine & Teak

Shelf Pieces: Iron

Butt Straps of Keelsons, Stringers and Tie Plates, double or single riveted: Triple in Keelsons & double otherwise.

Deck Beams, how secured to the side: Bracket ends on Beams riveted to frames 22½ in. long

Hold or Lower Deck, how secured to the side: do ribs

General Quality of Workmanship: Good

What description of Iron is used for the Frames, Beams, Keelsons, Stringer and Tie Plates: Hopkins & Co. Middlesbro, Beams and Angles Shotley Bridge Co. for Plates

We certify that the above is a correct description of the several particulars therein given.
 Builder's Signature: A. Stephen & Son
 Surveyor's Signature: Thomas Alexander

Her Masts, Bowsprits, Yards, &c. are in Good condition and sufficient in size and length.

Sails

2 Fore Sails

2 sets Fore Double Top Sails

2 Fore Topmast Stay Sails

2 Main Sails

2 sets Main double Top Sails and others in all 38 pieces

Standing and Running Rigging is of wire and hemp, sufficient in size, superior in quality

She has six boats, 25 to 37 feet in length

The present state of the Windlass is Good

3 Capstans and Rudder: Good

Pumps: Murdock Patent-double acting

1 Steam Winch

Cables

Chain	150 fathoms	1¾ in.
Iron Stream Cable	90 fathoms	$1^5/_{16}$
Hawser	90 fathoms	9½
Towlines	90 fathoms	8
	120 fathoms	6
Warp	120 fathoms	5
	120 fathoms	4

All of Good quality

Anchors	Weight Ex. Stock
	30. 0. 4
Bowers	30. 0. 4
	26. 1. 0
Stream	11. 3. 8
Kedges	6. 3. 0
	3. 1. 0

General Remarks

This vessel has been built in conformity with enclosed plan submitted 31/5/64 & the subsequent recommendations suggested in Surveyor's note of 3/5/64 complied with viz: Garboard Strake Crossbolted and adjoining strake each side edge bolted with yellow metal. Is fastened throughout from lower part of keel to 4/5 depth of hold with 1 inch mixed metal screw pointed bolts & nuts 6 inches long dowelled outside and above that height. All fastenings outside and in decks are of Iron Galvanized. Has been built under a roof conformable to rule. Has 5 pan each side diagonal trusses fromed of plate 12 x ½ applied outside of frames. Has also an additional course of lates 17½ x 9/16 applied in way of Fore and Main Chains. Upper deck has 10 pair diagonal trusses 12 x 11/16 and lower deck is trussed at Fore and Main Masts. Butt Plates in way planking extend from frame to frame riveted to frames and 11/16 thick.

In what manner are the surface of Iron Work preserved from oxidation: Portland Cement in bottom up to bilge and red lead paint above that.
Present condition of Caulking of Bottom: efficient
Deck: efficient
Waterways: efficient
If Sheathed, Doubled, Felted, Coppered: Yellow Metal Paper

I am of opinion this Vessel should be classed 15A1
The amount of the fee £5 is received by me Thomas Alexander

Character assigned: A1 for 15 years
26 July 1866

Note: A detailed list of the thickness of planking used throughout the ship together with sizes of bolts and fastenings is also given in this survey but not reproduced here. The enclosed plan referred to does not appear to have survived.

ROYAL NAVY

Many Royal Navy seamen were 'pressed' into service and others were enlisted for a period of years. Those who chose to remain in Australia were usually deserters. Crew lists (muster rolls) for Royal Navy ships are to be found among Admiralty documents at The National Archives, London. Some men who are listed did in fact leave the ship before she sailed. It should be noted that the supernumeraries listed include some passengers. These were presumably government officials.

Detailed plans of a large number of Royal Navy ships are kept at the National Maritime Museum, Greenwich (see Appendix 21). Part of the plans of HMS *Porpoise*, and of the *Coromandel* when converted to a prison hulk at Bermuda, are shown on pages 71 and 302. Detailed specifications for Royal Navy ships, and contracts for those built in merchant yards, are also held by the National Maritime Museum, in record class ref. ADM 168 and ADM 170. These classes of document are similar to each other, each providing a detailed description of the ship. Below are abstracts from the first two pages of the contract for HMS *Woolwich*, dated 1782, which was built at Bursledon near Southampton. This ship was a 5th Rate Ship of War with forty-four carriage guns, launched in December 1785. The 23-page long contract contains considerable detail of the construction of the ship.

NMM ref ADM 168/190

Heights	Of the Top Timber Line, or Upper Edge of the Waste Rail above the Upper Side of the Main Keel at the Beakhead 32 feet 4 inches, Midships 30 feet 6 inches, at the Stern Timber 36 feet 7 inches. Of the Rising in Midships above the Upper Side of the Keel 9 inches.
Gun Deck	Beams to round 4½ inches, Plank thick 3 inches. Height from the Plank of the Gun Deck to the upper side of the Upper Deck Beams at the Middle of the Beam, afore 6 feet 8 inches; Midhsips 6 feet 8 inches; Abaft 6 feet 8 inches. Height from the Upper Side of the Gun Deck Plank to the Upper Side of the Lower Port Sills 2 feet 1 inch. Ports deep 2 feet 6 inches, fore and aft 2 feet 11 inches. Ports from the Water in Midships 4 feet 10 inches. Hanging of the Deck at the Middle 1 feet 5½ inches.
Extreme Length	From the Fore Side of the Taffrail, at the height of the Fiferail, to the Fore Side of the Figure of the Head by a Line parallel to the Keel 165 feet 3 inches. From the Fore Side of the Stem, at the height of the Beakhead, to the Fore Side of the Knee of the Head 11 feet 4 inches. From the Fore Side of the Stem at the Height of the Beakhead, to the Fore Side of the Beakhead Bulkhead 5 feet 4 inches. Length from Aft Side of the Wing Transom to the Aft Side of the Stern Timber, at the Upper Side of the Plank of the Lower Counter at the Middle Line 5 feet 9 inches. Length from the Aft Side of the Wing Transom to the Aft Side of the Stern Timber, at the Height of the second Counter, or Lower Edge of the Rail under the Great Cabin Lights 7 feet 9 inches.
Keel	The Keel to be elm (except the After Piece, which is to be Oak, or Elm) not more than 5 pieces 15½ inches square in the Midships, sided Afore 13 inches, and at the Aft Part of the Rabbit of the Post 10 inches, the Scarphs to be 4 feet long, tabled one into the other, laid with Flannel or Kersey, bolted with 6 bolts of 1 inch diameter, the Lips of the said Scarphs not to be left more in thickness than 4⅛ inches.
False Keel	The False Keel to be 7 inches thick so as to make the Main and False Keels together 19½ inches below the Rabbit, not to have more than 5 pieces of proper Lengths to give Scarph to the Scarphs of the Main Keel, to be laid with Tar and Hair, thick Brown Paper dipt in Tar, put between the Main and False Keel, and sufficiently fastened with Nails and Staples, and the Bottom and Sides filled, as shall be directed.
Stem	The Stem not to be more than 2 or 3 Pieces of good sound Oak, quite free from defects of any kind, sided at the Head

(which is to be continued down to the lower side of the lower Cheek) 1 foot 9 inches below the Hance 15½ inches, and at the Fore Foot the bigness of the Keel at that place moulded at the Head 16 inches, and at the Fore Foot the bigness of the Keel, the Scarphs 4 feet long, tabled one into the other, laid with white Flannel or Kersey and bolted with 6 bolts of ⅞ inches diameter, the middle bolt to go through the False Stem and well clenched thereon, the Lips of the Scarphs not to be more than 4⅛ inches thick.

False Stem or Apron	The False Stem or Apron to be 8½ inches thick, to be in breadth as the Rabbit on the Stem may require, if the Rabbit of the Stem comes in the middle it must then be the same breadth as the Stem, but if the Rabbit comes on the aftside to be 1 foot 10½ inches broad as far down as the Knight Heads say to it, and below as the Body may require, the scarphs to be 12 inches long.
Stern Post	The Stern Post to be of good sound oak timber of the best kind, free from defects, square at the Head 18½ inches, fore and aft on the Keel (the Back or False Post, if any included) 2 feet 6 inches abaft the Rabbit at the Wing Transom 10 inches, and on the Keel 1 feet 8 inches not to have less than 10 inches Main Post abaft the Rabbit, the Breadth Athwartships at the Head to be continued down as low as the Deck Transom, and from thence to begin its tapering to 10 inches as before observed, that the Main Keel is to be wrought at that place, not to be bearded until the Back is on, and then to be no more than the tapering of the Keel requires. The Rabbit of the Main Post at the lower end to be sunk no deeper than 2½ inches.
Inner Post	The Inner Post to run up to the under side of the Deck Transom to be 10 inches fore and aft there 14 inches on the Keel, to be of the same breadth athwartships as the Main Post from the lower Transom up, from thence down as the Body requires.
Wing Transom	The Wing Transom to be sided 12 inches and moulded at the ends 16 inches, in the middle 1 feet 9 inches, no Chocks to be admitted on the aft side, and to be bolted to the Post with 2 bolts of ⅞ inches diameter, or (if the standard bolt comes into the Wing Transom) as shall be directed.
Filling Transom	The Transom between the Wing and Deck to be sided 8 inches, to the left for air between the Wing and Filling 2 inches, between the Filling and Deck Plank 2 inches, and to be bolted to the Post with one bolt of 1¼ inches diameter.

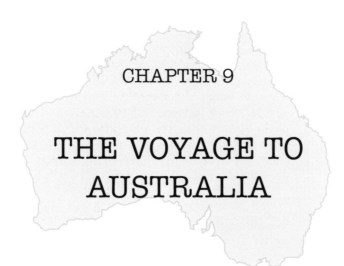

CHAPTER 9

THE VOYAGE TO AUSTRALIA

SHIPS' JOURNALS, PORT RECORDS, CONSULATE LETTER BOOKS AND RELATED CORRESPONDENCE

(See Appendix 19)

Ships' journals contain all manner of detail, not just about the navigation of the voyage, but also records of the people on board, including the convicts. Surgeons' journals are of particular interest, giving details of the sick passengers, crew and convicts. Letter books written by the various British Consulates at ports where the ships called on their voyage, sometimes contain interesting details. The Privy Council was concerned with foreign affairs and its records sometimes refer to the voyages of ships and any incident that was of particular interest. The Colonial Office records for New South Wales include references to the voyages of various ships. The Ministry of Transport records include surgeons' superintendent journals for convict ships. All these records are held at The National Archives, London.

The following is recorded in the Privy Council papers relating to the *Eden* convict ship before she sailed for New South Wales.

TNA ref PC 1/2715

Eden Convict Ship
Sheerness
8th July 1840

Sir

Having discovered in the course of yesterday that attempts has been made to remove a bar from the after hatchway in the prison of this ship, I was induced to have the irons of all the convicts embarked carefully examined. I found that the rivets of some of them had been tampered with, that the barrels of some were so large as to admit of being drawn over the foot entirely and that in a particular individual, Richard Gould, both defects existed so that had the opportunity for escape offered he could readily have divested himself of his irons altogether. I have had these faults rectified by the carpenter of the ship, as far as possible but I consider it my duty to report the circumstances and offer a suggestion that in future more attention be paid to the size of the barrels made use of in ironing the convicts as they appear to be often much larger than is consistent with security, and as there are at present for convicts on board whose irons do not admit of being re-applied from their great size I have to request that a few additional pairs may be sent on board this ship, and beg to suggest at the same time that in future a proportion beyond the numbers absolutely required be furnished to sea-going convict ships, to provide against casual deficiencies or misfits.

I have the honor to be
G.E. Foreman
Surgeon Superintendent

Consulate Letter Books

TNA ref FO 772/1B

Spain, Canary Islands – Consulate Letter Book

Santa Cruz
Teneriffe
January 23rd 1833

My Lord,
I have the honor to inform your Lordship that the *Diana* Transport, with female convicts, Ellis surgeon, touched here on Monday last the 21st, the surgeon came to the Mole in a boat intending to purchase some refreshments but the quarantine[1] being still rigorously inforced he could not come on shore to choose what he required, he did not therefore wait. The ship proceeded forthwith to its destination.

I am,
Richard Bartlett, Consul

Santa Cruz
May 8th 1834

My Lord,
I have the honor to inform your Lordship that His Majesty's Ship *Rainbow*, Captain Bennett, anchored in this Bay on Thursday the 1st instant, and having taken on board some water and fresh Provisions sailed in the evening of Saturday the 3rd. The *Rainbow* is the first British Man that has been admitted to Pratique since the beginning of the year 1832. The ship *John Barry*, John Robson master, with 320 convicts and a detachment of the 50th Regiment (every person on board in perfect health) anchored on the 28th April, the iron work of the tiller having become loose from friction and requiring repair. The *John Barry* proceeded on the voyage in the evening of Saturday the 3rd.

The ship *Medora* with Government stores on board for the West Indies anchored the 28th April took on board 800 pipes of wine, and sailed in the evening of Saturday the 3rd instant.

I have the honor to be &c
Richard Bartlett, Consul

1. There was a cholera epidemic.

TNA ref CO 201/73

Report on the Voyage of Three Transportation Ships to New South Wales

Sydney, New South Wales
September 30th 1814

Sir

Some days since, in a conversation with your Excellency on the subject of the calamitous state of disease in which the convicts on the Transports, *General Hewitt*, *Three Bees, and Surry*, arrived in the Country, Your Excellency expressed a wish that I should communicate to you my sentiments on the probable cause of the diseases which appeared among the convicts on these Transports on the means of preventing similar occurrences in future, or of counteracting their effect.

In obedience to this wish I have now the honor of submitting the following detailed observations to Your Excellency's consideration.

In the order in which I now propose to myself to lay before Your Excellency the observations I am about to make, I shall beg leave to call Your Excellency's attention to the various circumstances connected with these Transports according to the priority of their arrival in this Colony, making occasionally, as I proceed, such remarks as seem naturally to arise out of the subject.

It appears from the best information I have been able to obtain, that the *General Hewitt*, a ship of 960 tons, Earl, master, received on the 28th July 1813 from the Hulk at Woolwich, one hundred and twenty four Convicts. She then dropped down to Gravesend where she remained sixteen days whence she went to the Nore and received forty eight Convicts from the hulk at Sheerness, on the 22nd and 23rd August. Two days after her arrival at Portsmouth, she completed her number three hundred by one hundred and twenty four Convicts from the Hulks at Portsmouth and Langston and finally sailed from England on the 26th of the same month, having on board in addition to the Convicts, seventy Soldiers, fifteen Women, eight children and one hundred and four Ship's Company, besides several passengers, in all five hundred and fifteen, having been twenty seven days from the embarking of the first of the Convicts to the day of her sailing, during the whole of which time it is to be observed and regretted the Convicts were closely confined below.

That they were divided into messes of six men each, six of which messes were admitted on deck in rotation during the day for the benefit of air. This practice was continued till, she arrived at Madeira, when the prisoners were again kept below for nine days the time of her stay at that Island. On proceeding to sea they were again admitted on deck in the same number and usual manner until they made Rio Janeiro, when they were once more closely confined for ten days, by which time the sickness which had commenced shortly after their quitting Madeira had increased to an alarming degree. In consequence of this sickness the Convicts were very properly allowed access to the deck during the day for the remaining part of the voyage. It was alas too late; no care, no exertion however it might lessen, could now remedy the evil!

That there were two days in the week appointed for shaving and cleaning the convicts, but this regulation was not furnished in with any regularity, they were, however obliged to appear clean every Sunday on the quarter deck in order to attend divine service, till they arrived at Rio Janeiro, when this salutary practice was neglected, and the Convicts were suffered to become exceedingly filthy. There was no fresh water allowed for washing any part of their linen and the allowance of water was reduced to three pints per man per diem, that the soap (about twelve ounces) was served out once a month to each mess.

INSTRUCTIONS

RELATIVE TO FREE PASSAGE.

I. **Persons** eligible for Free Passage, are Married Agricultural Labourers, Shepherds, Carpenters, Smiths, Wheelwrights, Bricklayers, and Masons, and Unmarried Female Domestic and Farm Servants, being of competent skill, sound health, and good character.

II. **Married Persons**, 40 years old and upwards, and Unmarried Persons 30 years old and upwards, are **not eligible** for Free Passage.

III. **Unmarried Males** under 18, and Females under 15, are **not eligible** for Free Passage; but will be taken out with their Parents, on payment of £3 each, if their Parents are approved for Free Passage, and not otherwise.

IV. **Married Men** cannot obtain Free Passage, unless accompanied by their Wives; nor Married Women without their Husbands.

V. **Unmarried Females** cannot obtain Free Passage, unless they proceed, under the care of Married relatives, connexions, or friends.

VI. **Unmarried Males,** of the classes above named, between 18 and 30, will be taken on payment of £5 each.

VII. **Brother and Sister,** provided they are proved to be actually so connected may obtain Free Passage.

VIII. **Emigrants,** on application for Free Passage, and before the printed forms of application are furnished to them, are required to pay into the hands of Mr. W. WILLIAMS, a deposit of One Pound each Adult (15 years old and upwards), which will be returned to them, if they are not approved of.

IX. **Emigrants** are supplied with the necessary Box, 15 inches square, containing a knife and fork, a table and a tea-spoon, a metal plate, and a hook-pot, for the One Pound each deposited as above.

X. **Emigrants** should not encumber themselves with much luggage, as they will be charged freight for any quantity over ten cubit feet (that is, one box not exceeding 3 feet long, 1 foot 9 inches wide, and 1 foot 6 inches deep, in addition to the Box of 15 inches square); they are not required to bring provisions, and are not allowed to carry with them any beds or bedding, for use on board, sheets only excepted.

XI. **Emigrants** must arrive at the port of embarkation (Bristol) at least two days before the day advertised for sailing, on which day they will be embarked with their luggage on board the Ship in which they are to sail, **free of expence;** which being done, the Emigrants are supplied with good and wholesome provisions, according to the scale laid down in the Prospectus, and continue to be so supplied until their arrival at PORT PHILIP. Beds and bedding are also supplied the Emigrants, **free of charge;** and if from stress of weather, or any other cause, they should be prevented embarking on the day advertised, they will, from and after that day, be maintained on shore.

XII. **Emigrants** will forfeit their deposits, if they do not join the Ship as above.

XIII. **Baptismal** Certificates from the Registry Books of the Parish, are indispensably necessary for all the Emigrants, of whatever age.

WILLIAM WILLIAMS,

COOPERS' HALL, KING-STREET, BRISTOL.

A ship's 'Instructions – Relative to Free Passage'. (The National Archives CO 201/363)

That the first issue of wine was on the day they left Madeira when half a pint was served to each man; no more was issued for three weeks, (when a quarter of a pint was issued to each man), till they arrived at Rio Janeiro. About a month after their departure from that Port the issue was recommenced and continued, but very irregularly, and my information states that it is calculated there was a deficiency in the issue of at least three hundred gallons.

The decks were swept every morning, scraped and swabbed twice a week; they were sprinkled with vinegar weekly until they made Rio Janeiro when this was discontinued. The ship was also fumigated once a week for the first six weeks, but was afterwards much neglected.

No vinegar was issued to the Prisoners, and mustard but three times, about 12 ounces to each mess. That three weeks previous to their arrival at Rio Janeiro their bedding was thrown overboard in consequence of having been wetted from want of which the Convicts, when they came into a cold climate suffered exceedingly.

It also appears that Captain Earl purchased the Convicts ration of salt beef for nine weeks, paying them for it after they left Rio Janeiro in the following articles at most shamefully enormous prices, viz. coffee four shillings, sugar one shilling and sixpence, tea twenty shillings, tobacco five shillings per pound which was not less than six or seven hundred per cent on prime cost.

As there is a wide difference between several essential points of this statement, the truth of which there is little reason to doubt, and that given by Mr Hughes, the Surgeon of the *General Hewitt*, before the Court of Enquiry, instituted by your Excellency in March last on this subject, I feel myself called upon to detail, as concisely as possible, the substance of Mr Hughes testimony, viz:

That there were three hundred Convicts received on board the *General Hewitt* from the hulks at Woolwich, Sheerness, Portsmouth and Langston. That some of them were in a state of debility; to 15 or 16 of whom he would have objected had there been time previous to the sailing of the ship, as being unfit for the voyage; that the Convicts were not examined after their embarkation by any inspecting Medical Officer, but that they were accompanied by health certificates from the Surgeon of the respective Hulks, and that, though he did not coincide with the opinions contained in these certificates, he admitted there were none labouring under contagious diseases. That the ship remained three days at Spithead after the completion of their number, that about a fortnight after quitting Madeira 12 or 14 were attacked with dysentery which he conceived arose from the Convicts being confined below by the bad weather which prevailed for some time before and during the time of them being alluded, and also from the bedding having been wetted on deck, and imprudently used before it could be dried. That the dysentery continued to increase with typhus fever; that on their arrival at Rio Janeiro the Convicts were in a very sickly state, and reduced to extreme debility; that the articles of comfort &c which were put on board were duly served out, and that the Convicts were formed into three divisions, one of which possessed the deck in rotation, so that the whole were on it in the course of the day and that at the times of fumigating the prison the whole were on deck at once, that after quitting Rio Janeiro all the Convicts had access to the deck during the day at pleasure, that they were supplied with fresh beef and vegetables while at Rio, but on being examined as to the sufficiency of it, he admitted that it had been issued at first in too small a quantity, but that an augmentation had been made by Captain Earl on his representation which silenced all complaints on that head.

He also admitted that Captain Earl had purchased the Convicts ration of salt beef, observing that he had known it to have been the custom with the Master of several

Transports to salt ration during their passage through the tropics, and, finally that thirty four Convicts died on the voyage.

Remarks on the *Three Bees*

The Convicts from the New Prison, Dublin, joined those from the Northern jails, who had embarked two days before on board the *Atlas* hired Brig, on the 28th August 1813. The weather was sultry, and as they were exceedingly crowded in a close hold the nights were truly suffocating. During their stay here one of the prisoners died, where fatal termination, it was said, was accelerated, if not solely occasioned by the foulness of the place, necessarily attendant on crowding so many together. They sailed from the Canal Docks, Dublin the 20th September and anchored in the Cove of Cork on the night of the 22nd. Next day they were examined by Doctor Harding, inspecting Physician, and were removed on board the *Three Bees* as fast as they could be conveniently cleaned and dressed. This service was completed on the 2nd October. The Cork and the Southern Convicts with those of the *Atlas,* completed their number two hundred and nineteen. On the 27th they sailed from Cork and anchored at Falmouth on the 30th. The weather during the time they were at Falmouth was exceedingly cold and the prisoners suffered severely. They finally sailed from England the 7th December.

They were while in harbour, supplied with fresh beef, their rations were uniformly and justly served out. A gill[2] of wine was issued every Sunday to each man when at sea till they drew nigh the end of the voyage, when it was served out twice a week. During the prevalence of cold, damp or rainy weather fires were lighted in the prison. It was every morning cleaned and was fumigated with sulphuric acid and nitre as long as they lasted, when these failed camphor, vinegar &c were used.

The convicts were formed into five divisions, each having a portion of the day on deck when the weather would admit. In the Harbour of Rio Janeiro they were all on the deck together every day, on which occasions the mercury in the thermometer fell in the prison to 7 and 8 degrees. Here a case of fever appeared and as it bore all the marks of common ship fever every precaution was used to prevent the contagion from spreading. The subject of the fever died. They arrived at Rio Janeiro on the 3rd February and left it the 17th. On the 27th a strange sail appeared and as she bore down, had the appearance of an enemy. The Prisoners bedding was used on this occasion as a barricade and being kept on deck all night was quite drenched with rain. After several fruitless endeavours, on as many days to dry the bedding it was put into the Prison; at the same time the Prisoners were cautioned not to use it. This injunction was disregarded and scurvy which had been long lurking among them, made its appearance. Seven men died of it ere they reached Port Jackson, and fifty five were sent to the Hospital in a dreadful state. Nine Convicts died on the passage.

Remarks on the Scurvy

It appears from the Ship's and Surgeon's journals that they completed their number two hundred Convicts on the 21st January 1814; that they were admitted on deck in divisions of twenty five men each in rotation; that the Prison was regularly cleaned and fumigated; that vinegar, mustard and soap were issued; that divine service was read to the Convicts in the Prison; and that half a pint of wine was served out to each man every Sunday during their stay in England.

---

2. A quarter of a pint.

On the 22nd February they sailed, having formed the Convicts into nine divisions of twenty one men each, one of which was admitted on the deck in turn during the day; in addition to this number there were fourteen who being appointed to perform little offices for the others, had constant access to the deck. On the 17th March the Surgeon's journal records the case of John Stopgood who seems to have been the first that laboured under a well defined case of Typhus fever or common ship fever. On the 12th John Ranson died of fever; from which time it seems to have been kept up more or less till their arrival here.

The Surgeon, although his journal is very uninteresting, containing no remarks of importance, or indicating much thought, seems to have paid all the attention in his power to cleaning and fumigating the Prison up to the 2nd June when his journal ceases. And at this point I am sorry to observe from all I have been able to learn on the subject, that neither his representations nor his efforts met with that attention or assistance from the Captain and his officers, which it was their duty to have afforded him. For notwithstanding that another fatal termination of fever occurred on the 22nd May, no attempt appears to have been made towards ventilating the prison.

The ship's journal contains a regular registry of the times of cleaning and fumigating the Prison, of admitting the Convicts on deck, of Divine Service being read to them in the Prison; and of issuing the wine. On the 18th March it states that the Convicts were formed into eight divisions, one of which had access to the deck in turns during the day, and that Tuesday and Friday were appointed for washing days, which seems from the Journal entries to have been pretty regularly observed till they made Rio Janeiro on the 11th April. While they lay in Rio they were supplied with fresh beef, vegetables and fruit. And it states that on the 16th as no shore boat was permitted to go along side, Captain Paterson sent on board tobacco, coffee and sugar for such of the Provisions as had the means and wish to purchase any.

On the 21st April they left Rio Janeiro and the Journal goes on to state the times of admission of the Convicts on the deck, cleaning and fumigating the prison, and issuing the wine, the last issue of which took place on the 1st May. From Sunday the 24th May no more mention is made of Divine Service having been read to the prisoners.

On the 22nd May Isaac Giles died of fever, the last case mentioned above from the Surgeon's journal. Nothing worthy of notice occurs in the Ship's journal, being merely a registry of transactions similar to those in the last paragraph to the 9th June, when Aaron Jackson died of fever from which period the deaths become awfully frequent.

On the 26th July they fortunately fell in with the Transport *Broxbornebury* and being reduced to the greatest distress requested Captain Pitcher to send some person on board to take charge of the ship. Next day Mr Nash from the *Broxbornebury* went on board and took charge of the *Surry,* the Captain two mates, the Surgeon, twelve of the ship's company, sixteen Convicts and six Soldiers were lying dangerously ill with fever. Captain Paterson died the same day. They anchored on the 29th in Port Jackson Harbour when the ship was immediately put under quarantine regulations.

The sick were landed and taken into tents prepared for their reception. Every plan was adopted and carried into effect, that had a tendency to cut short the progress of contagion. The measures adopted proved so effectual that but one case of infection took place after the sick were landed.

There died in all thirty six Convicts, four Soldiers and seven Seamen among whom is included the Captain, Surgeon and two Mates.

That the death of the Captain, Surgeon and Mates may operate as an awful lesson in future on the minds of the Officers of Transports is a communication devoutly to be wished.

Having thus detailed the various circumstances and operations connected with the management of the Convicts on board the above named Transports as fully as the means of information and the harassing professional duties in which I have been for some time engaged, will admit, I shall proceed to point out the errors which appear to have existed, and as time will not permit me to enter into a separate train observations on the conduct observed in the management of the Convicts on board of each, I shall review my subject under the following heads. Clothing, Diet, Air, and Medical Assistance: applying the reasoning which may arise from the consideration of these subjects to practice in, those vessels either collectively or separately as the case may seem to require.

Clothing

Will embrace every thing regarding personal cleanliness as well as dress.

It must have been obvious to your Excellency, that not withstanding the great difference of the temperature of the different seasons of the year of the various climates through which they must pass, the clothing of the Convicts on their arrival in this Country has been hitherto of not quite the same, namely blue cloth, or kersey[3] jackets and waistcoats, duck trousers, check or coarse linen shirts, yarn stockings and woollen caps.

When a ship quits England in the summer months from the usual length of the voyage, she arrives here also in the summer, thus nearly or entirely avoiding the winter; but when she leaves England in the winter the reverse of this takes place, having instead of two summers the rigor of two winters in latitude 52 N and not less than 45 or 46 S to support, in both which our own personal feelings have taught us the comfortable and pleasing accommodation of warm clothing.

The Convicts when about to be embarked on the Transports are collected from the various prisons and hulks in which they may have been confined, are stript of their former clothing, washed and dressed in the clothing above enumerated, if it be the winter season the change must be great, sudden and striking, more especially as we know that they are not prohibited wearing such warm apparel as they or their friends can find the means of furnishing.

Experience the best of guides, has long taught mankind the knowledge, that the human body does not possess the power of instantaneously adapting itself to very great and sudden transitions, nor of supporting their effects with impunity. With this fact in view it will be readily admitted that the great and sudden change of dress to which the Convicts are thus subjected, must, in a winter's passage, be one source of disease. The common and invariably effects of this change are colds, pneumonic complaints and rheumatism which together with the means requisite to subdue these complaints are highly calculated for the production of debility the predisponets [sic] of scurvy fever and dysentery.

That the want of warm clothing had a very considerable share in the production of the inveterate degree of scurvy, under which the Convicts in the *Three Bees* laboured, will require but little proof. They were on board the ship from the 2nd October to the 7th December, lying in the Ports of Ireland and England, stript of their clothing generally consisting of coarse cloth, or friese[4] coats, waistcoats, breeches or trousers

3. Coarse woollen cloth.
4. Coarse woollen cloth.

and not uncommonly with addition of a friese great coat, dressed in the light clothing mentioned above with trousers of a thin kind of brown or unbleached linen known in Ireland by the name of 'harn' which is much thinner and less calculated to resist cold and severity of weather than even the Dutch trousers of the English Convicts. In such a dress, having undergone such a change, exposed to the rigor of two winters, incapable from a variety of causes too obvious to require mentioning, of taking exercise with but a single blanket the only covering on their beds at night, to the eye of common sense, not to say to that of medical acumen, the probable effects must exhibit too strong a figure to be easily doubted or mistaken.

For a summer voyage no dress can be more suitable than the present for they can be as lightly clothed as they please by discumbering themselves under the pressure of heat, of their jackets and waistcoats, when the shirts and trousers will be found quite pleasant and amply sufficient.

Far, very far from arrogantly wishing to propose useless innovations in a system already as nearly perfect as possible, yet with the importance of the subject pressing on my mind, and urged too, by a strong sense of duty, I shall take the liberty most respectfully, to submit to your Excellency's consideration the propriety of suggesting and recommending to his Majesty's Government, the following trifling change and addition in the present clothing for the winter voyage.

That the duck or ham trousers be exchanged for cloth ones, that flannel waistcoats and drawers be supplied, and that an additional blanket be issued to each person. This change and addition of the trousers, flannel waistcoats and drawers at no very great expense, would affect the means of resisting cold during the day, and that the blanket would contribute warmth in the night and supersede that baneful custom which is but too common of sleeping in their clothes; a practice which cannot be too strongly deprecated, since by confining the effluvice arising from the human body constantly about it thus rendering it more virulent it tends directly to supply the most effectual means of generating and diffusing contagion.

In objection to this charge and addition of dress it might perhaps be urged, that a flannel or woollen cloth is in most circumstances generally less cleanly than linen, and as woollen clothes possess in a high degree the property of imbibing and retaining the principles of contagion, the benefits derived from their power in counteracting the effects of cold, and affording warmth, would be inadequate to risque of favouring the diffusion of contagion. The answer to this objection leads me to the second division of this head.

Personal Cleanliness

Altho the strength of this argument must in some degree be admitted, yet it cannot be denied but that either cotton or linen, if worn on the person till it become filthy will retain fomites and communicate contagion as certainly as woollen. But fortunately we possess even on board ship, the means of preventing the generation and diffusion of contagion with as much certainty as any place else. To effect this object all that is necessary is cleanliness and ventilation.

In detail of the transactions respecting the management of the Convicts on board the *General Hewitt,* I am sorry to be obliged to observe that however well they commenced by appointing proper days for attending to the personal cleanliness of the Convicts, and by insisting on their being shaved and clean in order to attend Divine Service on the quarter deck every Sunday in the early part of the voyage, they did not consider these circumstances of importance enough to merit being steadily carried into effect, since long ere the termination of the voyage, they suffered these most useful and salutary regulations to sink into neglect so that we find the Convicts becoming exceedingly filthy.

Whatever good excuse might be urged for not supplying the prisoners with a certain portion of fresh water for the purpose of washing their linen at sea, surely none can be offered why it was withheld in harbour. It would perhaps be equally difficult to assign any solid reason, in a passage of less than six months, for putting them on an allowance of three pints of water per man per diem.

The soap. I am concerned to find, was not issued to them in the proportion in which it should have been, as it appears from the calculation of twelve ounces to each mess of six men per month that not more then 150 lbs was issued during the passage. On the subject of the practice with regard to soap, I shall have occasion to animadvert below.

It is also to be regretted that sufficient attention was not paid to the personal cleanliness of the Convicts on board the *Three Bees,* as those who were landed ill of scurvy before their clothing was changed were extremely dirty both in person and dress. On enquiry into the cause of this I was told that only one man could have access to the head at a time, which was the place appointed for them to wash themselves, and that the soldiers composing the guard threw as many difficulties in their way on these occasions as possible, so that in the midst of the ocean they could not for want of a little common management obtain, even, salt water enough to wash themselves once a week.

The Convicts in the *Surry* did not, from quitting England in February, suffer so much from want of warm clothing as those of the *Three Bees* but from the wretchedly dirty and squalid appearance of their person and dress, there was much reason to suppose that they had been as great if not greater strangers to wholesome ablution as those of either the *General Hewitt* or *Three Bees.*

In occurrence demonstrative of the highly improper practices carried by the masters of some of the Transports with regard to the articles of comfort &c fell within my own immediate observation, and which I cannot pass over in silence. When the Convicts were landed from the *Surry* in order that the ship might be fumigated, and it was deemed proper to wash the prisoners persons as frequently as possible previous to the quarantine restrictions being removed; a little soap was requested from the Purser or Steward for this purpose. 'There was none, it was all expended' was the reply. A few days after it was discovered that a quantity of soap was inserted in the invoice of goods they had for sale. In consequence of which it was suggested that an enquiry was likely to be instituted concerning the proper expenditure of the articles of comfort &c put on board for the use of the Convicts on the passage. This produced the desired effect and five boxes of soap were sent to the General Hospital as remains of unexpended stores. This fact speaks for itself.

Having thus shewn that the personal cleanliness of the Convicts on board these Transports did not obtain the degree of attention corresponding to the importance of the subject. I shall reserve the suggestion I mean to throw out on this part of the case for the conclusion of this paper. In the meantime I must beg leave to observe that experience has shewn that the effusion of cold water over the body is a powerful means of preventing the generation of contagion by washing off the effluvia from the body and enabling it to resist cold and even contagion itself when present. I could therefore recommend that as many as possible should every morning undergo the cold effusion but if it could not be complied with every morning then it should alternate with the days of cleaning and shaving, that they might every day have something to do, that would require some exertion of body and afford some amusement to the mind.

Diet

Diet including food and drink, is the next object of enquiry according to the plan proposed, and on this part of our subject Government having already made arrangements so well calculated for the health and comfort of the Convicts that there is little room for observation The allowance of food, I am warranted in asserting from practical observation, is quite sufficient, provided it be duly served out. That this has not always been the case is to be lamented. For although it is granted that it is amply sufficient, yet it does not follow that it will admit of any subduction. On the contrary I am convinced as well from information as observation, that no subduction whatever can take place without producing visible effects by debilitating the body and disposing it for disease. It has been stated above from unquestionable Authority that the matters of several Transports have purchased the Convicts ration of salt beef on their passage through the tropics, and that one at least paid them for it in a manner disgraceful to himself and injurious to them. This practice is probably in imitation of a similar one that sometimes takes place in the Navy and Company's Service wherein the salt meat ration in warm climates, by desire of the people, is retained in the Purser's hands, for which they are paid according to the established rules of the service, or they receive flour, suet and plumbs in return. To this practice in either the Navy or Company's Service there can be no possible objection, as the ration bearing a proportion to that of the Convicts is as six to four, will account of such subduction or exchange. The exchange in either case would be serviceable, but the subduction would, we know, in the one be injurious, in the other it might perhaps be harmless, and therefore Government might give instructions for the exchange of salt beef for flour, suet and plumbs between the tropics according to the usage of the Navy. But the circumstances of the muster of the Transports purchasing any part of their rations deserving of the most serious representation. It is pregnant with danger, as it affords them when so disposed, every facility for peculation, and for applying certain articles of the Convicts provisions and comforts to their private use or emolument. A transaction of this kind seems to have occurred not long since, although it failed to be proved. The Steward of the *General Hewitt* gave an information that the Captain with held a quantity of the butter put on board as part of the Convicts' ration, but when called upon to prove the fact he declared that he had served out the usual proportion of sugar in lieu of butter according to the rules of the Navy. Butter appears to be the only thing in the ration table that is unfit to form an article of diet in a voyage through the tropics. It is an expensive article and as it sells well here it is more the subject of speculation than perhaps any other put on board for the Convicts' use. Molasses might, I conceive, be substituted with advantage to Government as well as to the Convicts.

With regard to the allowance of two gallons of wine for each man during the voyage, it appears from the usual mode of administering it to be somewhat difficult to define the intention with which it is given, or the utility likely to be derived from it. Half a pint is commonly served out, or said to be so every Sunday, or some one day in the week. Of what benefit is this? I know not. Would it not be much better to reserve it for the purpose of serving out half the quantity during the prevalence of cold and bad weather?

If I might presume to suggest the result of my reasoning on this subject I should beg leave most respectfully to offer for your Excellency's consideration the fitness of recommending to His Majesty's Government to increase the quantity of wine to six gallons which would allow an issue of one fourth of a pint to each person daily. This quantity would be amply sufficient and would be attended with the most beneficial consequences, as it would by assisting to maintain the vigor of the system, counteract debility arising from bad weather, confinement below and despondency. It ought to be detailed with an equal quantity of water to which might be added a small portion of lime juice and sugar and served out and drunk at the tub by each individual that was able to come upon deck. In this manner of preparing and issuing it, it would furnish an article highly antiscorbutic[5] and as each Convict would them know the quantity he was daily entitled to, it would prevent the shameful practices which have not unfrequently taken place with regard to this article. Two instances of which are deducible from the remark made on the issue of this article in the *General Hewitt* and *Surry*. In the former it was stated there was a deficiency in the issue of 300 gallons. In the latter it is proved by the ship's journal that there is a deficiency of 240 $7/16$ gallons. Each issue of wine is regularly recorded in the ship's journal, commencing on the 30th January and terminating on the first of May during which period there were about 169 $9/16$ gallons issued, which being subtracted from 400 gallons, the quantity put on board being two gallons for each man, there remains the above deficiency of 240 $7/16$ gallons. This fact is fully and fairly recorded in the ship's journal without a single attempt at explanation.

Air

An object of still greater importance than any of those already touched on is Air, the grand Pabulum of Life, without which existence can scarcely be maintained for a minute; and from ignorance or inattention in regulating its influence in the management of the Convicts on the passage; the ill state of health and great mortality are chiefly to be attributed.

That the bodies of men when chiefly confined in considerable numbers possess a power of generating a most subtle poison, the nature of which is cognizable but in its effects, not only injurious and deleterious to the bodies of those by whom it is generated, but spreading its baneful influence far and wide among all who come within the sphere of its action, is fully evinced by the many lamentable instances on record.

The case of Mrs Howitt and others who escaped from the Black Hole in Calcutta and were afterwards seized with the fever was generated during their confinement and the seeds of which they carried with them is in proof of the first part of this position; and the second will be equally certified by the relation of one of the most striking instances of the kind on record which happened on the 11th May 1750 at the Old Bailey. The Prisoners were kept for nearly a whole day in small, ill ventilated and crowded apartments; some of them laboured under jail fever. When they were brought into Court the windows at the end of Hall opposite to the place where the Judges sat were thrown open; the people on the left of the Court, on whom the wind blew were infected with the fever, while those on the opposite side escaped. The Lord Chief Justice and the Recorder, who sat on the Lord Mayor's right hand escaped, while the Lord Mayor and the rest of the bench who sat on his left were seized with the distemper. Many of the Middlesex Jury on the left side of the Court died of it, while the London Jury, who sat on the opposite to them received no injury. But why should we go so far back and quote cases in proof of that of which we have got a melancholy instance before our eyes? In the Transport *Surry* the poison was generated by the close confinement of the Convicts in the Prison. It diffused its malignant influence through a every part of the ship and spared none who came within the sphere of its action.

5. Scorbutic: having scurvy.

SCHEME

For Victualling Convicts on board Convict Ships.

The Rations of Provisions which have been established for each Mess of Six Convicts, for Seven Days, successively, on the Passage to New South Wales, is as follows, viz.

Days of the Week.	Bread, Pounds.	Flour, Pounds.	Beef, Pounds.	Pork, Pounds.	Peas, Pints.	Butter, Pounds.	Rice, Ounces.	Suet, Pounds.	Raisins, Pounds.	Oatmeal, Pints.	Sugar, Ounces.	
SUNDAY	4	4	8					½	1			
MONDAY....	4				3	½	4			2	2	
TUESDAY ..	4	4						¼	1			Vinegar, One Quart per Week.
WEDNESDAY .	4			6	3	½						
THURSDAY ..	4	4						½	1	2		
FRIDAY	4		8		3	½						
SATURDAY ..	4				3		4			2	2	
TOTAL	28	12	16	6	12	1½	8	1½	3	6	4	One Ounce of Lemon Juice and the same quantity of Sugar is also to be issued Daily to each Convict, after the Ship has been at Sea from three to four Weeks.

And the Period for which it has been usual to put the same on board the Vessels transporting the Convicts has been Eight Months, besides which, each Convict is allowed One Hundred and Twenty Gallons of Water, and Two Gallons of Wine during the Voyage ; and the Women have the same Proportion of Provisions as the Men, with an addition of Three Pounds of Muscovado Sugar, and Half a Pound of Black Tea, per Week, for each Mess of Six Women.

The only Provisions which have been forwarded to New South Wales for the Service of the Convicts, for Three Months after their arrival, have been the Articles of Beef and Pork, which have been sent agreeably to the following Rations, viz.—1¾lb. of Beef and 3¼lbs. of Pork, making 5lb. of Beef and Pork conjointly for each Person for the Week.

N. B.   One of these Copies is to be stuck up between Decks for the Information of the Convicts.

TRANSPORT-OFFICE, *Deptford,*
Day of   18

To Mr.
Master of the
          Convict Ship
          Tons.   }

'Scheme – For Victualling Convicts on board Convict Ships', filed in 1822. (The National Archives CO 201/118)

RULES

TO BE OBSERVED

By Masters and Commanders of His Majesty's hired Transports,

IN

VICTUALLING LAND FORCES.

	Bread. Pounds.	Beer. Gallons, or ½-Pints of Spirits, or Pints of Wine.	Beef. Pieces of 8 Pounds.	Pork. Pieces of 4 Pounds.	Pease. Pints.	Oatmeal. Pints.	Butter. Pounds.	Cheese. Pounds.	Vinegar.
Sunday	4	4		1.	2				
Monday	4	4				4	½	1	
Tuesday	4	4	1 or 6 Pounds of Flour, ¼ a Pound of Suet, and One Pound of Raisins.		2	4	½	1	
Wednesday	4	4			2	4	½	1	
Thursday	4	4		1	2				
Friday	4	4			2	4	½	1	
Saturday	4	4	1 or as above.						

Six Soldiers, or Four Seamens' Allowance for every Day in the Week. or four Soldiers when embarked on board transport ships. One Quart in a Week.

The above are to be served out by full Weights and Measures.

When Flour, Suet, and Raisins are put on Board, they are to be served in equal Proportion with Beef, *viz.* one Half in Beef, the other in Flour, Suet and Raisins, on each Beef Day.

Four Pounds of Flour, or Three Pounds of Flour, with Half a Pound of Raisins (or Quarter of a Pound of Currants) and Quarter of a Pound of Suet, are equal to Four Pounds of Beef, or Two Pounds of Pork with Pease.

Half a Pound of Rice is equal to a Pint of Oatmeal; Half a Pound of Sugar is equal to Half a Pound of Butter, and a Pound of Rice is equal to a Pound of Cheese; a Pint of Oil is equal to One Pound of Butter, or to Two Pounds of Cheese, that is a Pint of Oil for the Proportion of Butter and Cheese.

A Pint of Wine, or Half a Pint of Brandy, Rum, or Arrack, is equal to a Gallon of Beer.

One Pound of Fresh Beef is equal to One Pound of Salt Beef, and One Pound and a Half of Fresh Beef equal to One Pound of Pork.

'Rules – To Be Observed by Masters and Commanders of His Majesty's Hired Transports', filed in 1822. (The National Archives CO 201/119)

To prevent the generation of this subtle, malignant and indescribable poison, every effort should be directed, and that it is possible in, perhaps every instance of bringing Convicts from England to this Country, the numerous examples of those arriving in health, having lost few or none on the passage, render extremely probable, if not quite certain. In this point however it is to be regretted that those ships which are the subject of this investigation have most miserably failed. Whether this failure arose from timidity, ignorance or inattention to their duty, this is certain, that had they intended to have favored the propagation of contagion and to have given full force to its virulence, they could not have devised a more effectual plan for their purpose.

It is recorded above that 20 or 21 of the Convicts composing one of the nine divisions, into which the whole were formed, with fourteen privileged persons were admitted on deck in their turn, when the weather and the duties of the ship would permit, and it is no where recorded either in the Surgeon's or Ship's Journal that the Convicts were at any one time, from their first embarkation to the period of their arrival in this port, all on deck at once. Hence it follows that 165 persons, or nearly that number, were locked up in the Prison or Hospital. The word ventilation is never once mentioned. No provision of windsails. The stove is removed at an early stage of the voyage. The bedding was never once brought on deck. Here is a combination of circumstances favouring the generation of contagion, with out one rationally directed effort to counteract it. To have escaped contagion under these circumstances would have been miraculous. It is only to be wondered at that so few died.

Forming the Convicts into these small divisions and admitting but one on the deck at a time to embrace a twofold intention; the safety of the ship and the health of the Convicts. That the first part of this intention might be effected by other means, remains to be shewn, but that the second is entirely defeated by its own operation will require but little proof.

It will be taken for granted that what has been once done, can be done again. It is mentioned above that the Convicts, however badly managed in other respects were at least on deck all at once every Sunday, when the weather and the duties of the ship would admit, in order to attend Divine Service. And during the time they were fumigating the ship for the first six weeks. It is also stated those of the *Three Bees* were all on the deck together every day while in Rio Janeiro. Here are 300 Convicts in the former and 200 in the latter all on deck at once, yet nothing was attempted to endanger the safety of the ships. Had this been practiced every day on board those three ill fated ships, there would have been no occasion for those observations. There would have been but little scurvy fever or dysentery. To effect this object the plan is simple and easy of execution. It only requires to put no more Convicts on board each Transport than the deck is capable of holding; to choose such time of the day when the officers and ship's company shall be most disengaged, to place the guard in a state of preparation, and in the most favourable position to command the deck in case of any attempt to gain possession of the ship.

The custom of admitting 20, 30 or 50 of the convicts on the deck at a time in rotation, is on the principle of benefiting the health of each individual and of guarding the whole against contagion. It might, perhaps, be wrong to assert that the prisoners individually receive no benefit from the very short time they are on the deck, but it might be easily proved that the advantage is not so great as is generally supposed.

Granting that the whole 2 or 300 men shall have been on the deck by 30 or 50 at a time during the day, what does this effect as to the state of the prison? Does it cause a thorough change of air? That it neither does or can requires no proof. If it fall short of this, it is of no utility, disease will be as infallibly generated by 165 persons constantly remaining in the Prison as if the whole had remained there.

To effect a complete renovation of air in the Prison and to prevent the generation of contagion let the whole of the prisoners with heir bedding be taken on deck daily when admissible and detained there some time in the meantime let the Prison be well cleaned and fumigated, and that not in the common manner of performing this operation, but let the hatchways, ports and scuttles, fore and aft be shut in and covered down in order that the fumigation be rendered as perfect and general as possible. When this shall have gone on a sufficient length of time let the hatchways, ports and scuttles be thrown open, let fires be lighted in the Prison and when the whole shall have been thoroughly aired and dried the convicts, with their bedding may be sent below. Keeping in mind that the longer they are on the deck in a body the more certain the prevention of contagion. In addition to this the Prison and Hospital ought to be white washed every two or three weeks with quick lime. I would earnestly contend for the diffusion of the nitre or muriatic acid[6] in the form of gas, in the peculiar case of a Transport carrying prisoners, although I might under other circumstances, concur in opinion with the intelligent and spirited author who says that 'The long catalogue of fever exorcisms (from the explosive devils that used to render the between decks of our ships so many miniature representations of tartarus, down to the more elegant antiloimic farce of oxymuriatic incantation) is now superseded by the simple application of three elements that are always at hand: water, air, fire. And thus what was decided in the senate to be deserving of a national reward, is known in the cockpit to be the veriest phantom of imagination.'

On what principle is it to be accounted for that not one of the Transports employed exclusively in bringing out female Convicts has had a contagious disease among them? The answer is obvious. From the women there is nothing to apprehend with regard to the safety of the ship, they have therefore unrestrained access to the deck and are generally on it, so that a perfect renovation of the air of their person is constantly taking place. On this principle and on this alone is the absence of contagion to be accounted for.

Medical Men

It becomes necessary to make a few observations respecting the medical men who are appointed to take care of the health of the Convicts on their passage. Those who have been hitherto appointed have been either students from the lecture room, or men who have failed in the respective lines of their profession. If from the first class, they are without experience and however they may be fraught with the instructions conveyed in the various lectures they have attended, or with the contents of the numerous volumes they have read, they are but ill qualified to take charge of the health of two or three hundred men about to undertake a long voyage through various climates and under particularly distressing circumstances, without a sense of conscious rectitude to support them; dissatisfied with the past, repining at the present and apprehensive of the future, deprived of power of enjoying the air and exercise &c necessary of maintenance the due equilibrium of temper and spirits so essential to the well being of man. If from the second it but too frequently happens that either from the cause or consequence of their failure, they totally devote themselves to sobriety. How little capable either the one or the other is for this important trust, is too self evident to require demonstration.

6. Hydrochloric acid.

Besides they are employed by the owners of the ships and placed immediately under the command of the masters of the Transports who with few exceptions, having little claim to education, refined feeling, or even common decency, generally treat their surgeons as they do their apprentices and men with rudeness and brutality.

Incapable of appreciating the value of learning and despising all knowledge beyond what they themselves possess they avail themselves of every opportunity to insult and mortify their surgeons. Under this species of treatment with no means of redress during a long voyage the minds become paralysed; they view their situation with disgust and if they have the means should they not have been so before, they soon become confirmed drunkards. Hence their duty is neglected and the poor Convicts become the unhappy victims of the Captain's brutality and the surgeon's weakness want of skill or drunkenness.

Thus this picture is not surcharged the records of the Colony will furnish but too many proofs. Yet at the same time it is but fair and just to observe that although this is by much too frequent, it is not so general but that there is now and then an exception.

With a view therefore of providing skilful and approved Medical Men for this service it might not perhaps be deemed improper to suggest that the Surgeons ought to be appointed by Government, selected from the Surgeon in the Navy. Men of abilities who have been accustomed to sea practice, who know what is due to them as man and as Officers, with full power to exercise their judgement without being liable to the control of the Musters of Transports.

Previous to dismissing this part of my subject it may be right to observe that as disease has so often made its appearance among the Convicts during the voyage, and as it pays no more respect to the Surgeon than to any other person, he is therefore

The *Mount Stewart Elphinstone*, a convict transport ship, which sailed to Australia in 1848. (National Maritime Museum)

equally liable to become the victim of contagion in which event the ship is without any medical assistance. And indeed if there be much sickness and the Surgeon be fortunate enough to escape, the duty in attending upon many is too arduous and difficult for any one man to perform as it ought to be done. I should therefore most strongly recommend that an assistant Surgeon be also provided.

As it has sometimes happened that those concerned in bringing out the Convicts regardless of the principles of honesty and humanity and availing themselves of the unlimited power with which they are invested have withheld a portion of the rations and articles of comfort from the Convicts and appropriated them to their own use, instances of which are hinted at above. I trust it will not be conceived impertinent to recommend that an Agent for Transports be sent out in every ship. He might be selected from the Navy Surgeons, combining the Offices of Principal Medical Officer and Agent in his own person. An appointment of this nature filled by a person duly qualified, promises to be attended with incalculable advantage, and that too, at a trifling increase of expense.

Having thus taken an excursive, though I trust not useless view of the subject, I should beg leave to conclude by recapitulating the principle result of this enquiry and most respectfully, at the same time most strenuously recommending them to your Excellency's consideration.

1. That more warm clothing be provided for the winter passage.
2. That more regard be directed towards personal cleanliness by facilitating the means of washing and cleaning their persons and dress.
3. That cold effusion be employed as largely as possible.
4. That Masters of Transports be prohibited purchasing or exchanging, unless direct instructions from the Transport Board, any part of the rations of the Convicts.
5. That a different distribution, or rather an increase of the quantity of the Convict's wine be provided for.
6. That no reduction, unless under peculiar circumstances, of the regulated allowance of water be suffered.
7. That no part of their rations or articles of comfort be surreptitiously or fraudulently withheld.
8. That in order to prevent the generation of contagion it is absolutely necessary that the Convicts with their bedding should be admitted every day, when the weather will permit, on board the deck for a certain time. The longer the better.
9. That the Prison and Hospital be regularly cleaned and fumigated with nitric, or muriatic acid in a gaseous state. That the fumigation be as perfect and as general over the ship as possible, well airing and drying the Prison before the Convicts are sent below.
10. That for the better preservation of the health of the Convicts more eligible Medical Attendants and a different establishment, be provided.
11. That an Agent for Transports be sent out in whose person might be combined the two offices of Agent and Principal Medical Officer, invested with powers to cause the necessary regulations to be carried into effect.

I very much regret that time will not permit me to correct these observations. They are written without method or attention to arrangement or stile; and as Your Excellency is aware of the very short time I have had to prepare, owing to the pressure of professional business I trust that every allowance will be made for the imperfect state in which it meets Your Excellency's eye. If however, any thing contained herein should be the means of throwing any additional light on the management of the Convicts, and, by giving more effect to the benevolent intentions of His Majesty's Government, of ameliorating their condition or be the means of saving the life of a single individual, I shall feel more than amply compensated for any pains I have bestowed on the subject.

    Sir,

        I have the honor to be,

            With all possible respect,

                Yours Excellency's Most Obedient and devoted Humble Servant

                    Dr M.R. Gosern [?]

His Excellency Governor Macquarie

TNA ref CO 201/85

Report on the Ill-Treatment of Convicts on their Voyage to New South Wales

Government House

Sydney

12th September 1817

My Lord,

I am under the painful necessity of reporting to Your Lordship that on board the Male Convict Ship, *Chapman*, which arrived here from Ireland on the 27th July last, such a series of cruelty and oppression towards the convicts took place during the passage hither, as has induced me to appoint a Court of Enquiry to investigate the

The *Success* moored at Barry Docks, South Wales. This vessel carried many emigrants to South Wales, but never convicts. She was then converted into a prison hulk in 1852, and later became a women's prison and a reformatory for boys. (Somerset Heritage Centre ref DD/X/LES)

circumstances in order to my adapting such future measures as the nature of the case will authorize and demand at my hands.

It may perhaps be premature in me to brand the conduct of the Surgeon Superintendent (Mr Dewar), Captain Drake, Commander of the ship, his officers, and Lieutenant Bustead of His Majesty's 69th Regt who had command of the Military Detachment on board, with wanton indiscriminate and unprovoked cruelty towards the miserably unfortunate men who had been entrusted to their charge as the facts are now under investigation. I shall not therefore trouble Your Lordship with entering further into the detail until the result of that investigation which is now taking place before the Judge Advocate, my secretary, and the principal Magistrate of Police, shall enable me to give Your Lordship a full and circumstantial report thereon. In the mean time I do myself the honor to transmit Your Lordship a copy of the Official report made to me by Mr Secretary Campbell on the occasion of his mustering the convicts on board the *Chapman* in the usual way, previous to their being disembarked. Whereon the present investigation has been founded.

The killing of twelve of these convicts and the wounding thirty others, together with the killing two of the seamen, and nearly starving and destroying two hundred men, have to be accounted for by those to whose charge they have been committed, and although a plea of mutiny with a purpose of seizing the Ship by the convicts has been alleged in justification of the severities adopted yet it does not at all appear to me that any such object was in view with them, or if it even had, that it would by any means have warranted the extraordinary cruelties and punishments inflicted.

Not having any Court in this Colony competent to take final cognisance of crimes committed on the High Seas, I will feel it my duty to exercise so far the General powers with which I am invested for the protection of his Majesty's subjects in this Territory, as to send home prisoners, those persons who shall be deemed most criminal (if criminality be attached to the proceedings by the Court of Enquiry) for Your Lordship and His Majesty's Government to adopt such measures thereon as may appear due to the circumstances of the case.

I submit for Your Lordship's consideration whether it may not be expedient in the first instance to instruct the Transport Board to withhold the payment under the Charter Party for the ship *Chapman*, until such time as a full report shall be finally made from hence.

I have the Honor to be
My Lord
Yours Lordship's Most obedient and Humble Servant
L. Macquarie

To The Right Honorable Earl of Bathurst
His Majesty's Principal Secretary of State for the Colonies

Copy of Report

Sydney, 1st August 1817

Yesterday in pursuance of Your Lordship's Commands conveyed to me in the Government and General Orders of 28th ult. I proceeded at nine o'clock yesterday morning on board the hired male convict Transport Ship *Chapman*, John Drake master lately arrived from Ireland, to muster the convicts on board and to make report thereon to Your Excellency.

Altho' the master of the ship had been duly apprises of your Excellency's Government and General Orders for the muster being held at nine o'clock, yet he did not appear on board for fully one hour and one quarter after that time, during which time I remained on deck waiting his return on board, he having been on shore a very short time before my going on board. A wish to forward the Public Service induced in me to wait his arrival which took place at ¼ after ten o'clock, when I felt it due to Your Excellency's authority and to my own station, to tell him that his conduct was highly disrespectful and that I should not fail to report therein to Your Excellency. No apology was made, Captain Drake only asserting that his conduct was not disrespectful.

Having been informed by the Superintendent of Prisoners, Mr Hutchinson, and also by Mr Dewar the Surgeon Superintendent on board the *Chapman*, on the 29th ult. that Captn Drake would not release the prisoners from their irons previous to their being mustered (as it has ever been uniformly the custom) unless he should receive special orders to that effect from me, and concluding that this resolution must have been adopted in consequence of the danger he apprehended from the prisoners either in regard to security, or the safety of the ship. I addressed a letter to him (a copy hereof I now transmit for Your Excellency's perusal) on the 30th ult. informing him that his refusal to strike the irons off the prisoners had been reported to me, and if it was on the score of danger being apprehended I would not but approve of the precaution but requested to be informed by him what were the actual motives for his refusing to comply with the accustomed rule as to prisoners being relieved from their irons previous to their being mustered.

To this letter I received no answer and in consequence I asked Mr Drake if he had received it, to which he answered that he had, and did not answer it because he thought from the stile of it that I was offensive.

Shortly afterwards I asked Cptn Drake why he kept the men in irons at that time contrary to all usage and to the instructions conveyed to him by the Superintendent of Convicts to which he answered in an insolent tone that he received them on board in irons and would land them in irons. I did not feel it necessary to hold any further correspondence with him on that subject but asked for the County or Jail Lists in order to proceed on the muster and was told by him that he got none. I beg to remark here that as I was aware that much disturbance had taken place on board the *Chapman* with the Prisoners during the voyage I did not commence the muster until Captain Drake came on board in order that he might have an opportunity of meeting any complaints which the Prisoners should prefer against him, or any of the persons having authority on board and also that he might have the opportunity of reporting on the good or bad conduct of them as he felt them meriting of commendation or censure.

Owing to the melancholy circumstances which occurred during the voyage whereby twelve of the convicts had been killed and 22 wounded, my enquiries were necessarily rendered more minute than in ordinary cases, in order to ascertain as nearly as possible to what causes could be assigned the desperate measure of firing upon prisoners loaded with irons and close confined in their prison.

The general result of these enquiries fully convinces me that no plot or conspiracy existed among the convicts to seize the ship or to act in any way mutinously of their situations as prisoners. All such intention has been most solemnly denied by 174 out of the 176 whom I mustered. The other two, namely Michl Collins and John Ryan, no. 20 and 104 in my Muster Roll, being the persons who gave information and who persisted in their original statements. Surgeon Dewar and Captn Drake both gave good character to several of the prisoners, and those very persons. One and all of them denied that any plot or conspiracy had existed. I find that the prisoners had been well treated from the sailing (the 14th March) until the 17th April, and they have made few complaints previous to that day. An alarm was given on the 12th of April at

'On Board an Emigrant Ship – "Land, Ho!".' (The *Graphic*, 6 May 1871, p. 413)

night that the prisoners had got on deck, and that some of them were in the shrouds. Lights being procured it was discovered to have been altogether an unfounded, false alarm they being all found quiet in their cells. Suspicions were from thence forward propagated and on the 17th about or rather between 7 & 8 o'clock in the evening an alarm was given that the prisoners were forcing up the grating on the fore hatch. A sailor having said that he felt the grating rise under his feet. This report was deemed sufficient to warrant a general firing down the several hatch ways and the bulk heads for upwards of one hour on the miserable wretches in the Prison.

The soldiers and sailors all firing at them it was 9 o'clock before the firing ceased. On cries of mercy being sent up from the unfortunate sufferers; 3 were killed outright and twenty two wounded; the killed and wounded were nearly all naked in their beds or lying naked on the prison floor whither some of then had for coolness removed from their births, the weather being very hot in 14° N. Latitude. The dead were not removed or the wounded dressed until the next day. The sufferings and apprehension of these poor creatures cooped up as they were and fired on fore and aft need not be commented on and can scarcely be exaggerated.

Floggings on suspicion then commenced and I find that the same person has been repeatedly flogged on the most frivolous if not unjust charges. 74 to 100 men were chained naked to the Iron Cable, the first set for nearly 24 hours and never fewer than 74. Sometimes 106 were thus nightly chained to the Cable. The system of terror was carried to such a cruel excess that when these poor creatures were on the Cable they were afraid to express having a call of nature least a brutal fellow, the 3rd Officer called Baxter should beat them with his fist or cut them down with a cutlass or bayonet and if they voided their excrement under them rather than being beaten by one or other of the Ship's Officers they were sure to be flogged for filthiness.

If a man's chains were hard to rattle he was flogged and if he muffled them to prevent noise he was likewise flogged for disobedience of orders. After the 17th April they were not allowed knives to cut their meat with and some of the convicts broke off the tin handles of their mugs to use as knives for this they were also flogged. Thus were these most unfortunate men so tyrannized. Over that as many of them said on their examinations they would rather they had been hanged for their original offences than subjected to the hardships they endured. To aggravate their miseries they were nearly famished with hunger having been after the business of the 17th April deprived of one half their allowance in every thing and this severity was continued until the 10th or 11th of July last being a period of nearly three months. From the time of leaving Cork until they arrived in Sydney Cove they were never once allowed to be out of irons. Even those who were lame of Arms lost as Soldiers and Sailors in fighting the Battles of their Country at Copenhagen and Waterloo were thus starved, double Ironed and chained to the Iron Cable. Many fainted from pure weakness on the Cable arising from hunger. A hurried letter can but ill give an idea of these peoples various miseries. Let a humane man figure to himself a fellow creature double Ironed Chained to an Iron Cable and handcuffed for 3 months except when taken off to be flogged. He will then be able to form some idea of the sufferings these men endured.

Referring Your Excellency to the Muster Roll itself for many particulars in regard to the cruelties committed and too numerous to be contained in this letter I hereby declare that I consider the conduct of the Captain, his Officers and the Surgeon Superintendent and many of the crew, inhuman, barbarous and cruel beyond all reason or what even mutiny itself, if the Prisoners had been guilty of it, would have at all warranted. In including the Surgeon I have to observe that in every instance which has come before me in his professional character. He appears to have conducted himself kindly and humanely, but in his character of Superintendent he seems to have lost sight of all compassion and of all judgement in adopting the false accusations of a couple of informers and of some of the Ship's Petty Officers. When the Prisoners were stripped in order to be searched for weapons and tools their clothes were carried upon deck, and all the money they contained was plundered. Several articles of apparel were also kept from them. I pray Your Excellency to be pleased to order a full investigation of these atrocious circumstances to take place and that evidence may be called from among the prisoners themselves in order to the substantiating the charges I now submit to your consideration. Trusting that either by some evidence which I cannot anticipate the conduct of the Ship's Officers may be justified or that they may suffer condign punishment according to the overflowing measure of their cruelty and guilt.

I have the honor to be
Your Excellency's most Obt Hble Servant
J.T. Campbell

P.S. In the multiplicity of circumstances which I have been anxious to lay before Your Excellency I find I have omitted to state that this muster which detained me yesterday until nearly 5 in the evening was only finished this day a few minutes before 3 o'clock. To His Excellency Governor Macquarie

TNA ref CO 18/4

A Steam Ship to Australia in 1829

East Stockwith
near Gainsbro
22nd July 1829

Swan River [Western Australia]

Having been informed that His Majesty's Government are about sending a Steam Vessel out to the New Settlement on Swan River I have ventured to address you to solicit the situation of engineer on board of her. I have been regularly brought up in the management of engines, and as a smith. I have conducted one of the steam vessels between Hull and London, and for the last 3 years have been in the employ of Messrs Goodwins at this place in the capacity of engineer to a mill used for crushing bones for manure, and from whom I can have the most unexceptionable character.

I am 33 years of age, my family, a wife and six children. I should have no objection to remain in the Colony if required in either of the capacities above named.

Should this situation be filled up I shall be much indebted to you Sir if you could place me in the employ of any of His Majesty's steam vessels, in any other quarter of the Globe.

Humbly waiting your reply
I am Sir
Your Obedient Servant
Willm Longman

To Rt Honble Sir Geo. Murray, Bart

TNA ref CO 309/1   *Tables 9.1a, b, c, d, e, f: Ship Return for the vessel James T Foord.*

Ship Returns – Report on Immigrants

By the Ship *James T Foord*, John Hume, Master, which arrived at Port Phillip from Plymouth on the second of May 1851. – George Cream Esq., Surgeon Superintendent

Table 9.1a: Ship's details. *(TNA ref CO 309/1)*

Name of Vessel	*James T Foord*
Tonnage	790
Place of Departure	Plymouth
Place of Arrival	Port Phillip
Date of Sailing	December 29th 1850
Date of Arrival	May 2nd 1851
Number of Days on the Voyage	124
Superficies of Passengers' Deck	3621
Number of Adults admissible, computed to the Passengers' Act	241
Number of such Adults actually on board	235½ [sic]
Port at which the Vessel touched	nil
Date of Touching	nil
Days there	nil
If placed in Quarantine for what cause	No
Contract Price per Statute Adult	£10 – 19 – 0

Table 9.1b: Numbers of passengers, including births and deaths on the voyage. *(TNA ref CO 309/1 continued)*

	Adults		Children between 14 & 7		Children between 7 & 1		Children under 1		Totals	
	M	F	M	F	M	F	M	F	M	F
Numbers embarked	122	93	9	6	15	11	4	1	150	111
Total deaths	-	-	2	-	4	2	-	1	6	3
Totals	122	93	7	6	11	9	4	0	144	108
Number of births on the voyage	-	-	-	-	-	-	1	3	1	3
Total landed in the colony	122	93	7	6	11	9	5	3	145	111

Table 9.1c: Numbers of working people on board. *(TNA ref CO 309/1 continued)*

Number of adult labourers		177
Number of labourers hired at the place of landing		177
Number of labourers who left the place of landing		none
Amount paid to assist them on their journey		none
Number of agricultural labourers		115
Number of shepherds		2
Number of domestic servants	Male	0
	Female	54
Number of mechanics engaged in erecting buildings, or in obtaining or preparing building materials		2
Number of tradespeople making or selling articles of consumption	Male	0
	Female	0
Number of tradespeople engaged in making articles of clothing	Male	0
	Female	1
Number of other mechanics, &c, not included in the foregoing columns	Male	3
	Female	0

Table 9.1d: Nominal list of deaths on board the *James T Foord* on the voyage. *(TNA ref CO 309/1 continued)*

Name	Age	Date	Disease
Herrig, Mary	6 hours	January 24th 1851	Premature birth
Cain, James	2 years	February 8th	Measles
Malony, Michael	7 years	" 9th	do
Sheeham, Wm	3 years	" 14th	do
Shanahan, Judith	3 years	" 28th	do
Blakeley, Robt	9 years	March 1st	Debility & low fever
Pardy, James	2½ years	March 2nd	Debility and teething
Kennedy, Ellen	3 years	March 2nd	Measles and low fever
Stapleton, Roger	3 years	March 8th	do

Table 9.1e: List of births on board the *James T Foord. (TNA ref CO 309/1 continued)*

Mother's Name	Date 1851	Sex of the Child
Callagan, Bridget	January 18th	Male
Herrig, Bridget	January 23rd	Female
Hogan, Mary	January 31st	Female
Bamfield Harriett	April 18th	Female

Table 9.1f: List of passengers in the ship *James T Foord. (TNA ref CO 309/1 continued)*
N.B. This nominal List will require to be filled in the case of Persons assisted by Public Funds.

No.	Name	Calling	Married Persons Ages		Number of Children 7 to 14		1 to 7		Under 1	
			Husb.	Wife	M	F	M	F	M	F
1	Anderson, John	Labourer	24							
2	" Margt			20						
3	Barker, John	Labourer	26							
4	" Cathn			25						
5	Bamfield, Danl	Labourer	28							
6	" Harriett			21						
7	" M.A. Foord									Inft
8	Blakely, John	Labourer	39							
9	" Mary			38						
10	" William	Labourer			14					
11	" Joseph	do			14					
12	" Mary							6		
13	Pain, John	Labourer	30							
14	" Margt			32						
15	" Philip						5			
16	Bowland, Thos	Labourer	34							
17	" Ann			30						
18	Clampitt, Jno	Labourer	31							
19	" Margt			29						

Wives and Families of Pensioner Guard

Table 9.2a: A list of free passengers on board the Convict Ship *Merchantman* at Swan River on 15 February 1863. *(TNA ref MT 32/5)*

Names	Where Embarked	When Embarked	Conduct on Board
Mrs Smith	Gravesend	10th Oct. 1862	Very good
Wm Smith	"	"	"
Henry Smith	"	"	"
Sarah Smith	"	"	"
Mrs Calighan	"	"	"
Mary Calighan	"	"	"
J. Francis Calighan	"	"	"
Mrs Johnstone	"	"	"
Martha Johnstone	"	"	"
Wm J. Johnstone	"	"	"
Mary Johnstone	Born at sea	7th Novr 1862	
Mrs Ahern	Gravesend	10th Oct. 1862	"
Mary Anne Ahern	"	"	"
Mrs Stuart	"	"	"
John Stuart	"	"	"
Martha J. Stuart	"	"	"
Victor Stuart	"	"	"
Mrs McKee	"	"	"
Mrs Galbraith	"	"	"
Sarah Galbraith	"	"	"
Mary Anne Galbraith	"	"	"
Catherine Galbraith	"	"	"
Wm Jas. Galbraith	"	"	"
Mrs Atkinson	"	"	Was guilty on several occasions of foul and abusive language & is a woman of most passionate & violent temper
Wm Atkinson	"	"	
Thos. Atkinson	"	"	
Mrs Begley	"	"	Good except on one occasion, when she was most violent & noisy from the effects of liquor
Mrs Byrnie	"	"	Very good
John Byrnie	"	"	"
Mrs Carsons	"	"	Very good
Margaret Carsons	"	"	"

Names	Where Embarked	When Embarked	Conduct on Board
Rebecca Carsons	"	"	"
Moriah Carsons	"	"	"
Mrs College	"	"	"
Mrs Connolly	"	"	"
Elizabeth Connolly	"	"	"
Mrs Fitzpatrick	"	"	"
Mrs Anderson	"	"	Good on the whole, but a virago
Robt Anderson	"	"	Very good
Elizabeth Anderson	"	"	"
Mrs Mayberry	"	"	"
Mrs McDonald	"	"	"
Elizabeth McDonald	"	"	"
Mary McDonald	"	"	"
Margaret McDonald	"	"	"
Mrs McDonough	"	"	"
Mary McDonough	"	"	"
Margaret McDonough	"	"	"
Patrick McDonough	"	"	"
Mrs Milton	"	"	"
Janet Milton	"	"	"
Mrs Meehan	"	"	"
Mary Meeham	"	"	"
Mrs Monigham	"	"	"
Mrs McNeice	"	"	"
Thos McNeice	"	"	"
Wm McNeice	"	"	"
John McNeice	"	"	"
Mrs Pindar	"	"	"
Mrs Roberts	"	"	Good on the whole, but was guilty of a false and scandalous report
Richard Roberts	"	"	Very good
Catherine Roberts	"	"	"
Mrs Simons	"	"	"
Mrs Slattery	"	"	"
Wm Slattery	"	"	"
Mary Slattery	"	"	"
John Slattery	"	"	"
Mrs Slavin	"	"	Good, except on one occasion
Mary Slavin	"	"	Very good
James Slavin	"	"	"

Names	Where Embarked	When Embarked	Conduct on Board
Mrs Sincroix	"	"	"
Mrs Sullivan	"	"	"
Alice Sullivan	"	"	"
Richard Sullivan	"	"	"
Mich[l] Sullivan	"	"	"
Mrs Toole	"	"	"
Joseph Toole	"	"	"
Mrs Tooley	"	"	"
Mrs Welsh	"	"	"
Johannah Welsh	"	"	"
J. Merchantman Welsh	Born at sea	15th Dec. 1862	
Mrs McCourt	Gravesend	10th Oct. 1862	A violent and most unmanageable woman. She was reported to me by her husband for keeping company with single men on board and refusing to come below to bed at 10 p.m.
Hugh McCourt			
Timothy McCourt			
Mrs Power			Very good
Bridget Power	Born at sea	14th February 1863	
Mrs Hamilton	Gravesend	10th Oct. 1862	Very good
John Hamilton	"	"	"
Robt Hamilton	"	"	"

'Emigrants at Dinner', travelling to Sydney, *The Illustrated London News*, 13 April 1844. (Library of New South Wales)

The first page of the register of the convict hulk *Antelope* at Bermuda. (The National Archives ref HO7/3 67707)

Table 9.2b: Wives and families of warders. *(TNA ref MT 32/5 continued)*

Names	Where Embarked	When Embarked	Conduct on Board
Mrs Paisley	Bermuda	2nd Decr 1862	Very good
Thos W. Paisley	"	"	"
Mrs Robinson	"	"	"
Mrs Scott	"	"	"
J.W. Scott	"	"	"
David Scott	"	"	"
Elizabeth Scott	"	"	"
John Scott	"	"	"
Margaret Scott	"	"	"

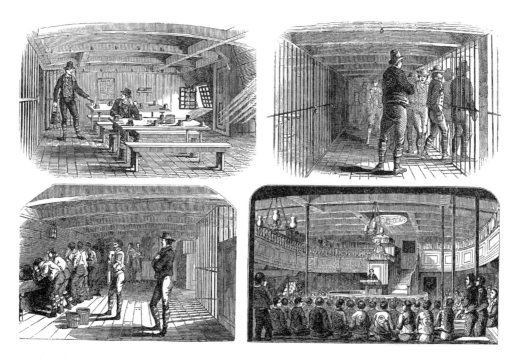

On board a prison hulk (*Clockwise from top left*): a convict ward; the gallery; the washing room; the chapel. (*The Illustrated London News*, 21 February 1845, p. 125)

Table 9.2c: A List of warders for convict duty embarked on board the *Merchantman* at Bermuda on 2 December 1862. (*TNA ref MT 32/5 continued*)

Names	Rank	Conduct on board
Thos Paisley	Princl Warder	Very good
James Scott	Warder	Very good
Wm Robinson	Asst Warder	Very good, with the exception of showing disrespect to me, in attempting to forward a letter clandestinely to the Comptroller General
John Mahon	"	
Daniel Harrington	"	
Dennis O'Brien	"	
Chas H. Horden	"	Insolence and disobedience of orders
John Harrison	"	Disobedience of orders

SHIPS' SURGEONS' JOURNALS

Including References to Convicts and Free Passengers on board Ship

To suffer the rigour and peril of the sea while battened below decks for much of the voyage to Australia was often a formula for sickness and disease among the convicts. In the early years of transportation, the diet did little to benefit their health, often consisting of nothing more than gruel, bread, biscuits and salt beef. Many convicts fell ill with scurvy or dysentery, and many never lived to see Australia.

A ship's surgeon was not only concerned with the health of the passengers and crew but also acted as Superintendent of Convicts. Ships' surgeons' journals therefore include much about the behaviour and treatment of convicts. Their journals are held at The National Archives (see Appendix 19). They vary considerably in content, depending on the character and conscientiousness of the surgeon concerned. In some cases a detailed account of the treatment of every sick person is given, whether convict, crewman, guard or emigrant. Some surgeons were so thorough that they also noted the daily weather conditions and even made notes of religious matters on board. There are sometimes lists giving the names of all free passengers, guards as well as convicts, presumably for the convenience of the surgeon concerned (see Chapter 10). Occasionally, there are lists recording the 'punishments awarded' to convicts who had misbehaved on board ship.

Although the medical treatment given must have been basic by today's standards, it is perhaps surprising that any treatment was given to convicts. In general these journals reveal a deep compassion for the sick and dying. Perhaps we should not be surprised at the appearance of such an emotion in ships' surgeons, who must have seen much suffering. The following abstracts give some idea of the wide range of material to be found in the pages of these journals.

Note: Many of the medicines prescribed for the patients were noted down by the surgeon in pharmaceutical symbols or in Latin. For ease of reading these have been omitted in the examples below and replaced with English translations.

TNA ref MT 32/5

Merchantman, 10 October 1862 to 24 February 1863: Gravesend to Swan River, Western Australia.

General Rules
To be observed by Convicts on board the *Merchantman*

The Surgeon Superintendent direct attention to the following Rules and Regulations which are issued for the general benefit and comforts:
1. You are strictly prohibited from holding intercourse with the crew or guard except in the discharge of duties directed by the Surgeon Superintendent.
2. The Surgeon Superintendent will select from the general body of men such persons as he may deem fit and will appoint them to assist in carrying on the discipline which he may think proper to direct. To these men, when appointed, the Surgeon Superintendent expects the same prompt obedience as he himself.
3. You are required promptly to obey all orders which may from time to time be issued by the Surgeon Superintendent or Religious Instructor, whether issued from them personally, or through those whom they may place in Authority.
4. You will be admitted on deck at such times and under such Regulations as the Surgeon Superintendent may direct.
5. The power or Prison deck to be kept clean and dry, no water to be spilt, the water kegs to be properly secured, and no person to wash anything below.
6. No prisoner is, on any account, to exchange or to sell his clothes or any article belonging to him.
7. No prisoner is allowed in any mode to gamble for his provisions or for any of his property.
8. No-one is allowed to keep any clothes or other description of property which he may find, but is to give it up immediately to the first Superintendent for the purpose of being restored to their proper owners.

9. It shall be the duty of the Superintendents to preserve order and good behaviour amongst the men in the department of the ship over which they may be stationed, and, in particular, to prevent all quarrelling, fighting, swearing, the using of obscene language, and the singing of immoral songs, and to see them all in their proper berths by 8.00 p.m. and after 8.30 p.m. no singing, speaking or noise of any kind will be permitted.

10. One man from each of two consecutive Messes to attend with the Principal Superintendent the weighing and issuing of provisions.

11. It is expected that every person will conduct himself in a quiet, orderly and respectful manner, as the Surgeon Superintendent begs distinctly to intimate that a record of the names of all defaulters will be kept for the purpose of being reported to the Governor on their arrival in the Colony, and that their future comfort very much depends on the report that, in discharge of his duty, he shall have to make concerning them.

William Smith, M.D.
Surgeon Superintendent
Jno. Williams
Religious Instructor

Daily Routine

Tuesdays and Fridays washing days

5.00 a.m.	The cooks are to come on deck and commence their duties. At daylight Prisoners are to roll up and stow their Hammocks and Bedding, the Hammocks to be lashed up and all stowed in their proper places. All hands to wash. At daylight the cleaners are to be mustered on deck and commence their duties washing closets, deck &c.
6.30 a.m.	The daily allowance of water to be used.
7.00 a.m.	The daily allowance of biscuits to be issued.
7.30 a.m.	The Surgeon Superintendent will visit the sick.
7.45 a.m.	The messmen are to be mustered on deck to receive the breakfast allowance, and all the other Prisoners will go below and sit down in a quiet, orderly manner, each in his own berth.
8.00 a.m.	Breakfast. Immediately after every meal the men whose day it is for messing are (on the upper deck) to wash the mess belonging to their respective messes & then return them to the messmen who are to remember that there is a place for everything and everything must be in its place. After breakfast all the Prisoners will be admitted on deck and the Prison is then to be cleaned throughout by the cleaners.
10.00 a.m.	Divine Service.
10.30 a.m.	School.
11.45 a.m.	The allowance of lime juice to be issued.
12.45 a.m.	The messmen are to be mustered on deck; all other Prisoners to go below in the same manner as at breakfast.
1.00 p.m.	Dinner. After dinner the Prisoners to be admitted on deck & her cleaners to sweep the whole of the prison deck.
1.30 p.m.	The daily allowance of wine to be issued.
2.05 p.m.	School. After school all the Prisoners on deck.
4.45 p.m.	Messmen to muster on deck; all Prisoners below.
5.00 p.m.	Supper. After supper the whole of the Prisoners to be admitted on

deck and the Prison to be again carefully swept by the cleaners. Before dusk the allowance of salt meat to be issued to the messes. At dusk the hammocks are to be taken below and the beds made.

8.00 p.m.   All in bed.

8.30 p.m.   No more talking or noise of any kind will be permitted in the Prison during the night.

William Smith, M.D.,
Surgeon Superintendent

Many surgeons kept notes on the conduct of the prisoners, the guards, and even of the wives and families of the guards. Reports of misconduct were passed on to the civil authority on arrival in Australia.

Table 9.2d: A list of Prisoners embarked at Bermuda on 2nd of Dec. 1862 on board the Convict Ship *Merchantman* for conveyance to Western Australia and reported to Captain Newland R.N. Comptroller General, as having committed themselves whilst on board together with a Statement showing the nature of the offences and the punishments awarded. *(TNA ref MT 32/5 continued)*

No.	Name	Class	By Whom Committed	Offences	Punishment
2134	Jas. Scott	1st	P.W. Paisley[7]	Insolence	Two hours confinement and 1 days wine and lime juice stopped
2131	Jas. Hodgkinson	"	Wm. Scott	do & threatening language	Wine stopped until further orders
1690	Wm. Snow	"	Prinl. W. Paisley[7]	Irregular conduct	do
2137	A. Marney	"	Wm. Scott	Disobedience of orders	7 days wine stopped
1985	Henry Marsden	"	Prinl. W. Paisley[7]	do	do
1616	Wm.L. Oliver	"	do	do	do
1469	Jno. Woolley	"	do	do	do
1759	Jas. Coleman	"	Asst W. Harrington[8]	Insolence	Wine stopped until further notice
2167	Austin Callaghan	"	Prinl. W.[7] Paisley	For concealing themselves having to avoid being looked at below	7 days wine stopped
2155	James Callaghan	"	do		
2021	Henry Taylor	"	do		
2121	Edward Kelly	"	do	Attempting to pass counterfeit coin	Wine stopped until further notice orders
2169	Alex McRae	"	do	Pulling down a notice posted by order of Surgeon Superintendent	7 days confinement

7. P.W./Prinl W: Principal Warder.

8. Asst W.: Assistant Warder.

Table 9.2e: Punishment List of the Pensioner Guard on board the Convict Ship *Merchantman* between the 10th of Oct. 1862 and the 17th of Febr. 1863. *(TNA ref MT 32/5 continued)*
Note: all those below held the rank of private.

Name	Offence	Date	By Whom Reported	Punishment Awarded
Jno. Hamilton	For insolence to Sgt. Major	Oct. 19	SM Smith[9]	7 days liquor stopped
Enock Pinder	Insolent language to Mr Caddy the Third Officer	Oct. 22	do	do
Patrick Meehan	Beating his wife	Nov. 5	do	do
Wm. Atkinson	Filthy and abusive conduct towards Mrs Toole	Nov. 6	do	do
Jno. Hamilton	Ringing the Ship's Bell when on duty	Nov. 9	do	2 days liquor stopped
Do	Threatening language towards Sergt. Major	Nov. 11	do	7 days liquor stopped
Jno. Roberts	Leaving his post when on sentry duty over the cook's galley and found lying down on the hatchway at 5 a.m.	Nov. 18	do	1 month liquor stopped
Chs. McCulloch	Being drunk when on sentry duty on the gangway at 3p.m. & making use of bad language on the Quarter Deck	Nov. 20	do	2 days in cell
Jas. Peddie	Being drunk		S. Callaghan[10]	7 days liquor stopped
Patk. Reynolds	Making a noise after hours	Nov. 19	S. Johnstone[10]	Admonished
Wm. McDonald	Being drunk and noisy	Nov. 28	Acting S.M.[11]	7 days liquor stopped

Wives and Families of Pensioner Guard

Table 9.2f: 'A List of the Free Passengers on Board the Convict Ship *Merchantman* at Swan River on the 15th February 1863.' *(TNA ref MT 32/5 continued)*

Names	Where Embarked	When Embarked	Conduct on Board
Mrs Smith	Gravesend	10/10/1862	Very Good
Wm. Smith	do	do	do
Henry Smith	do	do	do
Sarah Smith	do	do	do
Mrs Johnstone	do	do	do
Martha Johnstone	do	do	do
Wm. J. Johnstone	do	do	do

9. S M: Sergeant Major
10. S: Sergeant
11. Acting S.M.: Acting Sergeant Major

Names	Where Embarked	When Embarked	Conduct on Board
Mary Johnstone	Born at sea	7/11/1862	do
Mrs Ahern	Gravesend	10/10/1862	do
Mary Anne Ahern	do	do	do
Mrs Atkinson	do	do	Was guilty on several occasions of most foul abusive language and is a woman of most passionate & violent temper.
Wm. Atkinson	do	do	
Thos. Atkinson	do	do	
Mrs Begley	do	do	
Catherine Begley	do	do	Good except on one occasion when she was most violent & noisy from the effects of liquor
Mrs McCourt	do	do	A violent and most unmanageable woman. She was reported to me by her husband for keeping company with single men on board and refusing to come to bed at 10 p.m.
Hugh McCourt	do	do	
Timothy McCourt	do	do	
Mrs Power	do	do	
Bridget Power	Born at sea	14/2/1863	

TNA ref ADM 101/54/2

Medical Journal of the Convict Ship *Minerva*

5th September 1817 to the 8th May 1818, sailing to New South Wales, James Hunter, Surgeon.

December 23rd and 24th 1817
Michael McMahon, Edward O'Hara, Wm. McGuighan, Robt. Farrel, Edwd. Cunnningham, Saml. O'Hara, John Keon, Patk. Hickey, Patk. Fealy, Artr. O'Neal, Jno. Gallagher, James McGarrett, Owen Mullen, Patk. Graham.
Ulcers All these men had bad ulcers when they came on board, those which were in the sloughing state were treated until they became clean with powdered Peruvian bark and citric acid and afterwards adhesive straps applied. The rest were treated as their different appearances indicated. On leaving Port we experienced a heavy gale of wind which lasted some days, and the motion was so great as to make every Convict and many Sailors very sea sick this I think has a very good effect upon the ulcers as it had upon their general health. Many healed rapidly afterwards, 6 were well on the 14th Jany, 4 more 26th Jany, and the other 4 were well 20th February. There were a great number of others of minor consideration which were all within one month after our departure from Port.

December 25th 1817
On enquiring particularly into the state of health of the whole of the Convicts, found amongst other things that nearly the whole of them were constipated in their bowels many of them had not an alvine evacuation for more than a week. I prepared therefore

a large quantity of pills after the following form: calomel one drachm, powdered jalap [roots of a Mexican plant], two drachms gum Arabic, sufficient to make a pill, mixture makes 24 pills. Gave two or three of these pills as the urgency of the case required, followed up by a dose of the solution of sulphate of Magnesia. Many cases proved very obstinate, but as numerous were the complaints and of so little importance that I have not thought it worth while to particularise.

December 26th 1817
Jno. Cartwright, convict, aged 35
Typhus Mitior This man having a wife and many children had by anxiety and lowness of spirits reduced his strength very materially and the late fatigue and privation experienced in a tedious passage from Dublin has induced the low nervous fever which he has now upon him. Prescribed emetic draft to be taken at once. Some hours after the operation of which prescribed a solution of ammonium acetate 4 drachms, camphor mixture 1 drachm, mix to make a draught to be taken every four hours.
27th: Is rather better this morning but the bowels rather constipated prescribed a powder made from 10 grains calomel and 5 grains of jalap to be taken in the evening. The mixture has operated twice and the patient much relieved thereby. Powdered antimony 4 grains, pure nitre powder 5 grains, mix to make a powder, to be taken every 4 hours.
28th: The patient perspired a good deal during the later part of the day and this morning the pulse is nearly natural and scarcely any complaint of the head. Ordered Arrow Root and Wine.
29th: Great debility, but scarcely and other complaint. Supplied him amply with Wine and Arrow Root which is all his stomach can bear at present.
30th: No appearance of fever but great prostration of strength and his spirits at the lowest ebb.
Feb. 2nd: I find it will be necessary to keep this man in the Hospital as long as I have room to spare. His frame being too weak to remain in health amidst the crowded Convicts in the Prison, allow him therefore half a pint of Wine, tea, Arrow Root, &c., as he can fancy them.
Feb. 25th: Is in as good health as perhaps he will ever be but can eat no meat, his support depending wholly upon Wine, Arrow Root, Tea, &c..
March 5th: Remains free from disease still, but required to be kept separate, and allowed Wine, Tea, Rice, &c.
April 26th: As before
Feb. 2nd 1819: Well

Robert Marang, Convict
April 27th. 1818 **Debility** This man is a black, and of a weak, debilitated habit, he is of dull and sulky disposition, speaks to no one nor does he make any complaint. I find that he is extremely weak, and in a rapidly declining state of health. I shall put him into the Hospital rather against his consent, and give him Arrow Root, Wine, &c.
May 2nd: Now that we are at anchor in Sydney Cove I shall send him to the Hospital although he is some what better for the benefit of milk diet, &c.

TNA ref ADM 101/63/5

Medical Journal of the Convict Ship *Recovery*

Peter Cunningham, Surgeon. 7th July and the 30th December 1819 during which time the said ship has been employed in transporting Convicts from England to New South Wales.

George Breadman, Convict, aged 24
July 22nd 1819, River Thames
About five weeks previous to joining this ship was in consequence of exposure to wet and cold, attacked with cough attended with pain of the breast, expectoration of thick matter and diarrhoea. He was treated three weeks at the *Justitia* Hulk and two weeks at the Hospital Ship before joining the *Recovery,* being discharged from the latter only the day previous, much emaciated and debilitated with a hectic look, but denied having any complaint. I objected to receiving him but was told in consequence of his sentence being for life he could not well be exchanged. On application he laboured under cough attended with expectoration and dysenteric symptoms, to all of which he continued more or less subject until his discharge to Sydney Hospital. In about a fortnight after application he was obliged to keep his bed thro' the day, to which, excepting occasionally in fine weather, he was confined until leaving the Ship. Various modes of treatment were had recourse to but without being attended by any very permanent beneficial effect. The dysenteric and pectoral symptoms usually alternating with each other, but the dysenteric generally being the most urgent and requiring the most attention, the pectoral being alleviated by the occurrence of the dysenteric and vice versa. He had frequently griping discomfort but seldom pain on pressing the abdomen. Stools of various appearances, slimy and bloody indigested, dark and foetid, or clay coloured, the last being the most usual. The expectoration consisted principally of thick mucus blinded with purulent flakes and blood. Appetite always tolerable and frequently voracious. Pulse usually moderate. Skin hot and dry thro' the day with occasional hectic sweats in the afternoon and night. Thirst always more or less urgent. Cupping, blistering and fomenting the breast, pectoral mixtures and opiates for the cough. Hot fomentations to the abdomen. Opiate, enemas. Purgatives and opiates alterative or combined. Pill of mercury with lead and opium stimulant and mercurial frictions over the right side and abdomen for the dysenteric were the remedies chiefly employed. His strength supported throughout by supplies from the cabin table besides the articles of comfort allowed the sick, wine, porter, &c., but not withstanding continued gradually sinking until his removal to Sydney Hospital.

Francis Rhodes, Convict, August 3rd 1819, Gravesend
About nine weeks previous says that he caught a severe cold on his way from jail to the Hulk, since then he has never been well: it was aggravated in the Hulk by getting wet and since then he has been worse, never being free from headache, pains of the back and loins, shoulders and arms but chiefly the latter parts. Having led a very debauched life drinking usually from 13 to 14 pints of gin and beer daily, it is more than probable these complaints originate chiefly from want of his usual stimulus. Complains at present of sickness and frequent vomiting, thirst, pains and numbness in his limbs, but particularly in the superior extremities with bad taste in his mouth and thickly furred tongue in the morning, with obstinately constipation. Pulse natural, skin cool and soft, dejection vitiated.

Treatment: Proved a very obstinate perplexing case. From the large quantity of purgative medicine required to operate upon him and the difficulty with which they were retained, it was found necessary to trust to injections of cold salt water thrown up with considerable force to evacuate the contents of the Alimentary Canal. Warm bath, stimulant frictions and frictions with Mercurial Ointment, Mercurial Blisters, Sinapismus, bleeding from the arm, and Cupping were at different times had recourse to and for some time prescribed in, but he appeared to derive most benefit from Cupping of the neck and temples, blisters to the head and Infus Quassia [appetite stimulant] given in doses throughout the day. Porter and wine with every nourishment the Medical supplies or Cabin table afforded were liberally supplied him when he seemed to require it, but not withstanding these he continued to get worse, becoming daily weaker, and was reduced to a puppet on the ship's arrival at the Island of St. Paul's but having caught there a large quantity of fish, he eat of them with extraordinary avidity, and even after that would eat of almost nothing else, and having got a quantity salted for him I was able to indulge him in this respect until the arrival of the ship in Sydney Cove. From the time of his being put upon fish diet he mended rapidly and by the period of arrival at Port Jackson he had regained his former flesh and strength.

December 17th Discharged cured.

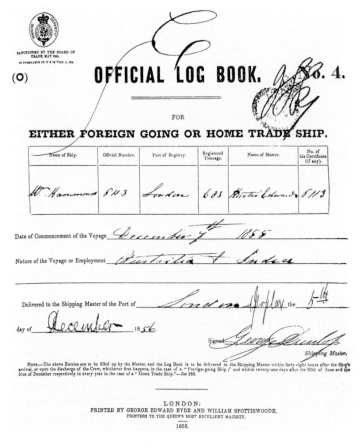

Cover page of the log book of the merchant ship *William Hammond*, which sailed to Western Australia in 1856. (The National Archives ref BT98/4614)

TNA ref ADM 101/13/1

Medical Journal of the *Borodino* Convict Ship

4th December 1827 to the 14th July 1828, on a voyage to New South Wales, George Thomson, Surgeon Superintendent.

Table 9.3: Sick List *Borodino* Convict Ship. *(TNA ref ADM 101/13/1)*

Entry	Name	Age	Decease	Discharge
1828				1828
Jan 28	Thos. Timmon	21	Phlogosis	12 Feb
Feb 1	William Mercer	40	Catarrhus	10 Feb
"	Maurice Hayes	33	"	9 Feb
Feb 4	Richard McHeugh	27	Constipatio	28 Feb
"	John Falvey	21	"	7 Feb
"	Mich. Spiller	33	Febris Inter	21 May
"	Mich. Neville	22	Ulcus	14 April
Feb 6	William Reagan	21	Constipatio	9 Feb
Feb 7	James Barry	52	Rheumatismus	24 July
"	Patrick Savage	22	Constipatio	10 Feb
Feb 9	Mich. Coughan	22	Ulcus	29 May
Feb 10	James Byrne	20	Constipatio	10 March
"	Robert Mearce	19	Ulcus	16 Feb
"	John White	18	"	"
Feb 11	James Fitzgerald	19	Diarrhoea	23 Feb
"	Mic. Gleeson	17	"	28 Feb
Feb 15	Tim. Costigan	19	"	23 March
"	William Ford	32	Constipatio	28 Feb
"	Maurice Kellegher	40	Cephalagia	22 Feb
Feb 18	Jno. Coyne	44	"	29 Feb
"	Edward Masterson	69	Diarrheoa	29 Feb

Note: All the men in the above were convicts.

George Thomson, the surgeon superintendent, like other convict-ship surgeons, treated anyone who required his services, as the following extract from his journal shows:

On the 17th March attended the wife of Sergeant McNamara during her confinement of a living male child. On the 19th March at midnight was called to attend George Wallace, seaman, who ruptured himself while working in the hold during the day. After bleeding to syncope in the recumbent position the rupture was reduced and a truss supplied him for which the Master gave a receipt. On the 27th was called to attend the child of Hugh Coffee, private, 57th Reg. which I found in *articulo mortis* in a convulsion fit caused by teething during which it expired. In consequence of the loss of the Iron Tiller on the 21st Feb. during a severe gale of wind obliged us to put into Lisbon, the voyage was protracted to an unusual length, the Guard having been on board 232 days and the Convicts 200, which caused a considerable expenditure of Medicines and Medical Comforts and require much attention to preserve their Health. The Irish Convicts in my opinion do not bear the voyage as well as Englishmen but the former are more easily managed. My former voyage with English Convicts was 135 days without touching, and no case of Scurvy or any other disease except trifling complaints occurred. On the last voyage although John Ryan was the only one confined with Scurvy yet towards the end of the voyage a number had spongy gums and loose muscle to whom I issued Medical comforts. Strict attentions was paid to see the Convicts drink their Sherbet at the Tub (as many would have exchanged it) and I am satisfied that it is not now an antidote for Scurvy. I attribute my not losing any of the Convicts on two voyages to keeping them on deck whenever the weather would permit between sunrise and sunset, to keeping the Prison dry and well ventilated, to prohibiting the Convicts from using the water closets during the day (which are generally badly fitted), to frequent fumigation, great attention to cleanliness and obliging them to take as much exercise as their situation would admit.

George Thomson

TNA ref ADM 101/60/1

Medical Journal of the *Platina*

12th March to the 19th November 1837 transporting female convicts from London to Van Diemen's Land, George Ellesy Forman, Surgeon.

Jane Duffy, aged 18, April 28th 1837
Oesophagitis produced by swallowing a pin. Swallowed a pin by accident last night, which lodged in the gullet immediately behind the thyroid cartilage, producing pain and some spasm. I endeavoured to extract it but could only succeed in moving it to the stomach, and then administered a dose of castor oil. She now complains of such pain in swallowing, which extends from the point formerly occupied by the pin, downwards into the stomach, in which viscus there is also tenderness on swallowing, and pain on taking nourishment of any kind. She is hoarse and has some cough and fever. Bowels open by physic. Take a warm mixture of salt with magnesia three hourly.
29th: Much the same.
30th: Less
May 1st: Free disengagement of mucus from oesophagus, and improvement in all respects. From this period she continued to do well, there was no recurrence of inflammatory symptoms, and in a few days she commenced the use of wine and tonics, under which treatment she became completely well.
May 27th: Discharged well.

M.A. Brady, aged 21. April 28th 1837
Gonorrhoea accompanied by acute rheumatic affection. Complains of the usual symptoms of Gonorrhoea which she says have existed for several weeks, but now give her more trouble than they did. Barley water with Carbonate of Soda. Frequent ablution of the genitals and occasional aperients. Under this treatment the scalding was relieved and the discharge diminished for some days when improved from day to day, but the state of the genitals remained the same, fluctuating much under the use of a variety of local applications, and eventually healing completely, but not until after repeated disappointment. The uterine functions were restored to their healthy state

and when she was discharged she had regained her health and embonpoint
Discharged well October 7th 1837

Richard Fisher, aged 19 days. Free Child. At sea July 4th 1837
Fatal Convulsions in an Infant. This child was born on board on the 15th June and for a few days appeared to be a healthy strong babe. The mother is a robust woman and was doing well with milk in abundance. The first appearance of disease was an apthus affection of the mouth, and diarrhoea. These were relieved by chalk mixture and caraminatives with linctus of nitre and sugar, but he lost flesh rapidly and was this day seized with convulsions. The warm bath was used twice daily and a bottle of hot water was applied occasionally to the feet and back but these were attended only by temporary relief, for the convulsive attacks became at length incessant and in the course of two days destroyed him.
Died July 6th 1837

TNA ref ADM 101/77/10

Medical Journal of the Emigrant Ship *Lady Nugent*

G. Roberts, Superintendent Surgeon, carrying emigrants to New South Wales. 10th July to 30th November 1838.

James Card, aged 32, Emigrant. August 7th at Sea.
Ambustio. While standing by the coppers a sauce pan containing boiling water was turned over upon his left leg scalding it anteriorly from knee to ankle joint. On removing the stocking the whole length of the limb was completely robbed of its cuticle. Cloths wet with vinegar were kept constantly applied over the injured part until a cessation of pain when it was dressed with the resin ointment softened with turpentine oil.
8th Limb inflamed and much swollen with considerable pain. Continued resin ointment.
9th Continues nearly in the same state, bowels have been freely purged.
10th The timefaction and inflammation of the limb reduced.
11th The surface of the sore looks well with secretion of healthy pus. Stopped resin ointment, applied simple ointment.
14th Sore healing kindly, continued as before.
18th Sore looks healthy and is nearly healed up, continued as before.
23rd Sore entirely healed up. Discharged.

TNA ref ADM 101/59/1

Medical and Surgical Journal of Her Majesty's Hired Convict Ship *Pestonjee Bononjee*

1st September 1845 to 12th January 1846, during which time the said Convict Ship has been employed in making a passage to Van Diemen's Land.

Peter Ohoo, aged 18, prisoner. September 12th English Channel.
Pericarditis. Was admitted into hospital on the 10th instant for an attack of diarrhoea brought on through eating of indigestible matter. A dose of castor oil was prescribed.

After clearing out his bowels he was ordered to have ten grains of powdered *ipecacuanha* [root of a South American shrub]. On the 11th in consequence on a continuance of the diarrhoea the compound chalk mixture was prescribed which completely checked the purging. This morning complains of dull pain with a sense of oppressions and weight in the Cardiac region with palpitation and dyspnoea [difficulty in breathing]. There is great anxiety depicted in his countenance, his pulse is 120, small and irregular at times almost imperceptible. Carried out venesection bleeding at once. Eight ounces [of blood] taken. Prescribed tincture of colchicum [alcoholic solution with meadow saffron] one drachm, wine of antimony potassium tartrate two drachms, water two ounces. Make a mixture. Received one ounce of this mixture every four hours.

September 13th The venesection of yesterday morning relieved the sence of oppression complained of in Cardiac region dyspucea became also more moderate. His improved condition he remained in until noon when he complained greatly of Cardiac pain. He stated that the pain was of a more acute from that it had been in the morning and that he experienced more difficulty in breathing. His pulse was 120 full and irregular. Venesection was immediately performed and the Antinomial mixture was ordered to be treated, this treatment was shortly followed by mitigation of all the acute symptoms and he continued easy until about midnight when he again experienced a return of the former acute symptoms. The lancet [for blood letting] was again had recourse to and ½ grain of the mercurous chloride with one of strained opium was prescribed after which he became more composed. This morning still complains of pain in the region of the heart but at the same time states that his most troublesome symptoms is the difficulty of breathing. His pulse is 100 small but regular. Applied crushed melon pumpkin seeds with iron to the left side. Received 6 grains mercurous chloride and 2 grains opium thrice daily.

September 14th Has passed a tranquil night, this morning complains of occasional dyspnoea with slight thoracic oppressions, his pulse is a 100 small and regular. Continued mercurous chloride and opium as before.

September 15th Has been gradually convalescing till this evening when suddenly he complained of a great Cardiac oppression with extreme difficulty in breathing. His pulse became very small and irregular intermitting very fourth stroke. Applied cantharides plaster to left side. Continued mercurous chloride and opium as before.

September 16th Has passed a very bad night at times incoherent, is rapidly sinking. Continued mercurous chloride and opium as before.

September 17th Became insensible last evening, he lingered on till four o'clock this morning when death closed the scene.

September 17th DIED.

Prudence Lilly, ages 8 months, child of Sergt. Lilly, 65th Regt. October 1st
[Ship's Position] Lat. 33, 47 N., Long 18, 39 W.
Since the cutting of her first tooth which took place about three months ago, her mother states that she has almost daily suffered from what she terms colic pain, and that her nights rest is always broken and irregular attended with more or less fever. That her bowels are irregular, she is alternately constipated and purged. When in the latter state her alvine evacuations are composed of a chalky looking matter without the slightest biliary tinge. Her abdomen is hard and prominent whilst the rest of her body is greatly emaciated. Her appetite is deficient, with a highly furred tongue. Prescribed mercury with chalk 5 grains, powdered rhubarb root 3 grains, mixed to

make a powder, gave at bedtime. Repeat on alternative days. Massaged the abdomen at bedtime with soap liniment.

October 15th Since last report her bowels have become more regular and her stools are of a more natural appearance but she continues to labour under hectic symptoms and is every day becoming more and more emaciated.

October 27th Died. Was attacked yesterday with severe purging for which repeated small doses of the compound powder of *Ipecacuanha* was prescribed but without any apparent benefit. Subsequently anodynes were tried both in the form of draughts and enemas but without palliating the symptoms. The diarrhoea continuing to run its fatal course until two a.m. this morning when death terminated her suffering.

MEDICAL HOSPITAL MUSTERS

Rio de Janeiro

Table 9.4: An account of the names and numbers of such sick and wounded seamen and marines as have been received into and victualled at the Naval Hospital at Rio de Janeiro between 1st day of July and 30th day of September 1810 according to the account thereof kept by Dr Geo. Roddam, surgeon and agent. This includes: Convicts bound to New South Wales from the *Indian* Transport per order of the Commander in Chief. *(TNA ref ADM 102/721)*

Men's Names	William Goodrich	Henry Meyet	William Feill
Quality	Convict	Convict	Convict
When Recv'd	Sept. 17	Sept. 17	Sept. 17
Quality of the Decease or Hurt	Ulcer	Hypatitis	Dysentry
D, DD or R	D	D	D
Time When	Sept. 25	Sept. 25	Sept. 25
What Ship returned to or How disposed of	*Indian* Transport	*Indian* Transport	*Indian* Transport
No. of Days Victualled in the Quarter	9	9	9

The following list gives the stores carried to relieve the sufferings of emigrants and convicts.

Table 9.5: Transport Office, 11th July 1816. A list of stores, shipped on board the *Lord Melville* Convict Ship, T. Wetherall, Master, for the use of 100 female Convicts, and Passengers, during their voyage to New South Wales; and of clothing for the use of the Convicts upon their arrival at the Colony. *(CO 201/82)*

Articles of Comfort for Use during the Voyage

Mustard	125 lbs	Souchong Tea	340 lbs
Soap	375 lbs	Portable Soup	120 lbs
Combs	18 large; 18 small	Lemon Juice	81 gallons
Needles	1000 no.	White Thread	10 lbs
Scissors	10 pairs	Coloured Thread	10 lbs
Moist Sugar	1625 lbs		

Articles in Case of Sickness

Tea	25 lbs	Ginger	10 ozs
Sugar	125 lbs	Allspice	5 lbs
Chocolate	7½ lbs	Black Pepper	2 lbs 8 ozs
Sago	15 lbs	Red Port Wine	90 Bottles
Scotch Barley	250 lbs		

Fumigating Articles

Tar	1 barrel	Extra Wicks	2 boxes
Brimstone Crude	30 lbs	Oil	4 gallons
Vinegar	30 gallons	Oil of Tar	10 gallons
Fumigating Lamps	2 no.		

Hospital Furniture

Calico Bedgowns	6 no.	Tin saucepans	6 no.
Calico Petticoats	6 no.	Tea Kettles	2 no.
Cotton Hose	12 pairs	Tea Kettles to serve as Tea-pots	17 no.
Linen Pocket-handkerchiefs	12 no.	Knives and Forks	12 of each
Nightcaps	12 no.	Bathing Tub	1 no.
Towels	12 no.	Water Purifier	1 no.
Cotton Sheets	10 pairs	Child-bed Linen	10 sets
Pillow Cases	10 pairs	Charcoal	24 bushels
Pewter Bed-pan	1 no.	Water Pails	4 no.
Pewter Urinal	1 no.	Airing Stove	1 no.
Closestool-pan and Chair	1 of each	Japanned Mugs	100 no.
Spitting-pot	1 no.		

Clothing for the use of the Convicts upon their Arrival

Brown Serge Jackets	100 no.	Shoes	100 pairs
Brown Serge Petticoats	100 no.	Neck-handkerchiefs	100 no.
Linen Shifts	200 no.	Beds complete	140 no.
Linen Caps	100 no.	Cotts	2 no.
Stockings	100 pairs		

CHAPTER 10

GUARDS ON CONVICT TRANSPORTATION SHIPS, THE NEW SOUTH WALES CORPS AND OTHER ARMY REGIMENTS IN NEW SOUTH WALES

(See Appendix 17)

The guards on convict transportation ships were often soldiers who had retired from the regular army and were receiving an army pension. Many of these men settled in Australia. Their records are to be found in the Army Pension Returns at The National Archives in document class WO 22. They date from 1842 to 1883.

The New South Wales Corps was set up to guard the convicts in Australia. Their muster rolls are to be found in TNA document class WO 12. The first men recruited to the New South Wales Corps arrived on the Second Fleet in 1790. The enlistment papers of soldiers who served in other regiments in New South Wales are to be found in TNA document class WO 97.

Pensioner guards (and free passengers) can also be found listed in the surgeon superintendents' journals kept by the Admiralty Department of the Ministry of Transport in TNA document class MT 32. They only cover the dates 1858 to 1867. The following are examples from these records.

Table 10.1: A list of Pensioners embarked as a Convict Guard on board the Convict Ship *Merchantman* at Gravesend on the 10th October 1862. *(TNA ref MT 32/5)*
Note: The *Merchantman* sailed to Western Australia in 1863 with 191 male convicts on board. All the convicts survived the voyage.

Names	Rank	Conduct on Board
Thos Smith	Sergeant Major	Very good
John Callaghan	Sergeant	Good
William Johnstone	"	Very good
William Galbraith	Corporal	"
John Ahern	"	"
John McKay	"	"

Names	Rank	Conduct on Board
Daniel Stewart	"	"
Thos Fitzpatrick	Private	"
James College	"	Good, except report as per List[1]
James Connolly	"	Very good
Enoch Pendar	"	Good, except report as per List
William Rawson	"	Very good
Joseph Grice	"	Very good & did duty as Hospital Serg[t]
John Simms	"	Good, except report as per List
Thos Byrne	"	Very good except report as per List
Thos McDonough	"	do
Wm Atkinson	"	Bad, see reports as per List
Patrick Toole	"	Very good
John Ward	"	do
James Pedie	"	Indifferent, see report
Richards Roberts	"	Very good
Stephen Melton	"	do
Philip St Croix	"	[blank]
Charles McCullock	"	Indifferent, see report as per List
William Hall	"	Very good
Patrick Meehan	"	Indifferent, see report as per List
William McDonald	"	Very good, except report as per List
Donald McAllister	"	do
William Purvis	"	Very good
William Dunn	"	Good, except reports as per List
Patrick Monaghan	"	Very good
John Roberts	"	Good, except report as per List
Thomas Mayberry	"	Has been on the Sick List nearly all the voyage – a malingerer
Geo. Knochton	"	Very good, except report as per List
John Finnessey	"	Very good
Patrick Bayley	"	Good, except report as per List
John Porrer	"	Very good, except report as per List
Michael Toohey	"	Indifferent, see reports as per List
Patrick Sullivan	"	Very good
James Slavin	"	Indifferent, see reports as per List
John Hamilton	"	Bad, see reports as per List
Michael Welsh	"	Very good
James Carsons	"	do except report as per List
John Slattery	"	Very good, except reports as per List
William Dunlop	"	do except report as per List
Francis Anderson	"	do

Names	Rank	Conduct on Board
John McNeice	"	Very good
Patrick Reynolds	"	do except report as per List
James McCourt	"	do
Richard Williams	"	Very good

1. The 'List' referred to in the above tabulation is presumably the Punishment List, which follows.

Table 10.2: Punishment List of the Prisoner Guard on board the Convict Ship *Merchantman*, between the 10th of October 1862 and the 17th of February 1863. *(TNA ref WO 22/226)*

Name	Quality	Offence	Date of Offence	By Whom Reported	Punishment Awarded
Jno Hamilton	Pte	For insolence to Serg^t Major	19th Oct. 1962	Serg^t Major Smith	7 days liquor stopped
Enock Pinder		Insolent language to Mr Caddy the 3rd Officer	22nd Oct. 1962		
Patrick Meehan		Beating his wife	5th Nov. 1962		
Wm Atkinson		Filthy and abusive conduct towards Mrs Toole	6th Nov. 1962		
Jno Hamilton		Ringing the Ship's bell when on duty	9th Nov. 1962		2 days liquor stopped
		Threatening language towards Sergt Major	11th Nov. 1962		7 days liquor stopped
Jno Roberts		Leaving his post when on sentry over the cook's galley & found lying down on the hatchway at 5 a.m.	18th Nov. 1962		1 month liquor stopped
Chas. McCulloch		Being drunk when on sentry on the gangway at 3 p.m. & making use of bad language on the quarter deck	20th Nov. 1962		2 days in cell
Jas. Peddie		Being drunk		Serg^t Callighan	7 days liquor stop^d
Pat^k Reynolds		Making a noise after hours	19th Nov. 1962	Serg^t John Stone	Admonished
W^m McDonald		Being drunk and noisey	28th Nov. 1962	Act^g Serg^t Major Callighan	7 days liquor stopped
Pat^k Begley		Being drunk & making use of improper language shilst a prisoner with p^{te} Carsons			2 days in cell and 1 month's liquor stop^d

Table 10.3: 'Pay List of Enrolled Pensioners in the Convict Ship *Clyde* from 27th January 1863 to 24th June 1863.' *(TNA ref WO 22/226)*
Note: The *Clyde* sailed to Western Australia in 1863 with 320 male convicts.

Regt from which Pensioned	Rate of Pension	Rank and Name	Period		No. of Days	Rate of Pay £ s d	Amount £ s d
			From	To			
Sergeant Major Acting							
96th Foot	1/7	Thomas Bryan	30 Jan	24 Feb	25	1/10	2 5 10
			25 Feb	24 June	120		11 0 0
Sergeants							
Canadian Rifles	1/6	Michael M. Cardle	30 Jan	24 Feb	26	1/10	2 7 8
			25 Feb	24 June	120		11 0 0
97th Foot	1/3	James Crowe	28 Jan	24 Feb	28		2 11 4
			25 Feb	24 June	120		11 0 0
Corporals							
8th Foot	1/5½	James Rolston	30 Jan	24 Feb	26	1/6	1 19 0
			25 Feb	24 June	120		9 0 0
1st Rifle Brigade	1/0	Matthew Rice	29 Jan	24 Feb	27	1/6	2 0 6
			25 Feb	24 June	120		9 0 0
E.I.Co.	1/0	John Arbuckle	29 Jan	24 Feb	27		2 0 6
			25 Feb	24 June	120		9 0 0
20th Foot	1/1½	William Bewsher	17 Feb	24 Feb	8		12 0
Privates							
1 Batt Art.	10d	Archibald Muirhead	30 Jan	24 Feb	26		1 12 6
			25 Feb	24 June	120		7 10 0
D.Bd Artillery	1/0	Robert Ireland	28 Jan	24 Feb	28		1 15 0
			25 Feb	24 June	120		7 10 0
D.Bd do	1/0	John Bennett	31 Jan	24 Feb	25		1 11 3
			25 Feb	24 June	120		7 10 0
16th Drags	8d	James Thompson (died in Military Hospital Gravesend 1863)	13 Jan 15 Feb	15 Feb	17		1 1 3
1st Foot	8d	James Keenan	30 Jan	24 Feb	26		1 12 6
			25 Feb	24 June	120		7 10 0
4th Foot	9d	Edward Kelly	31 Jan	24 Feb	25		1 11 3
			25 Feb	24 June	120		7 10 0
4th Foot	8d	William Warner	31 Jan	24 Feb	25		1 11 3
			25 Feb	24 June	120		7 10 0
9th Foot	9d	Timothy Connealy	30 Jan	24 Feb	26		1 12 6
			25 Feb	24 Jan	120		7 10 0
1/10th Foot	10d	Michael Walsh	31 Jan	24 Feb	25		1 11 3
			25 Feb	24 June	120		7 10 0

Regt from which Pensioned	Rate of Pension	Rank and Name	Period		No. of Days	Rate of Pay £ s d	Amount £ s d
			From	To			
10th Foot	1/0	Patrick McCann	2 Feb	24 Feb	23		1 8 9
			25 Feb	24 June	120		7 10 0
10th Foot	1/0	Patrick Hayes	30 Jan	24 Feb	26		1 12 6
			25 Feb	24 June	120		7 10 0
14th Foot	10d	Thomas Hogan	28 Jan	24 Feb	28		1 15 0
			25 Feb	24 June	120		7 10 0
20th Foot	9d	Patrick Healy	29 Jan	24 Feb	27		1 13 9
			25 Feb	24 June	120		7 10 0

When an army pensioner took up a position as a guard on a convict ship his change of address was recorded. The following is an example of a Certificate of Change of Residence.

TNA ref WO 22/226

Convict Ship *Norwood*

Pay List for the Period ending 31st July 1862

Certificate of Change of Residence
Private Thomas Grady
Out-Pensioner from the 4th Regiment of Foot
Private Thomas Grady an Out-Pensioner of the Royal Hospital at Chelsea from the 4th Regiment of Foot at 8d per diem, having applied to me stating that he is desirous of removing from this District, and to receive the next payment of his pension at Australia in consequence of Proceeding as Convict Guard. This is to certify that I have no doubt of his identity as the individual on the Out-pension List under the above name, and that I have every reason to believe the truth of his statement as to the grounds on which he wishes to remove to Australia. A description of his person, and the particulars of his Service are given in the margin [see below]. He has been paid by me up to the 31st day July 1862.
(signed) Robt McNair, Capt.
                Dated at Tilbury Fort the 20th day of February 1862
                        Signature of Pensioner X
                                Signature of another Pensioner to whom he is known as the
                                        Individual borne on the Pension List
                                                (signed) James Wood. Staff Serg. Major; 32nd Regiment

The following is the detail given in the margin of the original document:

Date of Admission to Out-Pension	*28th Oct 1856*
Present Age	*26*
Present Height	*5/5¼*
Color of Hair	*Dark Brown*
Color of Eyes	*Blue*
Color of Complexion	*Fresh*
Face	*Oval*

Figure	*Proportionate*
General Appearance	*Healthy*
Character on Discharge	*Very Good*
Wounds or Distinguishing Marks	*Wound left arm*
Present Trade or Occupation	*Labourer*
Married	*Catherine Devaney, Liverpool, 1856*
Number of Children	*above 14 -* *under 14 1*
Period of Service in Corps from which discharged	*2 8/12*
Service in any other Corps	*99th Foot 11/12*
Service abroad and at what Station	*East 1 year*
Cause of Discharge	*Wound left arm*
Date of Expiration of Pension if temporary	*Permanent*
Whether subject to Stoppages from Pension	*Nil*
Present Character and Habits	*Good*
Whether in possession of Medals or other Distinctions	*Crimea Distinguished & Turkish Medals & Victoria Cross*
Whether Enrolled, or Registered for Enrolment on a vacancy occurring, or for the Reserve, or as Unfit	*Was Enrolled*
Amount of Enrolment Money to be recovered, if not Re-enrolled for the remainder of the year	*Nil*

Born at Claddagh Galway, Parents Dead

Note: The convict ship *Norwood* sailed from Portland to Western Australia in 1862 carrying 290 male convicts.

TNA ref WO 12/11028

New South Wales Corps

Muster Roll of His Majesty's New South Wales Corps of Foot, commanded by Major Francis Grose, for 183 days from 25 December 1794 to 15 June 1795, both days inclusive.

Commissioned and Warrant Officers

Major	Francis Grose
Captains	Nicholas Nepean
	William Patterson
	Joseph Foveaux
	George Johnston
Lieutenants	John McArthur
	John Townson
	Edward Abbott
	William Beckwith
	John Thomas Prentice
	Thomas Rowley
	William Cummings
Ensigns	John Clepham

	John Piper
	Neil McKellar
	James Hunt Lucas
	Thomas Davis
	Anthony Kemp
	William Patillo
Chaplain	James Bain
Adjutant	Thomas Rowley
Q. Master	Thomas Laycock
Surgeon	John Harris
Mate	Edward Laing
Sergeants	James Brackenrig
	Richard Clench
	William Day
	Richard Evans
	William Field
	Richard Hudson
	John Haddick
	Obadiah Ikin
	Charles Jenkins
	William Janneson
	David Jones
	James McMullon
	John Palmer
	John Pollard
	James Plowman
	Joseph Radford
	Samuel Reddish
	John Stroud
	William Sherwin
	Thomas Whittle
	Sergeant William Jones died 17 Jany
	John Vernice[?] discharged 26 Feby
	John West died 2 Apl
	Robert Turner appointed 18 Jany
	Edward Haven appointed 27 Feby
	Robert Higgins appointed 3 Apl
Corporals	Jonas Bradley
	Peter Farrell
	William Goodall
	Richard Guise
	John Gardiner
	Thomas Jones
	Thomas Laurence
	Thomas Lucas
	John Melone
	William McLeod
	Samuel Porter
	Henry Parsons
	John Price

John Smith
William Tydeman
William Ternan
John Wexstead
William Webster
Robert Turner to Sergeant 17 Jany
Edward Haven to Sergeant 26 Feby
Robert Higgins to Sergeant 2 Apl
John Gowen appointed 18 Jany
William Parker appointed 27 Feb
John Hemming appointed 3 Apl
—

Drummers   Joseph Abbott
Thomas Bates
Thomas Brown
Thomas Brown 2d
Thomas Douglas
John Darke
Thomas Haddick
John Hammond
Obadiah Ikin
William Johnston
William Larking
Thomas Landsley
John Roberts
John Williams

TNA ref WO 97/1067

Army Enlistment Papers

(These are officially referred to as Attestation Papers.) The following is an example.

100th Regt of Foot
Whereof Lieut. Genl Sir Albert Gledstanes, Kt is Colonel
These are to Certify
That Richard Taylor born in the Parish of Hunmanbie in the County of York was enlisted for the aforesaid Regiment at Sydney, N.S.Wales on the 11th day of August 1800 at the age of thirty for unlimited service.
That he hath served in the Army for the space of seventeen years and 281 days after the age of eighteen, according to the subjoined.

Statement of Service

In What Corp	Period of Service		Private		Total Service	
	From	To	Yrs	Days	Yrs	Days
100th Regt	1800 11 Aug	1818 18 May	17	281	17	281

That in consequence of The Regiment being disbanded

HE IS HEREBY DISCHARGED

THAT he is not, to my knowledge, incapacitated by the Sentence of a General Court Martial, from receiving a Pension.

THAT his General Conduct as a Soldier has been very good.

THAT he has received all just Demands of Pay, Clothing, &c. from his Entry into the Service to the date of this discharge, as appears by his Receipt underneath.

I Richard Taylor do hereby acknowledge that I have received all my Clothing, Pay, Arrears of Pay and all just demands whatsoever, from the time of my entry into the Service to the date of discharge.

Witnessed by *T. Thomas, Ensn 100th Regt*   Signature of the Soldier

R. Taylor X his mark

To prevent any improper use being made of this discharge, by its falling into other Hands, the following is a Description of the said *Richard Taylor*. He is about *47* years of Age, is *5* feet, *7* Inches in Height, *D. Brown Hair*, *Grey* Eyes, *Swarthy* Complexion; and by Trade or Occupation a *Labourer*.

Given under my Hand and the Seal of the Regiment at *Chatham* this *17th* Day of *March 1818*.

Signature of the Commanding Officer   *F Harries Lt Col. Comy*

Horse Guards *18th May 1818*

CHAPTER 11

MILITARY CONVICTS AT ROBBEN ISLAND

Many British army offenders were sent to Robben Island, situated off the coast of South Africa, near the Cape of Good Hope. Some were later transported to Van Diemen's Land (now known as Tasmania). Records of these convicts can be found in the War Office Correspondence at The National Archives in document class WO 1. The following examples shows the detail to be found in these documents.

Table 11.1: Cape of Good Hope. Return of Military Convicts under Sentence of Transportation at Robben Island on the 30th November 1844. *(TNA ref WO 1/439)*

Date of Trial	Names	Of What Regiment	Period of Sentence
1840 June 23	Thomas Bowyer	75th Regt	5 years
1843 Augt 14	William Briggs	45th do	7 years
" Mar. 16	Martin Brogan	27th do	For Life
" " 14	Thomas Butler	27th do	do
1842 Decr 18	John Baker	St Helena Corps	do
1843 Mar. 16	Edward Coyle	27th Regt	do
1842 Novr 14	Hugh Culshaw	St Helena Regt	7 years
1843 Mar. 20	Geo. Cunningham	91st Regt	7 do
" " 13	John Divine	27th do	7 do
1841 Jany 1	Michl Donaghy	27th do	5 do
1843 July 13	Robt Duffus	91st do	14 do
1844 Feby 28	Thos Deveraix	91st do	10 do
1838 Mar. 13	Platje Adams	Cape Corps	7 years computed from 30 Aug. 1838
1843 June 21	Danl Ferral	St Helena Regt	7 years
1844 Feby 8	Henry Greenwood	45th Regt	For Life
1843 Mar. 17	James Hunt	27th Regt	For Life
" July 16	John Hamilton	27th do	14 years
1844 May 17	Joseph Hicks	45th do	For Life
1838 Mar. 13	Gezwind Jager	Cape Corps	7 years computed from 30 Augt 1838
1843 " 15	Patrick Keegan	27th Regt	7 years

Date of Trial	Names	Of What Regiment	Period of Sentence
" " 17	Patrick Kelter	27th do	For Life
" June 24	William Kelly	St Helena Regt	7 years
" Mar. 14	Mich. Maker	27th Regt	7 do
" " 18	Mich. Mc Guire	27th do	For Life
" July 13	John McDonald	91st do	7 years
1844 Feby 29	Samuel Millien	91st do	14 years
" " 8	John McGuire	45th do	For Life
1843 Mar. 20	Isaac Penfield	91st do	7 years
1839 July 23	Ths Sullivan	Cape Mounted Rifles	14 do
1843 May 3	Joseph Speakman	Royal Sappers	14 do
" June 23	Patrick Smith	St Helena Regt	7 do
" Novr 13	Samuel Smith	Cape M. Rifles	14 do
" Mar. 14	Patrick Walsh	27th Regt	7 do
" " 20	James Wray	91st do	14 do
1842 Decr 27	Robert Workman	St Helena Corps	7 do

Note: 35 in number.

Table 11.2: Military Convicts sent to the Road Stations. (TNA ref WO 1/439 contd.)

Date of Trial	Names	Of What Regiment	Period of Sentence
1838 Mar. 13	Klaas Busack	Cape Corps	7 years to be computed from 30th Augt 1838
1837 Septr 2	Alexander Philip	Cape M. Rifles	7 years
" " 25	Fredrik Twartboy	do	do

Colonial Office, Cape Town
16th December 1844
John Montagu

Robben Island
8th November 1844

Sir,
I regret to have to report to you a most outrageous act of Mutiny committed by the convict Michael Mc Guire, No 165, late a soldier in the 27th Regiment under sentence of transportation for Life to Van Diemens land.

The circumstances attending this melancholy case are as follows.

The sub-overseer, Benjamin Wiglesworth [sic] reported Michael Mc Guire for smoking and for resisting and offering violence to B. Wiglesworth when he endeavoured to take the pipe from him.

For the offence McGuire was brought before me, and B. Wiglesworth deposed on oath to having seen McGuire with a pipe in his mouth at half past 8 o'clock this morning, and that on going up to McGuire to take the pipe from him he struck his arm away and refused to deliver the pipe. His evidence was corroborated by a prisoner who saw the transaction. I therefore considered the offence proved and as McGuire had been before me on the 24th of last month for the same crime for which I ordered him a punishment twenty one days to work in Irons, and as he had been three times before me since April for disobedience of the Overseer's orders, I resolved to flog him this afternoon, and directed his being put in the Black Hole till quarter past 6 pm when I would punish him.

There happened to be another case of a trifling nature reported also by B. Wiglesworth and during the few minutes it occupied, McGuire stood outside my office door. On the conclusion of the latter case Mr Wolhuter, the Head Overseer (who I invariably have present at all examinations) and B. Wiglesworth [sic] left my office. Mr Wigglesworth [sic] went first, and Mr Wolhuter followed to take charge of McGuire, and lodge him in the Black Hole as ordered. Mr Wiglesworth had walked just fifteen feet from the corner of my office towards the Prison when McGuire followed him, threw a stone weighing one pound two ounces with all his strength, and hit him on the back part of his skull, inflicting a deep wound, and fracturing the skull. Mr Wiglesworth of course fell forward and with such force was he struck that he severely bruised his forehead in the fall.

That this was premeditated there is not a shadow of a doubt for there never is a stone any where near my office as big as a marble, and he must have brought the stone from the Quarry in his pocket with the determination of grievously injuring Mr Wiglesworth, and this is the more certain because 4 men in my employ who were standing outside my office wanting to speak to me and who saw him all the time with his arms folded, told me that he did not pick up the stone there, and the stone is similar to the stones at the Quarry, and McGuire was employed up to the moment he was brought to me, at the Quarry.

I am very sorry to say that the Surgeon informed me that B. Wiglesworth is in a very dangerous state and therefore called on Mr Wright to give me a certificate of the injury he has received which I have now the honor to enclose.

I have placed the convict McGuire handcuffed in the Black Hole till I hear from you how I shall proceed. If he is tried before the Supreme Court for the assault I know not what adequate punishment they can inflict upon a criminal already under the sentence of transportation for Life and there is no punishment I can inflict at all commensurate to the guilt of the prisoner.

It is a very serious crime at a place like this and calls for a most severe example.

I had thought of sending McGuire to Cape Town Gaol but I conceived it better to keep him here till I heard from you on the subject unless in the mean time Mr Wiglesworth dies, in which case I will send him over under escort.

McGuire has always been a lazy, idle, evil disposed man since he has been here. George Wolhuter, Head Overseer, Henry Clarke, William Cameron, John Getzen and Marthinus Solomon, free men in my employ were present; saw the assault committed and the whole affair.

I have &c
Richard Wolfe
Commandant

Robben Island
8th November 1844
These are to certify that upon examination of the second Overseer Benjamin Wiglesworth, I this day found him suffering from a lacerated wound of the scalp and fracture of the outer table of the right Parietal bone of the skull, also a very severe contusion of the Forehead and that he is, in my opinion, in a very dangerous state.
(signed) Lee Wright
Resident Surgeon

Government House

Cape of Good Hope
23rd December 1844

My Lord

I lately intimated my intention of addressing Your Lordship respecting the Military Convicts waiting under sentence of Courts Martial at Robben Island for transportation to Van Diemen's Land.

On the 1st January 1834 their number was 4, and 107 have since been added to them. 57 have been removed to their destination; 3 have died; 3 have absconded; 13 have served out their sentences, and 35 remain at the present time a list of whom is enclosed.

Since the stricter regulations were introduced for the discipline of the convicts this portion of them has evinced much dissatisfaction with their position and been urgent with me for their removal to Van Diemen's Land as their sentences require, and they have become restless and troublesome, complaining with some degree of truth, that while they are detained at Robben Island their conduct, however exemplary, is of no advantage in improving their condition, as it would be under the Probation System in Van Diemen's Land, or even here if they were included in the Ordinance which enables the Government to remove the well behaved Convicts to the Road Parties.

By the enclosed report of a serious outrage committed by one of them upon our Overseer, Your Lordship will perceive how necessary it is that some definite arrangement should be made respecting them.

In stating to Your Lordship the two modes of dealing with them, which occur to me, I will premise that, in my opinion, it is immaterial to the men whether they are sent to Van Diemen's Land or detained here so long as uncertainty of their destination is removed and they are enabled to enjoy the benefits resulting from good conduct.

Should Your Lordship decide to remove them, I would beg to suggest that Convict Ships be directed to call at Table Bay for that purpose, in the summer months to avoid the great expense, inconvenience, and risk of sending them to Simons Bay for embarkation, or else that I should be empowered to engage passages for them in private ships which might easily be arranged and would probably be the more economical method could its safety be ensured. But if Your Lordship should prefer to leave them here, by virtue of an ordinance which could be passed to legalise it and to which plan this Government has no objection to make, I would propose an alteration in the mode of disposing of them. The usually determined character of the Military Convicts has rendered it necessary for their safety and management to have always a Military Guard consisting of a Subaltern and 33 men stationed on Robben Island under the charge of a Military Commandant by which a considerable expense is occasioned to the Home Government which pays the salary of this Commandant, also of a Commissariat Storekeeper amounting together to £220.

The Colony is also subjected to a heavy charge for the maintenance of the Military Convicts for which their labor on Robben Island yields a very inadequate return.

Now both the Home Government and the Colony would be relieved of these charges if the Military Convicts could be removed in a gang to the main land to be employed in road making or on Public Works in unfrequented situations for then there would be no need of the Commandant or Commissariat Storekeeper and the labour of the Convicts would compensate for the cost of their maintenance. In such an arrangement, however, the same Military Guard, as is now necessary at Robben Island, would be required for their safe keeping and subjection to rigid discipline.

Should this arrangement be adopted the presence of the Military Guard would supersede the necessity for the Civil Police, at present employed with an annual amount of salary of £434, and this sum I think should be paid by the Central Board into the Military Chest towards defraying the expense of the Military Guard, as the benefit of the Convict labor would belong to the Colony.

This plan I beg to recommend to Your Lordship and should it meet with Your Lordship's approval it would enable me to remove from the Island all the remaining Civil Convicts, and make their labor available to public purposes, and having evacuated Robben Island I should be enabled to put into execution the plan proposed to Sir George Napier, and transmitted in his despatch No. 49 of 15th March last of removing to that Island the chronic sick, lunatics and paupers maintained by the Colonial Government and who are now dispersed over the Colony in a most unsatisfactory and expensive manner.

In conclusion I beg to suggest that, should Your Lordship's decision be that the Military Convicts should be detained at Robben Island, Your Lordship may, perhaps, be disposed to relieve the Colony from the charge of their maintenance.

I have &c

P. Maitland

CHAPTER 12

RECORDS OF OFFICIALS, EARLY SETTLERS AND PARDONED CONVICTS IN NEW SOUTH WALES

(See Appendix 18)

There is much detail concerning early settlers and pardoned convicts in the Colonial Office correspondence. These records include the estates of deceased persons. The following are some examples.

TNA ref CO 201/23

Recommendation for a Surgeon in New South Wales

Grosvenor Square
June 26. 1802

My Lord
Understanding from Mr Balmain, who is just returned from the settlement at Botany Bay, where he had been Chief of the Medical Staff, that some additions are to be made to that Staff. I take the liberty of recommending Mr John Savage for one of the appointments. Mr Savage was surgeon to the *Melville Castle* East Indiaman, when your Lordship was at Madras, on his return to England. He became Surgeon's Mate to my Regiment of Militia during the four years he acted as such. He gave great satisfaction in every point of view, his professional skill being highly thought of by his principal, who is himself a person much superior to his situation. I mention these circumstances as proofs of Mr Savage's ability to fill the situation with advantage to the Colony.

I have the honor to be
My Lord
Your Lordship's most obedient humble Servant
Wentworth Fitzwilliam

Lord Hobart

TNA ref CO 201/61

Registered Baptisms

Account of Baptisms Registered at the Parish Church at Windsor in New South Wales from 30th June to 30th September 1812. [*Note*: the date of birth is also given.]

Margaret daughter of Matthew and Mary Hughes, born 27 March 1812 and Christened 3rd July 1812.

John Kenedy son of John and Jane Howl, born 5th April 1812 and Christened 5th July 1812.

William son of Henry Treadaway and Elizabeth Dring, born 14th December 1811 and Christened 12th July 1812.

Edward son of Joseph and Sarah Craft, born 27th March 1812 and Christened 5th July 1812.

William son of James and Ann Clark, born 20th August 1811 and Christened 16th August 1812.

Elizabeth daughter of Benjamin and Mary Singleton, born 9th May 1812, and Christened 13th September 1812.

Sarah daughter of William and Mary Douglas, born 22nd August 1810 and Christened 13th September 1812.

Charles son of William and Mary Douglas, born 31st July 1812 and Christened 13th September 1812.

James son of James Kable and Elizabeth Tailby,[1] born 23rd January 1805 and Christened 13th September 1812.

David son of David and Catherine Roberts, born 5th July 1812 and Christened 13th September 1812.

Pierce son of John and Mary Lyons, born 30th December 1811 and Christened 20th September 1812.

Sophia daughter of James and Sarah Morris, born 24th May 1812 and Christened 27th September 1812.

Elizabeth daughter of John and Susannah Randall, born 30th August 1812 and Christened 27th September 1812.

    Signed Robt Cartwright
    Asst Chaplain

Account of Burials

Table 12.1: Account of the Burials.

When Buried	Name	Age	
1812 July 14th	John Clark	7 years	Born in the Colony
" " 16th	Jane Yeoman	3 weeks	do
" " 17	Patrick Kirwan	70 years	Per *Tellicherry*
August 1	Dennis Malone	30 years	Per *Ann*
"	Patrick Clark	42 years	Per *M. Cornwallis*
" " 16	Jonathan Holdsworth	47 years	Per *Barwell*
" " 26	Robert Faithful	2 years	Born in the Colony
" Sept. 3	Willm Fitzgerald	32 years	Per *Duke Portland*
" " 28	Joseph Kearns	65 years	Per *Tellichery*

    Signed Robt Cartwright
    Asst Chaplain

1. Elizabeth Tailby married John Hawkins (see Chapter 19).

Illustrated emigration correspondence to The Right Honourable Lord Howick MP, *c.* 1831. (The National Archives ref CO 384/28)

Public Baptisms

Table 12.2: Public Baptisms, Sullivan Cove, River Derwent, Van Diemen's Land, 1810–11.

1810

John son of George and Dorothy Oakley (late Dorothy Barrisford)	Jany 14th
Elizabeth and John daughter and son of Margaret Eddington	Jany 14th
William son of William and Jane Womack (late Jane Gilmore)	Jany 21st
Edward Mellows son of Edward and Ann Risbey (late Ann Gibson)	Jany 21st
Sarah & Maria daughters of Samuel and Sarah Sheers (late Sarah Johnstone)	Feby 19th
William John son of Michael & Sophia Mansfield (late Sophia Childers)	Feby 19th
Robert son of Samuel and Ann Thorne (late Ann Luckwell)	March 17th
Ann daughter of Jacob and Ann Billett (late Ann Harper)	March 18th

George son of Ann Priest	March 19th
Ann daughter of do	March 19th
William son of John and Rebecca Ingle (late Rebecca Hobbs)	March 23rd
Dorothy Elizabeth daughter of William & Ann Garigil (late Ann Skilhorne?)	March 26th

During His Honor Lt Govr Collins, Commandant

Sarah Ann daughter of Samuel and Jannett Gunn (late Jannett Patterson)	May 26th
John son of Henry and Catherine Dutton (late Catherine Sullivan)	April 6th
John son of Edward and Maria Lord (late Maria Risely)	April 9th
Jacob Native of Van Diemen's Land	June 25th
Mary Ann daughter of Maria Hopper	July 6th
Derwent son of Thos & Ann Hibbins (late Ann Clarke)	July 6th
Emmiline daughter of Richard & Elizabeth Carter (late E. Billett)	July 29th

During Edwd Lord Riall, Commandant

George son of John and Elizh Herbert (late Elizh Smith)	July 30th
Charlotte daughter of William & Frances Nichols (late Frances Davis)	Augt 1st
John George William son of John and Ann Cummings (late Ann Boyton)	Augt 2nd
James Boyton son of John and Ann Cummings do	Augt 2nd
Mary Ann Ellinor daughter of do do	Augt 2nd
George John a native boy aged about 7 years	Sepr 22nd
Robert son of William and Mildred Williams (late Mildred Harrison)	Sepr 24th
Michael son of John and Mary Shillingbourne (late Mary King)	Sepr 30th
James son of Robert and Elizabeth Washart (late Elizabeth Allen)	Oct 16th
Rebecca daughter of Elizh Bradshaw	Oct 21st
Eliza daughter of do	Oct 21st
Sarah daughter of Elizabeth Meredith	Oct 22nd
Thomas Russel son of Thos Russel & Mary Crowder (late Mary Smith)	Oct 28th
Thomas son of Thomas and Elizh Green (late Elizh Fawkner)	Oct 31st
Ann daughter of Thomas William & Sarah Birch (late Sarah Guest)	Nov 6th
Mary Ann daughter of Thomas and Mary Ann Peters (late Ann Warwick)	Nov 7th
James son of Robert and Elizh Wispers (late Elizh Allams)	Nov 10th
William George son of William & Judith Symonds Hopley (late Judith S. Hobbs)	Nov 13th
James son of do do do	Nov 13th
William son of John and Ann Marshall (late Ann McDonald)	Nov 14th
Thomas son of Mary Barrisford	Dec 5th
Elizabeth daughter of Edward and Elizabeth Fisher (late Elizh Gregory)	Dec 24th

1811

Ann a native of Van Diemen's Land	Jany 4th
Mary do do do	Jany 4th
Lucy Murray daughter of Ann the native as described	Jany 4th
Susannah daughter of Thomas & Mary McCluer (late Mary S. Windon)	Jany 12th
Mary Fitchett Farum native V.D.L.	Jany 14th
James son of Ann Fowler	Jany 20th
Catherine daughter of William and Margaret Longshaw (late M. Myers)	Jany 31st
John son of Joseph and Elizh Patterson (late Elizh Roberts)	Feby 1st
Ann Riley daughter of Thomas William and Sarah Birch (late S. Griest)	Feby 5th
Margaret daughter of Mary Martin	April 16th
John son of Peter and Catherine McGuire (late Catherine Lemmon)	May 24th

William Michael Anthony John and Francis sons of Joseph and Catherine (late Catherine Burn)	June 3rd
Robert son of Samuel and Ann Thorne (late Ann Luckwell)	June 7th
Constantia Elizh daughter of Thomas and Ann Hibbins (late E. Clarke – sic)	June 18th
George son of Mary Ann Moody	June 18th
Sophia daughter of John and Elizabeth Dunscombe (late E. Hamley)	June 22nd
William son of Elizabeth and William Hervey (late Elizabeth Cole)	July 10th
Susannah daughter of do do	July 10th
Malvina daughter of George Prideaux and Ann Jane Harris (late Ann Jane Hobbs)	July 15th
Andrew son of Robert & Jane Beaty (late Jane Millar)	Sept 5th
John son of John and Ruth Blachlow (late Ruth Thompson)	Sept 6th
Daniel son of Danl & Margaret McCoy (late Margaret Young)	Sept 9th
Sarah May native of Van Diemen's Land	Sept 23rd
Mary Ann daughter of Danl and Maria Stanfield (late M. Kimberly)	Sept 24th
John Henry son of John and Rebecca Ingle (late Rebecca Hobbs)	Oct 8th
John son of Thomas and Frances Williams (late Frances Reardon)	Oct 20th
Jane daughter of John and Mary Grierson (late Jane Birch – sic)	Nov 16th
Elizh daughter of Samuel & Susannah Wiggins (late Susannah Welch)	Nov 28th
Orison son of Thomas and Mary Craham (late Mary Monk)	Dec 8th
Catherine daughter of Mary Martin	Dec 23rd
Rebecca daughter of Francis and Sarah Cox (late Sarah Edge)	[blank]

TNA ref CO 201/93

A Complaint against the Governor of New South Wales

3 Fleet Street
April 16th 1818

My Lord,

I have been induced to address the following particulars to you from a mere sense of imperative duty when I had the honor to hold a situation by Your Lordship's appointment at N.S. Wales. I had very good opportunities to be minutely acquainted with the circumstances I am about to detail, and on my leaving that Colony I was particularly urged by several of the most respectable inhabitants to submit them to Your Lordship which hitherto I have forborne to do lest I should appear troublesome or obtrusive. Lately however I have received further information and solicitations to the same purpose and on consulting with some very grave and pious friends I have been induced to consider the subject in the point of view above stated. I trust therefore that your Lordship will not misunderstand me and, however these particulars may seem to reflect upon the present Governor, that your Lordship will see that my object is not so much to complain of him as to procure redress to the settlers at large, and that the only aim I have in pointing out the faults of the present Government is to assist as far as may be in preventing them for the future.

The general plan pursued under the present Government is not to raise the convict to the rank of the settler but to degrade the free settler to the rank of a convict. In confirmation of this I need only state that there is the same general order respecting the free settlers as there is respecting the convicts. If they have business at the stores they must both come on the same day and at the same hour. If they have petitions to present, and nothing can be done without them they must both attend on the same day and at the same hour. The same system is universally pursued and it has happened that a Gentleman Magistrate and his emancipated convict, after being raised to the magistracy have been associated together in the same colonial employment. In all things too the convict has been indulged in preference to the free settler and the recommendation of a convict magistrate has been found to prevail in the most desperate cases when that of the most worthy and universally lamented magistrate, the late Ellis Bent, Esqr. has proved ineffectual. In illustration of this article I must state to you Lordship that convicts at the recommendation of D'Arcy Wentworth have had as great allowances of spirits as Ellis Bent Esqr. himself although those convicts were still in a menial capacity. Individuals also on whom the sentence of the law was pronounced recommended to mercy were pardoned who committed more murders after their restoration to society than before their conviction. On the contrary many persons really reformed at the instance of D'Arcy Wentworth have been persecuted and punished for nominal crimes while others of the most abandoned character have escaped. Instances of the former will be given lower down. One of the latter which occurred at the time of my leaving Sydney will be sufficient to state for the present. George Wakeman alias Parsons was many years ago an accomplice with D'Arcy Wentworth in the most nefarious practices and has been transported three times. Yet this man was pardoned by Governor Macquarie at the request of D'Arcy Wentworth and actually left the Colony in the ship in which I took my passage for England. It is evident that such inducements to convict magistrates are sufficiently strong to buy them over to the Governor's views however dishonourable or unjust they might be.

In order the more effectually to depress the free settler and to secure not only a monopoly of power but also a monopoly of interest the Governor was used to apply to foreign markets to encourage foreign shipping, and in order to disguise the motive for this traffic it has been laid down on a general matter that the Government never receives a present nor any thing for which he does not pay at least the prime cost. Those however that have been on the spot, that have been familiar with the parties concerned cannot but see the consummate cunning of such a plan and the more than mischievous tendency of it. Political traders whose interest it is to have the patronage of the executive government understanding the general maxim which is laid down take care to bring an investment united to the taste of the Governor and invoiced at a price so low as to be a very considerable present. In this manner they insure a large premium on their remaining investment and find it worth their while to come from America and India to pay their court to N.S. Wales while no one in the Colony is benefited except the Government. A more flagrant instance of this perhaps I need not point out than the trade to India for wheat when the Colony is able to provide not only for home consumption but even for exportation. Even at the very period, 1813, that the Government published proclamations in Sydney and compelled the clergymen to read them in their churches stating that the Colony was in a state of starvation, Mr H. Baldwin, Mr H. Kable and others offered to procure any quantity if the Governor would promise to receive it into the stores to prevent the necessity of applying to a foreign market; but the monopoly of the sale of spirits allowed by the Governor to the Indian merchants enabled them to furnish a supply of wheat cheaper than it could be grown in the Colony, and this is said to be the foundation of all the misery which the poor settlers have ever since suffered and in one communication which I have received on this head, it is said 'That the Governor had a present of ten thousand gallons of rum by the Governor General of India as a return for two hundred tons of coals' and in another communication 'That the contract for the Hospital, which was connected with the monopoly of the sale of spirits secured to each contractor at least ten thousand pounds.'

Besides this oppression of a general nature there are others extending to individuals. The Governor whips some free persons without the formality of a trial, imprisons others with as little ceremony, and in some instances prevents persons from marrying without assigning any lawful impediment. In conformation of these particulars I will take the liberty in this place to transcribe part of a very important letter which was addressed to me a little before my departure.

You know the breach in the Government wall was actually left open as a trap to catch people. You know that the reward of two bottles of rum is great enough to tempt the bad men such as the most of our police are to condemn innocent persons. You know the innocent circumstances under which the poor blacksmith was seized and unheard, imprisoned, whipt, and fined. You know that decent and reformed men have more than once without a trial or even a charge on oath been exposed to the same shameless treatment and how even some poor free settlers have been tortured whose character was never so much as tinged with a trial. You remember also the case of Mr Philip O'Connor a gentleman yet in the British confidence and bearing arms in His Majesty's service. You know that he came from India to this place to fulfil an honourable engagement in a religious manner. You know that his Banns of Marriage were published on Sundays May 12th, 19th and 26th after being refused a Licence without any lawful impediment assigned and yet that he was forcibly detained on board the Brig *Tweed* from May 21st or 22nd till that Brig sailed for no other reason whatever than to prevent the solemnization of an honourable union and which was thereby prevented.

Besides these individual cases I can certify your Lordship of other monstrous improprieties which affect both the public character of the Colony as well as its private character. Anthony Best and Mrs Powell are now living together in unauthorized wedlock because the Governor would not allow them to be married, considering that the woman was too old for the man. I was also particularly requested by the postmaster at Sydney to say how much he felt oppressed in his situation by the conduct of the Governor in always opening the mail himself and taking what letters he pleased out before the postmaster had them to deliver, by which he bore the blame of many things of which he was entirely innocent. The credit of Deputy Commissary General Attan has been most foully blasted by insinuations of the Governor through the Sydney Gazette, and he must have sustained an injury for which perhaps nothing can compensate. Mr Commissary Palmers has been most illiberally and unjustly persecuted by the Governor on the subject of a piece of ground, with the particulars of which as Government is concerned, I think your Lordship ought to be acquainted. The Governor succeeded to some property of one Andrew Thompson emancipated convict among which was a brewery and a certain piece of ground. This brewery and ground the Governor offered to Mr Palmer in exchange for a certain hill which Mr P declined. The Governor then offered £100 as a more valuable consideration but threatened at the same time, in case of non compliance to take it by force on the part of the crown. Mr G.T. Palmer however declined accepting the £100 and the Governor deserted his original plan for the following. The Governor bought the brewery and ground which was his own property for Government at the enormous sum of £500 which was afterwards sold by auction for a mere trifle. The whole of the correspondence respecting this affair was transmitted to me like the other particulars to state to your Lordship if I happened on an opportunity; the original correspondence

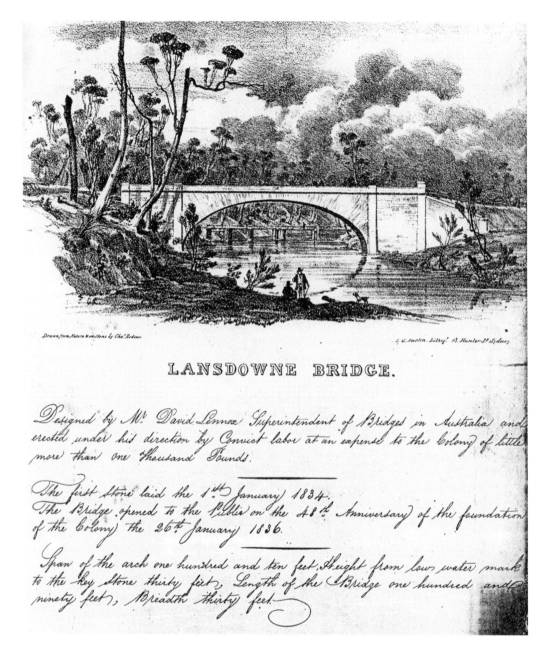

An illustration of Landsdowne Bridge, erected under convict labour between 1834 and 1836. (The National Archives ref CO 201/252)

can therefore no doubt be easily procured. The dates of the letters are April 8th 1815, April 14th 1815, May 7th 1815, March 25th 1816, March 27th 1816. I have known a hundred or more convicts sent to Van Diemen's Land, I believe by that Captain.

Jeff —— [missing] who is lately returned, but certainly, by Captain Forster of the Emu, without the least partition to separate the males from the females and when the females only were furnished with beds so that the strongest inducements were even held out to immorality. It is true that some of the worst of the population of N.S. Wales are compelled to attend Divine Service but the encouragement held out to those who are likely to reform is extremely inconsiderable. There is but one church at Sydney where the bulk of the convicts are and there is no accommodation in it for the greater part of those who are not compelled to attend, much less for those emancipated: and except at Parramatta, the rest of the clergy are either placed in situations where there are no people to reform as Mr Fulton, or where there is little or no accommodation for the discharge of their duties, as in Liverpool and Van Diemen's Land; and these are then likely to be removed from place to place, as I was for three months at a time by the will of the Governor, or be commanded on the most unpleasant duties at the most remote distances without sufficient notice to provide for personal or family safety and without any remuneration for the extraordinary expenses which the performance of those duties must incur; besides which their proper influence is prevented by the dread of martial Law in all places; and at Van Diemen's Land, now, by example of the Governor who attends on Divine Service, when it is performed with a kept woman on his arm.

What poor encouragements there are to virtue; are more than overbalanced by such incentives to vile and absolute oppressions as I have now mentioned, for the instances I have quoted are far from being solitary or the worst. I understand there is no place of separate confinement for females sentenced to Sydney Jail, but this I certainly know, that so contracted is the provision for the accommodation of female convicts in general, that the greater part are compelled to prostitute themselves in order to find a place for their nightly shelter; a case even worse than any of these occurred while I was at Sydney. Two thoughtless girls of honest reputation who were sauntering about with their mistress' or mother's children stepped over a part of the wall belonging to the government domain (which is a full quarter of a mile from the government house, and was not above seven or eight inches high, occasioned by a breach in the wall which had been there to my knowledge several weeks) merely as they said to shew the children the pretty daisies, were seized by two constables and conveyed to Sydney Jail where they were received without any ceremony. The constables received two bottles of rum for their exertions, and the poor girls were compelled to spend a night or two in that Jail exposed to all the insults which the worst of convicts chose to offer them.

Mr Moore Senr had his land taken away after he had bought horse, cart, &c for improving it, because he filed an information in the Supreme Court against an American Vessel trading unlawfully to that Colony, to the aggrandizement of the Governor and the oppression of the Settlers. Mr Moore Junr has lately had his land taken away because he signed a petition stating these or some of these grievances to the House of Commons and praying their assistance. I never had any land till the day I left the Colony at that late period the Governor who had used me so cruelly all the time of my residence there gave me a certain portion which I left in the hands of an agent to get cultivated &c according to the terms of receiving it. This has since, I understand, been taken away from me, because I was supposed to have had a hand (as the Governor said) in that petition; and by letters which I have received many are said to have been oppressed in a similar manner.

Besides the interference with Church matters, as in the case of marriages, the Clergy are obliged to read a variety of proclamations in the midst of the church service which in some instances are exceedingly burdensome. Some of these pass high encomiums upon the greatest oppressors of the people who are both immoral and unjust in their deportment. Some of these reflect on and censure the most industrious and worthy tho' poor oppressed settlers. Some of these have wholly a reference to the black natives respecting their carrying waddies[2] &c. and some of these refer to the sale, the prices &c. of spirituous liquors and licences to public houses.

Many a time have the people wished to petition parliament for some relief, especially for a council to act in concert with the Governor but the dread under which they lie will not permit them to do that publicly. Requisitions even for things of less moment, common market place meetings signed by the most sensible and pacific among the people, stating their object before hand to the Governor, have been most ungraciously rejected. The effort which a few lately privately made I am informed has not succeeded because it was made privately. In the moral government of the world God accepts a man's person according to what he has and not according to what he has not, and I trust your Lordship sees the propriety of acting on the same rule. The obligations these people have laid on me compel me to intercede for them in this respect. If they cannot send a public petition, surely a private one ought to have some weight, till arrangements can be made for the pore proper executions of such an instrument. Let me then entreat your Lordship to give the weight of your sanction to the best endeavours of which the people are at present capable, being confident of this; that they seek only what is the subject of our continual prayers, the good of the Church, the safety, honor and welfare of our Sovereign and his Dominions.

I will take the liberty of subjoining one more quotation from a letter to me, which will perhaps inform your Lordship more nicely of the general wishes of the people, & of the justice of these remarks which I have made. 'The Government at home is no doubt deceived; grossly deceived. Strangers come here whose interest it is to please the Governor and whom to please the Governor finds his interest. They pass away and tell a tale little according with the woeful experience of the more stationary. It might be worth the consideration of the British Government to give encouragement to the export of agriculture and to distillation and to the maritime speculations of N.S.Wales. For want of exports our youths, devoid of more suitable employment here, are drained from the Colony, by which means the Colony loses the benefit which would otherwise be derived to it, from their knowledge of the soil and the advantages or disadvantages of certain localities. If exports were encouraged men might be employed in procuring tobacco, flax, timber, grain of every description, oil, skins, sandal wood, &c. and this might be done by the Convicts sent from England, who would, in proportion as the consequence and opulence of the Colony increased, be taken from the ships and employed in this way by the persons engaged in such speculations. The colonists would thus be improving the circumstances of their situations and be remunerated, at the same time that they saved Government the expense of the Colony after they had once landed the convicts. But all these things are only consistent with a much greater degree of liberty than we at present enjoy. There ought to be some arrangement for the security of private property, that is, landed property, so as to protect it from arbitrary invasion, and we trust that we shall not long be permitted to be subject to the oppressive feat of one bad man.'

Having suggested these particulars to your Lordship I shall not, having satisfied my conscience, attempt the least commentary upon them. They all admit of the most lucid confirmation and seem to call for the most prompt correction. If this suggestion should be the means of making our oppressed fellow creatures more comfortable in their worldly circumstances, more willingly obedient to those in authority, and more

2. A waddy is a native war-club.

at liberty and encouraged to cultivate piety and virtue, I shall think myself happy and be your Lordship's obliged servant more on this account than on that which formerly brought me so much honor.

I am My Lord,

Your Lordship's obliged, obedient & devoted servant,

[Rev.] Benjamin Vale

Acknowledge receipt and acquaint him that Lord B will not fail to give it his immediate attention.

TNA ref CO 201/93 part 4

A Letter from Christopher Webb to his Wife

Sydney Port Jackson

New South Wales

April 11th 1817

Dear Wife

I received your ever welcome letter and was glad to hear of you all being in good health as it leaves me at present thanks be to God for it. Dear Wife I ham very sory to hear of old age over taken you so as not to be able seace to get subsistence but I hope in the course of a short time I shall be able to get my total Freedom so that I shall be able to return to England to spend the remainder of our lives together in a comfortable existence but if you think proper to come to me I can get you more comfortable liven here then I could if I whus in England so you must let me now if you deu not meen to come but if you meen to come you must make applycation to Earl Bathurst Office Transport Office, 44 Parliament Street, London as you are my lawfull wife and if my two sons wishes to come with you the may be able to get a vary good liven as shoe maken is the one of the first trades in The Colony. Therefore it is my harty wish that the should come if the can make it convenient to themselves therefore make up your minds and due as you think proper as for a liven I provided all ready, as I have got a good house or two of my own and no rent to pay so I hope you will not delay in coming or letting me having the result of your mind. Please to give my best wishes to all enquiring frends and in so doing I conclude your ever Affectionate Husband Till Death.

Christopher Webb

Eather Inquire for me or direct if you Rite

   Christopher Webb, Sydney

   Port Jackson

   New South Wales

as I [am] well known in the Town by every one.

Dear wife

when you go to the Transport Office before you come or start from England be shure and ask Earl Bathurst for your Instructions for so many Acres of Land and to put you upon the Stores for such a lenth of time as his Lordship may think proper when you get here and the same for my sons if the[y] are inclined to come with you and the[y] had no occations to bring any leather with them as leather is very cheap here.. Best inform them the[y] must bring some hemp as that is very deere. Be shure and get your instructions for the above.

My Lord

In consequence of a letter received by me from my Husband (which I enclose) who has been a settler at Sidney, Port Jackson, New South Wales near ten years I am emboldened to apply to your Lordship for your sanction and authority to take my passage together with my two sons John Webb (aged 40) and Christopher Webb (aged 38) both of No. 5 Parsonage Walk, Newington Church, Surrey, shoemakers, and their wives and two children to join my husband at Sidney above mentioned. As neither myself nor my sons is in a situation to pay for or support ourselves on the passage to Sidney we must request your Lordship to order our passage free of expence and proper necessaries during the voyage and that upon our arrival at Port Jackson we have a Grant of such a number of Acres of Land and that we may be put upon the Stores for such a length of time as to your Lordship may seem meet. Trusting to your Lordships Pardon for the liberty I am thus taking I request an answer may be addressed to me and my sons.

   C. Webb
   No. 5 Parsonage Walk, near Newington Church, Surrey
   I am with the greatest Submission
   Your Lordship's Most dutiful humble Servant
   Margaret Webb

                                                   Newington Surrey
                                                   17th April 1818

Acquaint her that Lord B has no objection to giving her a passage to New South Wales to join her husband but that with respect to her sons Lord B. cannot give them the same advantages. She must understand however that she will not be victualled at the public expense.

TNA ref CO 201/81

A Petition for a Return Passage to New South Wales
The Humble Petition of Anthony Fletcher

Humbly sheweth that your petitioner in the year 1802 went from Mr Welch's painter and glazier, no. 25 Cleveland Street, London, a free settler, sailed in the *Ocean* in company with the *Calcutter*, Captain Woodriff, intending to make a settlement at Port Phillips. After stopping some months finding we could not git no harvest by reason of the hot winds was oblige to return to Port Jackson ware Governor King was Governor he told he should like to send me to the Back Settlements for fere the Natives should due me an injery. Advise me to go to work for my selfe till I have an opertunity to settle. I did in the course of fore month he send for me said he had a place to sute he then provided pervision for me my wife and two children to go to Norfolk, New South Wales. When I came there Major Provest was Governor I wated on him he told me there was a Ship in the Harbour had brought an account that that place was given up to Government for pig iron. I ask the liberty of a few weeks to stop, my wife being very near her lying in. In a month after Major Provest advise me to content my self till he sent to Governor King. Major Provest loveing Norfolk and returning England left me in the hands of Capt. Piper Governor King word for me to receve Pantonys Farm. Capt. Piper had settled an other person in it unknown to me. It was still him about my settlement. He told me I must work for Government and I might remain there teell I could gain my settlement. I wanted to git to head quarters, a Schooner came in for pork by wich I got [to] Port Jackson and Major Provost was Governor. I told him my case but [he] youse me in a very abrubt manner and sworn he thought me an imposter on Government said go to Kings Executor and bring him here to over haul the books wich he did, and finding all right that I had said and Pantony where farm was to obtain, stood by me at the same time.

When found that would answer, Major Provest advise me to go thare which I refuse as Pantony could not due in it. The Major then told [me] to [go] about my business and not see him any more. I went to one Sir George Page and hired myself for twelve months. After three months one of the gards came to me said I must go to the Governor. I attended at 8 o'clock the next morning when Bodyly Sarjant seised me I went with him he ask me if my name was not Fletcher. I answered yes, he ask ware I wish to be settled. I answered at Darwin, New South Wales. He vittled me from Port Jackson to Norfolk from thare to Darwin ware I obtained my farm but never obtain my prevelage such as cows, sheep and pigs not any but one for nine months stock wich I should have had, had not the Governor dide.

I then returned to England and as my property has been so long in other peoples hands I should be glad to go back and know how to recover my property. I should be glad to git my passage. I am willing to due any thing on board to work my passage but I am no sailore and to have an order to receve my prevelage as before I hope Honerable Sir you will excuse my begging my passage as I am a very poor man and not able to pay for it for wich I shall be bound to pray and am Sir Your Very humble and obedient Servent.

Anthony Fletcher

If you plese Sir refer for a carracter to Mr Welch No. 15 Cleveland Street, Fitzroy Square, or Mr Hatton. No. 41 Henry Street, Hampstead Road.

PETITIONS FOR LAND GRANTS

The following petition is undated, but is filed in the year 1838.

TNA ref CO 201/282

To Her Most Gracious Majesty the Queen
The Humble Petition of John Augustus Manton

Sheweth

That your Petitioner is the son of the late Joseph Manton, gun maker, from whose numerous improvements in Fire Arms, during forty years of experimental research, may be mainly attributed the present advanced position of the Gun Trade.

That in consequence of his late Father's numerous and expensive experiments, not only connected with the Gun Trade, but in other branches of the Arts and Sciences, added to the defective state of the Patent Laws during the period of his Improvements, he did not receive that reward which the importance of his Inventions entitled him to expect; that in One thousand eight hundred and thirty five he died having expended a fortune in the advancement of Science.

That your Petitioner, in order to convince Your Majesty of the importance of his late Father's improvements, and the estimation in which they are held throughout the World, has obtained the signatures, with only one or two exceptions, of the whole of the Master Gun Makers of London and Birmingham, which he hopes will be sufficient evidence to induce Your Majesty to authorize Your Petitioner to select a Grant of Ten Thousand Acres (or a less quantity) of the uncultivated Land in Australia, whither

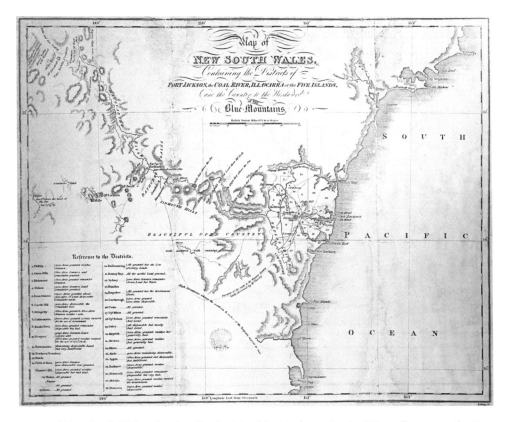

A map of New South Wales, showing the districts of Port Jackson, the Coal River, Illawarra or the Five Islands, and the country to the west of the Blue Mountains. (The British Library ref 90100(34))

your Petitioner, with a wife and young family, are about to emigrate for the purpose of establishing a General Store and Steam Flour Mills in the vicinity of Port Philip in consideration of the services rendered to the Country by his late father's numerous and scientific inventions which were only effected at great personal sacrifices.

And Your Petitioner as in duty bound will ever Pray.

To Her Most Gracious Majesty the Queen

We the Undersigned, Your Majesty's most dutiful subjects Master Gun Makers, residing in London and Birmingham, hereby certify that we consider the numerous improvements effected in Fire Arms, by the late Joseph Manton, and the spirited manner in which he, regardless of expense, brought forward the first rate Talent, as connected with the Gun Trade, to have been mainly instrumental in placing that Trade in its present advanced position, and that in One thousand eight hundred and thirty five he died, having expended a fortune in the prosecution of Scientific Discovery.

We have subscribed our Signatures to this Document, in the hope that by furnishing our humble Testimony to the worth of his numerous Inventions, and the Stimulus they have given to the advancement of Trade Your Majesty will be pleased to consent to Prayer of Your Petitioner, which will have the effect of increasing the exertions of Your Majesty's subjects for the promotion of Science by a knowledge that they do so under the protecting influence of a liberal and enlightened Government.

The following Signatures are attached by the written Authority of the Parties they represent. [The following are some of the gun-makers in London who are listed in this petition. The total list includes 76 gun-makers in London, and 137 in Birmingham.]

James Purdy, Oxford Street
Charles Lancaster, 151, New Bond
    Street
Thomas Smith, 55, Parliament Street
Joseph Lang, 7, Haymarket
Thomas Boss, 76, St. James Street
David Egg, 10 Opera Arcade, Pall
    Mall
Henry Fatham, 37 Charing Cross
W.F. Mills, The Board of Ordnance
    and the East India Company, 120
    High Holborn
John Lissant, 53 Drummond Street
John Blissett, 321 High Holborn
James Beattie, 52 Upper Marylebone
    St.
J.E. Barnett, 134 Minories
Barnard Denyer, 21 Percy St.
William Parker, 233 High Holborn
Edward London, 51 London Wall
James Seddon, 78 Lower Sloane
    Street, Chelsea
Thomas Potts, 70 Minories
William Lucy Sharp, 7 Little Alie
    Street, Goodmans Fields
Thomas Stevens, 43 High Holborn
John D. Field, 61 Leman Street
Richard Ellis Prichett, Goodmans
    Fields
Archibald Reed, City Road
Robert Ridley, 33 Munsell Street
E. Baker & Son, 24 Whitechapel Road
W.J. Watson. 17 Seymour Crescent

Joseph Charles Reilly, 316 High
    Holborn
William More, 78 Edgeware Road
James Yeomans & Sons, 66 Chamber
    Street, Goodmans Fields
Cephas Penn, 7 Upper Dorset Street,
    Bryanston Square
Richard Jackson, 19 Princess Street,
    Portman Market
George Walters, 7 Guildford Place,
    Clerkenwell
John Smith & Son, 4 Thavies Inn,
    Holborn
John Probin, 29 Lisle Street, Leicester
    Square
John Roberts, 6 Crown Court, Dean
    Street, Soho
J. Hill, 76 Tooley Street
Robert Braggs, 36 High Holborn
William Bond, 59 Lombard Street
I.J. Lightfoot, 25 Compton Street
J.W. Leigh, 49 Leman Street
William Green, 4 Leicester Square
James Glaysher, 3 Chapman Place,
    Dover Road
David Lock, late of Eagle Street
James Holland, 44 Great Prescott
    Street, successor to the late M.
    Wright
G. & J. Wilbraham, 123 Leadenhall,
    City and 146 Great Charles,
    Birmingham
etc., etc.

John Augustus Manton Esq.   22nd Decr '38

Sir,
I am directed by Lord Glenely to Acknowledge the receipt of your letter of the 13th Inst. with the copy of a memorial addressed to the Queen.

   His Lordship regrets that it is not in his power to comply with your application for a grant of land in Australia as H.M. Govt are strictly pledged to the existing Regulations by which the Crown Lands are sold at public auction.

                                                                          R

Land Grants

Table 12.3: Return of Persons formerly Convicts holding Land by Grant in purchase in Liverpool, Brimgelly, Cooks, Minto, Airds, Appix and Cabramatta Districts distinguishing the quantity held by each. *(TNA ref CO 201/123)*

1820 Names	Free by	Grant	Purchase
John Farley	C.P.	50	110
John Leighton	C.P.		140
John Metson	A.P.	50	
John Campbell	C.P.	40	
Henry McCaddon	C.P.	75	
Hugh Burn	C.P.	70	
Thos. Burk	C.P.	165	140
Luke Brinnan	C.P.	30	
Michl Conroy	C.P.	50	
Danl M c Lucas	C.P.	100	
Joseph Ward	C.P.	200	300
Willm Welsh	C.P.	50	
David Morris	C.P.	30	
Michl Grant	C.P.	50	
John Bent	C.P.	50	50
Michl Murphy	C.P.	35	50
Willm Davis	A.P.	80	
Patk Pendergrass	C.P.	50	
Moses Brennan	C.P.	40	
Michl Brennan	C.P.	50	
James Everitt	C.P.	60	
Antonio Vitrio	C.P.	40	
Andrew Byrne	A.P.	60	
Michl Woolhaghan	A.P.	50	
Michl Kallaghan	C.P.	30	
John White	C.P.	30	
Thomas Lewis	C.P.	30	
Joseph Scott	C.P.	60	
Jas Keargey	C.P.	30	
John Cogan	C.P.	50	
Isaac Dowse	C.P.		50
Saml Fairs	C.P.	60	
John Trotter	C.P.	50	
Thos Kennedy	A.P.	40	
Phillip Hogars	C.P.	120	

1820 Names	Free by	Grant	Purchase
Thomas Gilbert	C.P.	50	
John Marnagh	C.P.	100	
Darby Murray	C.P.	56	60
Malachi Ryan	C.P.	50	
Nicholas Beyan	C.P.	50	50
John Treman	C.P.	30	
Abraham Herne	C.P.	30	30
Michael Dwyer	A.P.	100	520
Michl Ryan	C.P.	40	140
Morris Hallaghan	C.P.		110
Thos Andlezark	A.P.	30	
Lachlan Monaghon	C.P.	50	
Patrick Daley	C.P.		30
Edwd Magee	C.P.	50	
Richd Morgan	C.P.	50	
Patk Flynn	C.P.	30	
Martin O'Hearn	C.P.	40	
Michl O'Hearn	C.P.	30	
Willm Bradbury	C.P.		289
John Neale	C.P.	50	
Willm O'Meara	C.P.	100	
Willm Hill	F.S.	30	
John Tindall	C.P.		600
Willm Marson	F.S.	50	90
Edmund Wright	F.S.	50	380
Robert Sells	F.S.	50	
Thomas Herbert	A.P.	100	
James Neale	C.P.	20	
William Wells	F.S.	40	
Banow Jackson	F.S.	40	
Thomas Galvin	F.S.	40	
Christopher Ward	F.S.	40	
Daniel Handshaw	F.S.	40	
Roger Doyle	F.S.	40	
Owen Connor	F.S.	40	

Key: A.P.: Absolute Pardon; C.P.: Conditional Pardon; F.S.: Free by Servitude.

TNA ref CO 201/263

Male Convicts Assigned to Free Settlers, 31st May to 15th June 1837

[The names of the convicts assigned are not given.]
  1. Arndull, Thomas, Pitt Town, 1 errand boy
  2. Australian Agricultural Company, Newcastle, 1 laborer, 2 miners, 2 colliers
  3. Briggs, Henry, Harrowly, 1 errand boy
  4. Brown, David, Jerry's Plains, 1 boatman
  5. Bowman, William, Richmond, 1 laborer
  6. Biddulph, Edward, Newcastle, 1 mason, 1 weaver and 1 laborer
  7. Brown, W.H., Shaolhaven, 4 laborers, 1 groom and soldier
  8. Bland, William, Pitt Street, 1 groom
  9. Burne, W.P. & Co., Port Macquarie, 1 ladies boot and shoe maker
 10. Blaxland, William, Merton, 4 laborers
 11. Bennett, William, Paramatta, 1 baker
 12. Barker, John, Windsor, 1 butcher
 13. Balcombe, William, Murray, 1 locksmith and blacksmith
 14. Bigge, E., Phillip Street, 1 indoor servant and cook
 15. Blaxland, Charles, Merton, 1 cook
 16. Broad, Robert, George Street, 1 watchmaker
 17. Berry, Alexander, Shoalhaven, 1 publican and brewer
 18. Brodie and Craig, South Creek, 1 bargeman, 1 porter
 19. Burt, John, Cook's River, 1 warehouseman, 1 errand boy
 20. Burns and Hickey, Port Macquarie, 1 shopman, 1 slater and 1 farm laborer
 21. Cohen, P.J., Maitland, 1 soldier
 22. Clements, Henry, Bathurst, 1 cloth dresser and laborer, 1 soldier
 23. Cadell, Lieutenant, Parramatta, 1 groom
 24. Clarke, William, Market Street, 1 butcher
 25. Campbell, A.E., Merton, 1 carpenter and joiner
 26. Craig, Robert, Bridge Street, 1 letter-press printer
 27. Cristy, Abel, King Street, 1 whitesmith
 28. Campbell, Robert, Maitland, 2 farm laborers, 1 stockman
 29. Campbell, J.K., Maitland, 1 blacksmith and farrier
 30. Carmichael, John, York Street, 1 baker
 31. Davis, Hart, Hunters River, 1 brickmaker
 32. Dearing, James, Castlereagh Street, 1 butcher
 33. Frier, Lieut., Windsor, 1 groom and laborer
 34. Ferriter, J.S., Fort Street, 1 in-door servant
 35. Finlay, M.S., Bathurst, 1 groom
 36. Forbes, Francis, Patrick's Plains, 1 weaver and soldier
 37. Forbes, Campbell, Sydney, 1 in-door servant
 38. Gamock, A., Goulburn, 1 groom
 39. Gibson, Andrew, Goulburn, 1 bargeman
 40. Gannon, Richard, Kissing Point, 1 weaver's boy
 41. Graham, James, Campbelltown, 1 groom
 42. Hindmarsh, Michael, Illawarra, 1 shoemaker's boy and servant
 43. Hanna, Quartermaster, for his farm, 1 shoemaker
 44. Hill, Richard, Meryon, 1 laborer
 45. Hamilton, John, Philip Street, 1 baker
 46. Hyadrian, G.R., Port Macquarie, 1 carpenter

47. Hardy, James Richard, Australian Office, 1 letter press printer
48. Hyam, Michael, Illawarra, 1 tanner
49. Hynds, Thomas, Sydney, 1 groom
50. Hayes, Richard, Prince Street, 1 chairmaker & turner
51. Hanna, William, Murray, 2 farm laborers, 1 laborer, 1 farm servant and shepherd
52. Jay, W.T., Raymond Terrace, 1 glover, 1 iron-moulder, 1 laborer
53. King, John, Murray, 2 laborers, 1 sweep
54. Kerr, Thomas, Peterson, 1 shoemaker's boy, 3 laborers
55. Larnach, John, Hunter's River, 1 saddler's boy, 1 ploughman
56. Lesslie, Patrick, Cassilis, 1 weaver, 1 farm servant, 1 farm laborer
57. Long, Perry, Castlereagh Street, 1 groom
58. Lang, Andrew, Dunmore, 1 groom and soldier
59. Manning, J.E., for his farm, 2 laborers, 1 weaver and soldier, 1 laborer
60. Maclehose, James, Hunter Street, 1 parasolmaker
61. M'Donald, Captain, Yass, 2 laborers and 2 laborers
62. Mein, J.S., Patrick's Plains, 1 laborer
63. Moore, Thomas, Liverpool, 1 in-door servant
64. Mackie, John, George Street, 1 soapmaker
65. M'Queen, T.P., Segenhoe, 1 farm laborer, 1 farm servant, 1 butler
66. Moore, Henry, Maitland, 2 laborers
67. Newton, William, Patrick's Plains, 1 laborer
68. Newton, Jacob, Williams' River, 1 weaver
69. Nichols, R., Concord, 1 farm servant, 1 blacksmith
70. Neville, John, Junior, Bathurst, 1 footman, groom and soldier
71. O'Neil, Owen, Bathurst, 2 laborers, 1 shoemaker and soldier
72. Osborne, Henry, Illawarra, 1 topsawyer
73. Prisley, William, Parramatta, 1 butcher
74. Panson, John, Windsor, 1 groom
75. Prentice, Thomas, junior, Maitland, 1 laborer
76. Patten, William, Sydney, 1 errand boy
77. Palmer, Edward, Illawarra, 1 waiter in public house
78. Popham, Richard, Argyle, 2 laborers
79. Price, W.T., Penrith, 2 laborers
80. Ryrie, James, Bungonia, 1 sawyer
81. Rens, Edward, Williams' River, 1 in-door servant
82. Snodgrass, William, Williams' River, 2 laborers, 1 wool-comber
83. Stephen, G.M., Nepean, 2 laborers, 1 farmer's boy
84. Sparke, Edward, junior, Ravensfield, 1 gardener
85. Smith, William, Lower George Street, 1 optician
86. Somerfield, William, Sydney, 1 iron turner
87. Styles, J.R., Argyle, gardener and wool manufacturer
88. Steele, Henry, Bathurst, 1 groom
89. Smeathman, Henry, Bong Bong, 1 soldier and house servant
90. Sparke, John, Sydney, 1 cook and confectioner
91. Schofield, John, Eastern Creek, 3 laborers and soldiers, 1 farm servant
92. Smith, James, Illawarra, 1 soldier and laborer
93. Street, S., Hunter Street, 1 groom
94. Terry, John, Box Hill, 1 in-door servant, groom and soldier
95. Teale, John, Windsor, 1 weaver
96. Threlkeld, Reverend L.E., Lake Macquarie, 1 sweep

97. Todhunter, William, Hunter's River, 1 laborer, 1 carter and fisherman
98. Tilson, Thomas, Brisbane Grove, 1 lacemaker, 1 sweep, 1 laborer, 1 shoemaker
99. Townsend, J.M., Patrcik's Plains, 1 shoemaker
100. Tom, William, Bathurst, 1 shoemaker
101. Taylor, Joseph, Sydney, 1 in-door servant
102. Wood, George Pitt, North Richmond, 1 farm servant
103. Woore, Thomas, Sydney, 1 ostler
104. Whitty, J.C. Windsor, 1 groom
105. Williams, John, Windsor, 1 baker
106. West, John, senior, Bathurst, 1 gardener
107. Whitfield, George, King Street, 1 gun-stock maker
108. Wiltshire, A.H., Sydney, 1 fellmonger
109. Wentworth, George, Lachlan River, 1 butcher and soldier
110. Whright [sic], Samuel, Hunter's River, 1 farm laborer, 1 farm servant
111. Walker, James, Vale of Clwyd, 1 laborer
112. Walsh, Donald, Port Macquarie, 1 farmer's boy, 1 laborer
113. Executors of the late Edward Wolstencroft, Shoalhaven, 1 lace manufacturer and 1 laborer

INTESTATES' ESTATES

Records of the unclaimed money left by deceased people in New South Wales who did not make a will are recorded in the Colonial Office correspondence. Table 12.5 and the following are examples.

Money in a Savings Bank left by Intestates

Table 12.4: IN THE SUPREME COURT OF NEW SOUTH WALES
A Return of the Sums of Money paid into the Savings Bank of New South Wales, by the Master in Equity of the said Court arising from the Insolvent Estate of J. E. Manning, Esq., lately Registrar of the Court aforesaid. (TNA ref CO 201/380)

Name of Intestates	Amount Paid in £ s d	Date of Payment	Remarks
William Atkinson	2 0 0	14 Aug. 1846	These several sums arise from a dividend of 4d in the pound paid in the Insolvent Estate of J.E. Manning, after deducting certain Office expenses
Robert Ayres	3 0	"	
James Bates	16 12 0		
George Brett	6 2 0		
G.G.Berrie	9 7 0		
James Chapman	3 0		
George Clarke	1 0		
J. Cleland	13 0		
Henry Coulson	2 0 0		

Name of Intestates	Amount Paid In £ s d	Date of Payment	Remarks
Morgan Donaghue	2 15 0		
John Doyle	2 0 0		
E. L. Fell	3 18 0		
W.J. Fitz	18 0		
Hodgson Good	1 15 0		
James Gibb	15 0		
J.J. Gregory	1 16 0		
Edward Hodgson	14 0		
George Hamstead	1 0		
Grayson Hartley	12 0 0		
James Kippen	7 0 0		
George Kendall	1 4 0		
Timothy Leyden	1 10 0		
James Luker	12 0		
Captain M'Auliffe	8 15 0		
James Maher	1 10 0		
J.N. Macnamara	5 0		
John Matthews	1 12 0		
James Minton	3 10 0		
William M'Echnie	11 10		
William Morris	2		
Francis Moore	9 2 0		
Hugh Niven	4 10 0		
Patrick Nugent	5 0		
Paul Pochlman	5 0 0		
James Quinn	12 0		
J.N. Richardson	11 0		
Moses Rochetz	7 0		
Francis Shires	1 6		
Duncan Sinclair	6 6		
G.W.C. Stapylton	10 0		
Ann Still	7 0		
George Thompson	1 9 0		
Eleanor Turner	9 0		
William Were	2 3 0		
Captain Webster	7 0 0		
William Wilton	3 16 0		
James Winten	6 0 0		
	£132 12 0		

Table 12.5: In The Supreme Court of New South Wales. A True and Perfect Schedule of all Moneys belonging to the Estates of Deceased Intestates placed under the charge of the Registrar of the said Court for collection under the Act of Parliament 9 Geo. IV Chapter 83 Section 12 remaining deposited in the Saving Bank of New South Wales on the Thirty First of December, A.D.1842.
(TNA ref CO 201/331)

No.	Names	Colonial Residence of Deceased	Supposed British Residence of Family
1	Anderson, Adam	Isabella Watson	Scotland
2	Alexander, John	Hunter's River	Scotland
3	Bell, David	Dungog, Hunter's River	unknown
4	Bell, Edward Cooke	Ship *Nelson*	unknown
5	Breane, Michael	Hunter's River	Ireland
6	Burns, Jeremiah	Merton, Hunter's River	unknown
7	Blizard, William	Bathurst	unknown
8	Cochrane, Herman	Surgeon in H.M. Navy	London
9	Connelly, James	Newcastle, Hunter's River	unknown
10	Connington, John alias Harry Hill	Liverpool	unknown
11	Campbell, Malcolm	Camden	unknown
12	Chapman, Miles	Piercefield, Hunters' River	unknown
13	Chesser, William	Barque *Mary Ridgway*	unknown
14	Cavendish, William Joseph	King Street, Sydney	London
15	Cope, Robert Camden	Custom House, Sydney	unknown
16	Corrigan, Hugh	Sydney	Ireland
17	Davis, David	Clarence Street, Sydney	Wales
18	Davis, John Job	Colo: North Richmond	Gloucestershire
19	Drake, John	Concord	England
20	Daley (or Daly), Patrick	Appin	Ireland
21	Darcy, Thomas	Argyle	unknown
22	Donohue, Thomas	Windsor	Kilmain, Ireland
23	Ellis, Charles	Sydney	unknown
24	Ennes, Philip	Campbell Town	Ireland

Moneys in the Savings Bank £ s d	Remarks
22 10 7	Died about the latter end of 1840; late passenger per *Isabella Watson* from Scotland to Port Philip
0 9 2	Died about January 1833, late free Mariner – deceased's brother is a Merchant at Kinross, Scotland
116 14 2	Late of Dungog, Hunters River
5 16 8	Died about 5th February 1832 at the Bay of Islands, New Zealand. Late chief officer of ship *Nelson*
187 1 9	Died about 1828. Formerly of Droumsteagh near Kenturk, County Cork
30 11 7	Died about 16th January 1837. Late Ticket of Leave holder and Constable
1 7 8	Died about 17th February 1832. Late publican at Bathurst
165 17 3	Died about July or August 1828
23 0 0	Died about 8 November 1831 in Sydney. Late free settler
5 19 11	Died about August 1832. Late assigned servant per *Norfolk* September 1829
1 13 10	Died about July 1832; late Superintendent to James Macarthur, Esq.
0 8 1	Drowned about September 1829 at sea. Late Ticket of Leave holder
57 7 3	Died about 13 February 1840 at Melbourne; late Master of *Mary Ridgway*
15 10 3	Drowned about 26th January 1839. Deceased's real name was Costell
7 2 7	Died about 27th September 1838
85 7 5	Died about 27th March 18344. Arrived in the Colony per *Isabella*. Left widow residing at Priorstown, County of Louth, Ireland
66 19 7	Died about 26th October 1836. Family address to care of Mr Jones, surgeon, Seaforth near Liverpool
42 14 5	Died about 15th August 1839. Free
9 16 4	Died about 11th March 1838. Deceased's father's address: Henry Drake Esq., solicitor, Barnstaple, England
87 0 3	Arrived about 1812, formerly of Drowcullagh, County of Limerick, Ireland
11 18 8	Died about April 1831, late Superintendent at Elligoug, County of Argyle
14 5 0	Died about April 1834. Late Turnkey in H.M. Gaol at Windsor
13 6 5	Died about 29th June 1827, late seaman
22 7 2	Widow's address at Rathcoffy, care of Sir G. Ayhurs, Donadee Castle, Kildare
£995 6 0	

A Schedule of the Estates of Intestates

Table 12.6: IN THE SUPREME COURT OF NEW SOUTH WALES
A true and perfect Schedule of all Estates of Deceased Intestates placed under the charge of Samuel Frederick Milford, Esquire, Master in Equity of the Supreme Court of New South Wales, under an Act of Parliament 9 Geo.IV, chap. 83, sec 12, from 1st July to the 31st December, 1846 both days inclusive. *(TNA ref CO 201/380 continued)*

Names of Intestates	Their Colonial Residence	Payments Made £ s d		
John Macdonald	McLeay River		12	0
John Farrell	ditto		3	6
Joseph Ward	Broulee		6	0
H.N.C. Matcham	Murrumbidgee	125	11	10
Henry Williams	Moreton Bay	1	1	9
Robert King	Dabee	1	14	8
Patrick Macnamara	Scone		10	0
Samuel Chard	Macdonald River		12	6
Richard W. Brogis	Jerry's Plains	2	9	2
William Johnston	Goulburn	—		
James Cooper	Kent Street, Sydney	10	0	0
Charles Raven	Scone	3	17	6
Oswald Wotherspoon (Scotland)[1]	Colonial Secretary's Office		3	0
John Lamey (Ireland)[1]	Singleton	1	1	8
William Guilliam	Liverpool	2	17	11
William Cherry	Yass		5	0
Henry Coulson	Sydney	2	0	0
William Perry	Mudgee	9	15	0
Nicholas Rourke	Lunatic Asylum		7	6
John Daly	River Hume	2	10	0
Patrick Morrissey	Port Macquarie	1	15	3
Louis V. Piarget	Sydney		5	0
John Dent	Maitland	4	2	1
James Lovett Howard	Minto		5	0
William Brown	Cassilia	1	4	8
Patrick Keenan	Yass	11	13	6
Elizabeth Wenham	Sydney	6	18	6
Francis Conway	Queanbeyan	9	19	0
Thomas Hatfield	Maitland	6	13	7
Malinda S. Rivers	Sydney	7	15	8
Mark Blucher	ditto	38	1	7
Michael Wright	Queanbeyan	36	0	5

Names of Intestates	Their Colonial Residence	Payments Made £ s d
James Tegg	George Street, Sydney	303 14 5
Henry Wilson	Wellington District	16 0
Nicholas Wallace	Queanbeyan	2 8 11
John Billet	Sydney	4 14 5
John M. Steele	Murrundi	20 12 2½
William Smith	Sydney	4 11 0
Nicholas Carpenter	Shoalhaven	1 5 3
Michael McCann	Paterson	15 2 6
William Dawson	Monaroo District	12 19 0
John Morrison	Audit Office	7 10 0
William Thompson	Moreton Bay	16 15 6
Benjamin Bulmer	Maitland	11 6 2
Joel Burford	Liverpool	1 2 9
William Southey	Moreton Bay	7 8 0
Michael Moore	Wollombi	9 4 2
Isaac Wakefield	Port Stephens	3 13 11
Stephen Tougher	Clarence River	16 10
Robert Johnson	Lachlan River	1 8 8
Michael Kelly	New England	13 6
Henry Smith	Mudgee	1 3 4
Thomas Jackson	Windsor	5 7 8
Patrick or Peter Henry Kearney (Sydney)[1]	Sydney	5 12 4
William John Fitz	Windsor	30 15 8
	Total	£901 11 11½

Note: The tabulation from which the above has been copied also has five other columns: Money Received, Moneys Paid into the Savings Bank, Moneys in The Savings Bank, Moneys in the Hands of The Master and Remarks. These have not been included in the tabulation above.

1. Another column headed Supposed British Residence has only entries against three names. These are identified in the above tabulation by [1] and the place name is given in brackets.

RECORDS OF OFFICIALS

TNA ref CO 201/73

A Heavy Storm at Sydney

Government House
Sydney
28th May 1814

My Lord,

A most violent and destructive hail storm took place here on the 10th of March last, which from the injury it has done, both to the houses of private persons, and to the Government Buildings, I feel myself under the necessity of representing it to Your Lordship.

This storm which came on nearly at mid-day, lasted about fifteen minutes, the wind blowing strong from the south west. The hail stones so far surpassed in size and varied so much in shape from any other hail that I have ever seen, that I think I should better describe them as irregular fragments of Ice than as hail stones. Many of them being from 2 to 3 inches in length, and nearly as much in circumference. These being drifted by a very stormy wind struck with such violence against the windows to the southward and westward, that almost every pane of Glass throughout the Town, in those directions was broken to pieces.

That aspect of the town which received the injury, presented on the following day just such a shattered appearance as might be expected from a great explosion of Gun Powder.

The quantity of glass thus destroyed in the Government Buildings demanding a large supply to make good the injury, and having accommodated some private persons who had suffered severely by the storm, from the supply of Glass in the Government Stores, which was almost the only Glass at that time in the Colony, the quantity now remaining in it is at a very low ebb. In consequence of this circumstance I am under the necessity of forwarding by the present occasion for your Lordship's approval, a supplementary estimate for window Glass, which will be required for New Barracks and other Public Buildings now in progress, and in contemplation at Sydney, and I respectfully solicit Your Lordship to give the necessary directions for its being complied with.

Since closing my despatch respecting Mr John Hartley, that person has applied for and received the pecuniary remuneration which had been formerly tendered him by my order for the disappointment he had suffered in not succeeding to the situation of Naval Officer. In consequence of his receiving this remuneration a Release and Acquittance has been signed and perfected by Mr Hartley in triplicate, whereby he has relinquished all further claim on Government on this account, one of these Releases I now transmit herewith for Your Lordship's information and guidance. Mr Hartley now proceeds to England on board the *James Hay*, which is the vessel I have now the honor to address Your Lordship by.

With a view to the inducing the Bandittis of run away Convicts in Van Diemen's Land (whose depredations I have in a dispatch by this occasion communicated to Your Lordship) to return to their duty and allegiance, I have issued a Proclamation under date the 14th Inst. holding out an Indemnity for their past crimes (murder excepted) provided that they shall surrender themselves within the time in the Proclamation.

Your Lordship will receive herewith a printed copy of this Proclamation, which I trust Your Lordship will approve of.

I have the Honor to be
My Lord
Your Lordships
Most obedient and Humble Servant
L. Macquarie

A List of Immigrants who came by the ship *New York* in 1841

Table 12.7: List of Immigrants (British Subjects) who have been introduced into the Colony of New South Wales under the Regulations of 3 March 1840 by John Miller Esquire of Glasgow, in pursuance of the unconditional authority conveyed to that Settlement in the Letter of the Colonial Secretary dated 21 October 1840 and who arrived at Port Jackson in the ship *New York* Packet, Captain Charles Dorning from Greenock under the Medical Superintendence of John Aitkin Esqr on the 23 October 1841. *(TNA ref CO 201/320)*
[The following is part of the tabulation]

No.	Name	Age		Occupation	Bounty		Remarks
					H	F	
1	Anderson	George	36	Farm servant	-	-	Died in Quarantine
		Elizabeth	37	House servant	19		
		John	16	son	15		
		William	14	son	10		
		Joseph	12	son	10		
		Jane	10	daughter	10		
		Alice	8	daughter	10		
						£74	
2	Byrne	John	37	Labourer	19		
		Eliza	34	Farm servant	19		
		Charles	12	son	10		
		Francis	6	son	5		
		Catherine	10	daughter	10		
		Mary	5	daughter	10		
						£73	
3	Bogan	John	18	Farm Servant	19		
		Mary	22	do	19		
						£38	
4	Boodle	Robert	31	Farm labourer	19		
		Anne	25	House servant	19		
		Robert	3	son	5		
		William	1½	son	5		
						£48	
5	Bagg	John	20	Carpenter	19		
		Christine	21	Dress maker	19		
						£38	
6	Bruce	Thomas	36	Farm Servant	19		
		Elizabeth	35	do	19		
						£38	
7	Carmichael	Donald	25	Trade carpenter	19		
		Margaret	29	Servant	19		
						£38	

No.	Name	Age		Occupation	Bounty		Remarks
					H	F	
8	Craig	Thomas	23	Joiner	19		
		Sarah	21	House servant	19		
						£38	
9	Campbell	John	25	Blacksmith	19		
		Margaret	22	House servant	19		
		John	2 mo	son	–		
						£38	
10	Clarke	Robert	25	Farm servant	19		
		Martha	24	do	19		
						£38	
11	Collins	John	26	Farm servant	19		
		Janet	24	do	19		
		Margaret	2	daughter	5		
						£43	
12	Donnell	William	22	Farm labourer	19		
		Rosanna	22	do	19		
						£38	
13	Dingwell	David	35	Mason	19		
		Margt	32	House servant	19		
		William	12	son	10		
		Elizabeth	10	daughter	10		
		Barbara	7	do	10		
		Janet	5	do	5		
		Margt	2¾	do	5		
						£78	
14	Devlin	James	33	Farm servant	19		
		Ann	32	do	19		
		John	10	son	10		
		James	4	do	5		
		Rosa	6	daughter	5		
		Mary A.	2	do	5		
						£63	
15	Elder	Chas. D.	29	Farm servant	19		
		Ann G.	28	do	19		
						£38	
16	Fraser	William	38	Farm Servant	19		
		Jane	37	do	19		
		James	17	son	15		
		William	4	do	5		
		Mary	14	daughter	10		

No.	Name	Age		Occupation	Bounty		Remarks
					H	F	
						£68	
17	Guinn	George	27	Farm servant	19		
		Elizabeth	25	do	19		
						£38	
18	Goodson	William	33	Farm labourer	19		
		Elizth	33	Weaver	19		
		David	10	son	10		
		John	8	do	10		
		Edward	3	do	5		
		William	1	do	5		
		Martha	6	daughter	5		
						£73	
19	Goodwin	Thomas	31	Farm Servt	19		
		Sarah	21	do	19		
		John	2	son	5		
		Henry	9 ms	do	-		under age
						£43	
20	Henry	John	24	Farm servant	19		
		Jane	25	do	19		
		John	2	son	5		
						£43	
21	Hore	William	37	Farm servant	-		died in quarantine
		Margt	35	do	19		
		William	13	son	10		
		Henry	3	do	5		
		Stanley	1¾	do	5		
		Catherine	5	daughter	5		
						£44	
22	James	Robert	24	Farm Servant	19		
		Mary A.	22	do	19		
		James	2 ms	son	-		under age
						£38	
22	Kerr [sic]	Andrew	33	Shopman	-		
		Elizabeth	24	Farm servant	-		
		James	6	son	-		
		William	3½	do	-		
		Jane	5	daughter	-		
23	Kyle	Thomas	39	Carpenter	19		
		Elizabeth	34	House servant	-		died in quarantine
		William	15	son	15		

No.	Name	Age		Occupation	Bounty		Remarks
					H	F	
		James	11	do	10		
		Thomas	7	do	10		
23	Kyle	Henry	4	do	5		
		Elizabeth	12	daughter	10		
		Dorothy	2	do	5		
						£74	
		Thomas	23	Farm servant	19		
24	Kearney	Catherine	25	do	19		
		Sarah	9 ms	daughter	-		under age
						£38	
		Patrick	37	Mason	19		
		Cecilia	33	Farm servant	19		
		John	17	son	15		
		James	11	do	10		
25	Moey	Peter	9	do	10		
		Patrick	7	do	10		
		Hannah	5	daughter	5		
		Alice	3	do	5		
		Cecilia	1	do	5		
						£98	
	etc., etc.						

Persons Purchasing Pigs on Norfolk Island

Table 12.8: (undated *c.* 1792)
Government
To the undermentioned persons the sums expressed against their names, being for sows purchased by order of the Lieutenant Governor, for the purpose of delivering to the Settlers on Norfolk Island. *(TNA ref CO 201/9)*

From whom Purchased	No. of Sows Purchased	Sum Valued at	Sum Paid	To whom paid
Saml Hussey	6	19 - 7 - 0	19 - 7 - 0	X^2
Nathl Lucas	2	7 - 0 - 0	7 - 0 - 0	X
Martha Baker	1	2 - 16 - 0	2 - 16 - 0	X
Henry Hathaway	1	3 - 5 - 0	3 - 5 - 0	X
Patk Connell	1	3 - 0 - 0	3 - 0 - 0	signed
Edwd Garth	3	10 - 7 - 0	10 - 0 - 0	X
James Davis	1	3 - 10 - 0	3 - 10 - 0	X
Elizabeth Lee	4	7 - 10 - 0	7 - 10 - 0	X
E.B. Perrott	2	6 - 16 - 0	6 - 16 - 0	signed

From whom Purchased	No. of Sows Purchased	Sum Valued at	Sum Paid	To whom paid
John Boyle	1	4 - 0 - 0	4 - 0 - 0	X
Jno Harris	3	8 -10 - 0	8 -10 - 0	signed
Jno Rice	1	2 -10 - 0	2 -10 - 0	X
Noah Mortimer	1	3 - 3 - 0	3 - 3 - 0	X
Wm Knight	1	2 -15 - 0	2 -15 - 0	X
Geo. Legg	3	10 -10 – 0	10 -10 - 0	signed
Saml Hussey	3	6- 10 - 0	6 -10 - 0	X
Thos Crowder	2	4 -12 - 0	4 -12 - 0	signed
etc., etc.				

2. X indicates that the person signed with a cross because they could not write.

ARCHIVES OF NEW SOUTH WALES

The records held at the Archives of New South Wales are extensive. Some of the early records are now available online at www.records.nsw.gov.au. The following is an example showing the detail that can be found.

SRANSW – Registers of Coroners' Inquests, 1796 to 1942; ref 2/8287, Roll 5607

A Coroner's Inquest

Evidence touching the death of Fanny Pentony taken before me Thomas Hobby, Coroner, May seventh 1822.
Elizabeth Taleby being duly sworn deposeth that she was in the house of Paul Randall the whole of the day May the sixth and that the deceased came in on the afternoon about two hours after sun set, she came there to the Public Tap Room into the kitchen which is at the back of the house and begged that she (Taleby) would not acquaint Mr Randall of her being there and a man who was with her whom she called Thomas asked for a Gill of Brandy which Taleby delivered to him and she saw Mrs Pentony standing behind him in the same place when she left the house which she conceives was eight o'clock but cannot say whether she (Pentony) left the house during the time specified, and she cannot say whether the deceased was in a state of intoxity or not.

The mark of
Elizabeth X Taleby[3]

Thomas Skinner being sworn stated that he was in company with the deceased yesterday in the afternoon about three o'clock in the Town and I asked her would she have a glass of spirits and she replied 'yes' and 'thank you.' I brought her into Paul Randall's Public House and gave her some spirits but cannot recollect what kind of spirits. She called for both brandy and gin of which she partook whilst he was in the house. He finally states that he remained with her the whole of the time to the best of his knowledge up to the period of her death, but he acknowledges he was not sober himself when he brought the deceased into the public house and he says he can give no further satisfactory testimony in consequence of his own inebriety

3. Elizabeth Taleby married John Hawkins (see Chapter 19).

but upon being called again to his recollection he says he laid down drunk in the Tap Room and the deceased lay by him with her head upon his thighs and in that position she was found dead, he came to the knowledge of her being dead by the servant of Paul Randall whose name is John Egleton, and another person of the common appellation Black John.

his
Thomas X Skinner
mark

John Egleton being sworn stateth that the deceased came into Paul Randall's with Thomas Skinner and they went into the kitchen and Skinner asked for half a pint of brandy which he (witness) gave to him and on it being brought he asked witness to take a glass out of it in the presence of the deceased. When immediately she took up the brandy in the glass and said 'I think there is not half a pint' and the inference he observ was that she was not sober or she would not have made the remark has [sic] a sober person would have seen and noticed the glass taken out of the half pint. At the normal time of the house being aloud [sic] Mrs Randall said to witness (the servant) that the parties asleep in the Tap Room (namely the deceased and Skinner) would soon get up she supposed the deceased would go home and desired witness to see her safe when she requested and told him the man would lay there until he became sober and attended to what was directed and went to bed himself. After he had been in bed to the best of recollection about two hours he was awaked by the shuffling and noise of a person stiring in the room and he found Black Joe close to the deceased and he heard the noise or jangling of money and witness enquired 'What you are doing to those persons asleep?' and he conceived from his speech that he had something in his mouth and on pressing his chin and cheek Black Joe dropped some copper coin namely a farthing and a crooked halfpenny of old English coin which he said was his own and he went and felt in the pockets of deceased if she had any money in them, but found none. Witness considered her at this time asleep, he then went to his bed again and Mr Seymour being out visiting a patient he had to get up to let him in and when Mr Seymour went into his bedroom witness thought he would endeavour to get her home as Mrs Randall had requested, he then found she was cold and alarmed the proprietors of the house from an apprehension she was dead and it proved unfortunately this was the case.

John Eggleton (signed)

Thomas Giles being sworn stated that he was in the house of Paul Randall in the evening of yesterday when he saw a female lying upon the thighs of a man and he was told by Mrs Randall that the female was Mrs Pentony that he was awoke in the night by John Egleton stating that he thought she was dead and he called Mr Seymour out of bed who said she was dead.

Thos Giles (signed)

Joseph Ryan a man of colour and a Canadian states (not on oath, being objected by the Coroner) that he slept in the Tap Room of Paul Randall last evening and seeing and knowing a woman laying in the same room drunk he wished to have a connection with her and said he would. He then told the servant of John Egleton that this was his intention and Egleton told him he should not but he persisted in endeavouring to complete his purpose. He approached the deceased and found the man upon whom she laid making a noise and he desisted for a short time and then he went a second time and found her thighs cold and says to the servant Egleton 'She wont do, she is cold, she is dead.' Then he says Egleton alarmed the house and Mrs Seymour got up and said she was defunct.

his
Joseph X Ryan
mark

Mrs Margaret Seymour being sworn states that she recollects the deceased came into the house of her father Paul Randall in the afternoon yesterday and she saw her drink a glass of brandy in the company of Skinner and that deceased was with Skinner the whole of the evening and during that time he had four or five half pints of brandy and she has no doubt but she, the deceased partook of those quantities having seen her after drinking the first glass of brandy in a state of perfect intoxication.

Margaret Seymour (signed)

Henry Francis Seymour states upon oath that he was called out of bed last night to look at the person of the deceased who was reported to him in a lifeless state and on examination of the body he found she was actually dead, and considers she came by her death from apoplexy brought on in all probability from intoxication knowing her for years past to be in the habit of drinking ardent spirits occasionally to excess.

Hy Fras Seymour (signed)

Cumberland

An inquisition indented taken before me at Richmond in the County aforesaid, in the third year of the reign of our Sovereign Lord the King, before me Thomas Hobby, Coroner on the seventh day of May, on the view of the body of Fanny Pentonny, then and there lying dead, upon the Oaths of

George Bowman	Joseph Baylis
Peter McAlpin	James Paget
John Wm John	James Roberts
Robert Martin	Matthew Hughes
James Vincent	Wm Carlisle
John Baylis	John Watts

Good and lawful men of the County aforesaid who being summoned and charged to enquire on the part of our Lord the King when, where and after what manner the said Fanny Pentony came to her death, do say upon their oath that the said Fanny Pentony came to her death on the evening of the sixth day of May in the year aforesaid from the excessive drinking of ardent spirits, and so the Jurors aforesaid do say that the said Fanny Pentony came to her death by the means aforesaid and not otherwise.

In witness whereof as well the aforesaid Coroner, as the Jurors aforesaid have to this Inquisition put their seals on the day and year and at the place first above mentioned.

Thomas Hobby (signed)
Coroner

CHAPTER 13

RECORDS OF CONVICTS AFTER THEIR ARRIVAL IN THE COLONY

(See Appendix 18)

The Colonial Office, Home Office and Privy Council records contain much detailed information about convicts after their arrival in Australia. These include pardons and tickets of leave granted in the colony, some of which outline the convicts' conduct during their time in Australia. Records are available which give the names of individuals to whom convicts were assigned, and there are lists of men assigned to government employment in dockyards, etc. There are also applications made by convicts to have their families sent over from Britain, and documents recording the deaths of convicts. Below are some examples from these documents.

COLONIAL OFFICE RECORDS

Sydney, New South Wales – Pardons from 1810

Table 13.1a: A List of Free Pardons granted by His Majesty and by His Excellency Governor Macquarie from 1810 to 1819 inclusive. *(TNA ref CO 201/118)*

Name	Year arrived	Ship arrived by	Date of sentence	Sentence
John G. Cradock	1809	*Adm. Gambier*	1807	Life
Wm Henderson	1798	*Barwell*	1797	Life
John Holden	1806	*Fortune*	1803	Life
W. Fielder als.Tubbs	1790	*Scarborough*	1789	Life
Eleanor Emmett	1807	*Sydney Cove*	1806	7 yrs
Sarah Mosse	1806	*Alexander*	1804	7 yrs
Sarah Townsend	1794	*Surprise*	1793	Life
Eleanor Leonard	1806	*Tellichery*	1804	7 yrs
William Eades	1807	*Duke of Portland*	1806	7 yrs

Name	Year arrived	Ship arrived by	Date of sentence	Sentence
Jerh Cavanagh	1800	*Friendship*	[blank]	Life
Mary Kell	1808	*Aeolus*	[blank]	7 yrs
Elizth Taylor	1806	*Alexander*	1805	7 yrs
Ann Nightingale	1808	*Aeolus*	[blank]	7 yrs
Richd Phillips	1799	*Hillsborough*	1798	Life
Mary Dorman	1808	*Aeolus*	[blank]	7 yrs
James Flannery	1802	*Atlas*	[blank]	Life
Elizth Kenworthy	1808	*Speke*	1805	7 yrs
Thomas Blake	1808	*Gamblin*	1806	Life
James Wright	1806	*Fortune*	1803	14 yrs
Sarah Brown	1804	*Experiement*	1803	7 yrs
James Cameron	1806	*Duke of Portland*	1806	7 yrs
Christr Kennedy	1796	*M. Cornwallis*[1]	1793	Life
Sush Harrison	1800	*Speedy*	1799	Life
Wm Barnfield	1800	*Royal Admiral*	1799	Life
Roger Gavin	1806	*Minerva*	1790	Life
Mary Crump	1809	*Indispensable*	1808	14 yrs
Thomas Barton	1796	*M. Cornwallis*	1793	Life
Cathe Jones	1806	*William Pitt*	1804	7 yrs
Anne Price	1806	ditto	1809	7 yrs
Sarah Mackenzie	1809	*Experiment*	1808	7 yrs
Mary Hands	1806	*William Pitt*	1804	7 yrs
Mary Baynon	1801	*Nile*	1797	Life
John Buckley	1803	*Calcutta*	1802	Life
Anne Smith	1808	*Aeolus*	1807	7 yrs
Richard Jones	1808	*Admiral Gambier*	1808	7 yrs
Jane Williams	1806	*William Pitt*	1804	7 yrs
Eleanor Hall	1808	*Speke*	1807	7 yrs
Mary Beckwith	1801	*Nile*	1800	Life
Thomas Tait	1806	*Duke of Portland*	1806	14 yrs
Thomas Robson	1806	*Fortune*	1804	7 yrs
etc., etc.				

Table 13.1b: A List of Conditional Pardons granted by His Excellency Governor Macquarie, from 1810 to 1819 inclusive. *(CO 201/118 continued)*

Year granted	Name	Year arrived	Ship arrived by	Date of Sentence	Sentence
1810	William Healey	1800	*Minerva*	1798	Life
"	John Birchall	1804	*Calcutta*	1802	Life

1. The ship *Marquis Cornwallis*.

PUBLIC NOTICE.

THE undermentioned Persons have obtained Certificates of Freedom during the last Week; viz.—

Agamemnon	*Barnard Glover*
Ditto	*William Butcher*
Asia (1)	*William Kitchen*
Ditto	*George Nish*
Baring (2)...............	*Joseph Davis*
Earl St. Vincent (2)	*William Brannan*
Henry	*James Power*
John Bull	*Celia Cox*
Ditto	*Eleanor Nolan*

Colonial Secretary's Office, March 9, 1827.

(The following was omitted in our last.)

Agamemnon	*Abraham Polack*
Ditto	*John Jacobs*
Ditto	*Henry Cook*
Ditto	*Samuel Wooller*
Ditto	*Samuel Myers*
Ditto	*Robert Leighton*
Ditto	*William Hanson*
Ditto....................	*J. Grummitt*
Asia(1)..................	*Patrick Collons*
Ditto	*William Bailey*
Ditto	*James Drover*
Dick....................	*Michael Robins*
Ditto	*Michael Sullivan*
Ditto...................	*John Griffis*
Dorothy	*James Horan*
Eliza(2)	*William Henry Lunnun*
Elizabeth(2)	*Henry Williams*
Ditto	*William King*
Guilford (6)	*Alexander Maguire*
Hebe	*Samuel Spruce*
Ditto	*William Green*
Morley (3)	*Margaret Oldham*
Ditto	*Sarah Downs*
Neptune (3)..............	*John Abwell*
Richmond	*Benjamin Morris*
Shipley (3)	*Francis Heniss*
Ditto	*Thomss Warburton*
Ditto	*Stephen Warren*
Ditto	*John Brown*
Ditto	*John Moore*
Ditto	*William Blackfield*
Ditto	*Francis Davy*
Ditto	*Samuel Gregory*
Speke(2).................	*Lazarus Barnett*
Surrey(3)................	*Joseph Gates*

Colonial Secretary's Office, March 2, 1827.

By His Excellency's Command,

ALEXANDER M'LEAY.

A public notice announcing Certificates of Freedom in *The Monitor*, Friday 16 March 1827. (The National Archives ref CO 201/181)

Convicts in New Holland, from *Malaspina Expedition Drawings*, 1793. (Library of New South Wales)

Table 13.1c: A List of the Tickets of Leave granted by His Excellency Governor Macquarie from 1810 to 1819 both inclusive. *(CO 201/118 continued)*

Granted		Name	Tried		Sentence	Arrived by	
Month	Year		Where	When		Ship	When
June	1810	John Drake		—		Coromandel	1804
		John Johnston		—		Anne	1810
		Simon Isaacs	Kingston	—		Cormandel	1804
		Sol. Wiseman	Old Bailey	Oct 1805	Life	Alexander	1806
		George Jubb	Leicester	—	Life	Fortune	1806
		Rd Anderson	Halifax	—	—	D. of Portland	1807
		Jas. Bendall	Surrey Sns	—	do	do	
		Wm. Waishman	Old Bailey	—	Life	Anne	1810
		Cr Coleman	Dublin	—	Life	Minerva	1799
		John Fowler	Limerick	—	Life	Atlas	1802
July	1810	Wm. Hathaway	Gloucester	—	Life	Glatton	1803
		John James	Worcester	—	Life	Coromandel	1802
		Jas. Ansell	Maidstone	—	—	Fortune	1806
		Wm. Burbridge	Old Bailey	—	—	Albermarle	1791
		James Lane	do	—	—	Fortune	1806
		Morris Connor	Middx. G.D.	—	14 yrs	do	do
		Pat. Daveron	Tipperary	—	Life	Atlas	1802
		John Town	Warwick	—	Life	Rl Adml	1800
		Sam. Read	Old Bailey	—	Life	Ganges	1797
		Jas. Carney	Clonmell	—	Life	Atlas	1802
		Wm. Davis	Kings Co.	—	Life	Friendship	1800
		Willm Silk	Waterford	—	Life	Britannia	1796
		John Waldron	Maidstone	—	14 yrs.	E. Cornwallis	1801
		Lawe. Baley	Dublin	—	Life	Tellicherry	1804
		Tho. McKeevey	Ireland	—	Life	Anne	1801
		Thos. Green	Worcester	—	14 yrs	Glatton	1803
		John Crawley	Bedford	—	Life	do	do
		P. Lutherborrow	York	—	Life	Barwell	1798
		etc., etc.					

Table 13.2: Account of Prisoners victualled by Government in the service of Gregory and John Blaxland Esqrs [dated 1814]. *(TNA ref CO 201/81)*

When received	Names	When discharged	No. of days victualled	Remarks
1806 May 15	William Cosgrove	12 Jan 1808	608	Govt Employ
ditto	Walter Power	11 Feb 1811	1733	Died
1807 April 27	Denis Riley	16 Feb 1808	296	Sydney Gaol
ditto	Owen Black	17 April 1808	355	Died
1808 May 15	Thomas Mahar	6 Oct 1810	1605	Govt Employ
1808 July 1	William Tumble	22 Aug 1808	783	Absconded
1808 May 15	William Smith	28 April 1810	1444	Free
1808 July 1	James Cavannah	7 April 1808	646	Free
1807 Oct 25	James McDonald	8 May 1818	201	Free
1806 July 1	John Fiztpatrick	8 May 1818	677	Free
1806 Aug 1	Thomas Roche	21 Aug 1806	21	Govt Employ
1806 Aug 1	William Webb	15 Sept 1806	46	Govt Employ
1806 Aug 1	Peter Millington	3 April 1807	246	Govt Employ
1807 Ap 27	John Cain	1 Nov 1807	189	Free
1806 Aug 1	John Newman	15 Aug 1806	15	Killed
1806 Aug 1	Joseph Bather	4 Jan 1812	2012	Sydney Gaol
1806 Aug 1	John Rogan	20 Jan 1812	2028	Free
1806 Aug 1	Patrick Shehan	28 Jan 1809	941	Absconded
1808 Oct 24	Christr Coleman	8 July 1809	258	Free
1808 Dec 24	Thomas Smart	24 Oct 1809	304	Govt Employ
1810 Oct 17	James Davis	4 Aug 1812	657	Free
1810 Mar 3	Robt Chapman	9 March 1812	736	Free
1810 Ap 28	Patrick Mahar	14 May 1810	17	Govt Employ
1810 Mar 3	Thomas Weedon	23 Jan 1813	4057	Free
1810 April 21	Thomas Glover	25 April 1810	5	Hospital
1810 May 10	ditto	11 Jan 1811	247	ditto
1811 Jan 25	ditto	4 Dec 1813	1043	
1809 Oct 24	John Bliss	4 Dec 1813	1502	
1810 Mar 3	Thos Chester	4 Dec 1813	1372	
1810 Mar 3	William Walker	4 Dec 1813	1372	
1810 Mar 3	George Higgins	4 Dec 1813	1372	
1810 Mar 3	Richd Kebble	4 Dec 1813	1372	
1812 Mar 9	Willm Hunt	4 Dec 1813	636	
			25876	

A list of forty-seven convicts is also given for Mr John Blaxland. Then follows:

Memorandum
It appears from Mr Gregory Blaxland's Agreement he was to have the number of forty men to be clothed and victualled at the expense of the Crown for the space of eighteen months, and by Mr John Blaxland's Agreement he was to receive the labor of eighty men to be clothed and victualled in like manner for eighteen months. Mr John Blaxland left the Colony for England in September, but Mr Gregory Blaxland who was the Partner and Agent to his Brother John, occasionally made Draughts of men in his absence from the Convicts which arrived from England, making no distinction at the time of drawing them, with regard to the number intended for each, but received them for the joint concern, and appropriated their Labor to such purposes as he thought proper, consequently no account but a joint one could be kept. It however appears from their own Returns on which this Account is formed that Mr Gregory Blaxland appropriated 3896 days labor for one man beyond what he was entitled to by his Agreement to his separate use and advantage which was a circumstance the Government of this Colony could neither foresee or prevent and as Mr John Blaxland made choice of his Brother as an Agent for his concerns during his absence he must of course look to him for renumeration of the labor appropriated for this separate use and advantage of his said Brother.

40 men for Mr Gregory Blaxland or 18 months is equal to	21,900 days
80 men for Mr John Blaxland for 18 months is equal to	43,800 days
	65,700
Mr Gregory Blaxland has received the Labor, Provisions & Clothing for	25,796 days
Mr John Blaxland has received do for	37,996
	63,792
Number of days labor and provisions due	1,908
	65,700

It appears by Mr Blaxland's returns which are corroborated by the Storekeepers that there are now twenty one men in his employ victualled at the expense of the Crown they will of course be entitled to be victualled up to the first of March 1815 which will complete the victualling as per Agreement.

It is necessary to observe that the List on which Mr Gregory Blaxland's Account is formed was not signed by him but Mr John Blaxland.

W. Broughton
D.A.C. Genl

Sydney
25 November 1814
Approved L. Macquarie

Convicts Employed at Sydney Station, Dockyard

Table 13.3: Sydney the 1st January 1822. Return of the Number of Convicts in the immediate Employ of Government at each Station, specifying the name of the Mechanics, date of Arrival and Period of Sentence. *(TNA ref CO 201/119)*

No.	Trade	Name	Arrived by Ship	Date of Arrival	Sentence Life 14 years	7 years
1	Shipwright	Robert Urcall	*Canada*	September 1819		1
2	do	Peter Penny	*Tottenham*	October 1819	1	
3	do	Jos Hannah	*Prince Regent*	August 1817		1
4	do	Jn O'Neil	*Guildford (3)*	January 1820		1
5	Caulker	Thos. Russell	*Recovery*	January 1820		1
6	do	Edwd. Ross	*Tottenham*	October 1818	1	
7	Blockmaker	Jos. Nipe	*Malabar*	October 1819	1	
8	Nailer	Wm. Hardy	*Tottenham*	October 1818		1
9	do	Geo. Hue	*Atlas (4)*	October 1819		1
10	do	Josh Bradley	*Agamemnon*	September 1820		1
11	do	Geo. Walsh	*Canada*	September 1819		1
12	do	Saml Lewis	*Marquis of Wellington*	January 1815	1	
13	do	Peter Perkins	*Larkins*	November 1817		1
14	do	Thomas Pardon	*Neptune (1)*	May 1818	1	
15	Hammerman	Edwd. Torin	*Mary*	August 1819		1
16	do	Jos. Walters	*Recovery*	December 1819	1	
17	do	Jas. Moxham	*Prince Regent*	January 1820	1	
18	do	Peter Henslow	*Globe*	January 1819		1
19	Blacksmith & fireman	Jas. Kenny	*Ocean (1)*	January 1816	1	
20	do	Thos. Andrews	*Atlas (4)*	October 1819		1
21	do	Wm Ashford	*Batavia*	April 1818		1
22	do	Jno Butle	*Tyne*	January 1819		1
23	Sawyer	Thomas Harford	*Gen. Stuart*	December 1818	1	
24	do	Willm Wallis	*Sir W.Bensley*	March 1817		1
25	Awl Maker	Wm Fowler	*Eliza*	January 1820	1	
26	Turner	Jno Neale	*Atlas (3)*	July 1816	1	
27	Boy Learner	Jno Puton	*Genl Stuart*	December 1818	1	
28	do	Thos Polter	*Malabar*	October 1819	1	
29	do	Wm Cameron	*Canada*	September 1819		1
30	do	Jno Lewdy[?]	*Daphne*	September 1819		1
31	do	Pat. Kullagher	*Mary*	August 1819		1
32	do	Philip Hide	do	August 1819		1

No.	Trade	Name	Arrived by Ship	Date of Arrival	Sentence Life 14 years	7 years
33	do	Henry Carment	Mariner	October 1816		1
34	do	Anty F. Kemp	Atlas	October 1819		1
35	do	Thos. Anderson	Alexander	April 1816		1
36	Sail Maker	Jas. Stewart	Larkins	November 1817	1	
37	do	Geo. Wood	Jno Barry	September 1819	1	
38	do	Saml Sheppard	Coromandel	April 1820	1	
39	Rope Maker	Thos. W. Hawke	Globe	[January]² 1819		1
40	do	Hugh Gigney	Mary	August 1819		1

There follows lists of men employed in the lumber yard: carpenters, bellows master, chair-maker, blacksmith and fireman, deputy overseer, hammerman, tool-sharpener, locksmith, vice-man, nailers, wire drawer and cordmaker, farrier and horse-shoer, iron-plate worker, tinman, gimblet-maker, brass-founder, brass-finisher, brass-moulder, iron-founder, overseer of brass and iron foundry, coppersmith, wheelwright, millwright coopers, shoemakers, tailors, saddlers, painter and glazier, plasterer, bricklayer, stone-cutter, blasters and rough mason.

Deaths Recorded in the Colony (Including Free Settlers)

The names of convicts, such as Stephen Wilfoil, who died in the colony were recorded and sent to the Colonial Office in Britain:

> Liverpool 28th March 1816: Stephen Wilfoil a Government Servant of Mr Oakley (slain in a sudden quarrel by a blow given on 17 March), came to the Colony by the ship *Three Bees*, aged about 50 years, a native of Sligo, about 5ft. 9 inches high, stout made.

Table 13.4: Liverpool for the quarter ending 25 March 1819. *(TNA ref CO 201/138)*

Name	Free or Convict	If Convict by what Ship	Age	When Deceased	Sudden Death
James Kale	Free	—	64	Jan 4	
Elizabeth Fletcher	Free	—	68	Feb 4	
Margaret Skinner	Free	—	55	Feb 24	
Samuel Jackson	Prisoner	Ocean	27	Feb 27	Killed by the fall of a tree
Patrick Hickey	Prisoner	1st Surrey	34	March 6	Dysentry
Joseph Sorton	Prisoner	1st Surrey	25	March 5	Drowned
Patrick Ward	Prisoner	Chapman	25	March 14	Shot
Samuel Croker	Prisoner	Isabella	20	March 19	Cramp in the stomach

2. The month is not given.

Table 13.5: Return of Prisoners who have died in the Colony of New South Wales from the first day of January 1840 to the thirty first of December 1840, inclusive. *(TNA ref CO 201/309)*

Name		Ship	Date of Burial	Year of Arrival
Aylett	John	*Barossa*	7 Jany 1840	1839
Atkinson	John	*Minerva (5)*	5 Feby 1840	1824
Agg	David	*Barrossa*	3 " "	1839
Ashurst	Nathaniel	do	8 " "	1839
Aston	David	*Genl Hewitt*	16 March "	1818
Archer	William	*John II*	9 June "	1827
Austin	William	*Woodbridge*	24 June "	1840
Austin	James	*Eden*	22 Novr "	1840
Ahern	Michael	*Brampton*	17 Novr "	1823
Ansell	John	*Mangles*	28 April "	1824
Braddick	William	*Royal Sovereign*	Jany "	1835
Blackburn	Henry	*Woodbridge*	1 July "	1840
Burt	Henry	do	26 July "	1840
Beale	Robert	*Jas Pattison*	9 July "	1837
Blansdon	Richard	*Asia (9)*	21 Jany "	1832
Braks	Stephen	do	10 Jany "	1832
Bell	John	*John Barry*	9 Mar "	1839
Burke	Patrick	*Blenheim*	21 Mar "	1839
Bodell	Thomas	*Barrossa*	21 Mar "	1839
Brophy	Michael	*Augusta Jessie*	22 Mar "	1840
Barlow	Thomas	*Barrossa*	22 Mar "	1839
etc., etc.				

The Principal Superintendent of Convicts in New South Wales often reported in the *Monitor* and the *Government Gazette*. Some copies of these publications are to be found bound together with colonial correspondence in TNA document class CO 201.

The following is taken from the *Monitor*, 16 March 1827:

TNA ref CO 201/181

Public Notice

The undermentioned Persons have obtained Certificates of Freedom during the last week, viz:

Agamemnon	Barnard Glover
Ditto	William Butcher
Asia (1)	William Kitchen
ditto	George Nish
Baring (2)	Joseph Davis
Earl St. Vincent (2)	William Brannan
Henry	James Power
John Bull	Celia Cox
ditto	Eleanor Nolan

Colonial Secretary's Office, March 9, 1827

The following was omitted in our last:

Agamemnon	Abraham Pollack
ditto	John Jacobs
ditto	Henry Cook
ditto	Samuel Wooller
ditto	Samuel Myers
ditto	Robert Leighton
ditto	William Hanson
ditto	J. Grummitt
Asia (1)	Patrick Collins
ditto	William Bailey
ditto	James Drover
ditto	Michael Robins
ditto	Michael Sullivan
ditto	John Griffis
Dorothy	James Horan
Eliza (2)	William Heney Lunnun
Elizabeth (2)	Henry Williams
ditto	William King
Guildford (6)	Alexander Maguire
Hebe	Samuel Spruce
ditto	William Green
Morley (3)	Margaret Oldham
ditto	Sarah Downs
Neptune (3)	John Atwell
Richmond	Benjamin Morris
Shipley (3)	Francis Heness
ditto	Thomas Warburton
ditto	Stephen Warren
ditto	John Brown
ditto	John Moore
ditto	William Blackfield
ditto	Francis Davy
ditto	Samuel Gregory
Speke (3)	Lazarus Barnett
Surrey (3)	Joseph Gates

Colonial Secretary's Office
Alexander M'Leay

TNA ref CO 201/263

Superintendent of Convicts

The following is taken from the *Government Gazette* for Wednesday, 28th June 1837.

June 27, 1837

The undermentioned Prisoners having absconded from the individuals and employment set against their respective names, and some of them being at large with stolen Certificates and Tickets of Leave, all Constables and others are hereby required and commended to use their utmost exertion in apprehending and lodging them in safe custody. Any person harbouring or employing any of the said Absentees will be prosecuted as the Law directs.

John Ryan BRENAN
Principal Superintendent of Convicts

Taylor, Thomas, alias Henley, Thomas, *Minerva* (5), 30 Newcastle-upon-Tyne, writing master, 5 feet – 7¾ inches

Tickets-of-Leave Cancelled

The Tickets-of-Leave granted to the following persons have been cancelled for the reasons set against their respective names, viz:

Byrne, John, *Captain Cook* (1), drunkenness.

Bagnall, John, *Minstrel* (2), out of his district without a pass.

Hancock, Charles, *Malabar* (1), bad character.

Kenny, Patrick, *Mariner* (3), neglect of muster and absent from district.

Mercer, Martin, *Marquis of Huntly* (2), sentenced to be worked in irons for 12 calendar months, for an assault.

Parsons, William, *Lord Eldon*, out of district without a pass.

By His Excellency's Command,
E. Deas Thomson

Colonial Secretary's Office
Sydney, 19th June 1837

The undermentioned articles, which were in the possession of James Woodgate, a prisoner of the Crown, by the ship *Norfolk*, who lately held a Ticket-of-leave for the district of Bathurst, when that indulgence was withdrawn, having been detained by the Police: Notice is herby given, that the same will be sold by Auction at Bathurst at twelve o'clock on Wednesday the 5th day of July next, for the benefit of the parties to whom the said Woodgate was indebted, who will render an account of their claims to the Police Magistrate of the District for investigation, within ten days from the date of the Sale, namely:

One Mare
One Horse
Two Saddles
Two Bridles and other Articles.

Also, at the same time and place will be sold, thirty head of Cattle found in the possession of John Carter, per ship *Vittoria*, a Prisoner of the Crown.

By His Excellency's Command.
E. Deas Thomson

HOME OFFICE RECORDS

Records of the deaths of convicts were often sent to the Home Office. The following are examples.

'A Government Jail Gang. Sydney N.S. Wales. 1830', from A. Earle, *Views of New South Wales and Van Diemen's Land* (London, 1830). (Library of New South Wales)

Table 13.6: Returns of all Convicts deceased in New South Wales so far as known to the Principal Superintendent of Convicts for the year 1829. *(TNA ref HO 7/2)*

No.	Name	Ship	Age	Date of Burial or Death	District or Parish	Remarks
				1829		
1	Ardis, Robert	*Dick*	60	Feb. 23	St. Johns, Parramatta	
2	Allen, George	*Baring* (2)	29	Feb. 26	St. James, Sydney	
3	Arthur, Alexander	*Atlas*	66	Feb. 30	Windsor	Free
4	Aspinall, Robert	*Larkins*	67	April 18	St.Philip, Sydney	
5	Allen, Thomas	*M. Hastings*	–	April 18	–	
6	Allen, John	*Mangles*	40	July 25	Moreton Bay	
7	Allman, Wm. E.	*Cornwallis*	59	Dec. 3	St. James, Sydney	
8	Atkins, George	*Guildford*	26	Nov. 11	Newcastle	
9	Birmingham, Benjn	*Malabar*	44	Jan. 5	St. Philip, Sydney	
10	Brown, George	*Hadlow* (1)	55	Jan. 19	St. James	

No.	Name	Ship	Age	Date of Burial or Death	District or Parish	Remarks
11	Brown, Wm Henderson	Hooghley	38	Feb. 27	Marellan	
12	Balden, Thomas	Genl Stewart	56	Mar. 2	St. Johns, Parramatta	
13	Brown, John	Morley	40	Mar. 7	Castlereagh	
14	Brignell, Rebecca	Lord Sidmouth	42	Mar. 9	St. James	Free
15	Boxo, John	Came Free	43	Ap. 25	Macquarie	A Convict
16	Byrne, Patrick	Cts. Harcourt	30	Ap. 30	Moreton Bay	
17	Browne, John	Royal George	35	May 1	Bathurst	
18	Barlow, James	Eliza	27	May 12	Parramatta	
19	Bradley, John	Surprise	95	May 16	Windsor	
20	Ball, John	Prince Regent	28	May 21	Moreton Bay	
21	Bias, Thomas	Prince Regent	34	May 13	Liverpool	
22	Burridge, Robert	Atlas (3)	49	June 11	Liverpool	
23	Bunyan, John	Champion	–	May 16	At The Manning	Reported 16 May 1829
24	Bishop, William	Somersetshire	61	June 17	St. James, Sydney	
25	Brennan, Peter	Hadlow	52	July 1	Liverpool	Free
26	Banks, Thomas	Prince of Orange	50	July 4	St. James, Sydney	
27	Bowman, Margt Wilkinson	Canada	32	July 4	Liverpool	Free
28	Burke, John	Indefatigable	71	Aug. 19	Windsor	
29	Baker, William	Neptune	58	Sept. 1	Windsor	
231	Reilly, James	Cs Harcourt	24	June 6	Moreton Bay	Killed by the natives
237	Simmons, Henry	Coromandel	63	Mar 25	Windsor	Ticket of Leave
238	Smith, Stephen	Asia (1)	–	June	Norfolk Island	Drowned
241	Swift, James	Mangles (1)	–	July		Accidentally shot while assisting the constables in search of bushrangers
243	Smith Benjamin	Fame	39	May 10		Ticket of Leave. Suicide
247	Smith, John	Albion	–	July 7		Drowned in the Parramatta River by the upsetting of a Govt. Boat to which he belonged
etc., etc.						

Table 13.7a: Return of One Thousand Four Hundred and Forty Two Tickets of Leave granted in New South Wales between the 1st day of January and the 31st day of December 1834 inclusive. *(TNA ref HO 10/31)*

Name	Ship		Tried		Sentence
			Where	When	
Martin Murphy	Lonach		Kilkenny	21 Aug. 1824	Life
John Moore	Minerva (5)	1824	Middx G.D.	7 April 1824	14 yrs.
Charles Rodins	Sarah	1829	Westminster Q.S.	3 April 1829	7 yrs.
Ann Goldie or Hughes, wife of Bernard Hughes	Louisa	1827	Glasgow C I	7 May 1827	14 yrs.
Henry Price	Baring (2)	1819	Monmouth Ass.	10 Aug. 1818	Life
Michl Buckley	Recovery (2)	1825	County Cork	19 Aug. 1822	Life
Joseph Clarke	Royal Charlotte	1825	Worcester Ass.	31 July 1824	Life
Ann Manby or Wales	Louisa	1827	Glasgow C I	7 May 1827	7 yrs.
John Fleming	Eliza (5)	1829	Cork County	28 Aug. 1828	7 yrs.
William Bell	Waterloo	1820	Cambridge Q.S.	14 July 1828	7 yrs.
Ann Getgood alias Getwood	Asia (7)	1830	Armagh	Spring 1829	7 yrs.
Garrett Kavenhagh	Govr Ready	1829	Carlow	23 Mch. 1828	7 yrs.
Mary Bates	Prins Royal	1829	Warwick	13 Oct. 1828	7 yrs.
Patk Goulden	Sophia	1829	Cavan	8 Mch. 1828	7 yrs.
Jas. Mackenzie	Minerva	1821	Nottingham Ass.	16 Mch. 1821	Life
Thos Forrester	Surry (4)	1823	Warwick Ass.	30 Mch. 1822	Life
John Bridger	John (2)	1829	Middx G.D.	12 July 1827	7 yrs.
Jas. Farmer	Eliza (4)	1826	Lancaster Q.S.	21 Jany 1828	7 yrs.
Thos Sears	Guildford	1824	Sussex Special G.D.	23 Dec.1823	Life
Jas. Haslom	America	1829	Lancaster Q.S.	21 July 1828	7 yrs.
Thos. Cooper	Sesostris	1826	Suffolk Ass.	28 July 1825	Life
John Collins Firman	John Barry (2)	1821	Kildare County	29 Mch.1820	Life
Matthew Todd	Jas. Pattison	1830	City Dublin	22 Sept. 1829	7 yrs.
John Fox	Regalia	1826	Antrim	20 July 1825	14 yrs.
George Burghall	Albion (2)	1828	Chester Q.S.	14 Jany 1820	7 yrs.
Thos Brown	Recovery (1)	1819	London G.D.	13 Jany 1819	Life
John Geo. Jelf alias George Jelfe	John (2)	1819	Middx G.D.	29 May 1828	7 yrs.
Nathaniel Davies	Bl Merchant (1)[3]	1828	Middx G.D.	21 Feb 1828	7 yrs.
Thos Bolt	Norfolk (1)	1825	Devon Ass.	22 Mch. 1824	Life
Adam Finch	Norfolk (1)	1825	Essex Ass.	2 Aug 1824	Life
Richard Franklin	Hercules (2)	1825	Berks Ass.	26 July 1824	Life
Danl Leahy	Eliza (5)	1825	Cork County	8 Aug. 1828	7 yrs.

| Name | Ship | | Tried | | Sentence |
			Where	When	
Michl Murphy	*Eliza* (5)	1829	Limerick Co.	24 July 1828	7 yrs.
William Pratt	*Waterloo* (1)	1829	Hertford Q.S.	13 Oct. 1828	7 yrs.
Edwd Sharpe	*Asia* (5)	1825	Suffolk Ass.	5 Aug. 1824	Life
John Beck	*Sophia*	1829	Down	14 Aug. 1827	7 yrs.
Patk Howard	*Eliza* (5)	1829	Kings County	13 Mch. 1828	7 yrs.
Thos Toomey	*America*	1829	Lancaster Q.S.	21 July 1828	7 yrs.
Isiah Bently	*Eliza* (4)	1828	York Ass.	2 Mch. 1828	7 yrs.
Willm Aldridge	*Minerva* (4)	1821	Hertford Ass.	7 Mch. 1821	Life
John Bayliss	*Hercules* (2)	1825	Stafford Ass.	11 Mch. 1824	Life
Charles Goodwin	*America*	1829	Lincoln Q.S.	19 April 1828	7 yrs.
Charles Husk	*Speke* (2)	1821	Gloucester Ass.	9 Aug. 1820	7 yrs.
William Beany	*Norfolk* (1)	1825	Sussex Ass.	22 Mch. 1824	Life
George Dorking	*Norfolk* (1)	1825	Suffolk - Sept G.D.	2 Aug. 1824	Life
Josh Garrad	*Norfolk* (1)	1825	Essex Ass.	2 Aug. 1824	Life
Jane Johnston	*Asia*	1830	City Dublin	23 Jny. 1823	7 yrs.
Patk Keegan	*Cambridge*	1827	City Dublin per M.R	1 Nov. 1826	7 yrs.
Denis Mallowny	*Lonach*	1825	Cork City per M.R.	Aug. 1824	Life
John Reagan	*Gov. Ready*	1829	County Cork	31 Mch. 1828	Life
Saml Hall the yr	*Norfolk* (1)	1825	Norfolk Ass.	21 Mch. 1824	Life
William Mace	*Guildford* (7)	1827	Chester Ses.	3 Ap. 1826	7 yrs.
Thos Bridges	*America*	1829	Kent S.S. of G.D.	15 Dec. 1828	7 yrs.
Samuel Gent	*Mangles* (1)	1820	Lancaster Ass.	1 Sept. 1819	Life
James Sheirin	*Eliza* (5)	1829	Cork City per M.R.	8 Aug. 1828	7 yrs.
Saml Povey	*Waterloo*	1829	Sussex S.S. of G.D.	20 Dec. 1828	7 yrs.
Roger Dobson	*Ocean* (3)	1823	York Ass.	20 July 1822	Life
Willm Chambers	*Norfolk* (2)	1829	York Q.S.	15 Jany 1829	7 yrs.
Patk Dalton	*St. Vincent* (3)	1823	Meath County per M.R.	9 Aug. 1822	Life
Philip Hammet	*Norfolk* (1)	1825	Devon Ass.	22 Mch. 1824	Life
etc., etc.					

3. Bengal Merchant.

Table 13.7b: Schedule of Free Pardons granted in Van Diemen's Land, c. 1838. *(TNA ref HO 10/31 continued)*

Name	Ship	Date of Trial	Sentence	Period in the Colony	Period C.P.[4]	Observations
Wm Evans	*Recovery*	22 Mch 1819	Life	19 yrs	7 yrs	No offence recorded against this man since his arrival in the Colony and the Police Magistrate at Oatlands and others certify his character.
Robt Graham	–	Dec 1820	Life	17 yrs	5 yrs	Without offence since his arrival and recommended by several Gentlemen.
Rose Jones	–	21 July 1817	Life	19 yrs	4 yrs	No offence recorded since her arrival.
Henry Ashworth	–	23 Mch 1852	Life	15 yrs	[blank]	[blank]
Owen Maloney	–	1811	Life	20 yrs	4 yrs	Granted on the late King's Birthday being without offence since his arrival.
John Taylor	–	14 Mch 1822	Life	16 yrs	3 yrs	Granted on the late King's birthday being also without offence since arrival and possessing high testimonials of character
Martin Callaghan	*Minerva*	1817	Life	19 yrs	6 yrs	Very strongly recommended by Magistrates of his District and without offence since his arrival
Corns Jones	*Morley*	20 Mch 1822	Life	15 yrs	3 yrs	No offence on record since his arrival and very favourably recommended by the Sheriff and others
Robt Greenan or Graham	–	Aug. 1817	Life	19 yrs	7 yrs	Without offence since his arrival and strongly recommended
Stephen Dennings	*Countess Harcourt*	13 Sept 1820	Life	17 yrs	5 yrs	No offence recorded during the entire period of his service in the Colony and his character favourably certified by respectable individuals

4. C.P.: Conditional Pardon held for the following number of years.

Name	Ship	Date of Trial	Sentence	Period in the Colony	Period C.P.[4]	Observations
David Solomon	*Arab*	20 Feby 1822	Life	15 yrs	7 yrs	Without offence since his arrival and highly recommended by the chairman of Quarter Sessions and several Magistrates and other Gentlemen of Launceston
Michael McElhatton	*Minerva*	Aug 1817	Life	19 yrs	8 yrs	No offence recorded during the entire period of his service and his character strongly certified
George Rew	*Fanny & Pilot*	1814	Life	20 yrs	7 yrs	Without offence since his arrival and very highly recommended
Denis Currington Carin	*Minerva*	July 1817	Life	19 yrs	6 yrs	No offence on record and recommended by several respectable inhabitants in the neighbourhood of Pitwater
Michl Hanton	*Minerva*	July	Life	19 yrs	7 yrs	No offence on record and his Certificates of Character subscribed by the Sheriff and several respectable Merchant of Hobart Town

PRIVY COUNCIL RECORDS

TNA ref PC 1/67 (Oct 1819)

Petitions for Free Pardons

Hobart Town
Van Diemens Land
November 17th 1818

To the Right Honourable Lord Fitzgerald.
My Lord, I here take the liberty of troubling your Lordship with a letter to inform you that my conduct since I have been in this Colony has enabled me to obtain a Conditional Pardon. I was promised a Free Pardon but I fear it will be a considerable time. Before I left England I hope I may beg to intrude upon your goodness once more to precure me a free pardon in hopes that I may be enabled to see my native land and to prove my gratitude for your kindness. I wrote two letters to your Lordship before but as I heard nothing from you I was fearful my letters never come to your hands.

Part of the list of free pardons granted in New South Wales between 1810 and 1820. (The National Archives ref CO 201/118)

I return your Lordships many thanks for the letters of recommendations you gave mee to bring to this Colony, they were very serviceable to me and family. I gave them to Liet. Governor Col. Davey but he never return them to me again. I hope this will find your Lordship and all your good family in good health and I remain your Lordships most humble and grateful servant.

John McCoy

I gott my Conditional Pardon for discovering lime stone and I burnt a great quantity of lime for government and was promised a free but only got a conditional pardon.

PC 1/67 (Oct 1819) continued

Paris
October 5th 1819

My Lord,

I once took the liberty some years ago of troubling your Lordship respecting the unfortunate man the writer of the enclosed letter who stated to your Lordship was a person well known to me, and of exceeding good character until in a drunken frolic he fell a victim and became the Dupe of the worst of characters. Your Lordship, when he was condemned to transportation, very kindly allowed him the indulgence of taking his wife and child with him, if not in the same vessel at least in the same fleet. If your Lordship would extend your goodness to him so far as to make enquiry whether his statements are true whether, he continues a deserving person and finding them correct would grant the Prayer of his Petition. I firmly believe you could not find an object on whom Pardon could be better bestowed. I have the honour your Lordships most obedient and very humble servant.

Henry Fitgerald

Alphabetical List of Prisoners and others employed at His Majesty's Agricultural Establishment Emu Plains Nov.r 1820

	Time received	Ship came in	Names	N.o	Time received	Ship came in	Names
1	1820 Jan.y	1	Recovery	Ayres Isaac	33	1820 Oct.r	3 Dorathy	Brennan Phil.
2	1819 Nov.r	2 Granada	Askey John	34	"	"	Brien O. Robert
3	1820 Oct.r	3 Dorathy	Ansley James	35	"	"	Byrne Turner
4	1819 Nov.r	2 Granada	Bayes John	36	"	Agamm	Bush Joseph
5	"	"	Bagley Thomas	37	"	"	Barton Tho.s
6	"	"	Blackwell Wm	38	"	"	Brennan Van. Nb
7	"	"	Blackwell Jo.t	39	1819 Nov.r	2 Granada	Bots John
8	"	"	Bruce Thomas	40	"	"	Calkham Wm
9	"	"	Burges John	41	"	"	Carter John
10	"	"	Baker George	42	"	"	Clarke Wm
11	"	"	Baker Richard	43	"	"	Carpenter John
12	"	"	Bingley William	44	1820 Jan.y	1 Minerva	Clowry Tho.s
13	"	"	Bennett Rich.d	45	"	"	Clowry John
14	"	"	Bennett Tho.s	46	1819 Nov.r	2 Granada	Cleworth Henry
15	"	"	Bailey James	47	1820 Jan.y	1 Recovery	Constantine Tho.s
16	Jan.y	1 Recovery	Barrow James	48	Feb.y	3 Eliza	Charters John
17	"	"	Baird John	49	"	"	Cunningham Brien
18	"	"	Brooks John 1.st	50	July	31 Neptune	Catling Robert
19	"	"	Brooks John 2.d	51	Aug.t	17 Mangles	Carr Richard
20	"	Minerva	Brewer John	52	"	"	Pullen John
21	"	"	Brien Thomas	53	Oct.r	3 Dorathy	Connain Charles
22	1819 Nov.r	2 Granada	Boothroyd Wm	54	"	"	Colbolly John
23	1820 Feb.y	20 Eliza	Bennett Robert	55	"	"	Campbell John
24	Aug.t	17 Mangles	Brown William	56	"	"	Carcurran Luke
25	Sep.r	2 E.&.V.t	Bellamy William	57	"	"	Carroll James
26	"	"	Bucknell Henry	58	"	Agamm	Clarke Reuben
27	"	Chapman	Bennett Mic.l	59	"	"	Cook Henry
28	"	Isabella	Buckley Tho.s	60	"	"	Cordray Joseph
29	"	23 Daphne	Barry Thomas	61	"	"	Pope Thomas
30	Oct.r	3 Dorathy	Brien O Tim.o	62	1819 Nov.r	2 Granada	Daver Thomas
31	"	"	Baylen Richard	63	"	"	Deaton John
32	"	"	Barker Richard	64	"	"	Deaton William

Part of the list of prisoners employed at Emu Plains Agricultural Establishment, November 1820.
(The National Archives ref CO 201/119)

TNA ref PC 1/67 (April 1819)

A Letter Asking for Material Comforts

Portsea, April 19th, 1819

Sir,

The friends of John Curl at present a convict at Botany Bay have applied to me. I address a letter to you requesting you will have the goodness to submit before my Lord Sidmouth that he wishes them to send out for his uses a Pipe Mould, some books and Garden Seeds and understanding from the Customs House at this place that such cannot be permitted without an order from my Lord Sidmouth. This is therefore to pray his Lordship's goodness and philanthropy in granting it. The same signifies to me (as there are several ships bound to Botany) thro your polite attention addressed to me at Mr Beatties, Common Hard will oblige.

Sir, Your Respectful Hble Servant
Thomas Downer

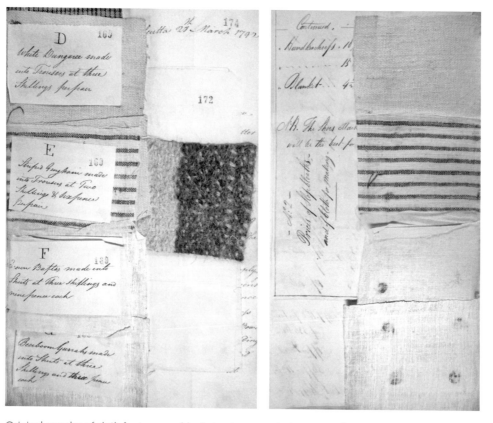

Original samples of cloth for trousers, blankets, etc., worn by transported convicts. Filed at The National Archives with Colonial Office documents for the year 1792, these are the earliest examples to be found. (The National Archives ref CO 201/7)

CHAPTER 14

FREE PASSAGE FOR THE FAMILIES OF CONVICTS

Many of the wives and children of convicts were given a free passage to be reunited with their husbands. There are numerous letters from convicts requesting that their families be allowed to join them. Sometimes a letter of application for a passage to the colony is found from the wife of a convict. These letters are to be found in the Colonial Office correspondence at The National Archives in record class CO 201. The following are some examples.

TNA ref CO 201/28 [undated, filed with the reports for the year 1808]

A List of the Wives of Convicts Given a Passage to New South Wales

List of Persons ordered on board the ship *Experiment*, for a passage to New South Wales, by Mr Secretary King.

Jane, wife of John Harman, a convict
Sarah, wife of James Stanton a convict
Maria, wife of Anthony Jonquay a convict, and 2 children
Catherine, wife of William Allen, a convict
Christiana, wife of Robert Beams, a convict
[blank], wife of William Lane, a convict
Ann, wife of John Roberts, a convict
Grace, wife of James May, a convict, and 2 children
Mary, wife of Thos McGrath, a convict, and 1 child
Ann, wife of Thos Brown, a convict
    10 women and 5 children

Table 14.1: List of Females who have prayed Permission to be sent to New South Wales in order to join their Husbands (Convicts) in that Colony. *(TNA ref CO 201/75; the list is undated but is filed in the year 1814.)*

Name	Age	Wife of	Sentence	No. of Children
Mary Ritchie		John Ritchie	Transported for 14 years	Five
Ann Moore		John Moore	Life	
Sophia Hart		Benjamin Hart	Life	
Harriett Godderd		John Godderd	Life	Three
Elizabeth Curl		Thomas Curl	Life	Two
Sarah Oatley		James Oatley	Life	One
Mary Thurston		— Thurston	Life	
Mary Thorby		William Thorby	Life	Three
— Hickey		John Hickey	14 years	Four
Hester Abraham	23	— Abraham	Life	Three
Hannah Dodman		Thomas Dodman	Life	Two
Martha Pinnell		James Pinnell	14 years	
— Scott		James Scott	Life	Three
Ann Saverson [sic]		Adam Sarverson [sic]	Life	Four
Cordelia Wheeler		Richard Wheeler	Life	Two
Jane Lees	28	William Lees	Life	
Ann Clements		W.R. Clements	Life	
Harriet Clements ·		John Clements	Life	
Dorothy Walker		Richard Walker	14 years	Five
Mary Spittle		Thomas Spittle	14 years	One
Sophia Mason		Squire Mason	14 years	
Mary Brown		John Brown	Life	
Susannah Jones	34	Thomas Jones	Life	
Sophia Ward		Michael Ward	Life	One
Charlotte Dixon		Thos Dixon	14 years	Two
Mary Moon		John Moon	Life	
Sarah Wheeler		Charles Wheeler	Life	
Susan Hill		Robert Hill	Life	
Mary Barnes	22	John Barnes	Life	
Esther Shevill (exception to general rule upon the ground that her father and mother are also at New South Wales – the former as a convict for Life)		John Shevill	7 years	
Eleanor Plomer		Peter Wm Plomer	Life	
Mary Russell		John Russell	Life	One
Ann Morley	22	James Morley	Life	Two

Name	Age	Wife of	Sentence	No. of Children
— Locke		John Locke	Life	Two
Harriett Herring	22	Henry Herring	Life	
Ellen Sewell		George Sewell	Life	Two
Ann Noble		— Noble	Life	Two
Maria Cribb		George Cribb	14 years	
Mary Huggins		— Huggins	Life	5 Children
Rachael Wyatt		Joseph Wyatt	Life	
Ann Riddell		J.R. Riddell	Life	5 Children
— Childs alias Giles		John Childs alias Giles	Life	

Mrs Bray wife of Wm Bray, Life, 3 Children
Mrs Hannam wife of Reuben Hannam, 2 Children
Mary Bradbury, daughter of — Bradbury
These three last under the authority of Earl Bathurst

Applications from Convicts for their Families to be sent out to Them

Table 14.2: An example from List of persons who have made Application for their Wives and Families to be sent out from England or Ireland. *(TNA ref CO 201/85; this example is undated but appears with the reports for the year 1817)*

		[now] free
Applicant's Name	Mary Plouright	
Ship	*Indispensible* (2)	
Date of Arrival	1809	
Tried – Place	Nottingham Assizes	
Tried – When	4 Aug. 1808	
Trade	—	
Sentence	7 years	
Childrens' Names	6 children	
Ages	—	
Place of Residence	Married in the name of Mary Pear to John Goddard at St. Mary's Church, Kegworth, Leicestershire about 32 years since, had issue 3 children christened at Loughborough in the same parish. Married 2nd time William Ploughwright to Mary Goddard about 20 years since, at St. Mary's Church, Nottingham. Issue 3 children: Elizabeth, William and Henry, christened at the same church; which 6 children she requests to be sent out. Apply to —— Goddard at Martletts Court, Bow Street, Covent Garden, London.	

TNA ref CO 201/408 [undated, filed in the year 1848]

The Wife of a Convict Requesting a Free Passage to New South Wales

My Lord,

Having received a letter from my husband Andrew Kehoe, formerly a convict for 7 years, but now a herd to George Wise Esq. near Yeses, New South Wales, he is upwards of 20 years in the colony his letter mentions 'that the Governor of the Colony has given out an order for any person that has a wife and family at home shall be sent out to their husband free of expense if they wish to come out. I have therefore given in an application for you and my family to be sent out to me and you will receive notice from the Home Government to that effect in due time.'

I now request my Lord, to know if the above statement is a verity, and to state that I have two sons and one daughter. One of my sons is in the constabulary, the other at home with me, and my daughter a farm servant, and that I can provide any certificates required if the statement be correct.

Your Lordship's answer will oblige
Yr Obt Servt
Mary Kehoe

Mr Elliot – This is one of many applications which will no doubt be made in consequence of the unqualified terms in which the recent notice of the local Government has been issued.

9 March

It is quite clear that this poor woman may be refused. Her husband was transported 20 years ago, for 7 years and now has been free for 13 years.

T.F.E.

Certainly say we cannot find to have the means of paying for her passage if he thinks proper.

20 March 1848

Mary Kehoe

I am directed by Earl Grey to acknowledge the receipt of your letter without date, requesting information in regard to the accuracy of a statement which you have received from your husband, formerly a convict in New South Wales, respecting the grant of a free passage to enable you, with the rest of your family, to join him in that Colony.

In reply to this application Lord Grey desires me to observe that the indulgence of sending out the wives and families of convicts, free of expense, is only granted in cases where the circumstances of the convicts themselves and of their friends or relatives in this Country are such as to render the assistance of H.M. Govt indispensable. In the present instance however it appears that your husband was transported 20 years ago for a period of 7 years. He must therefore have been a free man during the last 13 years, and has had sufficient opportunity to gain by his industry the means of paying for your passage to N.S. Wales should he feel so inclined to do so. His Lordship regrets therefore that he is unable to allow you to be sent out at the public expense.

[unsigned]

Immigration N.S. Wales
Chryh Baltinglass, Ireland

15th May 1848

My Lord

Having this day received a letter from my husband Andrew Kehoe dated Drummondiel near Yass, New South Wales 2nd Decr '47 purporting 'did you memorial this Home Government as I directed you in my last letter for a passage for yourself and family to this Colony as my Master Mr Wyse has been speaking to the Governor here who told him there was nothing to prevent you getting a free passage. I therefore beg leave to say that I forwarded a memorial to your Lordship on the 3rd March last and on the 9th I received a letter from the Colonial Land and Emigration Office stating or purporting "I could not get a Free Passage".'

The certificates alluded to in my husbands letter I could get in a few minutes as I am living in the townland where myself, my husband and children were born and although he was induced in one night through the influence of liquor and had company to convicts the such acts for which he was sent away for 7 years no man in this Parish will get a better character previous to that night. He is now nearly 21 years away and it appears that after the expiration of his sentence he resumed his former good character in being with the said Gentleman ever since. Should your Lordship deign to favour me with an answer I shall be grateful.

Humble subscribed by
Mary Kehoe

Inform the applicant that if it should be decided to send her and her family out to N.S. Wales due intervention will be given to her. Recommendation of her husband for this indulgence has not come from the Governor.

Table 14.3: Part of 'List of Persons who have made Application for their Wives and Families to be sent from England or Ireland'. *(TNA ref CO 201/85)*

Applicants Names	Ship Arrived In	Date of Arrival	Tried		Trade	Sentence
			Where	When		
Simon McGuiggan	*Britania*	1797	Co. Tyrone	1797	Labourer	[blank]
William Todhunter	*Morley*	April 1817	London	Sept. 1816	Clerk	14 yrs
Thomas Rollinson	*Fame*	March 1817	Exeter	March 1816	Smith	14 yrs
William Faulkner	*Atlas* (3)	July 1816	Warwick	July 1815	Labourer	14 yrs
William Cowley	*Earl Spencer*	1813	Maidstone	1812	Labourer	-
John Kidwall	*Surrey* (1)	August 1814	Exeter	Aug. 1813	Shoe Maker	Life
Thomas Lyon	*Atlas* (3)	July 1816	Chester	April 1814	Shoe Maker	7 yrs
John Phillips	*Fanny*	Jan. 1816	Newcastle	April 1814	Labourer	7 yrs
Henry Wood	*Fame*	March 1817	Taunton	March 1816	Wheelwright	Life
John Bicknell	*Shipley*	April 1817	Sussex	Aug. 1816	Shepherd	-

Wives Names	Childrens Names	Ages	Places of Residence	By Whom Recommended
Eleanor McGuiggan	Terence Isabella	-	Errigale Kirran, Tyrone. To be found addressing Sir John Stuart, Bart Ballygawley, Aughncloy	Dep. Com. Gen. Allan
Ann Todhunter	-	-	56 Great Portland Street, Mary-le-bone, Middx	do
Jane Rollinson	Matilda Emma	7 5	No. 9 Cannon Street, Plymouth, Devon	
Eliz. Faulkner	Henry Elizabeth	11 5	Warwick	Mr Rouse
Frances Cowley	William	1	Old Raddington Lane, Canterbury	do
Frances Kidwall	John William Mary Frank	12 10 8 6	Pilton near Barnstaple, Devon	Mr Wiltshire
Ann Lyon	Mary John Martha	9 7 5	St. Johns, City of Chester, Cheshire	do
Sarah Phillips	John Robert Louisa	8 7 5	Assen Street, Birmingham	Mr Nichols
Mary Wood	John Henry	3 2	Handy Cross near Taunton, in Somerset, Parish of Liddeard St. Lawrence	Captn Gill
Mary Bicknell	Two children names unknown	-	Henfield near Brighton, Sussex	Mr Wm Howe of Glenlee

CHAPTER 15

CRIMINAL OFFENCES IN THE COLONY

Details of crimes committed in New South Wales were sometimes reported to the Colonial Office and can be found in the correspondence files at The National Archives in document class CO 201. The following are some examples.

TNA ref CO 201/73

Four Men who Seized a Ship

Government House
New South Wales
7th May 1814

My Lord

1. Since closing my dispatches of the 28th and 30th ulto. some circumstances have been communicated to me, which altho' of no very serious importance at the present time I feel it my duty to appraise Your Lordship of.

2. In the course of the night of the 7th ulto' four convicts who had been sent from here to Newcastle as a punishment for various offences, seized upon a small vessel there called *The Speedwell* of Sydney, burthen 21 tons, and carried her off, having first severely beaten the Master and one Seaman, who happened to be the only persons on board at the time. As soon as they had got the vessel completely under weigh, and free of the Harbor, they sent the Master and Seaman on shore in a small Boat, which they had previously secured for the purpose of conveying themselves on board *The Speedwell*. This vessel being scantily supplied with provisions and water, it is not very likely that they will be enabled finally to effect their escape from hence, but they have not been yet heard of. The men who committed this Act of Piracy are of very desperate characters, and in order to their being apprehended and sent out hither again, if they should happen to return to England, I transmit your Lordship herewith a List of their names, with their Places and Times of Trial, Sentences and Ships arrived by.

3. At the Settlement in Van Diemen's Land, and particularly in the neighbourhood of Port Dalrymple, some very violent excesses have been lately committed by Bands of run away Convicts headed by two Persons who lately held Official and Creditable Situations under this Government, namely Peter Mills late acting Deputy Surveyor of Lands, and George Williams, late Acting Deputy Commissary of Provisions at Port Dalrymple. These Banditti support themselves by plundering the Houses and driving off the cattle of the unfortunate settlers who are not at present sufficiently numerous to defend themselves against these aggressions. Headed by two active and desperate Fellows such as Mills and Williams, it will be necessary to adopt some strong measure

to reduce these deluded wretches to submission and for this purpose I am now devising such as appears to me most likely to produce the desired object, without resorting to sanguinary proceedings.

4. Some Hostilities have been lately exhibited in the remote parts of this Settlement by the Natives, who have killed one soldier and three other Europeans. In consequence of this aggression I dispatched a small Military Party to the disturbed District, on whose approach the natives retired without being attacked or suffering in any degree for their temerity. In the course of this business I have caused enquiry to be made into the motives that might have produced it, and from thence I have learned that some idle and ill disposed Europeans had taken liberties with their women and had also treacherously attacked and killed a woman and her two children whilst sleeping, and this unprovoked cruelty produced that retaliation whereby persons perfectly innocent of the crime, lost their lives. Having had their revenge in the way they always seek for it I am not at all apprehensive of their making any further attacks on the settlers unless provoked as before, by insults and cruelties.

I have the Honor to be

My Lord

Your Lordship's most obedt and very humble Servant

L. Macquarie

Table 15.1: List of Four Convicts who Piratically seized and ran away with the sloop *Speedwell* from Newcastle on the 7th April 1814. *(TNA ref CO 201/73)*

Name	Tried Where	When	Sentence	Arrived by Ship
Joseph Burridge	Kent	March 1813	14 years	*Genl Hewett*: 1814
John Pearce	Surry Ass.	28 March 1810	Life	*Indian* Barclay, master 1810
Edward Scarr	Cambridge Ass.	13 March 1810	Life	*Ad. Gambier* 2nd[1] 1811
Herbert Stiles	Calcutta, Bengal	4 Decr 1809	Life	Brig *Eagle* Mackay, master 17 Feb 1811

1. *Admiral Gambier* 2nd indicates the second voyage of this ship to New South Wales.

Table 15.2: A List of Free Persons Fined for Various Offences, 1816. *(TNA ref CO 201/121)*

Date of Conviction	Person Fined	Offence	Sum Levied			How Disposed of			Presiding Magistrate
			£	s	d	To the King	To	Informer	
October 5	William Noble	For not registering Gov^t servant agreeably to General Orders		3	4		3	4	Revd R. Cartwright
October 7	John Town	do		3	4		3	4	Revd R. Cartwright & Revd H. Fulton

Date of Conviction	Person Fined	Offence	Sum Levied			How Disposed of						Presiding Magistrate
			£	s	d	To the King			To Informer			
						£	s	d	£	s	d	
October 9	Wm Lewis	Assault	2			2						Revd R. Cartwright & J. Mileham, Esq.
October 21	John Pendergast	Swearing in Court		3	4		3	4				
November 4	Thomas Frost	Selling spirits without Licence	10			5			5			Revd R. Cartwright & Revd H. Fulton
November 16	William Cussett	Assault		13	4		13	4				Revd R. Cartwright & J. Mileham, Esq.
December 16	Thomas Weyham	Harbouring a Runaway	10			5			5			Revd R. Cartwright
		For not registering Govt servant agreeably to General Orders		5			5					
		Working on the Sabbath & his 2 men		15						15		
December 16	William Powers	do		5						5		
December 17	James Kelly	Harbouring a Runaway	10			5			5			Revd R. Cartwright & J. Mileham, Esq.
December 26	John Brown	Harbouring Government Servants	1	6	8		13	4		13	4	
December 28	Robert Howard	Harbouring a Runaway	10			In consequence of this man's poverty this fine was forgiven						
			45	15	–	19	1	8	16	13	4	

TNA ref CO 201/238

Corporal Punishments Inflicted

Return of Corporal Punishments inflicted by Sentence of the Sydney Police Bench, from the 4th to the 30th September 1833, in the presence of E.A. Slade, J.P. Superintendent, Hyde Park Barrack.

1. William Graham, per ship *Camden*, absent without leave. 25 lashes. Shin lacerated at the 13th lash; at the 15th the convict appeared to suffer great pain, but during the whole of the punishment he did not utter a word, nor groaned; but when cast

loose from the table, the expression of his countenance indicated much suffering. The convict says that he never was flogged in this Colony before. I did not discover any marks of punishment on his back.

2. Calvin Sampson, *America*, stealing a pair of shoes. 50 lashes. Blood flowed at the 4th; the convict cried out at the 18th and continued crying for a few succeeding lashes; his skin was considerably torn and blood flowed during the whole punishment. This man groaned much and prayed whilst suffering his sentence; and afterwards declared seriously that he 'Would never come again.' I am of opinion that he was sufficiently punished at the 25th lash and I felt convinced that he suffered so severely as to become, henceforth, more careful in subjecting himself to the infliction of punishment in Hyde Park Barracks, under my superintendence. This convict says he was flogged once on the passage out but never before in the Colony.

3. Daniel Alone, *Andromeda*, grossly neglecting his duty. 50 lashes. The prisoner cried loudly at the 2nd, and repeated his cries at every lash; at the 12th lash the blood was flowing largely; the prisoner seemed to suffer intense agony. I am of opinion that this man was sufficiently punished at the 25th lash. Daniel Alone states, he was flogged last Saturday but the marks of punishment on his back were very slight indeed; this fact proves the necessity – not of increased punishment – but of the presence of some responsible Officer of character, whenever punishment is inflicted.

4. James Clayton, *Phoenix*, absent without leave and neglecting his duty, 50 lashes. The skin was lacerated at the 5th lash and there was a slight effusion of blood; the prisoner subdued his sense of pain by biting his lips. The skin of this man was thick to an uncommon degree; and both his body and mind have been hardened by former punishments; and he is also known to be what is termed 'flash' or 'game'; nevertheless I am of opinion that if all his former (or perhaps only his first) punishments had been as vigorously administered as this last, his indomitable spirit would have been subdued.

5. John Denning, *Parmelia*, neglect of duty. 50 lashes. The prisoner cried out at the 1st lash and continued crying loudly; at the 6th lash the flesh was lacerated considerably, blood was drawn but did not flow. This man says he was never flogged before and I did not discover any marks of former punishment on his back. It is my opinion he was sufficiently punished and that the number of lashes this man suffered has as much effect as to the intended end of punishment, as 100 lashes would have had.

6. Thomas Holdsworth, *Parmelia*, pilfering from his master. 50 lashes. At the 1st lash the prisoner uttered piercing screams and continued screaming at each succeeding lash, and appeared to suffer greatly; the 5th lash brought blood and the flesh was considerably lacerated at the conclusion of the punishment. This man says he was never flogged before, nor did there appear on his back any marks of former punishment. I am of opinion that he was sufficiently punished at the 25th lash, for his bodily strength was nearly exhausted as was manifested by his staggering gait when cast loose.

7. Joseph Kenworthy, *Camden*, accessory to pilfering from his master. 50 lashes. The first lash elicited loud cries from this prisoner; at the 18th lash the blood appeared; at the 25th lash the blood was trickling and at the 32nd flowing down his back; the bleeding continued until the end of the punishment. This man was very severely punished. I am of opinion that he would have been sufficiently punished at the 25th lash. He says he was never flogged before; his back exhibited no signs of former punishment; he was very fat, with a thin skin. The sufferings of this prisoner were evinced by his unnerved state of body when cast loose; he could scarcely stand.

8. Isaac Coats, *Mary*, insubordination. 25 lashes. At every lash this prisoner called loudly for mercy; the blood was drawn but did not flow. He says he was never flogged

before; when cast loose he was very pale and asked permission to sit down as he felt sick and faint; a sure evidence that his power of endurance of pain had been proved nearly to an extreme.

9. Edward Davis, *Dunvegan Castle*, drunk and making use of improper language before Mr Folkard's family. 50 lashes. This man was never punished before; he cried out loudly at the first lash; the skin was lacerated at the 14th lash and he continued

Table 15.3: Offences by Aborigines. *(TNA ref CO 201/369)*

Name	Supposed Offence	Where Committed	Date of Committal to Gaol	Put Upon Trial	Before Whom
Marrangobrun Abraham	Sheep Stealing	Colliban River	Jan. 1840		–
Pitchark	Felony	Portland District	28 Sept. 1840	Not Tried	–
Wendburn	Murder				–
Konghomarnee					–
Murrey	Felony	Goulbourn Dist.	17 Dec. 1840	6 Jan. 1841	Quarter Sessions
Pinc-gin-goon	Assault & Felony				
Nandermine	Felony				
Landermarkoon	Assault & Felony				
Cawing on lit					
Peebeep	Felony				
Larmibidernik					
Morrimallock	Assault				
Wiligan					
Tarrockminin	Assault & Felony				
Worwarrong	Assault				
Merryman	Suspicion of Felony				
Simon	Murder		1 Jany 1841	Not Tried	
Larry					
Jocky			7 Jany 1841		
Bon John		Jeelong District	23 Aug. 1841	16 Sept. 1841	Mr Justice Willis
Bob	Murder & Robbery	Western Port	30 Nov. 1841	21 Dec. 1841	
Jack					
Fanny	Accessory to do				

to cry out loudly. Twelve lashes would have been sufficient punishment; he continued crying after the flogging was over.

10. Alexander Somers, *John*, insubordination and absent without leave. 25 lashes. This man was never flogged before; the skin was lacerated at the 12th lash; he was sufficiently punished at the 12th lash. He did not cry out but he seemed to feel his flogging much.

Sentence	Remanded	Reason Why	Date of Discharge or of Execution Sentence	Grounds of Discharge
–	–	–	Discharged April 1840	No evidence
–	–	–	Discharged 4 Jan. 1841	No evidence
–	–	–	Died in Hospital 27 April	
–	–	–	do do	
–	–	–	Discharged 7 Jany 1841	No evidence forthcoming
	–	–		–
	–	–		–
	–	–		–
	–	–	Escaped when being transported	–
Ten Years Transportation	–	–		–
	–	–		–
	–	–		–
	–	–		–
	–	–	Discharged 20 May 1841	Some supposed Illegality in the Trial
Not Guilty	–	–	Discharged 6 Jany 1842	Not Guilty
–	–	–	Discharged 28 Dec. 1840	No evidence forthcoming
–	–	–	Discharged 2 Feb. 1841	No evidence
–	–	–		
–	Remanded	Incapable of Pleading	Discharged 16 Oct. 1841	Incapable of understanding the proceedings &c.
Death	–	–	Executed 20 Jany 1842	–
Death	–	–		–
–	–	–	Discharged 21 Dec. 1841	Not Guilty

11. William Gregg, *Norfolk*, absent without leave. 25 lashes. This man was punished with 50 lashes about the end of last month; his back was then sore; the unhealed skin broke at the first lash and at the 4th the blood appeared. This man did not cry out; he is a stout man and has a thick skin but the appearance of his back when the punishment was over sufficiently proved that he had endured much pain.

12. Robert Coakly, *Florentia*, insolent, disobedient, frequently drunk and absent without leave. 50 lashes. This man was never flogged before; he seemed to feel great pain at the 10th lash; the 15th lash drew blood; seemed to endure much pain at the 40th lash.

13. William Robinson, *Mary*, drunk and making away with a part of his dress which was given him by his master. 50 lashes. This man was never flogged before; he cried out at every lash; the skin was lacerated at the 12th lash; the blood appeared at the 20th. This man suffered intense agony. Twenty lashes would have been an ample warning to him.

14. George Mimden, *Asia*, gross neglect of duty. 25 lashes. This man was never flogged before; the skin was lacerated at the 16th lash; the blood appeared slightly; he did not cry out.

15. Jacob Gibbons, *Marquis Hastings*, absconding. 50 lashes. This man was punished with 50 lashes three years ago. At the 16th lash the skin was lacerated yet this man suffered in silence. The appearance of his back shewed the severity of the punishment. etc., etc.

Table 15.5: Escaped Convicts. 'Return of Persons supposed to have escaped from the Colony during the year 1840'. *(TNA ref CO 201/309)*

Name	Ship	Age	Native Place	Trade or Calling	Height	
					ft	in
Broad, Alfred Alias Frederick Johnson	*Bengal Merchant*	28	Wiltshire	Groom & Indoor Servant	5	2½
Scar left side of forehead						
Brown, W^m	*Mary Ridgeway*	24	Newcastle upon Tyne	Blacksmith 2 yrs	5	5½
Slight perpendicular scar top centre of Forehead. Diagonal scar on right eyebrow						
Colley, W^m	*Larkins* (1)	48	Doncaster	Weaver	5	5
Derbridge, W^m	*Hercules* (4)	49	Hertfordshire	Blacksmith complete	[blank]	
Nail of little finger of left hand split						

Table 15.4: Sample of 'Return of the Assignments revoked during the year 1850 showing the Cause of Revocation and the authority by which the prisoners have been withdrawn'. *(TNA ref CO 201/309)*

Name of Asignee	Residence	Prisoners Name	Ship	Cause of Revocation
Abbot, James	Portland Head	Thos Jackson	*Lady Kennaway*	Having been twice convicted of selling spirits without a Licence. No more convicts are to be assigned to him
Airds, William	Wollombi	Jas Barnes	*Roslin Castle*	Permitting his assignee servant to absent himself for ten months and not reporting him to the proper authorities
Bonner, R.	Wellington	James Simmons William Brown Walter Andrews Thos Hackitt Josiah Pary George Collins John Case Denis Stack John Chandler Henry Lee Jas. Manning Thos Burke Peter Menany	*Mary Ann* – first – do do do *John* (2) *Camden* (1) *Surrey* do do *Recovery* *Asia* (II) *Lady Kennaway* *Jas Laing* do	His establishment having been represented to be under very bad management, and also that two of his assigned servents are living in a state of concubine with black native women

Complexion	Colour of		From Whom	When	Remarks
	Hair	Eyes			
Ruddy & Freckled	Brown	Hazel	W.H. Kerr, Parramatta	26th July	–
Sallow & Freckled	Brown	Grey	Hyde Park Barracks	12th Aug.	Transported from Adelaide.
Ruddy	Brown	Hazel	John Solomons, Sydney	26th March	Supposed to have escaped to New Zealand
Sallow, much pockpitted	Dk. Brown	Hazel	Mrs F.A. Hely, Brisbane	26th Dec.	–

Name	Ship	Age	Native Place	Trade or Calling	Height		
					ft	in	
Deakin, Robert	*Kate*	44	Leicestershire	Labourer	5	10	
	Scar right side of chin. Breast hairy. Large raised mole centre of same. Mark of a bite right hand. Scar on left elbow, another below the same						
Fahy, John	*Middlesex*	35	County Galway	Labourer	5	5¾	
	Eyebrows partially meeting, small (sic) on bell of right ear, small on top of head (sic)						
Higgins, Wᵐ alias Silverlock	*Kate*	40	Liverpool	Labourer	5	6½	
	Diagonal scar centre of forehead. Horizontal scar under right eye, another under centre						
Kelly, John	*Marquis of Huntley*	53	Kerry	Gardeners Labourer	5	6¼	

| Complexion | Colour of | | From Whom | When | Remarks |
	Hair	Eyes			
Sallow	Brown	Blue	Stockdale, Illawara	22nd Sept.	Transported from Adelaide, South Australia

near right elbow. Two small moles below scar on thumb, another on third. Two on little finger of

Complexion	Hair	Eyes	From Whom	When	Remarks
Sallow	Brown	Blue	–	–	–

Complexion	Hair	Eyes	From Whom	When	Remarks
Sallow & Little pockpitted	Black	Brown	Escort 50th Regiment from Kiaccuty Wollongong	10th Sept.	Transported from Adelaide, South Australia & previously in the *York* in 1831 in the same name, prisoner for 7 years

of lower lip. Breast & arms hairy, scar ball of left thumb, blue dot back of left hand, large features

Complexion	Hair	Eyes	From Whom	When	Remarks
Ruddy & Freckled	Brown	Grey	Boats Crew Police Boat, Goat Island	1st July	–

CHAPTER 16

NORFOLK ISLAND

Norfolk Island, in the Pacific Ocean, lies 865 miles to the east of New South Wales. In 1855 convicts were transferred from Norfolk Island to Van Diemen's Land (Tasmania). Records of the inhabitants of Norfolk Island (officials, guards, free settlers and convicts) are to be found interspersed with the records of New South Wales in the Colonial Office correspondence at The National Archives in document class CO 201. Musters of the whole of the inhabitants of Norfolk Island for the years 1800–02 and 1805–08 have been published by Australian Biographical and Genealogical Record in 1988 and 1989 respectively (Baxter, Carol J.; see Bibliography). The following are some examples found in Colonial Office correspondence.

Table 16.1: List of Men whose Terms of Transportation are expired, and who left Port Jackson in the *Endeavour* with permission, but who remain on Norfolk Island on account of the loss of that ship on New Zealand. [1795] *(TNA ref CO 201/18)*

No	Names	How supported
1	Thomas Groves	By Government
	Michael Newhouse	By a Settler
	David Kincade	By Government
	Thomas Bateman	do
5	Thos Kerny	By a Settler
	John Edwards	do
	Joseph Morley	do
	John Kierman	do
-	Patrick Hart	do
10	Denis Newenham	do
	Peter Parker	do
	James Johnson	do
	John Nurse	do
	Daniel Gordon	do
15	Denis Mohair	do
	John Petit	do
	Terence Smith	do
	Joseph Meyrick	do

No	Names	How supported
	John Colley	do
20	William Osborne	do
	Geo. Holligan	By Government
	Philip Bone	By a Settler
	Robt Chalmers	do
	Willm Floyd	do
25	William Seals	do
	Thomas Invitt	By Government
	Thos Wood	By a Settler
	Joseph Ellis	do
	Elizabeth Heatherly	By Government
30	James Heatherley, a boy	do

(signed) Philip Gidley King

Table 16.2a: Victualling Book 1st July and 31st December 1804. Civil Department. *(TNA ref CO 201/42, Norfolk Island)*

Time of Victualling	Names	Quality	D or DD[1]	Time	Days Victualled
1st July 1804	Joseph Foveaux	Lieut. Govr	D	7th Sep. England	69
	Thomas Hibbins	D.J. Advo.			184
	Willm Broughton	Actg Dy Comd			184
	Martin Tims	Actg P.Master			184
	Henry Fulton	Chaplain			184
	Henry Williams	Actg Dy Survr			184
	John Drummond	Beach Master			184
	John Best	Superintendent			184
	Nathl Lucas	Master Carpr			184
	Robert Nash	Superintendent			184
	Zachh Clark	Depy Comy under suspension.	DD	6th Decr	159
	D'Arcy Wentworth	Asst Surgeon			184

1. D: discharged; DD: discharged dead.

Table 16.2b: New South Wales Corps. *(TNA ref CO 201/42, Norfolk Island, continued)*

Time of Victualling	Names	Quality	Days Victualled at Reduced Rations
1st July 1804	Joseph Foveaux See Civil Department	Lieut. Col.	—
	John Piper	Lieut	184
	Thomas Laycock	"	184
	Thomas Davis	"	184
	Willm Lawton	Ensign	184
	Edward Haven	Sergeant	184
	Robert Hall	"	184
	Isaac Champion	"	184
	Daniel Humm	"	184
	Willm Baker	Corporal	184
	John Howell	"	184
	Willm Charlton	"	184
	Richd Barnes	"	184
	Francis Howe	Drummer	184
	James Townson	"	184
	John Ainsworth	"	184
	Thomas Dean	Private	184
	George Plyer	"	184
	George Whittaker	"	184
	Prentice Coy	"	184
	John Matthews	"	184
	Thomas Asbury	"	184
	George Parker	"	184
	John Sturt	"	184
	John Roberts	"	184
	Willm Whiting	"	184
	Peter Wilson	"	184
	Willm Wright	"	184
	John Dubois	"	184
	James Archer	"	184
	Thomas Anderson	"	184
	John Barratt	"	184
	Saml Beachy	"	184
	James Capey	"	184
	George Eggleton	"	184
	Willm Llewellyn	"	184
	Joseph Lewis	"	184

Time of Victualling	Names	Quality	Days Victualled at Reduced Rations
1st July 1804	Richd Podmore	"	184
	Emanuel Parry	"	184
	Thomas Radcliffe	"	184
	John Vincent	"	184
	Willm Bohannon	"	184
	Neville Butler	"	184
	Joseph Mason	"	184
	Benjn Butcher	"	184
	etc., etc.		

Note: The total number of Privates listed is 104.

Table 16.2c: Settlers from Marines, Seamen, Freemen, &c. *(TNA ref CO 201/42, Norfolk Island, continued)*

Time of Victualling	Names	D or DD	Time	Remarks	Days Victualled
1st July 1804	Samuel King				184
	Thomas Lucas				184
	Thomas Cole				184
	James Ferguson	D	8 Sept.	Off Stores	69
	George Oakley				184
	James McCormick				184
	Thomas Gibson				184
	Patrick Waters				184
	Charles Fryer	D	24 Aug.	NSW Corps	55
	Thomas Williams	D	29 Sept.	Off Stores	91
	Anty Hitcher				184
	John Whitehouse				184
1st Sept.	— Bower				122
	— Oriou [?]				122

Table 16.2d: Settlers from Convicts. (TNA ref CO 201/42, Norfolk Island, continued)

Time of Victualling	Names	D or DD	Time	Days Victualled
1st July 1804	Jacob Billet			184
	Willm Jenner			184
	Aaron Davis			184
	Willm Atkins			184
	John Herbert			184
	John Owles			184
	Willm Sherburd			184
	John Walsh	D	13th September	75
	James Jordan			184
	Richd Morgan			184
	Edwd Kimberly			184
	James Triffett			184
	Thos Chaffey			184
	Willm Blatherhorn			184
24th Nov.	Willm Collins			38

Table 16.2e: Free Men from Sentences Expired. (TNA ref CO 201/42, Norfolk Island, continued)

Time of Victualling	Names	D or DD	Time	Remarks	Days Victualled
1st July 1804	Charles Repeat				184
	Thomas Priest				184
	Joseph Evans				184
	Henry Taylor				184
	Thomas McQueen				184
	John Smith				184
	Dennis Geary	D	27th July	Off Stores	27
	Jno Jones als Reilly				184
	Saml Free				184
	John Rawlinson				184
	Peter Woodcock				184
	James Hackett	D	14th Sept	Off Stores	76
	Thomas Hodgetts				184
	John Brown				184
	John Hatcher				184
	Thomas Stretch				184
	Joseph Harrison				184
	Saml Day				184

Time of Victualling	Names	D or DD	Time	Remarks	Days Victualled
1st July 1804	George Woodhead	D	14th Sept	Off Stores	76
	Thomas Newby				184
27 Oct. 1804	Willm Cartwright				65
3 Novr 1804	Charles Cooper				59
17 Novr 1804	Luke Normanton				45
24 Novr 1804	John Clapson				38
" "	John McKay				38

Table 16.2f: Male Convicts. *(TNA ref CO 201/42, Norfolk Island, continued)*

Time of Victualling	Names	D or DD	Time	Remarks	Days Victualled
1st July 1804	Samuel Baker				184
	Isaac Williams				184
	John Adie				184
	Thomas Alexander				184
	Robert Kingston				184
	John Bately				184
	James Waterson				184
	Henry Mullins				184
	Michl Murphy				184
	James Finnegan				184
	Willm Wybrow	D	13 Sept	Off Stores	75
	Thomas Carey				184
	John Sharp				184
	Stepn Skilling				184
	Barney Sands				184
	John Holmes				184
	Richard Burn				184
	Robert Thurley				184
	Thomas Dordon	D	14 Sept	Off Island	76
	Richd Baylis				184
	Pat. als Mich. Savage				184
	Patk Flynn				184
	Jose [?] McKinley				184
	Roger McGuire				184
	Edwd Tutty				184
	John Lacy	D	3 Aug	P. Jackson	34
	Dennis McGuire				184

Time of Victualling	Names	D or DD	Time	Remarks	Days Victualled
1st July 1804	John Walsh				184
	Richd Sydes				184
	John Walker				184
	James Blore				184
	Thos Hambleton				184
	Farrel Cuffe				184
	Wm Fitzgerald				184
	Michl Burn				184
	Michl Cox	DD	26 Septr		88
	John Rogers				184
	Richard Dry				184
	James Harrold				184

Table 16.2g: Free Women. *(TNA ref CO 201/42, Norfolk Island, continued)*

Time of Victualling	Names	D or DD	Time	Remarks	Days Victualled
1st July 1804	Cathe Davis				184
	Sarah Whitfield				184
	Margt Beachy				184
	Ann Benson				184
	Ann Fulton				184
	Harriet Hodgetts				184
	Sarah McHenry				184
	Hannah Barnes				184
	Mary Coleman				184
	Mary Fletcher	D	21 Decr		174

Table 16.2h: Free Women from Sentences Expired. *(TNA ref CO 201/42, Norfolk Island, continued)*

Time of Victualling	Names	D or DD	Time	Remarks	Days Victualled
1st July [1804]	Elizh Thomas				184
	Mary Wilson				184
	Elizh Goldsmith				184
	Hester Thornton				184
	Susan Pricket				184
	Ann Hill				184
	Ann Harper				184

Time of Victualling	Names	D or DD	Time	Remarks	Days Victualled
1st July [1804]	Ann Brooks				184
	Elizh Haywood				184
	Ann Fowler				184
	Dorcas Talbot				184
	Grace Maddox	D	21st Sept.	Off Island	83
	Olivia Lucas				[blank]
	Jemima Wasker				184
	Sarah Jones				184
	Mary Allen				184
	Abigail Cummings				184
	Elizh Smith				184
	Lucinda Woods				184
	Ann Hannaway				184
	Margt Hall				184
	Ann Gibson				184
	Mary Butler				184
	Elizh Harriman				184
	Elizh Bruce				184
	Maria Israel				184
	Mary Cavanagh				184
	Mary Randall				184
	Sarah Bond				184
	Mary Cooper				184
	Mary Hartley	D	3rd Aug	Off Stores	34
	Cathe Kearnon	D	24th Aug	Off Stores	55
4 July 1804	Mary Burn				181
15 Sept. 1804	Hanh Ronay				108
22 Sept. 1804	Ann Doyle				101
27 Oct. 1804	Ann Munday				66
24 Nov. 1804	Sarah Clayton				38

Table 16.2i:Female Convicts. *(TNA ref CO 201/42, Norfolk Island, continued)*

Time of Victualling	Names	D or DD	Time	Remarks	Days Victualled
1 July 1804	Cathe Rochford				184
	Mary Douglas				184
	Susan Ashman				184
	Cathe Burn				184
	Ann Wilson				184

Time of Victualling	Names	D or DD	Time	Remarks	Days Victualled
1 July 1804	Ian Whiting				184
	Mary Connelly				184
	Hannah Fisher				184
	Ann Watson	D	23 Nov.	Off Stores	174
	Mary English				184
	Ann Colesford	D	14 Dec.	Off Stores	167
	Mary Mills				184
15 Dec	Bridget Hickey				17

Table 16.2j:Orphans and Children above Ten Years. *(TNA ref CO 201/42, Norfolk Island, continued)*

Time of Victualling	Names	D or DD	Time	Remarks	Days Victualled
1 July 1804	Mary Reed				126
	Hannah Edge				184
	Mary Ann Edge				184
	Susan Gibson				184
	Sarah Fletcher	D	21 Dec	Off Stores	184
	Maria Hopper				184
3 Nov.	Charlotte Bolton				59

Table 16.2k: Children above Two Years of Age. *(TNA ref CO 201/42, Norfolk Island, continued)*

Time of Victualling	Names	D or DD	Time	Remarks	Days Victualled
1 July 1804	Richd Howard				184
	Geoe Goldsmith				184
	Susan Harper				184
	Willm Flannagan				184
	Mary Thomas				184
	John Poore				184
	Elizh Goldsmith				184
	Thomas Hoddy				184
	Mary Wishaw				184
	Elizh Thomas				184
	Maria Cole				184
	Mary Thornton				184
	Maria Hannaway				184
	Elizh Harrison				184
	Elizh Robley				184

Time of Victualling	Names	D or DD	Time	Remarks	Days Victualled
1 July 1804	George Robley				184
	John Howard				184
	Hannah Hoddy				184
	Sarah Smith				184
	Willm Thomas				184
	Jane Clarke				184
	John Brooks				184
	Ann Brooks				184
	Ann Harper				184
	John Thornton				184
	Willm Goldsmith				184
	Ann Grinslett				184
	Elizh Thornton				184
	John Flannagan				184
	Elizh Haywood				184
	Elizh Hannaway				184
	Margt Haywood				184
	James Bolton				184
	Jamima Bolton				184
	Nathl Howard				184
	Ann Flaharty				184
	Elizh Hoddy				184
	Isabella Oakley	D	21st Septr	Off Island	83
	John Wise				184
	Elizh Wise				184
	Mary Smith				184
	Saml Brooks				184
	Nathl Lucas				184
	Willm Grinslett				184
	Elizh Grinslett				184

Table 16.2m: Children under Two Years. *(TNA ref CO 201/42, Norfolk Island, continued)*

Time of Victualling	Names	D or DD	Time	Remarks	Days Victualled
1 July 1804	Thomas Beachy				184
	James Hodgetts				184
	Mary Goldsmith	D	21 Sept.	to Half	83
	John Harper				184
	George Lucas	D	21 Sept.	to Half	83

Time of Victualling	Names	D or DD	Time	Remarks	Days Victualled
1 July 1804	Jno Walker Fulton				184
	Willm Rochford				184
	Willm Smith				184
	James Jones				184
	Joseph Burn				184
	Sarah Lucas				184
	Mary Eliz. Hook				184
	Susan Brooks				184
	Mary Benson				184
	Ann Barnes				184
	John Bott				101
	Mary Flynn				101
	Willm English				101

Norfolk Island
            31st Decr 1804
                        William Broughton
                                    Actg Depy Comy

CHAPTER 17

POLICE IN NEW SOUTH WALES

The Colonial Office correspondence at The National Archives, document class CO 201, contains correspondence relating to the early policing of New South Wales and sometimes includes lists of policemen and others who worked for the Police Department. It is perhaps surprising to discover that some Australian Aborigines were employed as policemen.

TNA ref CO 201/121

Return of Constables compassing the Police at Parramata [1820]

Edward Dillan	John Kelly
Hugh Taylor	Martin Sweeney
Thomas Nugent	Francis Ainsworth
William Murray	Thomas Smith
Edward White	Thomas Healey
John Brown	John Lynch
John Riley	Benjamin Rattey
William Sully	Richard Grimshaw
Thomas Feaney	Thomas Pierce

District Constables

George Gore	Prospect District
Edward Jennings	Seven Hills
James McManis	Eastern Creek
Samuel James	Baulkham
William Smith	Castle Hill and Pennant Hills
John Martin	Northern Boundary
Edward McDonald	Field of Mars
William Small	Kissing Point
Thomas Baker	Sydney Road Constable

Sept. 11th 1820 A true Return
Wm Sherwin C. Constable

Table 17.1a: List of persons employed in the Police Department receiving salaries. *(TNA ref CO 201/121)*

			£ s d
D'Arcy Wentworth, Esq.	Principal Superintendent	per annum	200 0 0
Mr R.L. Murray	Assistant do		60 0 0
The same	Principal Clerk		45 0 0
Mr E. Wood	Assistant do		20 0 0
Mr I. Redmond	Chief Constable		60 0 0
Mr H. Thorn	Asst do		15 0 0
Six District Constables	Each		20 0 0
Fifty Constables without salaries			-

D. Wentworth
Superintendent of Police

Table 17.1b: Return of Constables compasing the Police Establishment at Parramatta up to the fourteenth day of September 1820. *(TNA ref CO 201/121 continued)*

Names	Free	Ticket of Leave	Convict	Remarks
Edward Dillon	free			Upwards of 3 years constable
John Kelly	"			"
Martin Sweeney	"			"
William Sully	"			"
Richard Grimshaw	"			"
Thomas Nugents	"			"
William Murray	"			"
John Brown	"			Seven months as a Constable
Thomas Feaney	"			Recently made Constable
John Lynch	"			Seven months as Constable
John Riley	"			Recently made Constable
Thomas Smith	"			Seven months as Constable
Francis Hainsworth	"			Upwards of 12 months Constable
Benjamin Rattey		Ticket of Leave		Recently made Constable
Edward Healey		"		Seven months Constable
Edward White		"		Watch House Keeper
Thomas Pawderly			Convict	Recently made Constable
Andrew Kenny			"	"

Wm Sherwin
C. Constable

TNA ref CO 201/121 continued

A List of the Sydney Constables

No. 1 Watch Houses

District Constable	William Spears
Constables	John Haslip
	George Kelly
	James Ball
	Thomas Lynch
	William Smith
	James Nickson

Dist. No. 2	Cumberland St. Rocks
Constable	George Pashley
Constables	Joseph Cradock
	William Hubbard
	William Wade
	Joseph Welch
	Richard Partridge
	William Kello

Dist. No. 3	Hunter Street
Constable	Thomas Austin
Constables	Richard McWorthy
	Thomas Bowers
	William Ogle
	Francis Wilde
	Abraham Bateman
	James Lane

Dist. No. 4	Pitt Street
Constable	Richard Dalton
Constables	Robt McAllister
	Thomas Byrne
	Andrew Murphy
	William Greenwood
	James Styles
	John Bell

Dist. No. 5	Brick Field Hill
Constable	Thomas Dunny
Constables	William Fowler
	Thomas Benton
	William Hazard
	William Massey
	James Hall
	John Smith

Dist. No. 6	Kent Street
Constable	John Butcher
Constables	Samuel Clemm
	William Brown
	Samuel Bowyer
	Peter Welch
	Thomas Cane
	John Bleatley

Mr Redman's Constables

William Goodwin
James Wilbow
Gilbert Baker
William Tristram
William Townsend
Matthew Miller
Joseph Redfern
John Price

Constables employed in Sydney

John Russell
T. Sullivan

William Wakeman constable in waiting.

Table 17.2: Return for the year 1842 of the number, names, age, character, conduct and services of the Party of Natives raised in the Port Phillip District in February 1842. Superintendent's Office 1st February 1843. *(TNA ref CO 201/344)*

Name	Age	Single or married	Children	If punished in what manner
Billibalang	45	Married 2 wives		Never punished
Buckup	18	Single	none	do
Cunumdigum or Redmouth enrolled in June 1842	22	do	none	do
Yamaboke	24	do	none	Frequently punished at first – Rations stopped
Berring	18	Single	none	Never punished
Nunupton	25	Married	two	Punished occasionally. Rations stopped and confined
Giminike	25	Single	none	Never punished
Barup or Gillibrand	30	do	do	Punished once – not allowed to ride
Yupton	20	do	do	Never punished
Nurmbinuck	22	do	do	do

Service	Conduct and remarks
Principally left in charge of the Camp and Stores when the Officers and Sergt. have been absent on duty. Never out on active service.	General conduct good – has a great deal of influence with his Tribe. Very useful in assisting to prevent quarrels and fighting.
On duty with Commissioner's Party in May when in pursuit of Bushrangers. On duty 3 months in the Western Port District. Several times handed drunken men over to the Police in Melbourne. On duty in the Portland Bay District. Often took and had charge of prisoners. Conducts himself exceedingly well in trying and dangerous circumstances. On duty with the Crown Commissioner's Party in the Western Port District. Deserving encouragement. Took 4 absconders at the Wannon 6th Jany and brought them to gaol.	General conduct extremely good. Obedient, quiet. Anxious to perform his duty well and to improve.
On duty in July with Sergt Bennett assisting to find and bring in the Van Diemens Land Natives. Ordered Flinders Island, on duty for three months in the Portland Bay District.	General conduct good; very trustable, cleanly, obedient to and respectful.
On duty at Narre Narre Warren in search of a woman & two children lost. On duty three months in the Portland Bay District. Out with the Crown Commissioners in the Western Port District.	At first much inclined to be subordinate. At the first information this man was dirty, indolent and insolent, but his conduct for the last 6 months is much altered; he is now cleanly, smart, active and obedient.
Was never on duty excepting about the Camp.	General conduct good; likely to make a good policeman.
On duty at Narre Narre Warren in search of a lost woman. Often employed as a messenger and on duty about the Camp.	General conduct not good at first fond of wandering. A pretty good messenger, likely to improve.
Sent after Bushrangers in May. On duty at Portland Bay.	General conduct very good. Steady & willing, rather stupid.
A good orderly. On duty at Windsor Port in June. Narre Narre Warren Portland Bay. Was very useful; took several Black prisoners. On duty with Crown Commr at Western Port.	General conduct good. Obedient, cleanly and useful.
On duty at Narre Narre Warren. Brought in the Van Diemens Land natives from the River Plenty. Three months at Portland Bay out with the Mounted Police.	General conduct very good. Quiet and tractable; cleanly, obedient & a good tracker but slow.
On duty after Bushrangers. On duty in the Weston Port District in June. At Narre Narre Warren in search of lost woman. Three months on duty in the Portland Bay District.	General conduct good. Active and intelligent of duty & cleanly and smart.

Name	Age	Single or married	Children	If punished in what manner
Borro-Borro or Jackey	26	do	do	Punished occasionally – Rations stopped & confined
Culpendurra or Robin	16	do	do	Punished occasionally – Rations stopped
Nangollibill or Turnbull	30	Married 2 wives	do	Punished occasionally – Rations stopped
Perrepoint or McHall	30	Single	none	Occasionally punished & put in confinement
Woverong or Murray	27	Married, 1 wife	1 child	Never punished
Wideculk or William	27	do do	do	Punished – Rations stopped sent to the lockup
Poky Poky	35	do do	Two	Never punished
Curra Curra or Davy	40	do 2 wives	Three	Punished; Rations stopped
Tournal or Tomying	18	Single	none	Never punished
Benbo Sergeant	35	Married; 1 wife	none	Never punished
Tomboko or Henry	25	do do	one	do
Mimmungé or Dr Bailey	20	Single	none	Never punished
Polligerry	20	do	do	do
Monce or William	24	do	do	Punished by confinement
Nurambeme	30	Married; 2 wives	two	Never punished

Service	Conduct and remarks
On duty at Narre Narre Warren in search of a lost woman. Not on duty since except at the Camp.	General conduct very bad; a great savage, careless, disobedient and dangerous.
On duty after Bushrangers. Not on duty since escaping at the Camp.	General conduct bad. Dirty & sometimes insolent, but likely to improve.
On duty at the Goulburn with the Sergeant. Took a prisoner of the Crown and brought him to Jail. Not on duty since except at the Camp.	General conduct pretty good. Cleanly & smart at drill but passionate & does not like much restraint.
On duty in December with the Crown Commr at Western Port. Conduct good. On duty at Mount Maudon & Narre Narre Warren. Assisted in taking on the 5th of January four absconders.	General conduct at first bad, can be very useful and intelligent if he likes. Not very clean. Conduct improved of late.
On duty at the Camp.	General Conduct good. Fond of rambling. Intellegent & cleanly.
On duty at the Camp a good messenger.	General conduct bad. Fond of rambling. Plausible and intelligent. Can behave very well if he likes. A great scamp.
On duty four months at the Police Station Mount Maudon.	General conduct good. Will do well about the Camp but useless on duty.
On duty only at the camp.	General conduct bad & perfectly useless.
On duty at Mount Maudon Police Station On duty at the Loddon and Western Port with Crown Commissioners.	General conduct very good. Active, intelligent, cleanly. Anxious to please, & smart.
On duty at the Mount Mauden Police Station and at the Loddon & Goulburn.	General conduct good. Cleanly, orderly, obedient and very useful in the Camp.
On duty at the Camp. Very useful and a good messenger.	General conduct very good. Cleanly, orderly and obedient.
On duty at Western Port and 4 months at Mount Maudon Police Station.	General conduct very good.
On duty at Narre Narre Warren. Three months at Portland Bay; on duty at Mount Rouse and at Port.	General conduct very good; smart, active and cleanly. Rather too fond of fighting.
On duty at Narre Narre Warren. Three months at Portland Bay. At Mount Rouse and Port Fairy with Mounted Police.	General conduct at first bad; now very good; at first slovenly & inclined to be disobedient. Now cleanly and anxious to please.
On duty only at the Camp.	General conduct good. Obedient, very determined but tractable.

CHAPTER 18

PERSONS RETURNING TO BRITAIN

Sometimes free settlers returned to Britain, and were listed in the Colonial Office correspondence. These lists also include discharged soldiers and some convicts whose sentences had expired.

Table 18.1: List of Names of Officers and other Free Persons who are to go Home as Passengers on board HM Colonial Brig *Kangaroo* to England – viz. *(TNA ref CO 201/84)*

No.	Names	Regiment	Remarks
1.	Captain W.G.B. Schaw	46th Regt	Not to be victualled at the Expense of Government
2.	Lieutenant Charles Dawe	do	
3.	Lieutenant G.A. Parker	do	
4.	Mr Thomas Hassall		
5.	Ensign Chas J. Bullivant	46th Regt	Going home to quit the Service and unable to pay his passage
6.	Mr W.J. Speedy		
7.	Thomas Alford[1]		
8.	John O'Hearne		These ten persons are to be victualled during the voyage to England at the Expence of the Crown, the last nine now free having come out originally as Convicts
9.	Edmond Flood		
10.	James Nangles		
11.	Bejamin Jacobs		
12.	Thomas Holder		
13.	John Bliss		
14.	Andrew Kane		
15.	James Byring	Private 46th Regt	Discharged Soldiers and Invalids with their Wives and Children to be Victualled at the expence of the Crown
16.	Charles Glass	do	
17.	Thomas Bate	do	
18.	Joseph Farley	do	
19.	Alex[r] McKenzie	do	
20.	John Matthewson	do	
21.	John Middleton	do	
22.	James Evans	do	

No.	Names	Regiment	Remarks
23.	Thomas McNabb	do	
24.	William Downie	do	
25.	Robert Thorn	do	
26.	John Frazier	do	
27.	James Farmer	do	Discharged Soldiers and Invalids with their Wives and Children to be Victualled at the expence of the Crown
28.	Joseph Craddock	do	
29.	James McMullen	do	
	Women		
30.	Mary Coglan		
31.	Mary Dowrie		
32.	Elizabeth Craddock		
33.	Patk Coglan, a child		
34.	Jane Scott		
35.	Hannah Pleasant Janes		
36.	Sarah Hills		
37.	Anne Coleman		
38.	Sarah Tillett		Free Women formerly Convicts to be Victualled at the expense of the Crown
39.	Anne Taylor		
40.	Sarah Atherley		
41.	Jane Ewen		
42.	Annastatia Lynch		
43.	Catherine Collins		

L. Macquarie
Government House
Sydney, N.S.W.
April 4th 1817

1. This is probably the Thomas Alford mentioned in Chapter 5.

CHAPTER 19

THE CASE STUDY OF JOHN HAWKINS CONVICTED OF SHEEP STEALING IN 1804

John Hawkins married Betty, the daughter of Robin Lock at Wiveliscombe, Somerset, on 2 October 1796, by whom he had two sons: Thomas, baptised in 1802, and William, baptised in 1804. Hawkins, together with Philip Cording, was convicted of sheep stealing on 29 March 1804. Both men were sentenced to death, but this was commuted to 'Transportation for Life'. Betty died in 1821.

Hawkins and Cording were held on the prison hulk *Captivity* at Portsmouth until January 1806 when they boarded the *Fortune* bound for New South Wales. They arrived in New South Wales in August 1806. Hawkins appears in various musters of convicts. The 1828 census of New South Wales records that John Hawkins was living with Elizabeth Hawkins and research in Australia revealed that they had married on 19 April 1824 at Richmond, New South Wales. Elizabeth was the widow of Thomas Taleby, and before that the widow of one Smith, whose first name has not been found. As Elizabeth Smith she was convicted at the Old Bailey on 4 July 1798 for 'Feloniously stealing on 8th June two guineas and three shillings in monies, the property of King George, having been paid two shillings and sixpence to sleep with him'. (A descendant of Elizabeth Taleby in Australia had assumed that this was in fact the King of England and spoke about her family's royal connection). The indictment document *(LMA ref. OB/SR 341)* records that 'King George' was actually a 'Bag Washer' from Bethnal Green Road.

King George gave evidence as follows: 'I was very much in liquor, I went home with the prisoner. I went to bed with her and when I was awaked in the morning I saw her hand in my breeches pocket; there was a knife lying upon the table and she took that up, and said she would run it into me.'

Prisoner's defence: 'I saw none of his money except half-a-crown that he gave me to sleep with him.'

Question [to King George]: 'How much money had you?'

Answer: 'Two guineas and three shillings, besides the half-crown that I gave her.'

Elizabeth Smith was sentenced to seven years' transportation. She was 27 years old. The Criminal Register for Middlesex for 1798 records that she was 5ft tall and lived on Tower Hill. She was held in Newgate Prison from the time of her arrest and conviction until 4 November 1799 when she was 'Delivered to the ship *Speedy*'. The *Speedy* arrived in

Sydney on 15 April 1800. By July 1805 her sentence had expired and she would have been free to return to England, but it is likely that she could not afford the cost of the passage. On 10 February 1807 she married Thomas Taleby (also a convict; see Chapter 4) at Parramatta, by whom she had two children. Thomas Taleby died at Richmond, New South Wales, on 19 May 1823. In 1822 Elizabeth Taleby gave evidence at a Coroner's inquest (see Chapter 12).

John Hawkins is recorded in New South Wales at different times as a carpenter, a clothier, and a wheelwright. It is probable that Hawkins was the brother of the author's ancestor Robert Hawkings [sic] who was a wheelwright. Was John Hawkins endeavouring to emulate his brother by working as a wheelwright?

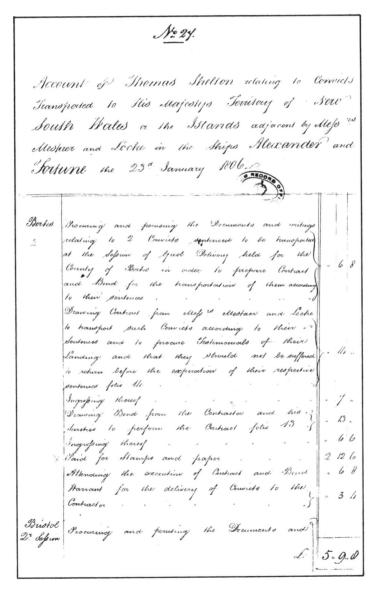

The first page of the account of Thomas Shelton (on behalf of Messers. Mestaer and Locke) for the transportation of convicts in the *Alexander* and *Fortune*, 23 January 1806. (The National Archives ref A03/291)

The 1828 census of New South Wales records that John Hawkins was living at Richmond, New South Wales, and was 55 years of age. The Calendar of Prisoners at the Taunton Assizes in March 1804 gave his age as 42 years. Assuming that his age was correctly recorded in the Calendar of Prisoners, he was in fact 66 years of age in 1828. There can, however, be no doubt about the identity of this John Hawkins because the 1828 census also records that he came by the ship *Fortune* in 1806. He is also recorded in this census as being a Protestant.

CP against his name indicates that he had been granted a Conditional Pardon. For a convict who was given a Life sentence it was necessary to have served a minimum of ten years of the sentence before an application for a pardon could be considered. John Hawkins was granted a Conditional Pardon in 1816. The official copies of original pardons held at The Archives Office of New South Wales give much detail. John Hawkins is recorded as being 4ft 11¼in tall, with dark sallow complexion, sandy hair and blue eyes. The date and place of his trial is given together with the ship he came by, and year of arrival. A Conditional Pardon gave a convict complete freedom in Australia, but he was not allowed to return to his native country within the period of his original sentence; to do so would mean facing the death penalty. As John Hawkins was given Life he had to remain in Australia for the rest of his life. Both John Hawkins and Elizabeth Hawkins died in 1838. Elizabeth was buried at Richmond on 11 June and John, who died in Windsor Poor House, was buried on 13 December. He was then recorded as a 'pauper'.

The following sets out the sequence of documents searched:

Stage 1: Criminal registers
(see Appendix 4)

Criminal registers (with the exception of those for the county of Middlesex and the Old Bailey) do not start until 1805 and therefore John Hawkins is not recorded in these registers.

Stage 2: Calendars of Prisoners
(see Appendix 5)

An incomplete series of Calendars of Prisoners for Taunton Assizes is held at the Somerset Heritage Centre, Taunton, Somerset. The following entry is recorded for John Hawkins and his partner in crime, Philip Cording:

SOM HC ref DD/MT Box 53

SOMERSETSHIRE

A

CALENDAR OF PRISONERS FOR THE LENT ASSIZES
to be held at the CASTLE of TAUNTON
In and for the County of Somerset
On THURSDAY THE 29th Day of MARCH, 1804
before
SIR ALEXANDER THOMSON, Knight
and
SIR ROBERT GRAHAM, Knight
two of the BARONS of his MAJESTY'S COURT OF EXCHEQUER

JOHN ROGERS, ESQ. SHERIFF
FOR TRIAL

John Hawkins, 42 years. Committed by E.T. Halliday, Esq., charged on the oath of one William Boucher, and on his own confession, with killing and stealing (in company with **Philip Cording**) one ewe sheep, the property of the said William Boucher. Warrant dated December 23.

Philip Cording, 42 years. Committed by E.T. Halliday, Esq., charged on the oath of William Boucher, and on his own confession, with killing and stealing (in company with **John Hawkins**) one ewe sheep, the property of the said William Boucher. Warrant dated December 23.

Drawn by J. Russell, R.A.   Engraved by H. Adlard

Captain William Bligh (see p. 291). (Rev. T.B. Murray, *Pitcairn*, 1854)

Stage 3: Legal proceedings

(see Appendix 8)

The following abstracts have been taken from Assize records.

TNA ref ASSI 25/2/15

Western Circuit Assizes – Indictments
Somerset

Thursday 29 March 1804 at the Castle, Taunton

Jury sworn: George Leeky, Amos Greenslade, George Bullock, Isaac Richards, John Bartlett, John Furze, Richard Trood, John Reynolds the younger, Joseph Andrews, James Bond, Thomas Hurman, Thomas Garland.

* **John Hawkins**,[1] *po se* [*ponit se super patriam*: pleaded not guilty and put himself at the mercy of the jury] – guilty, no goods; to be hanged.
* **Philip Cording**, *po se* – guilty, no goods; to be hanged.

For stealing on 21st December last at Wiveliscombe one sheep, pr [price or value] 30s., the property of William Boucher. 2nd Cot. [count] for killing sd [said] sheep with a felonious intent to steal the carcase thereof – against the State.

Reprieved. To be transported to the Eastern Coast of New South Wales or some one or other of the Islands adjacent for and during the term of their respective natural lives pursuant to Secretary of State's letter dated 11th April 1804.

[For details of this letter see Stage 8].[2]

Stage 4: Sheriffs' Assize Vouchers

(see Appendix 11)

These documents are bound in volumes and arranged annually county by county. The following records John Hawkins and Philip Cording.

TNA ref E 370/45/9

SOMERSET. The delivery of the Gaol of our Lord the King, of the County of Somerset of the prisoners therein holden at The Castle of Taunton in and for the said County on Thursday the twenty ninth day of March in the forty fourth year of our sovereign Lord George the Third by the Grace of God of the United Kingdom of Great Britain and Ireland, King, Defender of the Faith. Before Sir Alexander Thomson, Knight, one of the Barons of our Lord the King of His Court of Exchequer, Sir Robert Graham, Knight, one other of the Barons of our said Lord the King of his said Court of Exchequer and others their fellow Justices &c.

reprieved	**John Hawkins** ⎫	Attainted of sheep stealing, let them be severally
reprieved	**Philip Cording** ⎬	hanged by the neck until they are dead.
reprieved	John Way ⎫	Attainted of Burglary, let them be severally
reprieved	John Wood ⎬	hanged by the neck until they are dead.

1. A large asterisk against a name indicates the death sentence.
2. The *Western Circuit Assizes Gaol Book* for Somerset (*TNA ref. ASSI 23/9*), repeats identically the details given in the above indictment.

Stage 5: Prison records
(see Appendix 6)
As Hawkins and Cording were tried at Taunton it is likely that they were held at Taunton Gaol. There are no known registers for Taunton Gaol at this date (1804). Neither are there any registers for this date for the other Somerset prisons at Shepton Mallet and Ilchester. (The earliest known Taunton Prison register commences in 1807, Shepton Mallet 1809, Ilchester 1808.)

Stage 6: British newspapers

Newspapers invariably reported local crimes. The following is taken from the *Western Flying Post*, 9 April 1804:

BL/NL

> At the Assizes for Somerset, which ended on Thursday at Taunton, the following prisoners were capitally convicted and received sentence of death, viz. **John Hawkins** and **Philip Cording** charged on their own confession with stealing one ewe sheep, the property of William Boucher. John Wood, aged 15, for breaking and entering a dwelling house, and stealing money; John Way, for breaking and entering a dwelling house and stealing drapery goods, the property of R. Parkin; and William Dowder and William Needs, removed by Habeas Corpus from Exeter, charged with robbing John Pring of five guineas and half, and other articles. The four former are reprieved, but Dowder and Needs left for execution.

(Other criminal cases are reported in the same article.)

Stage 7: Petitions on behalf of convicted criminals
(see Appendix 9)
There are numerous petitions in various classes of documents at The National Archives, but no such document has been found for either John Hawkins or Philip Cording. (Examples of petitions are given in Chapter 5.)

Stage 8: Home Office warrants – pardons, reprieves and related correspondence
(see Appendix 10)
Both John Hawkins and Philip Cording were given a reprieve from the death sentence on condition that they were transported to New South Wales.

TNA ref HO 13/16

Whitehall 11 April 1804

To Justices of Assize for the Western Circuit
Gentlemen,
The following persons having been tried and convicted before you at the last assizes holden for the Western Circuit of the Crimes hereafter mentioned viz:

John **Hawkins** ⎫ **Philip Cording** ⎭	at the Castle Taunton in the County of Somerset on 29th day of March last of sheep stealing
John Way ⎫ John Wood ⎭	at the same time and place of Burglary

and you having by certificate under your hands humbly recommended them as fit objects of the Royal Mercy on Condition of their being Transported beyond the Seas for the Term of their Natural Lives; His Majesty has thereupon been graciously pleased to extend the Royal Mercy to the said several persons on Condition of their being transported to the Eastern Coast of New South Wales or some one or other of the Islands adjacent for and during the Term of their respective Natural Lives and has commanded me to signify the same to you that you may give the necessary directions accordingly.

I am,

C. Yorke

[A Principal Secretary of State]

Stage 9: Transportation Order Books

(see Appendix 8)

These are to be found for the Western Circuit of Assizes only, covering the counties of Cornwall, Devon, Dorset, Somerset, Southampton (Hampshire) and Wiltshire. The following entry records John Hawkins and Philip Cording.

TNA ref ASSI 24/27 Western Circuit Assizes – Transportation Order Book

LENT CIRCUIT – 1804 for Somerset

At the Assizes and General delivery of the Gaol of our Lord the King, holden at *The Castle of Taunton* in and for the *County of Somerset* on Thursday the twenty ninth Day of March in the Forty fourth year of the Reign of our Sovereign Lord George the Third, by the Grace of God of the United Kingdom of Great Britain and Ireland, Kind, Defender of the Faith. Before Sir Alexander Thomson, Knight, one of the Barons of our Lord the King of his Court of Exchequer, Sir Robert Graham, Knight, one other of the Barons of our said Lord the King of His said Court of Exchequer; and others their Fellow Justices of our said Lord the King, assigned to deliver his Gaol of the said *County of Somerset* of the prisoners therein being.

Whereas **John Hawkins**, **Philip Cording**, John Way and John Wood were at these assizes severally convicted of Felony for which they were excluded the Benefit of Clergy and His Majesty hath been graciously pleased to extend the Royal Mercy to them ON CONDITION of their being transported to the Eastern Coast of New South Wales or some one or other of the Islands adjacent for and during the term of their respective natural Lives and such intention of mercy having been signified by The Right Honourable Charles Yorke, one of His Majesty's Principal Secretaries of State:

IT IS THEREFORE, in Pursuance of an Act of Parliament, passed in the 24th Year of the Reign of His Majesty, King George the Third, entitled 'An Act for the effectual Transportation of Felons and other Offenders' and to authorize the Removal of Prisoners in certain Cases, and for other Purposes therein mentioned – ORDERED AND ADJUDGED by this court, that the said above-named Convicts be respectively transported to the Eastern Coast of New South Wales or some one or other of the Islands adjacent as soon as conveniently may be for and during the term of their respective natural Lives. And William Phelips, clerk, and Walter Wightwick, clerk, two of his Majesty's Justices of the Peace for the said *County of Somerset* are hereby appointed to contract with any Person or Persons for the Performance of the Transportation of the said convicts and to order sufficient Security to be taken for the same, pursuant to the said Act of Parliament: AND THIS COURT DOTH ORDER, that the said above-named Convicts be transferred to the Use of such Person or Persons, his or their Assigns, as shall contract for the due Performance of the said Transportation, which Contract or Contracts, and Security shall be certified by the said Justices to the next Court of General Delivery, to be holden for the said *County of Somerset* to be filed and kept among the Records of this Court.

By the Court

Stage 10: Sheriffs' Cravings

(see Appendix 11)

Sheriffs' Cravings are petitions to the Exchequer made by county sheriffs requesting payment of the expenses incurred in maintaining criminals in gaol and for conveying convicts sentenced to transportation from gaols to prison hulks. John Rogers, Sheriff of Somerset, requested the following payment for Hawkins, Cording and others:

TNA ref E 370/45

A Bill of Cravings in the Sheriffalty of John Rogers, Esqr. [Taunton] 1804	£	s	d
To paying [for] Wm. Dowder and Wm. Needs, two convicts from Lent Assizes from 29th of March to the 25th April being four weeks at 2s 6d pr. week each	1	0	0
To executing the above two convicts	4	0	0
To paying [for] **John Hawkins**, **Philip Cording**, John Way, John Wood, Saml. Chubb, Benjamin Cook, Thos. Bristow, Saml. Severn, Henry Emery, and Joseph Pearce, ten convicts from the above Assize from 29th March to the 7th June following, being 10 weeks and 1 day at 2s 6d pr week each. Then put on board the *Captivity,* Portsmouth.	12	13	4

Stage 11: Books of Sheriffs' Payments

(see Appendix 11)

In addition to Sheriffs' Cravings there are Books of Sheriffs' Payments that list payments made to county sheriffs by the Treasury and also list expenses for judges and gaolers. Unfortunately the Book of Sheriffs' Payments for 1804, which would have mentioned John Hawkins and Philip Cording, does not survive. The following is an example of sheriffs' payments.

TNA ref T 90/169

SOMERSET

John Legh, Esq. Sheriff for the said County for the year ending Michas 1811	£	s	d
Lodgings of Judges &c at both Assizes	63	0	0
Fitting up the Courts at do and for carpets, &c	5	0	0
Balloting Box & List of Juries	5	0	0
Dispg. Proclns (8th Feb. 1811) for a general Fast	2	0	0
Dispg. Proclns (8th Nov 1811) for proroguing the Parliament	2	0	0
Dispg. Proclns (8th Nov 1811) for holding the Audit	2	0	0
Attending persons to peruse Public Acts	2	0	0
Dispg Ploclns (18th Dec. 1811) for apprehending persons committing Riots	2	0	0
Dispg. Proclns (14th Jan 1812) for a general Fast	2	0	0

Justices Wages as per Affidavit	30	4	0
Poundage on leaving Taxes	199	5	0
For the like on £3195-16-2 in sums less than £100 at 1s	159	15	9
For Pipe fees thereon being 158 sums at ¾d	26	6	8
Tallies (No. 20)	7	0	0
King's Rem. Appl. Rec. & Certif ...	8	3	0

GAOLER'S BILL

Dietting John Biggs, George Shattock. John Hucklebridge, William Humphrey Hill & John Saw per 2nd April to 28th May 1811, 8 weeks at 2s 6d	5	0	0
Martha Parsons & Elizabeth Flemming from 23rd Aug to 13th Sept 1811, 3 weeks at 2s 6d per week		15	0
Thomas Jeffries, David Horler, Goerge Dix, John Smith, Charles Rowley & James Good from 23rd Aug to 13th Sept 1811. 3 weeks at 2s 6d per week	2	5	0
Executing Arthur Baily	2	0	0
Dietting John Carr from 2nd April to 10th Feb. 1812, 45 weeks at 2s 6d	5	12	6
	£531	**6**	**11**

> Sworn at Wells in the County of Somerset 27th April 1812 before
> Edmund Broderrip, undersheriff
> Robert Welsh, a commr. [commissioner]
> Allowed by Mr Baron Graham £130

Let the above Sheriff be allowed in full for this sum of Five Hundred & Twenty Eight Pounds, Six Shillings and Eleven Pence.

Stage 12: Treasury warrants
(see Appendix 11)
Treasury warrants include sheriffs' conviction money. John Hawkins and Philip Cording are again recorded.

TNA ref T 53/63 folio 302

> To Edmund Broderip, Undersheriff, County Somerset.
> Warrant dated 28th Dec. 1804
> To William Boucher et al for apprehending and convicting **John Hawkins**
> and **Philip Cording** of Fel. [felony] and sheep stealing.
> Cert. dated 2nd April 1804   £20
>   signed A. Thomson
>
> To Thomas Joyce et al for do, John Manners otherwise Maynard and Chas.
> Fuller of Fel. [felony] and Burg. [burglary].
> Cert. dated 14th Aug. 1804   £80
>   signed Ellenborough

Stage 13: Prison Hulk records
(see Appendix 7)
Home Office records list name, age and offence of each convict on board, together with the place and date of their trial and the sentence of the court. An additional note usually records the transfer of each convict to a transportation vessel.

Newgate prison, where Elizabeth Smith was confined prior to her transportation to New South Wales. (Courtesy of Guildhall Library, London)

Table 19.1: Prison Hulk *Captivity* at Portsmouth from 1 January 1802 to 19 September 1816. *(TNA ref HO 9/8)*

Received from Taunton the 7th June 1804

No.	Name	Age	Offence	When & Where Convicted	Sentence
1105	**John Hawkins**	45	Sheep stealing	Taunton 29 March 1804	Life. Sent on board the *Fortune*. 9 Jan. 1806
1106	**Philip Cording**	46	Sheep stealing	Taunton 29 March 1804	Life. Sent on board the *Fortune*. 9 Jan. 1806

Treasury Departmental Records, TNA document class T 38, include records of some prison hulks for the period 1802–18. They list the clothing and bedding issued to each convict. Details of any time spent by a convict in the sick bay are also recorded. The records include lists naming the crew and guards on the hulks (see p. 286).

Table 19.2: *Captivity:* Extracts from Quarterly Lists. *(TNA ref T38/311)*

	No. on Ship's Book	Entry	From Whence	Names	D [Dischar DD [Disch dead E [Escape
1 April to 30 June	1105	7 June 1804	Taunton Somerset	*John Hawkins*	
	1106	7 June 1804	Taunton Somerset	*Philip Cording*	
1 July 1804 to 30 Sept 1804	1105	5 June 1804 (sic)	Former Book	*John Hawkins*	
		5 June 1804	Former Book	*Philip Cording*	
1 Oct 1804 to 31 Dec 1804	1105	7 June 1804	Former Book	*John Hawkins*	
		7 June 1804	Former Book	*Philip Cording*	
	SICK BAY RECORDS				
	1106	20 Nov 1804		*Philip Cording*	D
	1105	12 Dec 1804		*John Hawkins*	—
1 Jan 1805 to 31 March 1805	1105	7 June 1804	Former Book	*John Hawkins*	
	1106	7 June 1804	Former Book	*Philip Cording*	
	SICK BAY RECORDS				
	1105	1 Jan 1805		*John Hawkins*	D
	1106	26 Feb 1805		*Philip Cording*	D
1 April 1805 to 30 June 1805	1105	7 June 1804	Former Book	*John Hawkins*	
	1106	7 June 1804	Former Book	*Philip Cording*	
1 July 1805 to 30 Sept 1805	1105	7 June 1804	Former Book	*John Hawkins*	
	1106	7 June 1804	Former Book	*Philip Cording*	
1 Oct 1805 to 31 Dec 1805	1105	7 June 1804	Former Book	*John Hawkins*	
	1106	7 June 1804	Former Book	*Philip Cording*	
1 Jan 1806 to 31 March 1806	1105	7 June 1804	Former Book	*John Hawkins*	D
	1106	7 June 1804	Former Book	*Philip Cording*	D

	Whither	No. of days Victualed	Jackets	Waistcoats	Breeches	Shirts	Pr. Shoes	Pr. Stockings	Hats	Handkerchfs	Beds	Blankets
		24						1		1		
		24			1	1		1		1		
		92	1			2			1			
		92	1			1	1	1	1			
		92		1		1	1					1
		92		1		1		1		1		1
c 1804		19 20										
		90	1			1		1	1	1		
		90	1			1	1					
1805 rch 1805		5 12										
		91			1	1	1	1				
		91			1	1		1		1		
		92	1					1	1	1		
		92	1				1	1				
		92			1	1	1	1				
		92				1		1	1			
uary	N.S.Wales	9										
uary	N.S.Wales	9			1					1		

Stage 14: Convict transportation records arranged by ships
(see Appendices 14 and 17)

1. Home Office records

Home Office lists of convicts on board transportation ships are recorded in TNA document class HO 11. Each convict has recorded against their name the place and date of trial and the term of their sentence.

Table 19.3: The *Fortune* and *Alexander* in the month of January 1806. *(TNA ref HO 11/1)* (Details of these ships are given on page 120.)

Names	Where convicted	When	Term
Philip Cording	Somerset Assizes	29 March 1804	Life
John Hawkins		29 March 1804	Life
Grace Knight		28 March 1805	7 years
William Ayshford		17 Aug. 1805	Life
Mary Hammett		17 Aug. 1805	14 Years
etc., etc			

2. Admiralty Transport Department: Out Letters

TNA ref ADM 108/20

T.O. [Transport Office], 6 Jan. 1806

Jno. King, Esq. [Home Office Official]
Sir,
I am directed by the Board to acquaint you for the information of the Right Honourable Lord Hawkesbury that the *Fortune* convict ship is now ready at Spithead to receive on board from the hulks at Portsmouth the convicts intended to be embarked in that ship for a passage to New South Wales and to request that the necessary direction be given accordingly.

I have the Honour to be,
Sir,
C.W.

A further letter of the same date requests 'a guard in place of the detachment which was lent from the Garrison at Sheerness'.

Lists of convicts on transportation vessels for the period 1842–67 are also to be found in Treasury Solicitor's contract records, TNA document class TS 18.

T.O. [Transport Office] 14 Jan. 1806

Jno. King, Esq.
We inclose for the information of the Right Honourable Lord Hawkesbury a list of convicts, guards, women and children of the guards and Ship's Company embarked on board of the *Fortune* convict ship for New South Wales. [Then follows the list of convicts from Woolwich, Portsmouth and Langstone hulks.]

The following is an extract from the list of convicts from Portsmouth:

Chas. Chambers
Wm. Greenwood
John Dunn
Thomas Child
William King
Wm. Docknell
Josiah Dodd
Matthew Smart
Wm. Ashford
Philip Cording
John Hawkins
Spicer Woodhouse
James Little
Jno. Newman
etc., etc.

Thirty guards are listed, several of whom are accompanied by their wives and children, all of whose names are given. For example: Corporal Isaac Dutton, accompanied by his wife Mary and his two-year-old son William; and private James Roche with his wife Elizabeth and ten-year-old daughter Eliza. There are forty-nine members of the ship's company listed with their specific rank or occupations, such as John Topling, second officer; Thomas Preston, boatswain; Andrew de Cruz, captain's cook.

'The Battle Previous to the Surrender of the Cape of Good Hope, 8 January 1806.' (Cape Archives ref M348)

3. Audit Department Accounts

A summary account for each county is then given, as in the following example.

TNA ref AO 3/291

Account of Thomas Shelton relating to convicts transported to His Majesty's Territory of New South Wales or the Islands adjacent by Messrs. Mestaer and Locke in the ships *Alexander* and *Fortune* the 23rd January 1806.

Somerset 13 convicts

Procuring and perusing the documents and writings relating to 13 convicts sentenced to be transported at the Session of Gaol Delivery held for the County of Somerset	6s 8d
Drawing Contract to transport them – folio 22	£1 2s 0d
Ingrossing thereof	11s 0d
Drawing Bond from the Contractors and their sureties to perform the Contract – folio 21	£1 1s 0d
Ingrossing thereof	10s 6d
Paid for stamps and paper	£2 12s 6d
Attending the execution of Contract and Bond	6s 8d
Warrant for the delivery of Convicts to the Contractor	3s 4d

[Other expenses are listed on the last page]

Instructions to prepare Assignment of the several Convicts from Messrs. Mestaer to the Governor of New South Wales for the remainder of the terms of their sentences	6s 8d
Drawing and ingrossing same	£1 0s 0d
Paid for stamp and paper	£1 11s 6d
Attending the execution thereof	6s 8d
Mailing fair copy list of such of the offenders as had been ordered to be transported beyond the seas in order that the same might be annexed to an order by His Majesty in Council appointing the Eastern Coast of New South Wales the place to which they should be transported	£1 0s 0d
Making fair copy list of all the offenders intended to be transported in order that the same might be annexed to a warrant under His Majesty's Sign Manual authorizing me to contract for the transportation of them	£1 7s 0d
The like for His Majesty's Secretary of State for the Home Department	£1 7s 0d
The like to annex the assignment to the Governor of New South Wales	£1 7s 0d
Examining lists, attendances at Secretary of State's Office and other places, letters, messages, postages, carriage of parcels, etc., etc.	<u>£4 4s 0d</u>
298 convicts	<u>£322 14s 6d</u>

Stage 15: Ships' records

Captains' papers preserved by the Admiralty include William Bligh's 'Order of Sailing', giving such details as his fleet's alternative formation to be adopted in the event of attack by the enemy (the French), and the distinguishing coloured pennants to be flown by each ship. The *Woolwich* was not included in this list. Part of the contract specification for this vessel is given on pages 124–125.

Table Bay *c.* 1790. (Cape Archives ref M226)

TNA ref ADM 1/2515 (a loose document)

ORDER OF SAILING
from Captain William Bligh

Weather or Starboard Division   **Lee or Larboard Division**
Lady Sinclair   *Porpoise*
Justina   *Fortune*
Alexander   *Elizabeth*

LINE OF BATTLE
Lady Sinclair
Justina
Alexander
Porpoise
Fortune
Elizabeth

Starboard Division will keep on the Starboard side of the Lee Division going before the wind.

Stages 16, 17 and 18: Ships' correspondence, captains' logs, masters' logs and lieutenants' logs
(see Appendix 19)

By piecing together information from various Admiralty papers, Colonial Office records and ships' logs, the story of the voyage can be revealed. The following chart summarises the main events on the voyage. (No logs for the *Fortune* and *Alexander* have been located.)

SUMMARY OF SELECTED SHIPS' CORRESPONDENCE

Note: (T.O.) = Transport Office, (H.O.) = Home Office, (A.O.) = Admiralty Office, N.M.M. = National Maritime Museum ref.

P.R.O. ref.	Date	From	To	Extracts from Correspondence
CO 201/39, f.106	15/11/05	J. Gambier, Philip Patton Garlies, by command of their Lordships, Wm. Marsden	Joseph Short, *Porpoise*	'You are hereby required and directed to take H.M. Ship *Woolwich* under your command . . . proceed to the store ship *Saturn* and the *Lady Sinclair* transport as expeditiously as possible to the Cape of Good Hope approaching with the greatest caution and taking particular care before you come to an anchor there, to be well assured it is in the possession of H. M. troops . . . then proceed with the *Porpoise* and *Lady Sinclair* to Port Jackson in New South Wales and upon arrival put yourself under the command of Captain William Bligh (whom His Majesty has appointed Governor of that Colony).'
ADM 108/20, p.264	6/1/06	A.W., (T.O.)	Jno. King	'*Fortune* now ready at Spithead to receive convicts.'
CO 201/41, f.5	6/1/06	*Fortune*, Portsmouth H. Moor		'No person here appears to know anything about the guard I am to have, who or where they are, and on Wednesday went the remainder of the convicts to embark.'
ADM 108/20	6/1/06	R.G., A.S., T.H, (T.O)		Request for a guard, in place of the detachment which was lent from the garrison at Sheerness.
CO 201/41, f.3	7/1/06	J. King, (H.O.)	Edward Cooke	Requesting 'that Lord Castlereagh be moved to give directions for embarking the Guard on the *Fortune*'.
ADM 110/50, f.19	9/1/06	J.M., G.P.T., C.C., W.B., R.P.T., Commissioners for the Transport Service	*Fortune*	Authorising the master of the *Fortune* to purchase fresh beef and water.
ADM 108/21	23/1/06	A.W., Portsmouth (T.O.)	Admiralty	'Convicts, wives and children, and ship's company embarked on the *Alexander* for New South Wales . . . the convict who died on the 19th instant is William Swain from Lincoln.'
CO 201/41, f.15	27/1/06	J. King, (H.O.)	Edward Cook	'Three hundred and six convicts on board the *Fortune* and *Alexander* – order to transmit list to the Governor of New South Wales'.
CO 201/39, f.116	30/1/06	Sir R. J. Strachan, Bt., Rear-Admiral of the Blue	Master of the *Lady Sinclair* transport	'His Excellency Captain William Bligh of His Majesty's Navy, Captain General and Governor in Chief of New South Wales embarked in the *Lady Sinclair* . . . the master of the *Lady Sinclair* is hereby authorised to wear a Pendant as a ship of War'.

ADM 51/1670	3/2/06	Captain's Log, *Porpoise*		'A boat from the *Fortune* with two soldiers, prisoners, and the Chief Mate, and an Officer to substantiate their crimes. Punished Edmd. Germany with 24 lashes and Levi Chance with 12 lashes for filthiness.'
ADM 1/2515	27/2/06	Joseph Short, *Porpoise*	Wm. Bligh, *Sinclair*	'*Alexander* and *Fortune* fearful of proceeding to the Cape as it is not confirmed as being in our possession'.
ADM 1/2515	27/2/06	Wm. Bligh, *Lady Sinclair* at sea off Canaries	Jo. Short, *Porpoise*	'*Alexander* and *Fortune* have not sufficiency of necessaries in case that the place [the Cape] is not in our possession, to proceed to Brazil'.
CO 201/39, f. 124	27/2/06	J. Short	W. Bligh	*Alexander*, 12 Sixes Carronades, 39 men, 12 weeks water. *Sinclair*, 10 Twenty Four Carronades, 4 Nines Long G., 49 men, 16 weeks water. *Justina*, 10 Long Sixes, 2 Twelve Carronades, 21 men, 12 weeks water. *Fortune*, 12 Long Sixes, 6 Long Nines, 60 men, 12 weeks water. *Elizabeth*, 8 weeks water.
CO 201/39, f.128	28/2/06	,,	,,	'*Fortune* running short of water, request transfer some convicts to us.'
CO 201/39, f.130	28/2/06	W. Bligh	J. Short	'Transferring some convicts to *Lady Sinclair* to help with the navigation – recommend you do not risk it . . . will tend to some danger of mutiny.'
ADM 1/2515	28/2/06	,,	,,	'Send Lt. John Putland to the *Lady Sinclair*. You to have command of the *Lady Sinclair*.'
ADM 52/3784	1/3/06	Master's Log, *Porpoise*		'Sent the boat on board the *Fortune*, 8 a.m. Returned with 12 convicts – employed working up the Junk.'
CO 201/39, f.. 144	11/3/06	J. Short	W. Bligh	'. . .unpleasant circumstances between myself and you . . . I have reported to my Lords Commissioners of the Admiralty.'
CO 201/39, f. 148	11/3/06	W. Bligh	J. Short	'James Russell and John Ashton of New South Wales Corps on board the *Fortune* found guilty of words tending mutiny.'
ADM 51/1670	12/3/06	Captain's Log, *Porpoise*		'Sent a boat on board the *Fortune* with Lt. Surgeon and Boatswain to attend punishment. Sent a boat manned and armed to examine a Brig. Continued the Chase at 7.40. – the *Fortune* and *Justinia* in chase. The Chase proved to be 3 Portuguese brigs from Sal a Mayo bound to Tescara laden with salt. Punished George Holland convict with 2 dozen lashes for contempt.'

ADM 1/2515	12/3/06	*Porpoise*, off Cape de Verde Islands	Wm. Marsden, Sec. (A.O.)	'*Justina* going to part company at St Helena, request Mr. Moor, Master of *Fortune*, to lend me 12 convicts . . . to find them well behaved. Ordered the *Fortune* to follow the *Canada* and West India convoy.'
ADM 1/2515	15/3/06	H. Moor, *Fortune*	J. Short	'Referring to surgeon's letter re convicts on *Fortune* . . . their dibilitated state from length of time embarked 14 weeks . . . should any alarming contagious disorder break out I should be unable to reach some port in time to save many lives.'
ADM 1/2515	15/3/06	J. Short	W. Marsden, Sec. (A.O.)	Complaining of . . . 'Captain Bligh not hailing this ship like he might with equal readiness he did the *Fortune* . . . Bligh claims that they discovered land which looking at the charts is impossible.'
CO 201/39, f. 150	15/3/06	W. Bligh	J. Short	'Mr. Moor Master of the *Fortune*, he will not wait with the convoy but proceed with the utmost despatch to Rio Janeiro on account of the convicts getting into bad health'.
ADM 51/1670	16/3/06	Captain's Log, *Porpoise*		'Sent a boat with 12 convicts to the *Fortune*'.
ADM 1/2515	16/3/06	J. Short	W. Marsden, Sec (A.O.)	'Necessary for the *Fortune* to leave the convoy on account of the sickness of the convicts on board and proceed to the nearest port for refreshment . . . via St Helena with the *Justina* which left at the same time.'
ADM 1/2515	26/3/06	Richard Brooks, *Alexander*, 'at sea'	J. Short	'Am obliged to quit the convoy for Rio to accomplish supplies'
ADM 1/2515	28/3/06	J. Short	W. Bligh	'Scurvey has begun on the *Alexander* amongst the convicts . . . the *Elizabeth* has only two weeks' water – will proceed to Rio Janeiro – will meet up with the *Fortune* lately parted from the convoy the addition of whose force in case of meeting the enemy may be essential service.'
ADM 1/2515	1/4/06	E. Bunker, *Elizabeth*, 'at sea'	J. Short	'We are short of wood and water, not more than 12 days [remaining] . . . proceeding to Rio Janeiro'.
ADM 1/2515	2/4/06	J. Short, Simmonds Bay, Cape of Good Hope	W. Marsden, Sec. (A.O.)	'*Fortune* parted for Rio Janeiro, sickness having begun.'
ADM 1/2515	9/4/06	W. Bligh	J. Short	'Proceed to the Cape of Good Hope with the greatest caution . . . it may not be in our possession. It is dangerous to anchor at Table Bay, proceed to False Bay which is on the East side of the Cape.'

ADM 1/2515	16/4/06	J. Short	J. Jackson, *Sinclair*	Instructions regarding the entry to False Bay and details of signals.
ADM 25/3784	26/4/06	Master's Log, *Porpoise*		'Condemned 2,630 pounds of bread and saw it thrown into the sea.'
ADM 52/3784	10/5/06	,,	,,	'Sent the boats armed and manned with the Master to see if the Cape was in the possession of the English. Boat returned with intelligence of the Cape being in the possession of the English; made signal to *Sinclair*.'
ADM 52/3781	14/5/06	Master's Log, *Porpoise*		'Sent the cutter manned and armed to board the Danish ship *Three Sisters* from Copenhagen bound for Tranquabor laden with Naval Stores and despatches for the Dutch Governor'.
ADM 1/2515	14/5/06	W. Bligh	J. Short	'You are hereby required to send the papers found on board the Danish ship to the Commandant, Major Tucker, to be forwarded to Lt. Gen. Sir David Baird, Commander in Chief of H. M. Forces in this Country.'
ADM 1/2515	15/5/06	J. Short Simons Bay, Cape of Good Hope	W. Bligh Simons Town	'You persist in sending me orders altho. you are not mustered on board any of H.M.'s ships on this Station . . . it may not be my fault you wanted to assume the command over me . . . the rules of H.M.'s Naval Service; I cannot obey until you are mustered or I am subject to Court Martial . . . I will report to the Lords of Admiralty.'
ADM 1/2515	21/5/06	,,	W. Marsden, Sec. (A.O.)	'Arrived at this place with *Sinclair*, 11 inst, on 14th sent boats into the Bay, boarded and detained *Three Sisters* Danish ship having Dutch property on board.'
ADM 1/2515	14/6/06	W. Bligh, *Porpoise*	J. Short, *Porpoise*	'I am proceeding to go on board the *Lady Sinclair* – you are required to still consider yourself under my command.'
N.M.M. ref. ADM/ L/P/190	6/8/06	Lieutenant's Log, *Porpoise*		'Tack'd Ship occasionally working up to Port Jackson. At 9.30 shortened sail came to with the small bower in fathom furled sails'.
N.M.M. ref. ADM/ L/P/190	8/8/06			'Came on board Captn. Bligh and ordered his Broad Pendant to be hoisted. Saluted the Governor going on shore with 15 guns.'
ADM 52/3784	13/8/06	Master's Log, *Porpoise*		'12.15 Saluted Governor King on his departure from the Colony as Governor with 15 Guns. At 1 saluted Governor Bligh on his taking command of the colony'.

Part of a list of pardoned convicts from 1816. Note John Hawkins is the first entry. (The National Archives ref CO 201/99)

Stage 19: Ships' surgeons' journals
(see Appendix 19)
No surgeons' journals have been found for this fleet. Some examples of this type of record are given in Chapter 9.

Stage 20: Foreign Office correspondence from the Canary Islands

No reference to any of the ships in this fleet have been found in these records.

Stage 21: Port records at the Cape Archives, South Africa

The following records the *Porpoise* at the Cape:

Ship's Name	*Porpoise*
Where from	Spithead
When sailed	28 January
Nation	English
Where bound	Port Jackson
Cargo	Provisions
Captain's Name	Short
Arrival	11 May 1806
Departure	17 June 1806

A similar entry is given for the *Sinclair*. None of the other ships in the fleet docked at the Cape.

Stage 22: Australian newspapers

Newspapers often reported the arrival of ships. No record of Philip Cording had been found in New South Wales and in the first edition of this book it was stated that he was assumed to be one of the three unnamed convicts who had died on the voyage. Subsequent research has shown that he did arrive in New South Wales where his name was recorded as Philip Cordon.[3] The following item is taken from the *Sydney Gazette*.

BL/NL Sydney Gazette [New South Wales],13 July 1806

SHIP NEWS

Yesterday arrived the *Fortune,* Captain Henry Moore, with 242 male convicts, and a Military Guard of 27 Rank and File commanded by Ensign Mullin of the 8th Veteran Battalion, from England; which she left the 28th January in company with His Majesty's armed vessel *Porpoise,* the *Alexander* transport, and *Lady Madeline Sinclair* with stores, Governor Bligh being on board the latter ship. The *Fortune* parted company with the above vessels at 9° north, on account of sickness: arrived at Rio Janeiro the 11th of April and sailed the 30th, leaving the *Alexander* and *Elizabeth* whalers at that port, which had parted company with the *Porpoise* and *Sinclair* about the 10th of April, the latter ship proceeding on to the Cape of Good Hope. The *Fortune* has lost only three convicts and one soldier, who were diseased on embarking.

The account we received of the last glorious exploit achieved by the late much lamented Admiral Viscount Nelson against the combined fleet of France and Spain is confirmed [by Captain Moore] with this difference, that instead of 23 ships of the line, the enemy's loss amounted to thirty-two, with the capture of three Admirals.

The death of the Right Honourable William Pitt, Captain Moor announces also; an event sincerely and universally regretted by the British Nation.

For the particulars of the investment imported in the *Fortune*, we refer to the Advertisement in the last column.

Goods for sale
FORTUNE'S INVESTMENT

Simeon Lord respectfully informs his Friends and the Public in general the valuable Investment imported in the ship *La Fortune* [sic], Captain Moore, will be open for sale on Commission on Thursday next, at his Warehouse in Sydney, consisting of the following articles, viz:

Ship's chandler's stores of various kinds
Anchors from ¾ cwt. to 7 cwt.
corkage from one to six inches
lines and twine, paint and oil
a small quantity of pitch, rosin and tar
gentlemen's hats, boots and shoes
ladies' shoes and straw hats
woollen cloths and trimmings
cutlery of various kinds

3. The Convict Muster for New South Wales and Norfolk Island for the years 1805–06 reads: 'Philip Cordon, came by the ship *Fortune*, Employed at Castle Hill.'

brass furniture for cabinet work
a small assortment of jewellery
tin in sheets with solder
a variety of tin ware
earthen and glass ditto
slop clothing, window glass
a few plated tea pots, &c
bridles, saddles and gig harnesses
loaf and Rio sugar, butter and cheese
oilmen's stores of different sorts
a small quantity of Brazil tobacco

and a number of other useful articles together with a small quantity of wine, spirits, rasberry [sic] and cherry brandy, perry and cyder, all of which must be sold subjected to His Excellency's permission.

Payment to be made on delivery in Government, Paymaster's or such other Bills as may be approved of, or Dollars at 5s each; in consequence of the Ship being under the necessity of leaving this Port in the course of a month.

The *Alexander*, a transport ship. (National Maritime Museum)

Taunton Castle, where John Hawkins and Philip Cording were tried and convicted of sheep stealing. (Courtesy of Somerset Archaeological Society)

Stage 23: Convict muster rolls in New South Wales

(see Appendix 15)

Various musters of convicts were made. The following tabulation lists the musters in which **John Hawkins** is recorded. Each muster also records that he arrived in New South Wales in July 1806 on the ship *Fortune,* after being sentenced to transportation for Life at the Taunton Assizes of March 1804. This information has been omitted from this tabulation.

Table 19.5: Muster roll entries recording **John Hawkins**. *(TNA ref HO 10)*

	Date of Muster	How Disposed of	Whether Resident in the Colony
1	1788–1789	Govt. Labour	In the Colony
37	1806	Govt. Labour, Castle Hill	
5	1811	(**John Hawkins** is recorded in this return but no other details are given)	
3	1816	Servant to J.Watts, at Richmond	In the Colony
8	1810–1817	Govt. Labour	In the Colony
12	1820	Govt Labour	In the Colony
36	1822	Wheelwright	Windsor (C.P.)[4]
19	1835	Carpenter	Richmond (C.P.)

John Hawkins is not recorded in the musters for 1818, 1821, 1828 or 1837.

4. C.P.: conditional pardon.

Stage 24: The 1828 census for New South Wales
(see Appendix 16)

Table 19.6: The 1828 census records John Hawkins as living with Elizabeth Hawkins. They are both shown to have been granted a Conditional Pardon (C.P.).

Name	Age	Free/ Bond	Ship	Year	Sentence	Religion	Employment	Residence
John Hawkins	55[5]	C.P.	*Fortune*	1800	Life	Protestant	Wheelwright	Richmond
Elizabeth Hawkins	56	C.P.	*Speedy*	1806	7 years	Protestant		Richmond

Stage 25: Pardons and Tickets of Leave
(see Appendix 10)

John Hawkins received a conditional pardon in 1816, as is shown in the following document from Colonial Office Records.

Table 19.7: A list of Conditional Pardons granted by His Excellency Governor Macquarie, from 1810–1819 inclusive. Sydney, New South Wales. *(TNA ref CO 201/118)*

Year	Name	Year Arrived	Ship Arrived By	Date of Sentence	Sentence
1816	William Holmes	1801	*Earl Cornwallis*	1800	Life
	Samuel Bales	1806	*Fortune*	1805	Life
	George Smith	1806	*Fortune*	1804	14 years
	B. Waterhouse	1806	*Fortune*	1805	14 years
	B. Marshall	1806	*Fortune*	1804	Life
	Tho. Hinton	1806	*Fortune*	1805	14 years
	John Hawkins	1806	*Fortune*	1804	Life
	M. Callaghan	1799	*Friendship*		Life
	D. Whitaker	1803	*Glatton*	1801	Life
	Thos. Stone	1812	*Guildford*	1810	Life
	etc., etc.				

Another list of Conditional Pardons, which also records John Hawkins, is given in TNA ref CO 201/84.

5. John Hawkins' age was misrecorded; he would have been 66.

Lent Circuit 1804

Somerset — At the Assizes and general Delivery of the Gaol of our Lord the King, holden at *The Castle of Taunton* in and for the County of *Somerset* — on *Thursday* the *twenty ninth* Day of *March* — in the *forty fourth* Year of the Reign of our Sovereign Lord George the Third, by the Grace of God ~~King of Great Britain and Ireland~~ *of the United Kingdom of Great Britain and Ireland King Defender of the faith* — *Before Sir Alexander Thomson Knight one of the Barons of our Lord the King of His Court of Exchequer Sir Robert Graham Knight one other of the Barons of our said Lord the King of His said Court of Exchequer* — and others their Fellows Justices of our said Lord the King, assigned to deliver his Gaol of the said *County of Somerset* — — — — — of the Prisoners therein being.

Whereas John Hawkins, Philip Cording, John Way and John Wood were at these assizes severally convicted of Felony for which they were excluded the benefit of Clergy and His Majesty hath been graciously pleased to extend the Royal Mercy to them On Condition of their being transported to the Eastern Coast of New South Wales or some one or other of the Islands adjacent for and during the term of their respective natural Lives And such intention of Mercy having been signified by The Right Honourable Charles Yorke + — one of His Majesty's principal Secretaries of State:

IT IS THEREFORE, in pursuance of an Act of Parliament, passed in the 24th Year of the Reign of his Majesty, King GEORGE the Third, intituled, " An Act for the effec-" tual Transportation of Felons, and other Offenders, and to authorize the Removal of Pri-" soners in certain Cases, and for other Purposes therein mentioned,"——ORDERED AND ADJUDGED by this Court, that the said above-named Convicts be ~~transported beyond~~ ~~the Seas remaining as soon as conveniently may be~~ *respectively transported* ~~to~~ *to the Eastern Coast of New South Wales or some one or other of the Islands adjacent as soon as conveniently may be for — and during the term of their respective natural Lives* — — — —

— — — — — — — — — — — —

— — — — — — — — — — — —

And *William Phelips, Clerk, and Walter Wighwick, Clerk;* — — — two of his Majesty's Justices of the Peace for the said *County of Somerset* — — — — — are hereby appointed to contract with any Person or Persons for the Performance of the Transportation of the said Convict *s* and to order sufficient Security to be taken for the same, pursuant to the said Act of Parliament :——AND THIS COURT DOTH ORDER, that the said above-named Convict *s* be transferred to the Use of such Person or Persons, his or their Assigns, as shall contract for the due Performance of the said Transportation, which Contract or Contracts, and Security, shall be certified by the said Justices to the next Court of General Gaol Delivery, to be holden for the said *County of Somerset* — — — — — — — to be filed and kept among the Records of this Court.

By the Court

A page from a Transportation Order Book listing (among others) John Hawkins and Philip Cording to be transported to New South Wales. (The National Archives ref ASSI.24 27)

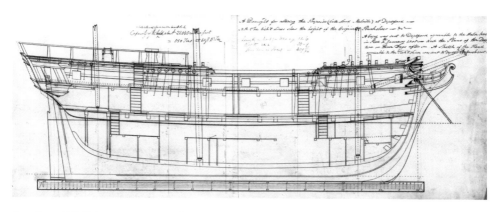

Drawing of HMS *Porpoise*. (National Maritime Museum)

The Archives in Australia contain further details of pardons:

S.R.A.N.S.W. ref 4/4430, page 97, Register of Conditional Pardons

DATE OF PARDON	1 January 1816
NAME	**John Hawkins**
SHIP AND YEAR	*Fortune* 1,[6] 1806
NATIVE PLACE	Somersetshire
PLACE AND DATE OF TRIAL	Somerset – Assizes, 29 March 1804
SENTENCE	Life
YEAR OF BIRTH	—[7]
HEIGHT	4 feet 11¼ inches
COMPLEXION	Dk. sallow
COLOUR OF HAIR	Sandy
COLOUR OF EYES	Blue

Stage 26: Miscellaneous convict records
(see Appendices 18)

No other records of John Hawkins have been found at The National Archives, London. A record of his death has been discovered. A search of Australian records found that John Hawkins died in Windsor Poor House, New South Wales, and was buried on 13 December 1838. John Hawkins' wife Elizabeth was buried at Richmond, New South Wales, on 11 June 1838.

---

6. The number following a ship's name refers to the number of voyages (and, therefore, year of arrival) to Australia; i.e. *Fortune* 1 refers to the first voyage and arrival in Australia, which was in 1806.
7. The year of birth or age is rarely given in these documents.

CHAPTER 20

HATTON PAPERS

This document collection was purchased by Joseph Hatton in 1868 and deposited at the Public Record Office (now The National Archives), by his daughter in 1943. Most of the documents relate to crime and punishment and are listed in Appendix 22. The following are some examples.

TNA ref PRO 30/45/1 folio 1

A Petition on behalf of John Evans of Hammersmith – 1779

Mr Grey Elliott

Plantation Office
July 14th 1779

Sir,

I am at a loss how to apologize for the Liberty I now take of soliciting a favor which I must acknowledge I have no right to do, but as it is an Act of Humanity I have to request of you I am from your very obliging behaviour in a trifling transaction that passed in this office, led to believe the goodness of your own heart will overlook any impropriety in an application which arises from the feelings of mine.

An honest neighbour of mine has an unfortunate son, now on board the Hulk at Woolwich, his name John Evans of Hammersmith, convicted in Feby 1778. His conduct since his punishment took place is said to have been truly exemplary, his crime I am told was not very heinous; and that he is a very likely stout young man and would gladly serve either in the Army or Navy. If Sir, thro your means he could obtain a discharge on condition of serving you will relieve his deserving parents from the distress they are now in, and confer on me an obligation so much the greater, as it will be without any merit of mine with you.

I am with true respect
Sir
Your most obedient Humble Servant
Grey Elliott

TNA ref PRO 30/45/1 folios 5 to 6

The Petition of Samuel Parker, a Convict – 1784

Recommended to the Royal Mercy by Sir Joseph Manley before whom he was tried.

To the Kings most Excellent Majesty
The Humble Petition of Samuel Parker
Sheweth
That at the Quarter Sessions holden at Southwark for the County of Surrey Your Petitioner was tried and convicted with one Samuel Totton upon an Indictment for Felony in Stealing some Turpentine the Property of Alexander Godwin Esquire in a yard belonging to him and was sentenced to be transported ten years.

That your Petitioner hath since his conviction remained a Prisoner in the New Gaol, Southwark where he has at all times behaved himself repentant of his Crime.

Your Petitioner has a Wife and five Children (the oldest of whom is not yet seven years old) who were all supported by your Petitioner's daily earnings and are now, with your Petitioner, reduced to the greatest and most deplorable distress.

That your Petitioner by reason of his long Confinement in Prison and the anguish of Mind on account of the Situation of his Family and himself, is greatly injured in his Health insomuch as to make his life very much in danger.

And your Petitioner sheweth that till the Commission of this Crime he always followed an honest, industrious and Laborious way of life; his character was never in the least impeached. And he was unwarily entrapped by the persuasions of the said Samuel Totton and his accomplice to be concerned in the Robbery, the only violation of the Law he ever committed.

And your Petitioner sheweth that your Majesty hath been pleased to extend your Royal Clemency in pardoning the said Samuel Totton.

Your Petitioner with the sincerest repentance and resolution never more to offend the Laws, most earnestly implores your Majesty's gracious Pardon (if the Almighty spares his Life) to his disconsolate Wife and Children.

And your Petitioner as in duty bound will ever pray.

Samuel Parker
X
His Mark

We your Majesty's most dutiful and loyal Subjects resident near the late Dwelling of the Petitioner Do most humbly certify to your Majesty that the Petitioner hath a wife and five children who were supported by his Labour. That he was always esteemed an honest man and was extremely industrious in his Business. We believe him to have been inadvertently drawn into a participation of the Crime. And not doubting he will again become a good Member of Society we do humbly recommend him as a proper object of your Majesty's most gracious Pardon.

[--- ? ---] Stp. Wright   Thos Carter

I most humbly certify that I have attended the Petitioner Samuel Parker in the New Gaol, Southwark, and find his Health very much injured by his imprisonment and therefore am of opinion if longer detained his life will be in danger.

Thos Walshman
Surgeon to the County Gaol

To the King's most Excellent Majesty I do most humbly certify that the Petitioner Samuel Parker hath behaved himself soberly and peaceably during his Imprisonment since which his Health is greatly impaired and I do think he is truly repentant of his offence.

B. Hall, Keeper

Grosvenor Street
May 28. 1784

I most humbly beg to report that the prisoner Samuel Parker was tried before me as chairman of the Quarter Sessions for the County of Surrey held at St. Margarets Hill and convicted on the clearest evidence. That I believe the report of his good behaviour in prison to be well founded and that after more than a year's confinement in prison I believe he may hereafter become a useful member of Society and therefore now recommend him as a fit object of Royal Mercy.

Joseph Mawbey

TNA ref PRO 30/45/1 folios 11 to 12

William Piggott sentenced to Death – 1786

R.A. Neville, Esq. in behalf of William Piggott,
a Convict under Sentence of Death in Newgate

Pall Mall
Mar. 27, 1786

My Lord
I am strongly requested by the Rev. Mr Tickell of Wargrave and many respectable persons in that neighbourhood to presume to make application to yourself in favor of William Piggot [sic] now under sentence of death in Newgate. If his unfortunate case can be thought worthy of mercy, and that your Lordship will be so kind as are your endeavors that his sentence may be changed to that of Transportation for Life. It will be the greatest comfort to a family of credit hitherto, and will be affording me the highest satisfaction. His crime is entering a cellar window and stealing some spoons and some halfpence. This lad is 20 yrs of age and just out of his time, and I understand it is his first offence.

I have many apologies to make to your Lordship for this interference but flatter myself you will forgive the liberty I am taking.

I have the honor to be with great Truth, My Lord
Your Lordship's most obdt and humble Servt
R.A.Neville

William Piggott was tried at the Old Bailey on 22 February 1786.

TNA ref PRO 30/45/1/5 folio 34

The Petition of George Batchelor late Surgeon in Coupar Angus – 1805
Now Prisoner in the Tolbooth of Edinburgh and of the other persons hereunto subscribing

Unto the King's Most Excellent Majesty
Most Humbly Sheweth
That your Petitioner George Batchelor was in Spring 1805 consulted by Ann Smyth a young woman who said she laboured under a certain Female disorder, but the

Petitioner having reason to believe she was with child administered some medicines which he knew would not injure her. It turned out that his suspicions were well founded and at the young women's earnest request he bespoke lodgings for her in Dundee believing that her object was to cover her shame and remain in private until after her delivery. But after going to Dundee this young woman applied to a person of the name of Katherine Stewart and an abortion took place. In July last the said Katherine Stewart and your Petitioner were indicted at the instance of His Majesty's Advocate for the Crime of causing the above Ann Smyth to abort and it appeared from the declaration of Katherine Stewart she had used means for that purpose. Ann Smyth was examined and deposed it was by those means the abortion was procured. She deposed that the medicines administered by the Petitioner did not injure her.

The jury found Katherine Stewart guilty of procuring the abortion and the Petitioner guilty Art and Part. In consequence of this verdict the Petitioner has been sentenced to be transported for the space of seven years. That your Petitioner in the unfortunate situation he now stands does not mean to arraign the justice of the sentence that has been passed against him; but he may mention that the bespeaking of lodgings for the young woman in Dundee was the chief point of dally proved against him and so conscious was he of the priority of his intentions that he had employed no Council and appeared voluntarily at the Bar on the day of Trial. That if others had not been deeply affected the Petitioner would have silently submitted to the sentence pronounced against him under the circumstances which have been mentioned and he has a virtuous wife and a numerous family whose fate are involved in his, and who must become utterly destitute should he be sent out of this Kingdom. It is this powerful consideration that induces him to make his unfortunate case known to your Majesty. The other Petitioners who have for many years been daily observers of his conduct here certify what they know of him and if he should be enabled through the Royal Clemency to contribute to the support of a numerous and helpless family he solemnly pledges himself that his conduct through life shall evince he was not an unworthy object of mercy. He being found guilty of an offence of a serious nature to society feels that the sentence which has been past against him ought not to be remitted. But he has humbly to mention that in his outset in life he was for several years employed as Surgeon in the Ships employed in the Greenland fishing and hopes on enquiry it will appear he would be useful on board the Navy. By thus commuting his sentence the Petitioner will be enabled to contribute to the support of his family and should your Majesty be generously pleased to interpose to that effect your Petitioner, his wife and family will be ever grateful and Pray.

The other Petitioners hereunto subscribing, residing in Coupar Angus and the vicinity Most Humbly beg to represent to your Majesty that George Batchelor practiced as a surgeon in Coupar Angus for the period of ten years and was personally known to us. We can with great truth assure your Majesty that his humanity and generosity to numerous poor families in this Town and Neighbourhood were conspicuous. He was a kind husband to a virtuous wife who is respected by all who know her and a dutiful parent to a numerous family, having their only dependence upon him. From our long acquaintance with George Batchelor we presume humbly to state to your Majesty that he is not one of those so depraved in mind and sentiment that ought to be viewed as an outcast from Society. We are satisfied that he sincerely regrets and repents of the error he has fallen into, and that it will be the object of his future life to attone therefor. On this unfortunate mans own account and that of his virtuous wife and numerous family we are induced to approach your Majesty. Should he be transported beyond Sea his wife and family will be unprotected and must become entirely destitute. The entirely innocent will suffer most. We know this cannot be your Majesty's intention and therefore we humbly implore the Royal clemency in favour of George Batchelor, his wife and family. In the hope our supplications will be listened to we will ever pray for your Majesty.

George Batchelor since five years as surgeon on board the *Rodney Greenlandman* under my command behaved with the greatest propriety.

Cornelius Froggett, Dundee
David Blair, JP
Cha. May, JP
James Crockatt, Surgeon

Charles Wood, Bleacher, Borking
David Whitlet, Redston
David Foot, Farmer, Kettens
James Halket, Lawton
John Halket, Buttergask, Farmer
Andrew Blair, Pattac, Farmer
Robt Gilray Smith, [?]
Peter Hay, Housekeeper, Cottens
Robert Davidson, Pointner
David Baxter, Pointner
John Eason, Brewer
John Craig, Baker
James Taylor, Brewer
James Porter, Housekeeper

John Hay, Bldr [?]
John Wright, Manft\u02b3
Da'd Young, Manft\u02b3
John Gallorerly, Broker
Robert Minzes, Watchmaker
John Par — [?], Merchant
Thos. Incher[?], Manr
David Lawson, Sadler
David Scott, Mercht
Wm Robertson, Mercht
James Duncan, Housekeeper
Alexr Ross, Dyer
James Dick, Mercht
John McDonald, Mercht

TNA ref PRO 30/45/1/9 folios 61 to 622

Letters from Mrs Jemott in favour of her husband William Jemott

Governor Macquarie has received Mrs Jemott's letter of date 19th Novr last [1812] enclosing three letters of recommendation in favor of her husband William Jemott.

Government House
Sydney
6th Feby 1813

The Governor has instructed Lt. Govr Davey, who now proceeds to the Derwent, to grant Mrs Jemott and her husband such indulgences as the situation of the latter can reasonably admit of. For some time to come nothing farther can be done for Mr Jemott than to exempt him from Government labour permitting him to employ himself in any honest respectable manner he pleases. In case he wishes it he will be allowed thirty acres of land to cultivate on his own account, and in case he has not the means of maintaining himself and family they will be victualled from the King's Store for the first twelve months from the date of their arrival at the Derwent.

TNA ref PRO 30/45/1/13 folios 204 to 205

The Petition of Mary Jemott on behalf of her Husband William Jemott

To His Royal Highness George Prince of Wales, Regent of the United Kingdom of Great Britain and Ireland

The petition of Mary Jemott

London June 1st 1816

Most humbly sheweth,

That in the year 1811 William Jemott the husband of your petitioner was capitally convicted for being concerned in the piratical embezzlement of the ship *Maria* and her cargo, but that circumstances transpiring after his condemnation, which appeared to exculpate him from having been of the original planners of this conspiracy, (although subsequently made an active instrument in carrying it into execution) his prosecutors, the Underwriters at Lloyds, recommended him to mercy, and his sentence was commuted by your Royal Highness into transportation for life.

That her husband through your petitioner, voluntarily made restitution to the underwriters of such part of the property as came into his possession, and gave them every information in his power as to the disposition made of the remainder by Mr Moore the master with whom he went the voyage in the capacity of Captain's Clerk, and that the prosecutors gave the strongest testimony of their satisfaction with the conduct of your petitioner by generously voting the sum of One thousand pounds out of the property so recovered, to be settled on her, and on her children.

That your petitioner accompanied her husband to New South Wales where his conduct has been meritorious and exemplary. That in April 1815 he volunteered on an expedition against the insurgents called the Bush Rangers and was severely wounded in that service. That Colonel Davey the Governor of Van Diemens Land, under whose jurisdiction he resides, recommended to your petitioner to return to Europe and endeavour to obtain the extension of some further mark of your Royal Highness's favour to her husband in confirmation of which your petitioner annexes to this her humble petition, a letter from the said Colonel Davey to General Tench requesting his interference on her behalf.

That while your petitioner's husband labours under his present sentence he is subject to various disabilities and disadvantages which prevent him from exerting himself usefully for the support of your petitioner and three helpless, innocent young children whom your petitioner as a fond mother and fully sensible of the value of that unblemished reputation which she has ever maintained, is anxious to relieve from the ignominy of being considered as the children of a convict.

Your petitioner therefore humbly prays that your Royal Highness on taking the premises into your Royal consideration would be graciously pleased to grant her husband William Jemott a pardon on condition of his continuing to reside in New South Wales as a free settler and never returning within the other Dominions of His Majesty.

And your petitioner as in duty bound will ever most humbly pray.

Mary Jemott

This petition is humbly recommended to the favourable consideration of His Royal Highness the Prince Regent by the Committee for managing the affairs of Lloyds.

Josh Harryat
Chairman

TNA ref PRO 30/45/1/16 folios 288 to 291

The Petition of Mrs Jemott in favour of her Husband

Right Honorable John Holby Addington

Great George Street
1st June 1816

Sir,

With this you will receive the petition of Mrs Jemott in favour of her husband respecting which I had the honor of speaking to you on Thursday last. The statements in it, as far as they relate to circumstances that took place in this country I know to be correct, and the others, I believe to be so.

Mr Jemott was formerly a Purser in His Majesty's Navy, and the ship in which he served being off Dantzic when that City was besieged by the French he volunteered his services in an attempt to supply it with ammunition but was unfortunately made Prisoner. While in captivity he became acquainted with Captain Moore in company with whom he made his escape and returned to England. Not being able immediately to procure another appointment as Purser and being without employment, he obtained leave of absence from the Admiralty and accepted the offer of Captain Moore to go a voyage [sic] with him as Captain's Clerk in the *Maria* to the command of which vessel he said he had been appointed and the greatest part of the cargo of which was to be consigned to his care.

Before the ship sailed a plot had certainly been laid to embezzle the cargo, and the owners, two persons of the name of Lazarus and Cohens were strongly suspected of having concealed it with the Captain. Instead of proceeding to the Brazils, the port of her destination, Captain Moore went to the Havannah where he sold a great part of the cargo and embarked with the proceeds on board a schooner for America leaving directions with Mr Jemott to sell the remainder and follow him with the amount. This schooner was oversett in a Squall before she was out of sight of the land, and all on board, as well as himself with his ill-gotten wealth, perished.

In consequence of this event Mr Jemott, after completing the sales of the cargo, returned to England where by this time some of the circumstances respecting the embezzlement of the *Maria's* cargo had transpired. Soon after his arrival he was apprehended and some of the effects found in his possession justifying his commitment, he was prosecuted, and when testimony of his having sold part of the cargo, convicted. Mr Jemott declared that having asked under the orders of Captain Moore, and being directed to account to him, he was at a loss, after his death, to whom to pay the money he held in his hands. Whether this was really the case or whether he meant to convert it to his own use is known to himself alone but some of Captain Moore's letters which were got hold of after his conviction appeared to relieve him from the cargo of having been originally implicated in the conspiracy.

This circumstance led to the interference of the underwriters in his favor, and the capital part of his sentence was remitted at their application.

Throughout the whole of these trying and painful events the conduct of Mrs Jemott was highly exemplary. Her attachment to her husband and the integrity of her principles were equally conspicuous. Through her entreaties he was prevailed upon to make restitution of all the property in his own hands and to give every information in his power, as to that part of it which had been disposed of by Captain Moore, and out of the funds thus recovered the underwriters appropriated One Thousand Pounds to her use and that of her children.

She accompanied her Husband to New South Wales and has now left him, only to exert herself for his benefit and that of her children. His good conduct has obtained him the recommendation of Governor Davey, who has encouraged Mrs Jemott to hope that she may now obtain a further remission of his sentence. As a convict he is now only incapacitated from exerting himself for the maintenance of her and her children, by various disabilities to which he is subjected, but that a certain degree of ignominy attaches also upon them, while he retains that character. Her pretensions extend no farther than the hope of his being relieved from the name of a Convict, and that obtaining a pardon, on condition of his continuing to reside in New South Wales, in the character of a Free Settler.

I sincerely hope that her application for this act of Royal Clemency will be successful and request that you will recommend it to the favourable consideration of Lord Sidmouth at the first opportunity, as Mrs Jemott wished to rejoin her Husband by the *Harriett* which she expects will sail the end of this month, no other opportunity being likely to offer for a very considerable period.

I have the honor to be very respectfully
Sir
Your most obedient and humble Servant
Jas. Harryatt
Chairman of The Committee of Lloyds

TNA ref PRO 30/45/1/8 folios 57 to 58

A Letter referring to a Petition on behalf of John Fanthom – 1813

The Right Honourable
The Viscount Sidmouth

Devonshire House
21st September 1813

My Lord,
I have the honour to transmit to Your Lordship the Petition of John Fanthom, now on board the hulks under sentence of Transportation for Horse Stealing. His case has been strongly recommended to my consideration by several Magistrates, and other respectable Gentlemen in the County of Derby in whom I can place the most perfect confidence, and whose wishes I am desirous of seconding by requesting that Your Lordship will have the goodness to lay the Petition before His Royal Highness the Prince Regent, hoping that His Royal Highness will be graciously pleased, in His Majesty's name, to extend to the Petitioners the Royal Mercy for which he has prayed, and to permit him to serve in any of His Majesty's Regiments, except those which are called West India Regiments.

I have the honour
My Lord
Your Lordship's most obedient
Humble Servant
Devonshire

TNA ref PRO 30/45/1/9 folios 91 to 94

A Letter referring to a Petition on behalf of the son of William Sandoe

J. Becket, Esq.

Heligan near St. Austell
July 18th 1813

Sir,

We beg leave to transmit to you the enclosed Petition which has been forwarded to us by several respectable neighbours of the Petitioner, with a request that we would lay it before Lord Sidmouth, in the hope that some mitigation of Punishment might be obtained for the person on whose behalf it is presented who is a Convict on board the Hulks at Portsmouth. They have been induced to make this Application in consequence of their knowledge of the good character which the Family of the Prisoner bear, his own being unimpeached till the present affair, and they have transmitted to us a Certificate from the Governor of the Gaol at Exeter that the Prisoner conducted himself during his confinement with great Propriety.

We have the Honor to be Sir,
Your most obedient humble Servants
Wm Lemon

TNA ref PRO 30/45/12 folio 165

Enquiry about Joseph Boneham in New South Wales

Cardington
Bedford
September 16th 1815

My Lord

Sarah Boneham of Turvey in the county of Bedford, wife of Joseph Boneham at present a convict in New South Wales, wishes to know if her husband was alive or dead. At the last accounts she is very unhappy about her husband and it will be doing her great kindness to let me know whether he is living or dead.

I have the Honor to be
My Lord
Yours Lordship's Obedt Servt
William Waldegrave

Right Honble Lord Sidmouth
Home Department
Downing Street

Joseph Boneham was found guilty of burglary at Lent Assizes at Northampton, 1809.

TNA ref PRO 30/45/12 folios 169 to 170

A Forger named William Bradford

Limehouse
Nov. 21, 1815

My Lord,

I take the liberty of addressing your Lordship on the case of an unfortunate young man of the name of Bradford who is now in Newgate under sentence of Death for the crime of forgery. I have seen him in the condemned cell on various occasions, since the sentence was passed and have endeavoured to administer to him all the consolation in my power. A circumstance by which his case is rendered mere melancholy is, that it is not many months since he was married at my church, and the lady with whom he was united is a young person of excellent character and exemplary conduct. On her account and on the account of an infant child, I should exceeding rejoice if this were a case to which the Royal mercy could be extended, and in which the punishment of death could be remitted to transportation for life. It has been my object to discourage in her mind any hope of mercy and not serving the contrition with which he contemplates his offence and feelings for the dreadful situation to which his wife and child are reduced. I have thought it to be my duty to exert myself in this melancholy business as much as I possibly could do. And under these impressions I have addressed your Lordship and I have humbly to entreat that your Lordship will be so good as to present to His Royal Highness the Prince Regent the Petition with which this letter will be accompanied, and if any thing can be done, I am persuaded that your Lordship will feel but too happy in using your interception and in exerting your interest.

Lady Pitt with whom the prisoner has been in the habit of staying, and from whom he has received various acts of kindness, has also petitioned in his behalf.

I have the honor to be, My Lord,
Your Lordships most dutiful
and humble Servant
James Budge[?]

William Bradford was found guilty of forgery at Clerkenwell Sessions, 28 October 1815.

TNA ref PRO 30/45/15 folios 235 to 238

A Petition on behalf of George Wheeler alias Ayres

The Rt. Honble
Viscount Sidmouth

Marston
April 14th 1816

My Lord
I must apologize to your Lordship for troubling you with the enclosed letter in behalf of George Wheeler alias Ayres, who was tried before Mr Rd Graham at the last Taunton Assizes condemned and left for Execution for time with another man (who has not been taken), who shot at and wounded my Game Keeper. The enclosed is from a very respectable Gentleman of the Town of Frome who has seen the unhappy man since his condemnation and to whom he solemnly states that he was not accessary to the Firing the Gun, nor knew of the intention; till he heard it go off. As I understand this unhappy man has always borne a good character amongst the neighbours and proved himself a good Husband and Father'd five Children. On this account and in commiseration for their sufferings I am induced to ask the favor of your Lordship to intercede with it before the Prince Regent for Mitigation of his Sentence.

I have the honor to be
Your Lordships
Obedient Servant
Cork

P.S. I beg leave to say I set out for London next Tuesday and expect to arrive in Hamilton Place on Wednesday.

Frome
April 12th 1816

My Lord

A very unforeseen occurrence having occasioned my passing through Ilchester on Wednesday last, and the Chairman of the Quarter Sessions, having requested the Gentlemen on the Grand Jury, when they had opportunity, to inspect the different Prisoners of the County. I embraced the opportunity and called on Mr Bridle the Governor of Ilchester Gaol. While I was there Mr Bridle spoke to me respecting the unhappy man Wheeler, condemned for the attack on your Lordship's Keeper, Wm Blacker. As I had had some slight knowledge of the Parties and had heard the Trial of Wheeler, I felt desirous of seeing him and Mr Bridle directed him to be brought from the Cell to the Chapel. On going to him accompanied by Mr Bridle I found him standing within the Rails of the Communion Table and in a very agonized distressed state of mind. I dropped a few hints to him on the exceedingly solemn situation he was then placed in, and on the necessity of an earnest and unremitted application by solemn Prayer to the Divine Being, for that mercy which could alone rescue him from a still greater Condemnation. I was pleased to see the attention he paid and the Impression it had on his mind. Bursting into Tears he told me he did endeavour to Pray in the best manner he could and hoped the Lord would be merciful to him, (as perhaps in common with all who heard his Trial). I considered that though he was not the Person who fired the Gun, yet that when he whispered to West immediately before, it was to instigate him to the horrid deed. I closely questioned him as to that fact. But this he most solemnly denied, asserting that as a Dying Man, and as he hoped for Mercy at that awful Bar, where he soon expected to appear, he was not privy to the Firing the Gun nor aware that West was about to do so, till the explosion took place. I asked him what it was he said to West when he whispered to him. He very promptly answered me, he said 'Let us go through the wood across the Park (meaning Witham Park) and into the further Woods.' Hoping (as he told me) that Blacker would give up the Pursuit of them. Aware that on this point hinged principally the Question of his Guilt or Innocence. I most earnestly conjured him not to say what was untrue as attempting to deceive his fellow creatures would not avail him, and to deceive GOD was impossible. Bathed in Tears and with increased earnestness he replied, 'It is no use now for me to deny the Truth, I was present when it happened, but as GOD is in Heaven I did not desire West to shoot Blacker, nor know he was going to, and when the gun went off I was so frightened that I immediately made the best of my way home, and knew not what became of Blacker or West.'

I must say my Lord, that the manner in which the unhappy Man made these declarations strongly impressed my mind that he was telling the Truth. As Wheeler knows that I did reside far from your Lordship, he most earnestly begged, I would implore your Lordship to recommend him to Mercy saying that if his Life was spared he hoped he should be a totally reformed person. He stated that he had a wife and five small children, and that naming them his grief became excessive. Since my return I have been informed that he has always been a kind husband and father, and my friend Mr Blunt informs me that he has lived in a house of his and worked for him as a weaver for some years, and he has always found him a very sober, civil, industrious man.

One circumstance escaped my recollection when I was leaving him, he desired me if I saw Blacker to tell him he owed him no ill will, or have any malice towards him, and hoped if they never meet again in this World they should in Heaven.

Under all the circumstances of this case permit me my Lord, most earnestly to second the Intreaties of the poor condemned culprit that you will have the goodness to intercede with the Judge on his behalf hoping that an extension of mercy in this case will not be defeating the important ends of Justice.

With the greatest Respect I remain My Lord
Your Lordship's Most Obt H'ble Servt
Geo. Kingdon

PS I was at Marston on Wednesday and found your Lordship was from home.

George Wheeler, alias Ayres, was found guilty at the Lent Assizes at Taunton in 1816. He was given a reprieve.

TNA ref PRO 30/45/1/16 folios 298 to 303

A Petition on behalf of John Hitchman

Portland Place
15 July 1816

My Lord
I have the Honor to transmit to your Lordship a Petition which I have received from a Prisoner in Lancaster Castle of the name of John Hichman [sic], who was sentenced at the County Sessions held at Liverpool in November 1816 to two years Imprisonment in Lancaster Castle for riotously resisting a Pressgang and inciting a Revolt in Liverpool. He was also sentenced to two years further Imprisonment unless he should in the mean time find two Sureties in £25 each for his good behaviour. At the time when I passed the sentence upon him I added the latter part chiefly to produce an effect on the Persons in the Court, many of whom were his associates and it was my intention to apply to Your Lordship to request His Royal Highness the Prince Regent to be pleased to remit the latter part of the Sentence. I the more readily do so now as according to the Testimony of the Keeper of Lancaster Castle, the Prisoner has behaved very well during the Term of his confinement with the exception of now making use of some improper expressions to the Turnkey, for which he was confined for two days.

I therefore have to request that at the expiration of two years John Hichman may be released without being obliged to find any sureties, except his own Recognizance for fifty pounds.

I have the Honor to be
My Lord
Your Lordship's Obedient Servt
Edward Booth Wilbrahan

Waterstock
Wheatley
Septr 20, 1816

My Lord
I have the honor to write your Lordship at the request of a respectable farmer of this neighbourhood in behalf of his brother now confined on board the Hulks at Woolwich. The man's name is Henry Hitchman [sic], convicted at the Old Bailey about 4 years since of having, with 2 other servants, stolen spirits from his Master, Mr Hodges, a distiller in Milbank. They were sentenced to be transported for 7 years and I am informed the servants are actually gone to Botany Bay; therefore it may be presumed there were some favourable circumstances in this young man's case that the sentence was not fully put in force against him. He has now been about 4 years at the hulks and is at this time on board the *Justitia* Hulk, Captn Smith, at Woolwich.

The man expressed great penitence and as he has been bred up in a very respectable way at home it may be hoped that he may return to a proper course of life, should your Lordship think it proper on an enquiry into the circumstances to recommend a remission of part of his sentence.

I have the honor to be my Lord
Your Lordship's most obedient humble servant
W.H. Ashhurst

TNA ref PRO 30/45/1/23 folios 495 to 496

A Petition in favour of John Horseman Drake under sentence of Death in the Gaol at Lancaster

Gilmore Park
April 10th 1819

My Lord

At the most earnest request of an afflicted family I take the liberty to address Your Lordship. A young man whose name is John Horseman Drake is to be Executed at Lancaster on Saturday next unless the Prince Regent might be induced to commute his Sentence from Death to Transportation for Life. His family are in the greatest possible affliction, are highly respected in this neighbourhood and their only object and anxious wish is to save him from an Ignominious Death and the consequent disgrace to his relations.

If His Royal Highness might be prevailed upon to spare his Life it would give great satisfaction to a very worthy class of Yeomanry who are connected by ties of Friendship with his Family. Shd any hopes of Mercy be extended to this unfortunate young man could I request the favor of Yr Lordship to forward the happy tidings to me by Express.

I entreat Your Lordship to excuse the great trouble I give you and have the Honor to remain My Lord with very great Respect Yr Lordship's Most Obedt and faithful Hum. Servt

[Lord] Ribblesdale

John Horseman Drake was tried at Lent Assizes at Lancaster, 1819.

TNA re PRO 30/45/1/28 folio 666

The Petition of Frederick Salmon, a Convict, of Swallow Street, St. James

Most Humbly Sheweth

That your Petitioner was tried last Sessions at the Old Bailey for being concerned with John Wilson and William Clark in Robbing a Lady in Hyde Park of her watch the day the Princess of Wales received the City Address at Kensington, and sentenced to be transported for Life.

That your Petitioner is only 19 years of age, is by trade a bricklayer and was never ever suspected of dishonesty until the present accusation, but on the contrary by a close attention to his Business has deservedly borne the character of an industrious lad, as can be testified by the Masters he has worked for and by others to whom he is known.

That your Petitioner being out of employment was actually in search of work when he accidentally met with Wilson and Clark and was so unfortunate as to accompany them to Kensington without having the least knowledge of their intention, neither had he the least idea when he was apprehended what he was accused of, being totally unacquainted with the characters of his companions.

That your Petitioner's former Master will readily employ him again if he should be so fortunate as to regain his Liberty or he will be happy to serve his Country in His Majesty's Navy and trust he should be able in a short time to retrieve his character and restore his unhappy Parents from the excessive grief they labour under at present, from the idea of his being separated from them for ever.

Your Petitioner humbly implores Your Lordship will be pleased to take his Case into consideration and restore him again to Society. And Your Petitioner as in Duty bound will ever Pray.

We the undersigned beg leave to recommend the Petitioner to Mercy
        Edwd Bennett, no.15 Holton Street, Clear Market
        John Bennett, no. 61 Marcham Street
        Frederick Salmons, Late Master
        John Dixey, Vine Street, Piccadilly
        Thos. Holliwell, 14 Vine St., Piccadilly
        John King, George Court, Piccadilly
        Henry Iles, George Court, Piccadilly
        George Lucy, Kings Street, St. James's
        Thos. Rogers, King Street, St. James's
        Geo. Guy, King Street, St. James's

Frederick Salmon was tried at The Old Bailey on 7 June 1813.

TNA ref PRO 30/45/1/29 folios 726 to 727

The Petition of Thomas Edgecombe, a Convict

To the Right Honourable Lord Viscount Sidmouth,
Secretary of the Home Department
The humble Petition of Thomas Edgecombe now a Prisoner in Newgate under sentence of Transportation for 14 years.

Humble sheweth

That your Petitioner hath resided in London for about the last twenty eight or nine years and has earned his livelihood as a Journeyman Taylor until the last two years and half when on account of work becoming scarce he was induced to keep a Rag Shop by his wife to help make up enough for their support in a House No. 10 Shorts Garden, Drury Lane, and which his wife principally attended to. That she purchased Rags at a low Rate of Taylors for whom he worked and was acquainted with, and by sorting them, sold them again at a very great Profit. That on the twelfth day of April last about half past four o'clock in the afternoon when your Petitioner returned to his house (having been absent for half an ounce of snuff for himself at Mr Grimpstons the corner of King Street) he found two men there and at the instant even before he had spoken to them two constables came into the house and finding there a Roll of Floor Cloth, which they had information had been stolen, they secured and took away the two men and ordered your Petitioner to attend in the evening at the Office in Marlborough Street, and which your Petitioner accordingly did voluntarily and unaccompanied, when to his surprise he was detained on suspicion for receiving the stolen property.

Your Petitioner most solemnly declares he never saw or had any knowledge of, or dealing, or conversation with either of the two men who brought the roll of Floor

Cloth into his house. That his wife informed him they ran into his house and threw it on the bed and asked her to buy it which she refused to do; and that from the time they came into the house until they were secured by the officers it was not more than three minutes and it appeared that a Boy came with the men with the above roll on their shoulder which he suspected they had stolen from the Floor Cloth Manufacturer in Bedford Street and he went to the House and a Roll of Floor Cloth being found missing he was ordered to follow and watch the men which the Boy did and saw them go into your Petitioner's House when the Boy immediately called at a Public House near, the Three Tons, where the Officers happened to be drinking and who found and took the men.

That the officers searched the two men and found only 3s/6d on them so that his wife could not have purchased the Roll which was worth upwards of four pounds.

That your Petitioner was tried at the last Old Bailey Sessions when several very respectable persons attended and waited for some time to give him a good Character but being in Business they could no longer stay and only one person remained when the Trial came on and your Petitioner was convicted and sentenced.

Your Petitioner most solemnly declares his innocence not only of the Crime of which he has been convicted but of any such Crime at any period of his life and he himself hopes that many Testimonials of his long and uniform good Character which will accompany this Petition will entitle your Petitioner to your Lordship's Belief and Pardon.

Your Petitioner is aware that although a Rag Shop may be conducted with Credit and Honesty yet that such shops are not generally so conducted. He has therefore given up his said shop and should he be so fortunate to receive a Remission of his present sentence he most solemnly promises never more to be concerned in such Trade but trust to what he may be able to earn in his own Trade as a Taylor in which some very respectable Tradesmen have in Compassion for his present situation and in consideration of his uniform good Character promised immediately to employ him.

And your Petitioner shall ever pray

Thomas Edgecombe

Christopher Savery of South Efford near Modbury, Devon, being in London, heard by mere accident last Tuesday evening that the Prisoner Thomas Edgecombe was confined in Newgate under sentence of Transportation and as the Prisoner was born in C. Savery's neighbourhood of very honest and respectable Parents and was well known and always respected by C. Savery he called on the Prisoner Wednesday morning and having very particularly questioned and examined him in presence of Mr Newman, the Keeper of the Prison, and believing him to be innocent of the offence for which he was convicted, and Mr Newman having expressed the same opinion C. Savery has since made it his business to call on and enquire of several Persons to whom among many others the Prisoner referred him, all of whom appeared to be Persons of great Credit and Respectability, and most readily testified their good opinion of his character as expressed in the Papers herewith delivered all of which were written and attested by C. Savery as well as the Prisoner's Petition which C. Savery firmly believes contains the whole Truth without any omission.

C. Savery would not have taken so much pains on the Prisoner's behalf but from a feeling of duty only to assist a Poor Man entitled to Assistance in an unfortunate situation.

The Prisoner referred C. Savery to many other Persons of great Respectability but he could not conveniently call on them nor did he think it material as C. Savery really believes the Prisoner can obtain, and very deservedly, as good a Character as any Person.

The Prisoner is so very poor that he has been obliged to sell his best cloaths to raise money for his and his wife's support since his confinement.

May 10th 1817

C. Savery at the Revd S. Savery's

St. Thomas's Hospital

Southwark

N.B. All the Persons who have given their Testimony to C. Savery of the Prisoner, will most readily attest the same on oath if necessary.

Christor Savery

TNA ref PRO 30/45/1/10 folios 119 to 120

A Letter on behalf of Jane Stanfield

Brighton

14th July 1814

My Lord Duke,

A case having within these few days come to my knowledge which has overwhelmed me and my family in the greatest concern, and knowing the benevolence of Your Grace's mind I will take the liberty of sending a brief statement of it.

A person of the name of Jane Stanfield, whose father was a Captain of a West Indiaman, he died, and his widow and daughter (the subject of this application) lived some years in one of the Trinity Houses in Deptford; the daughter married a man who afterwards failed in business and in addition to his misfortunes became blind. To maintain him and a numerous family she employed herself in attending different sales where she often bought bargains, which, I understand she carried about Town in order to dispose of them amongst her acquaintances. One day she met a Jew whom she had frequently seen at the sales, but did not know his name. He offered her a sample of skins for sale, which she took and immediately went to a Furrier's shop to dispose of them, when to her great surprise she found that they had been stolen. She was in consequence apprehended, and has since been tried with the house breaker, pronounced guilty and was sentenced to fourteen years transportation. She asserts her innocence in the most solemn manner and disclaims all knowledge of the people who committed the robbery, and all who know her character most firmly believe her protestations and have caused a petition to be signed by a number of respectable persons amongst whom is the name of the Prosecutor, and the principal evidence, which petition is laid before Mr Recorder who sat as Judge on the trial.

The above mentioned circumstance has occasioned great trouble to all who have known her for years, we recollect her living with her mother in innocence and peace, industriously employing herself at her needle, her mind adorned with every virtue which is estimable in the female character, and the admiration of all her friends, we now see her confined in Newgate surrounded by adepts in guilt without the means of rendering her husband and children the smallest help and with a dismal sentence hanging over her head, of being cut off from them for ever.

Upon the whole I declare upon my honor that I firmly believe her to be an object worthy of the greatest commiseration, and if Your Grace would have the goodness to render her any service I shall consider it the greatest of all the favors which you have had the kindness to confer on me, if Your Grace should think fit to take the case under your generous consideration, and should succeed in any application which you may deem proper to make, it would deliver her from her present miserable situation and it would restore her to the arms of her Family. You would have hers, and their blessings and the blessings of all who are interested for her.

Sincerely hoping that Your Grace will pardon me for this liberty.

I remain with the greatest respect

My Lord Duke

Your Graces

Most obliged and obedient servant

Edwd Scott

Jane Stamfield [sic], aged 40 years, was tried at The Old Bailey, 30 May 1814, and found guilty of stealing various animal skins.

TNA ref PRO 30/45/1/20 folio 414

Viscount Dewhurst Petitioning on behalf of Solomon Cohen

Piccadilly

16th May 1818

My Lord

I have the honor to lay before Your Lordship a Petition in favor of Solomon Cohen, under Sentence of Transportation for Seven Years, and now on board the *Bellerophon* Hulk at Sheerness.

The Petition is respectably signed and if your Lordship upon a perusal of it should see any ground for a mitigation of the sentence passed upon Cohen I have strong reason to believe such mercy will not be improperly extended to the unhappy Petitioner.

A Family wholly dependant of Cohen for support add their prayers to mine that the case may be taken into your Lordship's consideration.

I have the honor to be

My Lord

Most respectfully Your Obedient Servant

Dewhurst

Solomon Cohen, aged 33 years, was tried at The Old Bailey, July 1817, and found guilty of larceny.

TNA ref PRO 30/45/1/29 folios 683 to 684

A Petition on behalf of Edward Parker 1821

To: Nathaniel Conant

No.1 Portland Place

London

Durham, Summer Assizes, 1818

Death Sentence Commuted to 7 years Transportation

Rectory, Thorneyburn

22 Jany 1821

Sir,

I have been informed that sometimes the Term of a Convict's Servitude on board a Hulk, is by the Beneficence of His Majesty's Government, on the Convict's good behaviour and a proper representation thereof, considerably abridged. At the earnest request of his aged and widowed mother I would intercede for one Edward Parker, formerly of this Portion of Simonsburn Parish. I subjoin the character lately given him by the Captain of the *Retribution,* the Hulk in which he is confined, to which I would call your kind attention.

I trust you will excuse this trouble, and if my present application be addressed to a wrong person that you will not only pardon my intrusion, but assist me with your counsel in order that I may make a more formal effectual application in the poor man's favor.

An answer will much oblige.

Your most obedt Servt
William Elliot

On board the *Retribution*
Edward Parker came from the *Justitia* Hulk about two years since, with a good character. Since he has been here his conduct has been in every respect praiseworthy, and befitting his unfortunate degraded situation.

Edward Parker was tried at Durham Summer Assizes in 1818 and found guilty of larceny in a dwelling house.

TNA ref PRO 30/45/1/32 folio 771

Gaoler's Report on Isaac Simpson

J.H. Capper Esq.

Bellerophon
Sheerness
13th April 1823

Sir
The Gaoler's report of Isaac Simpson is as follows.

Well known to the Police of this Town as a noted Thief has been several times in Custody on charges of Felony but too experienced to come at until this offence. During the first part of his confinement his conduct was very disorderly, but lately has behaved himself well. Had a brother transported from this County a short time since. Others of his relations very respectable.

His general health have been good since he have been at this Ship with exception of his being 13 days in the Hospital last June, since which time he have been employed in the general work of the Dockyard in common with others.

I am Sir
Your Most
Obedt Servant
S. Owen

Isaac Simpson was tried at the October Sessions at Nottingham in 1821 and found guilty of larceny.

NOTES ON APPENDICES

1. The documents in the following departmental classes at The National Archives, London, referred to in the Appendices to this book, have been microfilmed and copies are available for researchers' use at the National Library of Australia, Canberra, and the State Library of New South Wales, Sydney. Microfilm copies are also available for consultation through most Australian State Libraries:

ADM 6	Appendix 7
ADM 108	Appendix 17
AO 3	Appendix 14
CO 201	Appendices 15 and 18
HO 7	Appendices 7 and 15
HO 8	Appendices 6 and 7
HO 9	Appendix 7
HO 10	Appendices 15 and 16
HO 11	Appendix 14
HO 13	Appendix 10
HO 16	Appendix 5
HO 26	Appendix 4
HO 27	Appendix 4
HO 130	Appendix 5
MT 32	Appendix 19
PC 1	Appendices 7, 9 and 15
PC 2	Appendix 7

2. A selection of only the following classes of documents referred to in the Appendices to this book are available on microfilm in Australia:

ADM 1	Appendix 19
ADM 51	Appendix 19
ADM 52	Appendix 19
ADM 53	Appendix 19
ADM 54	Appendix 19
ADM 101	Appendix 19
CO 386	Appendix 18
HO 7	Appendix 7
T1	Appendix 7
PC 2	Appendix 7

3. CO 207/1 to 8. These original documents have been transferred to the State Records Authority of New South Wales. Microfilm copies are held at The National Archives, London, with the references CO 207/9 to 11. See Appendix 18.

4. The references given in the Appendices to this book are references to The National Archives material unless otherwise stated.

5. Those documents listed in the Appendices which are available on microfilm in Australia are marked with an asterisk thus *.

6. Where only a part of a particular document has been microfilmed and is available in Australia, the document in the Appendices is marked thus §.

7. Microfilm reel numbers have been included where appropriate.

8. The transportation period quoted in this book refers to transportation to Australia only, 1787–1868.

9. Full details of all microfilm copies are listed in the Australian Joint Copying Project Handbook (in eight parts) published jointly by the National Library of Australia and the State Library of New South Wales.

THE ACT OF PARLIAMENT THAT RESULTED IN THE INTRODUCTION OF THE TRANSPORTATION OF CONVICTS TO NEW SOUTH WALES

An Act to authorise the Removal of Prisoners in certain cases; and to amend the Laws respecting the Transportation of Offenders

Anno Vicesimo Quarto King 24 George III [1784] Cap. XII

I   Whereas difficulties have occurred which have delayed the carrying into execution Sentences and Orders of Transportation of Convicts to places beyond the Seas and it may be some time before the said difficulties can be obviated. And Whereas, from the unusually great number of Offenders now under Sentence of Death and respited during His Majesty's Pleasure, or under Sentence or Order of Transportation, in the Gaols within England and Wales, there is such a want of convenient and sufficient room in many of such Gaols that very dangerous consequences are to be apprehended, unless some immediate provision be made for removing such Offenders to some other Place of Confinement. Be it therefore enacted by the King's Most Excellent Majesty, by and with the Advice and Consent of the Lords Spiritual and Temporal, and Commons, in this present Parliament assembled, and by the Authority of the same, that, from and immediately after the twenty fifth of March, one thousand seven hundred and eighty four it shall be lawful for His Majesty from Time to Time, by an Order in Writing to be notified by one of His Majesty's Secretaries of State, or for any three or more of such of His Majesty's Justices of the Peace acting in and for the County, City or Place, in which such Gaol shall be situated, as shall be authorised by His Majesty under his Sign Manual, to direct the Removal of any one or more Male Offender or Offenders who during the continuance of the Act shall be under Sentence of Death with a reprieve during

His Majesty's Pleasure, or under Sentence or Order of Transportation, and who, having been examined by an experienced Surgeon or Apothecary, shall appear to be free from any putrid or infectious Distemper, and fit to be removed from the Gaol or Prison in which such offender or offenders shall be confined, to such place of confinement within England, or the Dominion of Wales, either at Land, or on Board any Ship or Vessel in the River Thames, or any navigable or other River, or within the limits of any Port of England or Wales, as His Majesty, or any Three or more of such Justices authorised as aforesaid; and every Offender who shall be so removed shall continue in the said Place of Confinement, or be removed to and confined in any other said Place or Places as aforesaid, as His Majesty, or any other Three or more of such Justices, authorised from Time to Time shall appoint, until such Offender shall be transported according to Law, or by the Expiration of the Term of such Transportation, or otherwise, shall be intitled to his Liberty, or until His Majesty, or until Three or more of such Justices, authorised as aforesaid, shall direct the Return of such Offender to the Gaol or Prison from which he shall have been removed.

II   And be it further enacted. That the Sheriff or Gaoler, having the Custody of any Offender whose Removal shall be ordered in Manner aforesaid, shall with all convenient Speed after Receipt of the Notification of any such Order, convey, or cause to be conveyed, every such Offender to the place appointed, and there deliver him with a Certificate of his Christian Name, Surname and age, and of his Offence, and of the Court in which he was convicted, and also of the Purport of his Sentence, to such Overseer or Overseers as aforesaid, who shall give a proper Receipt in writing to the Sheriff or Gaoler, for the Discharge of such Sheriff or Gaoler.

III   And be it further enacted that all fees, on delivering out of the Custody of such Sheriff or Gaoler any such Offender so ordered to be removed, as hath usually been paid, and would have been due to them respectively if such Offender had been removed in order to have been transported, and all reasonable Expenses, which the Sheriff or Gaoler shall incur in every such Removal, shall be paid by the County, Riding, City, Borough, Liberty, or other Division, for which the Court in which the Offender was convicted shall have been held and the Sheriff or Gaoler shall receive the Money due for such Fees and Expenses from the Treasurer of such County, Riding, City, Borough, Liberty or other Division, such fees and Expenses being first allowed by the Order of the Justices of the Peace at their quarterly or other General Sessions of the Peace, who are hereby required to make such Order as shall be just in that Behalf.

IV   And be it further enacted, that after Delivery of any Offender under this Act, the Overseers who shall have the Custody of him shall, during the Term of such Custody, have the same Powers over him as are incident to the Office of a Sheriff or Gaoler; and in like manner be answerable for any Escape of such Offender; and also, during such Custody shall feed and clothe such Offender, and shall keep him in such Manner, and where the same can safely be done, permit him to labour at such Places, and under such Directions, Limitations, and Restrictions as His Majesty, or as any three or more of such Justices, authorised as aforesaid, shall from Time to Time, by any Order to be directed to such Overseer or Overseers for their Instruction, appoint; and shall allow him Half the Profits arising from such Labour for his own use; and in the mean time, as nearly in Conformity to the Treatment of Persons Committed to Houses of Correction as the Nature of the Case will allow.

V   Provided always, and be it further enacted, that nothing contained in this Act shall extend to Authorise putting to Labour any Person, Whilst he continues confined by virtue of this Act, who shall not consent thereto.

VI   And it is hereby declared, That all the Time during which any Offender being removed under the Provisions aforesaid, shall continue confined by virtue of this Act, shall be reckoned in Discharge, or satisfaction of the Term of his Transportation, so far as such Time shall extend.

VII   And be it Further enacted, that if any Offender shall, during such Custody under this Act, be guilty of any misbehaviour or disorderly conduct, it shall be lawful for such Overseer or Overseers, having the Custody of such Offender, to inflict or cause to be inflicted, such Moderate Punishment as may be inflicted by Law on Persons committed to a House of Correction, and if any such Offender shall break from, or unlawfully leave the Custody of such Overseer or Overseers, or if any person shall rescue, or attempt to rescue, or assist in rescuing any such Offender from such Custody, or shall supply any Arms or Instruments of Escape, or any Disguise, to such Offender, every such Offence shall be punishable in the same manner as if such Offender was in a Gaol or Prison, in the Custody of the Sheriff or other Gaoler, for the crime of which such Offender shall have been convicted.

VIII   And be it further enacted, that the Overseers of the several Places of Confinement to be appointed by virtue of this Act shall, from Time to Time, make Returns, specifying the Names of every Person in their Custody, the Offence of which he shall have been guilty, the Court before which he shall have been convicted, the Sentence of the Court, with his age, and bodily state, and his behaviour whilst in Custody; and also the Name of such Offenders who shall have died under such Custody, or shall have escaped, or have been lawfully released from same; which Returns shall be made the first Day of every Term to His Majesty's Court of King's Bench at Westminster, on the Oath of the Person or Persons making same; such Oath to be made before the said Court, or any Commissioner authorised to take Affidavits in the same.

IX   And whereas there are several Persons confined in the Country and City Gaols in England and Wales, under Sentences and Orders made by a Justice or Justices of Peace at their Sessions, or Otherwise, in a summary way, and not according to the Course of the Common Law; be it further enacted, That it shall and may be lawful for any Justice of Assize or Great Sessions, or any Two or more Justices of the Peace, within whose Jurisdiction the said Gaol is situate, to remove any such Person or Persons to any House of Correction within the said Jurisdiction there to remain in Execution of the said Sentence or Order.

X   And whereas the Security required by an Act, passed in the fourth year of the Reign of His Majesty King George the first, (intituled, An Act for the further preventing Robbery, Burglary, and other Felonies, and for the more effectual

Transportation of Felons, and unlawful Exporters of Wool; and for declaring the Law upon some Points relating to Pirates), relates only to the Transportation of Offenders to His Majesty's Colonies and Plantations in America; and whereas an Act, passed in the nineteenth year of His present Majesty (intituled An Act to explain and amend the Laws relating to the Transportation, Imprisonment, and other Punishment of certain Offenders), hath not provided any Security to be taken instead thereof; be it enacted, That it shall and may be lawful for any Court, having competent Authority to order the Transportation of Offenders, or any Person or Persons duly authorised for that Purpose to require and take from any Person or Persons who shall be willing to contract or agree for the Transportation of any Offender or Offenders, sufficient Security that he or they will transport or cause to be transported effectually, such Offender or Offenders to the Place which he, she or they, is, are, or shall be ordered to be transported; and that the said Offenders, or any of them, shall not be suffered to return from the said Place to any Part of Great Britain, by the wilful Default of such Person or Persons so contracting as aforesaid, or his or their Assigns; and instead of the Certificate required by the said Act of the Fourth Year of the Reign of His Majesty King George the First, to take Security for the Production of such other Evidence of the actual Transportation of such Offender or Offenders as shall appear necessary, and as the Nature of the Case may warrant.

XI   And whereas the Provisions of the said Act passed in the nineteenth Year of the Reign of His Majesty, (intituled, An Act to explain and amend the Laws relating to the Transportation, Imprisonment, and other Punishment of certain Offenders), are not sufficient to obviate the Difficulties which have arisen in carrying into Execution Sentences and Orders for transportation of Felons, and others now under Confinement: And whereas, in order to facilitate the Transportation of such Felons, and others, it is necessary that Authority should be given to transport them to any proper Place beyond the seas, although the said Place be not mentioned in the Sentence for their Transportation: Be it enacted, That if any Offender hath already been ordered to be transported to any Part beyond the Seas, or hereafter any Offender shall under the like Order, and such Order cannot be conveniently executed with respect to the place in such Order mentioned, it shall and may be lawful for the Court of King's Bench, or for the Court before which such Person hath been or shall be convicted, or any Court holden for the same County, City, Riding, Liberty, Division, or Place, having like Authority: or Whilst the Court of King's Bench is not sitting, for any Two Justices of the Court of King's Bench, Common Pleas, or Baron of the Exchequer, of the Degree of the Coif, if such Court, or such Two Justices or Barons, shall think fit to order that such Offender shall be transported to any other Part beyond the Seas, which shall appear to such Court proper for that Purpose, in such and the like Manner, and for the same Term of Years, As such Offender is or shall be liable to be transported to the Place mentioned in the original Sentence of Order for his or her Transportation; and such Order shall be considered as made at the same time, and shall be as effectual to every Intent and Purpose, and shall have all the same Consequences in every Respect, as the original Order for Transportation of such Offender; and such Offender shall be transferred, conveyed, and made over to any Person who will contract for the Performance of such Transportation, and to his or their Assigns, in like manner as if such Offender had been transported to the Place mentioned in the Original Order of Transportation and such Person or Persons so contracting as aforesaid, his or their Assigns, by virtue of such Order or Transfer as aforesaid, shall have a Property and Interest in the Service of the said Offender for the Remainder of the Term for which the Offender was originally ordered to be transported; for in case such Offender was originally ordered for Transportation shall be afterwards at large within any Part of this Kingdom of Great Britain, without some lawful Course, before the Expiration of the Term for which such Offender shall have been ordered to be transported, every such Offender, being thereof lawfully convicted, shall suffer Death as in Cases of Felony, without Benefit of Clergy; and shall be tried before such Judges, and in such Manner, and the same Evidence made use of for his or her Conviction, as are directed by the Laws now being for the Trial of other Felons found at large within this Kingdom before the Expiration of the Term for which they were ordered to be transported; and whoever shall discover, apprehend, and prosecute to Conviction of Felony without Benefit of Clergy, any such Offender so found at large within the Kingdom, shall be intitled to the like Reward of Twenty Pounds and Certificate, and in the same Manner as any Person may be intitled to for discovering, apprehending, and prosecuting to Conviction, any Offender Ordered to be transported and found at large within this Kingdom before the Expiration of the Term for which such offender was ordered to be transported: Provided always, that it shall not be lawful to order any Offender to be transported to the Coast of Africa, who shall be under Sentence or Order of Transportation to any other Place.

XII   And be it further enacted that the Expenses of carrying this Act into Execution, not otherwise provided for, shall be annually laid before both Houses of Parliament; and after deducting thereout the Profits, if any, arising from the Earnings of the Offenders who shall labour in any of the Places of Confinement to be appointed by virtue of this Act, shall be provided for in the next Supplies to be granted to His Majesty by Parliament.

XIII And be it further enacted, That if any Suit or Action shall be prosecuted against any Person or Persons for any Thing done in pursuance of this Act such Person or Persons may plead the General Issue, and give this Act, or the Special Matter, in Evidence at any Trial to be had thereupon, and that the same was done by the Authority of this Act: And if, a Verdict shall pass for the Defendant or Defendants, or for the Plaintiff or Plaintiffs shall become nonsuit, or discontinue his, her or their Action or Actions after Issue joined; or if on Demurer, or otherwise, Judgement shall be given against the Plaintiff or Plaintiffs, the Defendant or Defendants shall recover Treble Costs, and have the like Remedy for the same, as any Defendants have by Law in other Cases; and though a Verdict shall be given to any Plaintiff in such Action or Suit as aforesaid, such Plaintiff shall not have Costs against the Defendant, unless the Judge, before whom the Trial shall be, shall certify his Approbation of the Verdict.

XIV   And be it further enacted, That all Actions, Suits, and Prosecutions to be commenced against any Person or Persons for any Thing done in pursuance of this Act, shall be laid and tried in the County and Place where the fact was committed, and shall be commenced within Six Calendar Months after the fact committed, and not otherwise.

XV And be it further enacted, That the Provision of this Act, so far as the same extend to authorize the Removal of Offenders to temporary Places of Confinement, shall continue to be in force for One Year to be computed from the Twenty-fifth Day of March, One thousand seven hundred and eighty-four, and also to the End of the then Session of Parliament; or if the said Term of One Year shall not determine during any Session, then till the End of the then next ensuing Session of Parliament, and no longer.

APPENDIX 2

A CIRCULAR RECOMMENDING THE BRITISH PUBLIC TO EMIGRATE TO NEW SOUTH WALES

TNA ref CO 201/281

Sydney, New South Wales
1838

Believing as the writer does, that the British Public have not yet been made fully to understand the advantages they might derive from promoting an extensive emigration of the unemployed labouring poor from the Agricultural Counties in England, he takes this method to address to them a few topics for their consideration, with reference to so important a subject.

It is not necessary to direct attention to the fact that England labours under a heavy burden of taxes; that the poor's rates alone several millions of pounds sterling are annually expended; notwithstanding which there prevails at the present moment, and to a very great extent, a want of employment among large numbers of the labouring classes for which it is found impossible in the Mother Country.

Without entering into any *political* consideration of this, it may, at all events be stated that as the present condition of the English poor cannot be bettered without a still further increase of taxation, it is the duty of the Landlords to adopt means, when such may be found, of diminishing the numerical amount of the paupers population.

For this purpose they are invited to look to New South Wales and its Land Revenue, amounting, as it does at this moments, to between £300,000 and £400,000.

The appropriation of that fund has hitherto been made little else than a job, whereby certain parties have enriched themselves. England too, though possessing superior claims to the benefit of the Land Fund, New South Wales being radically an English Colony, appears to have slept while her neighbours took advantage of the proffered aid, and accordingly emigration from Ireland and Scotland has progressed, while a ship-load of English *agricultural* emigrants is still almost a rarity.

This somewhat anomalous fact can only be accounted for on the ground that the English landlords have not yet been made sufficiently acquainted with the inducements which New South Wales holds out to such of the labouring poor as not finding employment at home, would be willing to emigrate. To supply this want of information the Colonial Immigration Regulations are embodied in this Circular. The sum allowed by Government, as set forth in those Regulations will amply defray the expense of conveying to New South Wales a married couple having only *one* child. In cases where the children exceed that number the parish could defray, and it would be its obvious interest to do so, the surplus proportion of passage money, according to the same rate. It is proper to state however, that the Colonists discourage the emigration, at the public expense, of married couples having more than *one* child. To those parties who have no more, if not above the ages specified, of industrious, sober habits, and accustomed to agricultural pursuits, New South Wales offers ample employment and fair wages, let them come in what numbers they may.

But in order to make the Colonial Land Fund properly available to the English rate payers, they must take into their own hands the management of a well designed system of emigration. The landed proprietors and the parish authorities in the different districts must unite in carrying such a system into effect, instead of leaving the funds to be preyed upon by jobbers of every description. The population of England being so much more numerous than that of Ireland and the amount annually paid by the English public towards the support of the poor, combine to give them a paramount claim to assistance over the other sections of the United Kingdom, and the landholders therefore owe it to themselves to see that a due proportion of the Colonial Land Fund is applied to the purpose of promoting emigration from England.

The bounties offered to Emigrants by the Colonial Government (sanctioned by the Principal Secretary of State for the Colonies) are as follows:

With a view to the further encouragement of the introduction into the Colony of useful and respectable Emigrants from any part of Britain, His Excellency the Governor is pleased to revise the Government Notice of the 28th October 1835 and directs it to be notified that a pecuniary aid to the amount, and under the Conditions hereafter specified, will be granted to those Persons who shall be at the charge of bringing Emigrants to Sydney. The increased rates of bounty which are offered in this revised Notice will be allowed for those Emigrants who shall leave Europe after the first day of January next.

1. The Sum of Thirty-six Pounds will be granted as a bounty towards defraying the expense of the passage of every married man, whether mechanic, domestic or farm-servant, and his wife, neither of whose ages shall exceed on embarkation forty years, and the sum of five pounds for each of their children between the ages of one and seven years, and ten pounds for each of their children between the ages of seven and fifteen years, and fifteen pounds for every child above fifteen years.

2. A sum of eighteen pounds will also be allowed for every unmarried female whose age shall not be below fifteen nor above thirty years, who shall come out under the protection of the married couple as forming part of the family, and destined to remain with it until such female be otherwise provided for.

3. A bounty of eighteen pounds will also be allowed for every unmarried male mechanic, farm or domestic servant, above the age of eighteen and not exceeding thirty years, brought out by a person who at the same time brings out an equal number of females accompanying and attached to a family as herein-before described.

Before any such payments are made the Emigrants on whose account they are claimed, will be required to present themselves before a Board appointed by the Government to inspect persons of this description to whom the adults are to exhibit testimonials of good character, signed by Clergymen and respectable inhabitants of note in the places of their former residence, with which testimonials it is necessary that every family and single person for whom the bounty shall be provided. If the Board shall be satisfied with these testimonials and that the Persons presenting themselves are within the ages set forth in the foregoing paragraph, to be established, where possible, by the production of copies or extracts of the registry of their baptism, duly certified by the Parish Minister, or other proper officer, of good bodily health and strength, and in all other respects likely to be useful members of their class in society, a certificate to such effect will be granted by the Board which being presented at the Colonial Secretary's Office in Sydney, a warrant will be immediately issued for the payment of the sum to which the Person bringing the Emigrants out shall become entitled under the Notice.

Any Persons desiring to avail themselves of these bounties are required to transmit to the Colonial Secretary at Sydney, a list specifying as nearly as circumstances will permit, the number, condition and calling of the Persons they propose to bring out.

It is to be understood that the bounties will not be allowed for any Persons brought out unless the Claimant shall have transmitted to the Colonial Secretary the list required by the foregoing paragraph, and that he shall have received in reply an intimation of its being the intention of this Government to grant a bounty on the introduction of the Persons described therein. This document the claimant will be required to produce to the Board, and in order to guard against the inconveniences of long outstanding claim against the Government, bounties will not be allowed unless the Emigrants described in the application shall be presented to the Board within two years after the date of the notification by the Colonial Secretary.

It is also to be understood that no expense whatever, attendant upon the introduction of these Emigrants will be defrayed by Government excepting the bounties herein-before mentioned; and that the wives and families of soldiers in Regiments in this Colony, or in Van Diemen's Land, and of Persons serving under sentence of transportation in either Colony are excepted from the present regulation.

The foregoing regulations may appear to the English reader to be of merely local application; that is to have reference only to the mode in which Colonists on the spot are to transmit business connected with the importation of emigrants with the Colonial Government. But such is not the case. Persons in England desiring to send out emigrants will from them learn the principle on which the system is conducted, and every other necessary information may be obtained at the Office of the Secretary of State for the Colonies, Lord Glenelg having not long since, and with great prudence, sent out to this Colony under the above regulations, numbers of poor from his own estates in the Highlands as well as from those of his friend Lord McDonald, the whole of which emigrants have had their passage money, &c., defrayed from the Land funds of the Colonists of New South Wales.

An Anglo-Australian

APPENDIX 3

REGULATIONS REGARDING APPLICATIONS FOR PARDONS AND TICKETS OF LEAVE, ETC.

Abstracted from *British Parliamentary Papers, Colonies, Australia*, Vol. 3 Sessions 1816 to 1830, in the British Library.

Government Orders
Head Quarters,
Sydney
January 9th 1813

By Commands of His Excellency the Governor John Thomas Campbell, Secretary.
[This letter states that 'The former orders and public notices issued by him (his Excellency, the Governor) on these points ('Free Pardons, Emancipations or Conditional Pardons and for Tickets of Leave, and also for obtaining of lands and cattle —) — the former orders have not proved adequate — they are therefore rescinded and in their room the following standing Orders and Regulations are henceforth substituted.')]

First   Instead of receiving Petitions, Memorials and other applications heretofore on Monday of each week, he will in future receive such applications from individuals on the first Monday of each month only.

Second   Applications for lands and cattle are to be made in the month of June only in each year, and they will be received on the first Monday of that month, if it should not be a holiday; or in the event of its being a holiday on the second Monday of the said month and at no other time.

Third   Petitions or Memorials for Free and Conditional Pardons and Tickets of Leave, are only to be presented once in each year, and the first Monday in each succeeding month of December is hereby assigned for that purpose, at which time only applications will be received on these subjects.

Fourth   All Petitions or memorials for the extension of the above indulgences of Free and Conditional Pardons, and Tickets of Leave, and for lands and cattle, will be invariably required in future to be countersigned both by the Clergyman and Principal Magistrate of the District wherein the applicants reside, certifying that in their opinion they are deserving of the indulgences so solicited. And the Clergymen and Magistrates throughout the settlement are hereby enjoined not to sign or grant such Certificates to any person with whose real character they are not well acquainted; which certificates must express their considering the applicants sober, industrious and honest.

Fifth The granting of Absolute Pardons being the highest and greatest indulgence which can be extended to those under sentence of this law, and consequently of the utmost importance, it will be strictly confined to the industrious, sober, and strictly meritorious, and the most unquestionable proofs of rectitude of conduct, for a long series of years, will in all cases be required, his excellency therefore orders and directs that no person under sentence of Transportation for Life shall apply for Absolute Pardon until he or she have resided for the space of fifteen years in the Colony. And such persons as have been transported for limited periods, are desired not to apply for Absolute Pardons until they shall have resided in the Colony for at least three fourth of the original period of their Transportation.

Sixth Persons applying for Conditional Pardons or Emancipations, who are under sentence of Transportation for Life are required to have resided at least ten years in the Colony before they make such application: and those who are under sentence of Transportation for limited periods will be required to have resided therein for at least two thirds of their respective periods of Transportation before their applications for Conditional Pardons or Emancipation will be taken into consideration.

Seventh Tickets of Leave, enabling persons to employ their time off the Store [Government Establishment] for their own advantage, will not be granted to any person until they shall have been employed either by Government or private individuals, to whom their services may have been assigned for the full space of three years.

Eighth His Excellency having thus prescribed the terms on which the foregoing Indulgences can alone be obtained, orders and commands that no applications on those subjects shall be made to him in future, where those terms and conditions are not fully complied with; and the Clergymen and Magistrates, whose Certificates must be attached to all such applications, are required to be well informed of the circumstances before they join their signatures to them. Applicants who reside in Sydney will be required to have the Certificates of their good conduct signed by the resident Chaplain and Superintendent of Police there; and no application without such vouchers will be attended to.

Ninth His Excellency will receive Civil and Military Officers of Government, on business, each day of the week (Sunday excepted) between the hours of ten and twelve in the forenoon.

Tenth Applications for leave to purchase articles from His Majesty's stores, previous to their being made to His Excellency, must be submitted to the Commissary.

Eleventh All persons, whether free or convict, who by sickness require medical aid, and wish to be admitted into the general hospital for cure are to make their application in the first instance to the principal surgeon who is required to report thereon to His Excellency, in order to his insuring the necessary orders on the occasion.

APPENDIX 4

THE NATIONAL ARCHIVES, LONDON

CRIMINAL REGISTERS FOR THE TRANSPORTATION PERIOD TO AUSTRALIA

1. *HO 26 Criminal Registers – Series I. Middlesex only.
   HO 26/1 to 56. 1791–1849 (reel numbers 2730–52.).
Note: after 1849 Middlesex criminals are included with other counties in Series II.
2. *HO 27 Criminal Registers – Series II (reel numbers 2752–860.)
   All Counties in England and Wales, except Middlesex before 1850, which is to be found in Series I – HO 26.

Piece number	Year	Counties
1	1805	All counties
2	1806	All counties
3	1807	All counties
4	1808	All counties
5	1809	All counties
6	1810	All counties
7	1811	All counties
8	1812	All counties
9	1813	All counties
10	1814	All counties
11	1815	All counties
12	1816	All counties
13	1817	A to L
14	1817	M to Y
15	1818	A to L

Piece number	Year	Counties
16	1818	M to Y
17	1819	A to L
18	1819	M to Y
19	1820	A to L
20	1820	M to Y
21	1821	A to L
22	1821	M to Y
23	1822	A to L
24	1822	M to Y
25	1823	A to L
26	1823	M to Y
27	1824	A to L
28	1824	M to Y
29	1825	A to L
30	1825	M to Y
31	1826	A to L
32	1826	M to Y
33	1827	A to L
34	1827	M to Y
35	1828	A to L
36	1828	M to Y
37	1829	A to L
38	1829	M to Y
39	1830	A to L
40	1830	M to Y
41	1831	A to L
42	1831	M to Y
43	1832	A to L
44	1832	M to Y
45	1833	A to L
46	1833	M to Y
47	1834	A to L
48	1834	M to Y
49	1835	A to L
50	1835	M to Y
51	1836	A to L
52	1836	M to Y
53	1837	A to L
54	1837	M to Y

Piece number	Year	Counties
55	1838	A to L
56	1838	M to Y
57	1839	A to H
58	1839	K to R
59	1839	S to Y
60	1840	A to H
61	1840	K to R
62	1840	S to Y
63	1841	A to H
64	1841	K to R
65	1841	S to Y
66	1842	A to H
67	1842	K to R
68	1842	S to Y
69	1843	A to H
70	1843	K to R
71	1843	S to Y
72	1844	A to H
73	1844	K to R
74	1844	S to Y
75	1845	A to H
76	1845	K to R
77	1845	S to Y
78	1846	A to H
79	1846	K to R
80	1846	S to Y
81	1847	A to H
82	1847	K to R
83	1847	S to Y
84	1848	A to H
85	1848	K to R
86	1848	S to Y
87	1849	A to H
88	1849	K to R
89	1849	S to Y
90	[number not used]	[blank]
91	1850	A to F
92	1850	G to L
93	1850	M to R

Piece number	Year	Counties
94	1850	S to Y
95	1851	A to F
96	1851	G to L
97	1851	M to R
98	1851	S to Y
99	1852	A to F
100	1852	G to L
101	1852	M to R
102	1852	S to Y
103	1853	A to F
104	1853	G to L
105	1853	M to R
106	1853	S to Y
107	1854	A to K
108	1854	L to M
109	1854	M to Y
110	1855	B to K
111	1855	L to Mid.
112	1855	Mon. to Y & Welsh Co's
113	1856	B to K
114	1856	L to Mid.
115	1856	Mon. to Y & Welsh Co's
116	1857	B to K
117	1857	L to Mid.
118	1857	Mon. to Y & Welsh Co's
119	1858	B to K
120	1858	L to R
121	1858	S to Y & Welsh Co's
122	1859	B to K
123	1859	L to R
124	1859	S to Y & Welsh Co's
125	1860	B to K
126	1860	L to R
127	1860	S to Y & Welsh Co's
128	1861	B to K
129	1861	L to R
130	1861	S to Y & Welsh Co's
131	1862	B to K
132	1862	L to R

Piece number	Year	Counties
133	1862	S to Y & Welsh Co's
134	1863	B to K
135	1863	L to R
136	1863	S to Y & Welsh Co's
137	1864	B to K
138	1864	L to R
139	1864	S to Y & Welsh Co's
140	1865	B to K
141	1865	L to R
142	1865	S to Y & Welsh Co's
143	1866	B to H
144	1866	L to R
145	1866	S to Y & Welsh Co's
146	1867	B to L
147	1867	M to Suff.
148	1867	Sur. to Y & Welsh Co's
149	1868	B to K
150	1868	L to Som.
151	1868	South'ton to Y & Welsh Co's

Notes

Hampshire is listed as Hampshire 1805–37, and as Southampton 1838–68.

Shropshire is listed as Shropshire 1805–08, and as Salop 1809–68.

Welsh Counties: Anglesey, Breconshire, Caernarvonshire, Cardiganshire, Carmarthenshire, Denbighshire, Flintshire, Glamorgan, Merionethshire, Pembrokeshire and Radnorshire are listed after all English counties from 1805–14 and then alphabetically with English counties 1815–54. They are again listed after all English counties 1855–68.

Monmouthshire is always listed with English counties.

Website: both the above series of Criminal Registers are accessible at www.ancestry.co.uk

APPENDIX 5

THE NATIONAL ARCHIVES, LONDON

CALENDARS OF PRISONERS FOR THE TRANSPORTATION PERIOD TO AUSTRALIA

1.	HO 77	Newgate Calendar	1782 to 1853
	HO 77/1 to 61	Printed lists of prisoners at Newgate	
2.	PCOM 2	Calendars of Prisoners held for trial at Quarter Sessions and Assizes	
	301 and 367	Assizes & Q.S. Glamorgan	1863 to 1869
	304	Assizes, Wiltshire	1774 to 1789
	305	Assizes, Wiltshire	1790 to 1799
	306	Assizes & Q.S. Boro. of Leicester	1854 to 1865
	307	Assizes & Q.S. Boro. of Leicester	1864 to 1868
	311	Q.S. Louth and Spilsby	1854 to 1876
	312	Q.S. Kirton and Lindsey	1858 to 1878
	313	Assizes, Lincolnshire	1854 to 1878
	314	Assizes & Q.S. Lincolnshire	1858 to 1875
	319 to 328	Assizes & Q.S. Liverpool	1840 to 1863
	330 to 341	Liverpool Borough Sessions	1812 to 1843
	344	Sessions & Assizes, Newcastle	1860 to 1870
	346	Sessions & Assizes, Northumberland	1864 to 1866
	347	Q.S. North Riding of Yorkshire	1859 to 1881
	348	Q.S. Norfolk	1825 to 1857
	405 to 408	Sessions & Assizes, Somerset	1854 to 1869
	412 to 416	Sessions & Assizes, West Riding of Yorkshire	1853 to 1869
	417	Assizes, West Riding of Yorkshire	1864 to 1869
	418 to 420	Assizes, Hampshire	1816 to 1882
	421 to 422	Q.S. Hampshire	1829 to 1859
	423 to 424	Q.S. Winchester	1842 to 1867
	439	Q.S. Louth and Spilsby for part of Lindsey	1831 to 1863

	440	Debtors & Plaintiffs, Nominal Register, Lancaster	1792 to 1897
	441	Crown Cases, Nominal Register, Lancaster	1820 to 1826
3.	HO 140	County Calendars of Prisoners	
	HO 140/1	Angelsey to Gloucester	1868
	2	Hampshire to Lincoln	1868
	3	Merioneth to Rutland	1868
	4	Shropshire to York, Guernsey, Jersey, Isle of Man	1868
4.	*HO 16	Old Bailey Sessions	1815 to 1849
	HO 16/1 to 9	Returns of Prisoners committed for trial, charges and results of trials (reel numbers 1542 to 1545)	
5.	*HO 130/1	Calendars of Prisoners at Winchester Special Assize, 18th December 1830 (reel number 3128)	

APPENDIX 6

THE NATIONAL ARCHIVES, LONDON

PRISON REGISTERS FOR THE TRANSPORTATION PERIOD TO AUSTRALIA

HOME OFFICE RECORDS

Table App. 6.1: *HO 8 Quarterly Prison Returns (reel numbers 5167 to 5250).

Piece numbers	Prison	Place	Period covered Year/Quarter to Year/Quarter	
115 to 155	Boaz Island	Bermuda	1853 March	1863 March
126 to 178	Brixton (female)	London	1855 Dec.	1868 Dec.
159 to 178	Broadmoor	Berkshire	1864 March	1868 Dec.
130 to 178	Chatham	Kent	1856 Dec.	1868 March
106 to 178	Dartmoor	Devon	1850 Dec.	1868 March
131 to 178	Fulham (female)	London	1857 March	1868 March
121 to 178	Gibraltar		1854 Sept.	1868 Dec.
133 to 143	Lewes	Sussex	1857 Sept.	1860 March
162 to 178	Parkhurst (female)	Isle of Wight	1864 Dec.	1868 Dec.
98 to 178	Portland	Dorset	1848 Dec.	1868 Dec.
112 to 178	Portsmouth	Hampshire	1852 June	1868 March
102 to 109	Shorncliffe	Kent	1849 Dec.	1851 Sept.
140 to 174	Woking	Surrey	1859 June	1867 Dec

Table App. 6.2: HO 23 Registers of County Prisons.

HO 23/1	Aylesbury, Buckinghamshire	1864 to 1865
2	Bath, Somerset	1848 to 1855
3	Leeds, Yorkshire	1848 to 1864
4 to 7	Leicester	1848 to 1865
8	Northampton	1848 to 1855
9	Northampton	1863 to 1865
10	Nottingham	1864 to 1865
11	Preston, Lancashire	1848 to 1855
12	Reading, Berkshire	1847 to 1855
13	Somerset (Taunton)	1864 to 1865
14 to 20	Wakefield, Yorkshire	1847 to 1866

Table App. 6.3: HO 24 Registers of Government Prisons.

HO 24/1	Millbank	1843 to 1874
15	Parkhurst	1838 to 1863
16 to 19	Pentonville	1842 to 1871
20 to 8	Statistical information for various prisons in England and Wales. Names of prisoners are rarely given	1860 to 188

PRISON COMMISSIONERS' RECORDS

Table App. 6.4: PCOM 2 Prison Registers for the Transportation period to Australia (1787–1868).

PCOM 2/1 to 3 & 7	Chatham, Hampshire	1856 to 1871
10	Dorchester, Dorset	1853 to 184
11 to 19	Gibraltar	1851 to 1875
20 to 53	Millbank, Westminster	1837 to 1870
60	Millbank, Westminster	1816 to 1826
59	Parkhurst, Surrey	1853 to 1863
61 to 72	Pentonville, London	1842 to 1869
105 to 127	Portsmouth, Hampshire	1847 to 1875
138	Shornecliffe, Kent	1849 to 1851
139	Westminster Penitentiary [Millbank]	1816 to 1871
140	Westminster Penitentiary [Millbank] – burials	1817 to 1853
141 to 142	Woking, Surrey	1846 to 1867
160 to 161) 166 to 226)	Newgate, London	1770 to 1872
230 to 258	Wandsworth, Surrey	1858 to 1869
292	Bedford	1844 to 1857

302	Derby	1836 to 1844
303	Durham	1848 to 1850
308 to 310	Lincoln	1808 to 1846
342	Louth, Linclonshire	1852 to 189
343	Newcastle	1859 to 1860
350	Oxford	1845 to 1851
369 to 391	Portland, Dorset	1859 to 1865
392 to 395	Reading, Berkshire	1818 to 1883
396	Shrewsbury	1855 to 1861
400	Spilsby, Lincolnshire	1826 to 1848
401 to 403	Stafford	1841 to 1878
411	Wakefield, Yorkshire	1856
435	Birmingham	1799 to 181809
436	Birmingham	1849 to 1850
440	Lancaster	1792 to 1797

WAR OFFICE RECORDS

Table App. 6.5: WO 25 Savoy Prison and Prison Hulk Registers (Army Deserters).

WO 25/2956		1799 to 1806
2957		1803 to 1819
2958		1807 to 1812
2959		1809 to 1815
2960		1815 to 1821
2961		1821 to 1823

THE NATIONAL ARCHIVES, LONDON

PRISON HULK RECORDS USUALLY LISTING THE NAMES OF CONVICTS

HOME OFFICE RECORDS

1.   *HO 7/2 **Irish Hulks and Convict Establishments** (reel numbers 1541 to 1542)

Essex at Dublin, 1835; *Surprise* at Cove of Cork, 1823; Convict Department at Cork, 1835. Officers and individuals belonging to these. No convicts' names except invalid convicts on *Essex*.

2.   HO 7/3 **Hulks at Bermuda**

Antelope, 1823–26; *Coromandel* (undated, c. 1827–29); *Dromedary*, 1825; *Weymouth*, 1828–29.

3.   *HO 8 **Quarterly Prison Hulk returns** (reel numbers 5167 to 5250).

Table App. 7.1: *HO 8 Quarterly Prison Hulk returns.

Reel nos. 5167 to 5250					
Piece Numbers	Hulk	Place	Year/Quarter		to Year/Quarter
8/1	*Alexander Lamb*	Portsmouth	1824 Sept. only		
1 to 32	*Antelope*	Bermuda	1824 Sept.		1844 Sept.
1 to 6	*Bellerophon*	Sheerness	1824 Sept.		1825 Dec.
8 to 39	*Captivity*	Devonport/Plymouth	1826 June		1834 March
8, 16-114	*Coromandel*	Bermuda	1826 June		
			1828 June	and	1852 Dec.
23 to 37	*Cumberland*	Chatham	1830 March		1833 Sept.
9 to 32	*Dasher*	Woolwich	1826 Sept.		1832 June
100 to 108	*Defence*	Gosport	1849 June		1851 June
112 to 132	*Defence*	Woolwich	1852 June		1857 June
2 to 30	*Discovery*	Deptford	1824 Dec.		1831 Dec.
31 to 38	*Discovery*	Woolwich	1832 March		1833 Dec.
1 to 22	*Dolphin*	Chatham	1824 Sept.		1829 Dec.

1	*Dromedary*	Woolwich	1824 Sept. only	
8 to 55	*Dromedary*	Bermuda	1826 March	1857 June
7 to 78	*Euryalus*	Chatham	1826 March	1843 Dec.
92 to 110	*Euryalus*	Gibraltar	1847 June	1851 Dec.
38 to 79	*Fortitude*	Chatham	1833 Dec.	1844 March
1 to 61	*Ganymede*	Woolwich	1824 Sept.	1839 Sept.
1 to 39	*Hardy*	Tipner Lake	1824 Sept.	1834 March
1 to 111	*Justitia*	Woolwich	1824 Sept.	1852 March
64 to 66	*Leven*	Deptford	1840 June	1840 Dec.
1 to 88	*Leviathan*	Portsmouth	1824 Sept.	1844 Dec.
95 to 150	*Medway*	Bermuda	1848 March	1861 Dec.
74 to 127	*Owen Glendower*	Gibraltar	1842 Dec.	1856 March
6 to 10	*Racoon*	Portsmouth	1825 Dec.	1826 Dec.
1 to 39	*Retribution*	Sheerness	1824 Sept.	1834 March
63 to 81	*Stirling Castle*	Devonport	1840 March	1844 Sept.
82 to 111	*Stirling Castle*	Portsmouth	1844 Dec.	1852 March
112 to 129	*Stirling Castle*	Gosport	1852 June	1856 Sept.
77 to 119	*Tenedos*	Bermuda	1843 Sept.	1854 March
67 to 77	*Thames*	Deptford	1841 March	1843 Sept.
78	*Thames*	Chatham	1843 Dec. only	
82 to 120	*Thames*	Bermuda	1844 Dec.	1854 June
62 to 128	*Warrior*	Woolwich	1839 Dec.	1856 June
19 to 47	*Weymouth*	Bermuda	1829 March	1836 March
1 to 58	*York*	Portsmouth	1824 Sept.	1838 Dec.
59 to 111	*York*	Gosport	1839 March	1852 March

4.   HO 9 **Registers of Convict Hulks**

   HO 9/1   *Cumberland, Dolphin* and *Ganymede* at Chatham, 1820 to 1833

   2   *Euryalus* and *Fortitude* at Chatham, 1825 to 1836

   3   *Captivity, Ganymede* and *Discovery* at Devonport and Woolwich, 1821 to 1833

   4   *Prudentia* at Woolwich, 1803 to 1809; *Retribution* at Woolwich, 1803 to 1814; *Justitia* at Woolwich, 1814 to 1836

   5   Index to *Justitia*

   6   Index to *Retribution*

   7   *Retribution* at Woolwich, *c.* 1802 to 1834; *Bellerophon* at Sheerness, 1816 to 1825

   8   *Fortunée* at Portsmouth, 1801 to 1816; *Captivity* &/or *Laurel* at Portsmouth, 1801 to 1822; *Leviathan* at Portsmouth, 1810 to 1836

   9   *York* at Portsmouth, 1814 to 1836; *Hardy* at Portsmouth, 1824 to 1832; *Laurel* at Portsmouth, *c.* 1805 to 1836

   10   *Euryalus* at Chatham, 1837 to 1843

   11   *Fortitude* at Chatham, 1837 to 1843

   12   *Ganymede* and *Warrior* at Woolwich, 1837 to 1845

   13   *Justitia* at Woolwich, 1837 to 1844

   14   *Leviathan* at Portsmouth, 1837 to 1844

   15   *York* at Gosport, 1837 to 1845

   16   Convict Hulk Establishment Letter Book, 1847 to 1849

5.   Other occasional references to convicts on prison hulks are to be found in:

HO 6/1 to 25 **Judges' Circuit Letters**, 1816 to 1840: Returns by Judges and Recorders of convicted persons recommended for mercy, lists of convicts, letters from governors of convict prisons, etc.

6.   HO 47/1 to 75 **Judges' Reports on Criminals**, 1784 to 1829

TREASURY BOARD PAPERS

Treasury Board papers (document class T1) are arranged in bundles and boxes. There is an index (document class T2) to this series, which dates from 1777 and is arranged in annual volumes. The index gives the names of persons paid by the Treasury for all manner of contracts and includes names of persons petitioning the Treasury for agreement to perform certain tasks and duties. In many instances documents were moved by the Treasury clerks from one bundle to another, thus collecting together several papers all relating to the same subject. Movement and relocation of such documents is recorded in document class T3, which are the Annual Registers of document numbers. A tick against a document number indicates that it has not been moved from its original bundle and has been preserved. If it has been moved, the number of the document to which it has been attached is shown. It is then necessary to check this second number to ascertain whether the papers have been kept or have been filed with later papers. Many documents were weeded out and destroyed by the Treasury in 1852. Such documents have T.O. (*taken out*) against the number in T3.

It should be noted that some documents referred to as *taken out* in T3 have in fact survived, having been located in their rightful place in T1. Other documents that should be in place have not been found. Additionally, lists of convicts on hulks that are not listed in T2 have been found in T1.

Each prison hulk was maintained by a private contractor who was paid by the Treasury to guard, supervise, feed and clothe the convicts. Among these papers, with the name of each *overseer of convicts*, have been found documents which give the name of a prison hulk and usually list all the convicts on board. Very occasionally a payment has been found which was made to a coroner, listing the convicts who died on a hulk.

For the transportation period: T1/653 to T1/6848 (1788 to 1868; reel numbers 1083 to 1106, 1507, 3549 to 3569, and 4660 to 4665): the lists are usually recorded for a quarter year. The overall dates for each quarter are inconsistent. The last quarter of the year often overlaps into the following year. The following are examples:

1st quarter [1787]	*Dunkirk*	26 Dec. 1786 to 25 March 1787
2nd quarter [1789]	*Censor*	12 April 1789 to 12 July 1789
3rd quarter [1791]	*Fortunee*	21 June 1791 to 21 Sept. 1791
4th quarter [1790]	*Lion*	12 Oct. 1790 to 12 Jan. 1791

Table App. 7.2: A list of all the prison hulks that have been found in document class T1. The document piece number is given together with the dates covered for each hulk. This has been compiled from information supplied by the Australian Joint Copying Project and searches carried out by the author.

Year	Quarter	Censor	Ceres	Dunkirk	Fortunee	Justitia	Lion	Stanislaus
(1785 to 1792)								
1785	1st	619				619		
	2nd	622				622		
	3rd	626				626		
	4th							
1786	1st	630	630		638	630		
	2nd	634	637			634		

Year	Quarter	Censor	Ceres	Dunkirk	Fortunee	Justitia	Lion	Stanislaus
	3rd	637/638	637	635	638	637/638		
	4th	641	641	641	643	641		
1787	1st	645	644	644		645		
	2nd	648	648	647	646	648		
	3rd	650		661	649	650		
	4th	653	653	651	651	653		653
1788	1st	656	655	655	654	656		655
	2nd	658	658	657	657		658	658
	3rd	654		661	659	654		
	4th	665	665	663	662	665	665	665
1789	1st	667	667	667	666	667	667	667
	2nd	672	672	671/672	672	672	672	672
	3rd		672	672	672		672	672
	4th	677	685		678	677	677	677
1790	1st	680	680	680	680	680	680	680
	2nd	683	683		684	683	683	683
	3rd		685	685		685		685
	4th	690	691	689	690	691	691	691
1791	1st	693		693	693	693		693
	2nd	695			694		694	695
	3rd	696			696		696	696
	4th	701			698		698	701
1792	1st	703			701			703
	2nd							
	3rd				708		708	
	4th						711	

(1793 to 1803)

Year	Quarter	Fortunee	Lion	Stanislaus	Prudentia			
1793	1st	716	716	717	717			
	2nd	719		720	720			
	3rd	722	722	723	723			
	4th	725	725	727	727			
1794	1st	729	729	730	730			
	2nd	731	731	732	732			
	3rd	734	734	735	735			
	4th	739	739	743	743			
1795	1st	745	745	746	746			
	2nd	749	749	750	750			
	3rd	755	755	755	755			

Year	Quarter	*Fortunee*	*Lion*	*Stanislaus*	*Prudentia*			
	4th	757	757	759	759			
1796	1st			764	764			
	2nd	768	768	769	769			
	3rd	772	772	772	772			
	4th	776	776	778	778			
1797	1st			783	783			
	2nd	787/789	787/789	788	788			
	3rd	793	793	792	792			
	4th	797	797	797	797			
1798	1st	802	802	802	802			
	2nd	808	808	808	808			
	3rd	811	811					
	4th	816	816					
1799	1st	819	819	819	819			
	2nd	824	824	824	824			
	3rd	829	829	829	829			
	4th			835	835			
1800	1st							
	2nd	843	843					
	3rd	847	847	847	847			
	4th	853	853	853	853			
1801	1st			859	859			
	2nd			861	861			
	3rd	867						
1802	1st							
	2nd							
	3rd							
	4th			896	896			
1803	1st			901	901			
	2nd							
	3rd				916			
	4th							

In addition to those listed in the above tabulations the following have also been located:

Laurel at Portsmouth; 3rd quarter, 1801 – *ref T1/867*

Royal Admiral at Woolwich; 1st quarter, 1803 – *ref T1/901*

Retribution at Woolwich; 2nd quarter, 1803 – *ref T1/915*

Table App 7.3: The Geographic Location of the Prison Hulks, document class T1.

1785 to 1792	*Censor*	Woolwich
1785 to 1791	*Justitia*	Woolwich
1786 to 1787	*Ceres*[1]	Woolwich
1788 to 1791	*Ceres*	Langstone Harbour, Portsmouth
1786 to 1791	*Dunkirk*	Plymouth
1786 to 1801	*Fortunee*	Langstone Harbour, Portsmouth
1787 to 1803	*Stanislaus*	Woolwich
1788 to 1800	*Lion*	Portsmouth
1801 (July to September only)	*Laurel*	Portsmouth
1793 to 1803	*Prudentia*	Woolwich
1802 to 1803 (December to March only)	*Royal Admiral*	Woolwich
1803 (March to June only)	*Retribution*	Woolwich

1. The *Ceres* appears at Woolwich from 1786 to 1787 and then at Langstone Harbour, Portsmouth from 1788 to 1791. It is assumed that this is the same vessel that was removed from Woolwich and relocated at Portsmouth.

PRISON HULKS – QUARTERLY LISTS

T 38/310	*Bellerophon* at Sheerness	1816 to 1818
311	*Captivity* at Portsmouth	1802 to 1804
312	*Captivity* at Portsmouth	1805 to 1806
313	*Captivity* at Portsmouth	1807 to 1808
314	*Captivity* at Portsmouth	1809 to 1811
315	*Captivity* at Portsmouth	1812 to 1814
316	*Captivity* at Portsmouth	1815 to 1817
317	*Justitia* at Woolwich	1814 to 1818
318	*Laurel* at Portsmouth	1804 to 1806
319	*Laurel* at Portsmouth	1807 to 1809
320	*Laurel* at Portsmouth	1810 to 1812
321	*Laurel* at Portsmouth	1813 to 1815
322	*Laurel* at Portsmouth	1816 to 1818
323	*Leviathan* at Portsmouth	1817 to 1818
324	*Portland* at Portsmouth	1802 to 1804
325	*Portland* at Portsmouth	1805 to 1807
326	*Portland* at Portsmouth	1808 to 1810
327	*Portland* at Portsmouth	1811 to 1813
328	*Portland* at Portsmouth	1814 to 1816
329	*Retribution* at Woolwich	1810 to 1811
330	*Retribution* at Woolwich	1812 to 1814
331	*Retribution* at Sheerness	1814 to 1815

332	*Retribution* at Sheerness	1816 to 1818
333	*Retribution, Prudentia* and *Stanislaus* at Woolwich	1804
334	*Retribution, Prudentia* and *Savage* at Woolwich	1804 to 1806
335	*Retribution, Prudentia* and *Savage* at Woolwich	1807 to 1809
336	*Zealand* at Sheerness	1810 to 1811
338	*Zealand* at Sheerness	1812 to 1813
339	Inspectors' Accounts	1802 to 1815

Report by John Henry Capper, Messrs Bradley,
  Erskine and William Kinnard.

ADMIRALTY RECORDS

*ADM 6 **Registers and Indices of Convicts on Prison Hulks** (reel numbers 1760 to 1761).

ADM 6/418	*Cumberland*	1830 to 1833
419	*Cumberland* [2] – Index	1830 to 1833
420	*Dolphin*	1823 to 1833
421	*Dolphin*	1829 to 1835
422	*Dolphin* – Description Book	1814 to 1831
423	*Dolphin* – Index to 420 to 422	1825 to 1830

2. This item is a box containing an Index Book (marked 1a) to the *Cumberland*. The box also contains two other Index Books to the *Cumberland*, but a note in each states: 'Entries in red refer to convicts on Fortitude.'

PRISON COMMISSIONERS' RECORDS

PCOM 2 **Prison Books**

PCOM 2/131	*Defence*	1857 to 1860
132	*Defence*	1849 to 1851
	Stirling Castle	1842 to 1856
133	*Defence*	1856 to 1857
	Stirling Castle	1850 to 1852
134	*Stirling Castle*	1837 to 1850
135	*Retribution*	1837 to 1841
136	*York*	1841 to 1852
137	*Europa* at Gibraltar	1840 to 1856

PRIVY COUNCIL RECORDS

*PC 1/67 to 92 **Correspondence relating to Transported Convicts** (1818 to 1844; reel numbers 938 to 982).

*PC 2/132 to 269 **Privy Council Office Registers** (1787 to 1868; reel number 619). This series of registers begins in 1540 and finishes in 1901. The piece numbers given here cover the period of transportation to Australia.

AUDIT OFFICE RECORDS

AO 3/292 to 296   **Accounts of Convict Hulks** (1830 to 1837).

LEGAL PROCEEDINGS

RECORDS OF ASSIZES, OLD BAILEY SESSIONS, PALATINATE COURTS AND THE COURTS OF GREAT SESSIONS OF WALES

The overall covering dates of each group of surviving records are given below, but those groups of records which do not fall within the Australian transportation period have not been included.

1. **Assizes**

   Records at The National Archives, London.
   Records of the Justices of Assize are arranged in *Circuits*.
   The various *Circuits* are:

   1.1 *Home Circuit* (1558 to 1876) covering the following counties:
   Essex, Hertfordshire, Kent, Surrey and Sussex.

TNA class ref. ASSI 34	Cost Account Books	1791 to 1890
	Instruction Books	1783 to 1827
	Postea Books	1791 to 1856
	Presentment Books	1786 to 1804
	Process Books	1773 to 1822
	Rough Entry Books	1834 to 1884

   1.2 *Norfolk Circuit* (1558 to 1876) covering the following counties:
   Bedfordshire, Buckinghamshire, Cambridgeshire, Huntingdonshire, Norfolk and Suffolk. From 1864 to 1876, Leicestershire, Northamptonshire and Rutland were added to the Norfolk Circuit.

TNA class ref. ASSI 33	Gaol Books	1734 to 1863
" ASSI 34	Precedent Books	1831 to 1863
" "	Process Books	1831 to 1863

1.3 *South Eastern Circuit* (1876 to1971)

In 1876 the Home Circuit and Norfolk Circuit were combined to form the South Eastern Circuit. The following records survive under the heading of the South Eastern Circuit but commence well before its creation and must therefore include records from the earlier Home Circuit and Norfolk Circuit.

TNA class ref.	ASSI 31	Agenda Books	1735 to 1940
"	ASSI 32	Minute Books	1783 to 1943
"	ASSI 35	Indictments	1559 to 1957
"	ASSI 36	Depositions	1813 to 1943

(earlier depositions are filed with the indictments)

TNA class ref.	ASSI 38	Estreats	1770 to 1870
"	ASSI 39	Accounts	
		Appeals	
		Correspondence	
		Law Papers	} William III to 1891
		Nisi Prius Records	
		Notes on Cases	

1.4 *Midland Circuit* (1558 to 1971) covering the following counties:

Derbyshire, Leicestershire, Lincolnshire, Northamptonshire, Rutland, Warwickshire. From 1864 to 1876 the Midland Circuit covered Derbyshire, Lincolnshire, Nottinghamshire, Warwickshire and Yorkshire (previously in the Northern Circuit).

TNA class ref.	ASSI 11	Minute Books	1818 to 1945
"	ASSI 12	Indictments	1860 to 1957
"	ASSI 13	Depositions	1862 to 1945

1.5 *Oxford Circuit* (1558 to 1971) covering the following counties: Berkshire, Gloucestershire, Herefordshire, Monmouthshire, Oxfordshire, Shropshire, Staffordshire and Worcestershire.

TNA class ref.	ASSI 1	Minute Books	1803 to 1888	
"	ASSI 2	Crown Books	1656 to 1948	
"	ASSI 3	Crown Books	1847 to 1951	(Second Court)
"	ASSI 4	Postea Books		
		Process Books		
		Note Books		
		Fee Books	} 1660 to 1888	
		Certificates of Trial		
		Cost Books		
TNA class ref.	ASSI 5	Indictments	1650 to 1957	
"	ASSI 6	Depositions	1719 to 1951	
"	ASSI 8	Pleadings	1854 to 1890	
"	ASSI 9	Estreats	1746 to 1890	
"	ASSI 10	Returns as to Cases		
		Tried, Fees, etc.	1732 to 1890	

1.6 *Northern Circuit* (1558 to 1971) covering the following counties: Cumberland, Northumberland, Westmorland and Yorkshire. (In 1864 Yorkshire was transferred to the Midland Circuit.)

TNA class ref. ASSI 51	Indictments	1868
" ASSI 41[1]	Minute Books	1741 to 1889
" ASSI 42[1]	Gaol Books	1658 to 1811
" ASSI 43[1]	Postea Books	1830 to 1866
	Account Books } Note Books }	1730 to 1840
" ASSI 44[1]	Indictments	1607 to 1890
" ASSI 45[1]	Depositions	1613 to 1890
" ASSI 46[1]	Estreats	1843 to 1890
" ASSI 47[1]	Criminal Returns	1805 to 1890
	Nisi Prius Records	1830 to 1865
	Special Cases	1629 to 1890
	Miscellaneous Pleadings	1650 to 1890
	Correspondence of the Keeper of York Prison	1790
	Correspondence of the Clerk of Assize	1826 to 1874
	Miscellaneous Paper	1640 to 1890

1. These records are now listed under the North Eastern Circuit, which was created in 1876.

1.7 *Western Circuit* (1558 to 1971) covering the following counties: Cornwall, Devon, Dorset, Hampshire, Somerset and Wiltshire.

TNA class ref. ASSI 21	Crown Minute Books	1730 to 1953
" ASSI 22	Civil Minute Books	1656 to 1945
" ASSI 23	Gaol Books	1670 to 1824
" ASSI 24	Certificate Book	1876 to 1887
	Estreat Book	1740 to 1800
	Note Books	1629 to 1932
	Transportation Order Books	1629 to 1819
	Process Books	1717 to 1820
TNA class ref. ASSI 25	Indictments	1801 to 1953
" ASSI 26	Depositions	1861 to 1947
" ASSI 28	Pleadings	1812 to 1957
" ASSI 30	Miscellaneous Returns	1740 to 1902

1.8 *North and South Wales Circuit* covering the following counties: Anglesey, Brecknockshire, Caernarvonshire, Cardinganshire, Carmarthenshire, Denbighshire, Flintshire, Glamorganshire, Merionethshire, Montgomeryshire, Pembrokeshire, Radnorshire and Cheshire. This Circuit was created in 1830 before which all of Wales was covered by the *Court of Great Sessions of Wales*. Cheshire was, before 1830, covered by the *Palatinate Court of Chester*.

TNA class ref. ASSI 57	Civil Minute Books	1843 to 1878
" ASSI 61	Crown Minute Books	1831 to 1938
" ASSI 62	Crown Books (prisoners tried)	1835 to 1883

"	ASSI 63	Bill Books	1797 to 1816
		Cash Books	1835 to 1845
		Cost Books	1694 to 1821
		Day Books	1796 to 1812
		Fee Forfeiture	1844 to 1852
		Receipt Book of Fees	1856 to 1865
"	ASSI 64	Indictments	1831 to 1891
"	ASSI 65	Depositions	1831 to 1891
"	ASSI 71	Indictments	1834 to 1892
"	ASSI 72	Depositions	1837 to 1942
"	ASSI 74	Judgement Rolls	1846 to 1943
"	ASSI 75	Civil Minute Books	1846 to 1943
"	ASSI 76	Crown Minute Books	1844 to 1942

2. **Old Bailey Sessions** – London
   Records at The London Metropolitan Archives:
   2.1 Original documents for the City of London and for the county of Middlesex.
   2.2 A complete series of printed transcripts of Old Bailey Sessions cases for the Transportation Period is held at the London Metropolitan Archives.
   Records at The National Archives, London
   2.3 Printed transcripts of Old Bailey Sessions cases
   TNA ref. PCOM 1/1 to 95   1801 to 1868
   2.4 The Old Bailey court proceedings are also available at www.oldbaileyonline.org

3. **Palatinate Courts**
   The counties of Cheshire, Durham and Lancashire had their own courts, known as Palatinates Courts. These were the equivalent of the Assize Courts for other English counties.
   Records at The National Archives, London:
   3.1 *Palatinate of Chester*

TNA ref. CHES 24/1 to 225		Gaol Fines and Indictments	1341 to 1832

   3.2 *Palatinate of Durham*

TNA ref. DURH 15/1 to 10		Minute Books	1770 to 1876
"	DURH 16/1 to 7	Crown Books	1753 to 1876
"	DURH 17/1 to 197	Indictments	1582 to 1877
"	DURH 18/1 to 2	Depositions	1843 to 1876

   3.3 *Palatinate of Lancaster*

TNA ref. PL 25/1 to 317		Assize Rolls	1422 to 1843
"	PL 26/1 to 284	Indictments	1424 to 1868
"	PL 27/1 to 18	Depositions	1663 to 1867

4. **The Courts of Great Sessions of Wales**
   These were the Welsh equivalent of the English Assizes.
   The records are at The National Library of Wales, Aberystwyth.
   The following lists the records for the transportation period to Australia:
   4.1   ***Chester Circuit***
   4.1.1 Gaol Files

NLW ref.	WALES 4/1011/7 to 1022/6	Flintshire	1787 to 1830
	WALES 4/62/5 to 74/7	Denbighshire	1787 to 1830
	WALES 4/194/1 to 203/6	Montgomeryshire	1787 to 1830

4.1.2 Rule Books

NLW ref. WALES 14/5	Denbighshire and Montgomeryshire	1811 to 1830

4.1.3 Minute Books

NLW ref. WALES 14/7A	Denbighshire and Montgomeryshire	1783 to 1802
WALES 14/85 to 14/86	Flintshire	1741 to 1806

4.1.4 Crown Books

NLW ref. CHES 21/7 to 21/8	Flintshire	1759 to 1794
(NLW Film 790)	(with Cheshire)	1822 to 1830

4.2   North Wales Circuit

4.2.1 Gaol Files

NLW ref. WALES 4/255/2 to 261/6	Anglesey	1787 to 1830
WALES 4/276/4 to 284/6	Caernarfonshire	1787 to 1830
WALES 4/303/2 to 308/4	Merionethshire	1787 to 1830

4.2.2 Rule Books

NLW ref. WALES 14/14 to 14/18	Anglesey, Caernarfonshire and Merionethshire	1784 to 1830

4.2.3 Minute Books

NLW ref. WALES 14/87	Anglesey, Caernarfonshire and Merionethshire	1828 to 1830

4.3   Brecon Circuit

4.3.1 Gaol Files

NLW ref. WALES 4/388/1 to 398/8	Breconshire	1787 to 1830
WALES 4/526/5 to 538/8	Radnorshire	1787 to 1830
WALES 4/626/5 to 640/4	Glamorganshire	1787 to 1830

4.3.2 Black Books

NLW ref. WALES 28/34 to 28/36	Breconshire, Radnorshire and Glamorganshire	1771 to 1830

4.3.3 Rule Books

NLW ref. WALES 14/28 to 28/30	Breconshire, Radnorshire and Glamorganshire	1776 to 1830

4.3.4 Minute and Imparlance Books

NLW ref. WALES 14/37 to 14/38	Breconshire	1779 to 1830
WALES 14/43 to 14/44	Radnorshire	1781 to 1830
WALES 14/50 to 14/51	Glamorganshire	1783 to 1830

4.4   Carmarthen Circuit

4.4.1 Gaol Files

NLW ref. WALES 4/747/1 to 766/5	Carmarthenshire	1787 to 1830
WALES 4/823/3 to 837/6	Pembrokeshire	1787 to 1830
WALES 4/903/5 to 916/6	Cardiganshire	1787 to 1830

4.4.2 Rule Books

NLW ref. WALES 14/55 to 28/56	Carmarthenshire, Pembrokeshire and Cardiganshire	1782 to 1807

APPENDIX 9

THE NATIONAL ARCHIVES, LONDON

CONVICT PETITIONS

RECORDS CONTAINING PETITIONS FROM CRIMINALS AND THEIR FAMILIES

(See also List and Index Society publications in the Bibliography)

1. HO 17 Petitions, Series I (bundles of loose documents)
    HO 17/1 to 131   1819 to 1839

2. HO 18 Petitions, Series II (bundles of loose documents)
    HO 18/1 to 381   1839 to 1854

3. HO 19: Alphabetical Index to HO 17 and HO 18
    It should be noted that although this index dates from the year 1797 the petitions
    before 1819, to which this index refers, do not survive.

HO 19/1	1797 to 1812
2	
3	1812 to 1822
4	1823 to 1829
5	1830 to 1833
6	1834 to 1835
7	1836 to 1837
8	*c.* 1836 to 1839
9	*c.* 1840 to 1842
10	*c.* 1843 to 1846
11	*c.* 1847 to 1849
12	*c.* 1852 to 1853

4.   HO 47 Judges' Reports on Criminals (contain petitions)
        HO 47/1 to 75   1784 to 1830

5.   HO 48 Law Officers' Reports and Cases: Civil and Military (contain petitions)
        HO 48/1 to 50   1782 to 1871

6.   HO 49 Law Officers' Letter Books (contain petitions)
        HO 49/1 to 11   1762 to 1871

7.   HO 54 Petitions and Addresses, Civil
        HO 54/1 to 51   1783 to 1854

8.   HO 56 Various Petitions and Addresses
        HO 56/1 to 4   Indices to Letter Books
        HO 56/11 to 24   Letter Books, 1811 to 1871
        HO 56/25   Miscellaneous Petitions, 1836 to 1853

9. PC 1 The Privy Council Correspondence has information relating to convicts, including
   petitions from convicts' families. There are sometimes enquiries about convicts who have
   been transported. (These are arranged in monthly bundles.)

*PC 1/67   1818 (reel numbers 938–82)
     68   1820
     69   1821
     70   1822
     71   1823
     72   1824
     73   1825
     74   1826
     75   1827
     76   1828
     77   1829
     78   1830
     79   1831
     80   1832
     81   1833
     82   1834
     83   1835
     84   1836
     85   1837
     86   1838
     87   1839
     88   1840
     89   1841
     91   1843
     90   1842
     92   1844

APPENDIX 10

THE NATIONAL ARCHIVES

HOME OFFICE WARRANTS – PARDONS AND REPRIEVES, WITH CORRESPONDENCE

(See also Appendix 22)

1. *HO 13/1 to 98   Entry Books of Out Letters, 1782 to 1849
                          These include warrants and pardons
                          (reel nos 419–22 and 3082–116).
    Note: This series continues to 1871, but warrants and pardons are not included after 1849.

2. HO 15/1 to 7   Warrants Books, 1850 to 1898
                          Warrants in this series continue from HO 13.

3. HO 47/1 to 75   Judges' Reports, 1783 to 1830
                          Letters and reports from judges on criminals, with recommendations for pardons or commutation of sentences.
    Note: Details of these have been calendared by The National Archives Local History Group and published by the List and Index Society:

    Volume 304   Pardons and Punishments,
                          HO 47/1 to 12 – 1783 to 1830 Part A
    Volume 305   Pardons and Punishments
                          HO 47/1 to 12 – 1783 to 1790 Part B
    Volume 312   Pardons and Punishments – Part 2
                          HO 47/13 to 18 – 1790 to 1795
    Volume 330   Pardons and Punishments – Part 3
                          HO 47/19 to 24 – 1795 to 1800

THE NATIONAL ARCHIVES, LONDON

SHERIFFS' ASSIZE VOUCHERS, SHERIFFS' CRAVINGS, SHERIFFS' PAYMENTS AND TREASURY WARRANTS

1. *Sheriffs' Assize Vouchers* and *Sheriffs' Cravings.*
   These are requests for payments relating to hanging, whipping, the pillory and other punishments for prisoners. They give the prisoners' names. Sheriffs' Assize Vouchers and Sheriffs' Cravings appear together in the following:
   E 389/241 to 257   1714 to 1832

   Note: These documents were re-numbered. The references to this series were originally E 370/35 to E 370/51

2. *Sheriffs' Payments.*
   These are payments made by the Treasury to county sheriffs. They are arranged by county and include justices' expenses for keeping prisoners in gaol, conveying prisoners to prison hulks, executing, etc. They give the criminals' names. They commence in 1733. The following cover the period up to, and during, the transportation period:

T 90/163	1780 to 1781
164	1782 to 1783
165	1784 to 1787
166	1788 to 1798
167	1791 to 1794
168	1794 to 1799
169	1807 to 1813
170	1814 to 1822

   (end of series)

3.   *Treasury Warrants* T 53.
      Entry books of warrants for payment of moneys. They include Conviction Money,
      which are payments made to county sheriffs or under-sheriffs for the expenses
      incurred in apprehending and convicting criminals. They give the criminals' names.
      Each volume has an index at the back. The names of criminals are recorded in the
      index under Sheriffs' Conviction Money. This series commences in the year 1721.The
      following lists those for the transportation period:

      T 53/54   1777 to 1780
          55   1780 to 1782
          56   1784 to 1785
          58   1785 to 1787
          59   1787 to 1790
          60   1790 to 1793
          61   1793 to 1797
          62   1797 to 1801
          63   1801 to 1805
          64   1805 to 1810
      (no Conviction Money after 1805 but see T54 below)

4.   *Treasury Warrants* T 54.
      Entry Books of Treasury Warrants not directly related to the payment of moneys.
      These include Conviction Money from 1806 to 1827.

      T 54/50   1806 to 1808
          51   1808 to 1811
          52   1811 to 1814
          53   1814 to 1818
          54   1818 to 1824
          55   1824 to 1827

APPENDIX 12

PRISON HULKS – CHANGES OF NAMES

In some cases the names of prison hulks were changed. The following list gives name changes and also records the sale or break-up of some hulks.[1]

1. *Bellerophon.* Became a prison hulk in October 1815. Renamed *Captivity* 5 October 1827. Broken up December 1853 at Bermuda.
2. *Malabar.* Renamed *Coromandel* 7 March 1815. Became a prison hulk in October 1827. Broken up December 1853 at Bermuda.
3. *Dasher.* Broken up March 1838.
4. *Defence* (ex-*Maradon* renamed 1812). Burnt by accident 14 July 1857. Wreck broken up in January 1858.
5. *Discovery.* Broken up in February 1834 at Deptford.
6. *Howe* (ex-East Indiaman). Purchased 1805. Re-named *Dromedary* in 1808. Became a prison hulk in 1819. Sold August 1864 at Bermuda.
7. *Euryalus.* Sold 16 August 1860 at Gibraltar.
8. *Hebe.* French, captured 5 January 1809. Later named *Ganymede* prison hulk in 1822. Capsized in 1838 and broken up.
9. *Hebe.* Became a prison hulk in 1840. Broken up in March 1873 at Chatham.
10. *Leviathan.* Became a prison hulk in October 1816. Used as a target in October 1846. Sold 7 August 1848.
11. *Medway.* Became a prison hulk in October 1847.
12. *Owen Glendower.* Became a prison hulk in October 1842. Sold October 1884 at Gibraltar.
13. *Racoon.* Became a prison hulk in 1819. Sold 16 August 1838.
14. *Edgar.* Became a prison hulk in December 1813. Renamed *Retribution*.
15. *Stirling Castle.* Broken up September 1861.
16. *Tenedos.* Became prison hulk in April 1843. Broken up March 1875 at Bermuda.
17. *Thames.* Built at Chatham in 1823. Became a prison hulk in 1841. Sunk 6 June 1863 at moorings in Bermuda. Wreck sold.
18. *Warrior.* Broken up December 1857.
19. *Weymouth* (ex-East Indiaman *Wellesley*). Became a prison hulk in October 1828. Sold 10 March 1865 at Bermuda.
20. *York.* Became a prison hulk November 1819. Broken up at Portsmouth March 1854.

1. Abstracted from Colledge, J.J., *Ships of the Royal Navy*, vols 1 and 2 (Newton Abbot: David and Charles, 1969, 1970).

APPENDIX 13

PRISON HULKS IN USE IN 1830

Table App. 13.1: A list which purports to be all the prison hulks existing in England from 1 January 1830 to 30 June 1830. It is taken from TNA document *T 38/338*, which also gives the expenses of these hulks, rate paid to artificers and labourers, etc.

Name of Hulk	Station	Average number of Convicts daily on Board
Leviathan	Portsmouth	656
York	Gosport	571
Hardy	Tipnor	65
Captivity	Devonport	426
Retribution	Sheerness	598
Cumberland	Chatham	403
Euryalus	Chatham	403
Justitia	Woolwich	330
Ganymede	Woolwich	393
Discovery	Deptford	169

APPENDIX 14

THE NATIONAL ARCHIVES, LONDON

CONVICT TRANSPORTATION RECORDS ARRANGED BY SHIP

1. *HO 11   **Convict Transportation Records arranged by ships, giving the names of convicts** (reel numbers 87–93)

HO 11/1	1787 to 1809
2	1810 to 1817
3	1818 to 1820
4	1821 to 1822
5	1823 to 1825
6	1826 to 1828
7	1829 to 1830
8	1831 to 1832
9	1833 to 1834
10	1835 to 1836
11	1837 to 1838
12	1839 to 1841
13	1842 to 1843
14	1844 to 1845
15	1846 to 1848
16	1849 to 1850
17	1851 to 1852
18	1853 to 1863
19	1864 to 1867

2. *AO 3/291   **Accounts of Legal Expenses for Transportation to New South Wales, giving convicts' names 1789–1830** (reel numbers 1081 to 1083)

3. TS/18   **Contracts for the Transportation of Convicts, naming convicts, with date and place of trial, and sentence**

Table App. 14.1: Contracts for the Transportation of Convicts. *(TNA ref TS/18)*

Piece no.	Ship	From	Year of Departure	Destination
460	*Candahar*	Spithead	1842	V.D.L.
461	*Waterloo*	Sheerness	1842	V.D.L.
462	*Emily*	Sheerness	1842	V.D.L.
463	*Moffatt*	Plymouth	1842	V.D.L.
464	*Garland Grove*	Woolwich	1842	V.D.L.
465	*Duchess of Northumberland*	Sheerness	1842	V.D.L.
466	*John Renwick*	Portsmouth	1842	V.D.L.
467	*Gilmore*	Sheerness	1843	V.D.L.
468	*Emerald Isle*	Sheerness	1843	V.D.L.
469	*Lord Petre*	Woolwich	1843	V.D.L.
470	*Tasmania*	Woolwich	1844	V.D.L.
471	*Hydrabad*	Woolwich	1844	V.D.L.
472	*Sir George Seymour*	Woolwich	1844	V.D.L.
473	*Mountstuart Elphinstone*	Woolwich	1845	V.D.L.
474	*Tory*	Woolwich	1845	V.D.L.
475	*Theresa*	Woolwich	1845	V.D.L.
476	*David Malcolm*	Woolwich	1845	V.D.L.
477	*Marion*	Woolwich	1845	V.D.L.
478	*Equestrian*	Woolwich	1845	V.D.L.
479	*Lloyds*	Woolwich	1845	V.D.L.
480	*Stratheden*	Woolwich	1845	V.D.L.
481	*Mayda*	Woolwich	1845	V.D.L.
482	*Pestonjee Bomanjee*	Woolwich	1845	V.D.L.
483	*Joseph Somes*	Woolwich	1845	V.D.L.
484	*Emma Eugenia*	Woolwich	1845	V.D.L.
485	*Lady Palmira* [also recorded as *Palmyra*]	Woolwich	1846	V.D.L.
486	*Sea Queen*	Woolwich	1846	V.D.L.
487	*John Calvin*	[Dublin]	1846	V.D.L.
488	*Elizabeth & Henry*	[London]	1846	V.D.L.
489	*Pestonjee Bomanjee*	Woolwich	1846	V.D.L.
490	*Thomas Arbuthnot*	Spithead	1847	V.D.L.
491	*Asia*	Spithead	1847	V.D.L.
492	*Eden*	Plymouth	1848	N.S.W.
493	*Hashemy*	[Portsmouth]	1848	N.S.W.
494	*Fairlie*	[Plymouth]	1852	V.D.L.
495	*Sir Robert Seppings*	[Woolwich]	1852	V.D.L.
496	*Petsonjee Bomanjee*	[Plymouth]	1852	V.D.L.
497	*William Jardine*	[Plymouth]	1852	W. Aust.

Piece no.	Ship	From	Year of Departure	Destination
498	*Lady Montague*	[Plymouth]	1852	V.D.L.
499	*Oriental Queen*	[Plymouth]	1852	V.D.L.
500	*Pyrenees*	[England]	1852	W. Aust.
501	*Ramillies*	[London]	1854	W. Aust.
502	*Sultana*	[Plymouth]	1859	W. Aust.
503	*Palmerston*	[Portland]	1860	W. Aust.
504	*Lincelles*	[Portland]	1861	W. Aust.
505	*Norwood*	[Portland]	1862	W. Aust.
506	*Merchantman*	Bermuda	1862	W. Aust.
507	*Lord Dalhousie*	[Portland]	1863	W. Aust
508	*Clara*	[London]	1864	W. Aust.
509	*Merchantman*	[Portland]	1864	W. Aust.
510	*Racehourse*	[Portland]	1865	W. Aust.
511	*Vimiera*	[Portland]	1865	W. Aust.
512	*Belgravia*	[Portland]	1866	W. Aust.
513	*Corona*	[Portland]	1866	W. Aust.
514	*Norwood*	[Portland]	1867	W. Aust.
515	*Hougoumont*	[London]	1867	W. Aust.

Note: The places of departure given in square brackets have been added by the author, there being no place names given in the TNA class list. These additions have been taken from *The Convict Ships* by Charles Bateson (see Bibliography).

4.   PC 1   **Privy Council Correspondence**
     PC1/2715 Lists of Convicts embarked on the *Eden* for New South Wales,
              with correspondence, 1840.
     2716   Lists of Convicts embarked on the *Tortoise* for Van Diemen's Land, with
              correspondence, 1841.
     2717   List of Convicts embarked on the *Elphinstone* for Van Diemen's Land,
              with correspondence, 1842.
     2718   Lists of Convicts embarked on the *Anson* for Van Diemen's Land, with
              correspondence, 1843.

5.   ADM102   **Admiralty Hospital Musters**
     ADM102/1 to 920, 1740–1860

APPENDIX 15

RECORDS OF TRANSPORTED CONVICTS IN NEW SOUTH WALES AND VAN DIEMEN'S LAND

(See also Bibliography)

1.   *HO 10   **Musters, New South Wales and Van Diemen's Land**

New South Wales (reel numbers 59–72)

*HO 10/1	Males	1788 to 1819
2	Females	1788 to 1819
3	Males	1816
4	Females	1816
5	General Muster	1811
6	Convicts Embarked	1787
7	Convicts Embarked	1787
8	Males	1817
9	Females	1817
10	Males	1818
11	Females	1818
12	Males, A to K	1820
13	Males, L to Y	1820
14	Females	1820
15	Males, A to J	1821
16	Males, K to Y	1821
17	Females	1821
18	Males and Females	1822
19	General Muster, A to L	1825
20	General Muster, M to Z	1825

28	General Muster	1828
29	Convicts Arrived	1828 to 1832
30	Convicts Arrived	1833 to 1834
32	General Muster, A to C	1837
33	General Muster, D to J	1837
34	General Muster, L to Q	1837
35	General Muster, R to Y	1837
36	General Muster	1822
37	General Muster	1806

Van Diemen's Land (Tasmania) (reel numbers 72–80)

*HO 10/38	Ledger Returns, A to R	1846
39	Ledger Returns, S to Z	1846
40	Ledger Returns	1849
41	Lists of Convicts	1808 to 1849
42	ditto	1811
43	ditto	1817 to 1821
44	ditto	1820
45	ditto	1823
46	ditto	1826
47	ditto	1830
48	ditto	1832
49	ditto	1833
50	ditto	1835
51	ditto	1841

2. Pardons and Tickets of Leave, New South Wales and Tasmania (reel numbers 80–7)

2.1	*HO 10/31	New South Wales and Tasmania	1834 to 1838
	52	New South Wales	1838 to 1841
	53	New South Wales	1842 to 1845
	54	New South Wales	1846 to 1849
	55	New South Wales	1850 to 1859
	56	Tasmania	1840
	57	Tasmania	1841 to 1842
	58	Tasmania	1843 to 1844
	59	Tasmania	1845 to 1846
	60	Tasmania	1847 to 1848
	61	Tasmania	1849 to 1851
	62	Tasmania	1852 to 1853
	63	Tasmania	1854 to 1855
	64	Tasmania	1856 to 1859

2.2	*CO 201/118 Governor's Despatches, New South Wales (reel number 106)	
	Conditional Pardons	1810 to 1819
	Free Pardons	1810 to 1819
	Tickets of Leave	1810 to 1819

Further references to pardons in this series may be located by the use of the subject index, ref. CO 714/118 (Ind.18582).

3. *HO 7/2   Correspondence, 1823–35 (reel numbers 1541 to 1542). Includes returns of deaths of convicts in New South Wales (1829–34).

4. *PC 1/67 to 92 Correspondence relating to transported Convicts, 1818–44 (reel numbers 938 to 982).

APPENDIX 16

THE 1828 CENSUS OF NEW SOUTH WALES

(Includes Free Settlers and Convicts)

(Reel numbers 68–9)
*HO   10/21   A to B
          22   C to D
          23   E to H
          24   I to M
          25   M to Q (M appears in both HO 10/24 and HO 10/25)
          26   R to S
          27   T to Z

Note: The complete census for 1828 and other musters of convicts and free settlers have been published by The Library of Australian History, Sydney (see Bibliography).

APPENDIX 17

THE NATIONAL ARCHIVES, LONDON

SETTLERS, CONVICTS, GUARDS AND SHIPS' COMPANIES NAMED ON TRANSPORTATION SHIPS FOR NEW SOUTH WALES, 1803–16

(See also Appendix 19)

*ADM 108/10 (reel number 4398)

Pages 197–203	*Experiment* at Portsmouth and Spithead (1803). 129 Female Convicts named in health reports.
Pages 241–4	*William Pitt* (1805). Settlers and Convicts.
Pages 262–3	*Alexander* (1805). Female Convicts, and Male Convicts with Wives and Children.
Page 265	*Fortune* (1806). Convicts, Guards, Women and Children of Guards, and Ship's Company.

*ADM 108/21 (reel numbers 4400–1)

Page 1	*Alexander* (1806). Convicts, convicts' wives and children, and ship's company.
Pages 28–33	*Sydney Cove* (1806). Female convicts and their children, passengers and ship's company.
Page 44	*Duke of Portland* (1807). Convicts, guard, passengers and crew.
Page 47	*Duke of Portland* and *Young William* from Portsmouth (1807). Passengers (men, women and children with ages), and ship's company.
Pages 86–7	*Speke* (1808). Female convicts and their children.
Pages 105, 112	*Aeolus* (1808). Female convicts.

Page 112   *Admiral Gambier* (1808). Male convicts (gives gaol from whence).
Page 158   *River* (1809). Female convicts and their children.
Pages 182–3   *Ann* at Long Reach (1809). Male convicts.
Pages 219–21   *Canada* from Woolwich and Gravesend (1810). Female convicts.

*ADM 108/22 (reel number 4401)
Pages 59–60   *Friends* (1811). Female convicts (gives gaol from whence).
Page 62   *Admiral Gambier* (1811). Male convicts from the following hulks:
                  Retribution at Woolwich, *Zealand* at Sheerness, *Portland* at Langstone
                  Harbour, near Portsmouth, *Captivity* at Portsmouth.
Page 142   *Guildford* (1811). Male convicts from the hulks at Woolwich.
Pages 150–1   *Guildford* (1811). Male convicts from the following hulks: *Zealand* at
                  Sheerness, *Portland* at Langstone Harbour, near Portsmouth, *Laurel* and
                  Captivity at Portsmouth.
Page 266   *Minstrel* (1812). Female convicts and 19 children from Horsemonger
                  Lane and Newgate.

*ADM 108/23 (reel number 4401)
Pages 63–5   *Fortune* (1812). Male convicts from the following hulks: *Retribution* at
                  Woolwich, *Zealand* at Sheerness, *Portland* at Langstone Harbour near
                  Portsmouth. *Laurel* and *Captivity* at Portsmouth: list of convicts gives
                  names, age, where convicted and sentence.
Pages 137–40   *Earl Spencer* at Portsmouth (1813). Male convicts, giving name, age,
                  sentence and where convicted.
Pages 220–2   *Wanstead* at Portsmouth (1813). Female convicts and children.
Pages 241–5,   *General Hewit* (1813). Male convicts from hulks at Woolwich. *Zealand*
247   at Sheerness, *Portland* at Langstone Harbour, near Portsmouth, and
                  Laurel and *Captivity* at Portsmouth.

*ADM 108/25 (reel number 4401)
Pages 26–8   *Marquis of Wellington* (1814). Male convicts.
Pages 71–4   *Indefatigable* [convict ship] from Portsmouth (1814). Male convicts
                  from the following hulks: *Justitia* at Woolwich, *Retribution* at Sheerness,
                  Captivity at Portsmouth, *Laurel* at Portsmouth, *Portland* at Langstone
                  Harbour, near Portsmouth.
Page 150   *Northampton* (1814). Convicts, wives and children of convicts.
Page 223   *Baring* at Portsmouth (1815). Male convicts.

*ADM 108/26 (reel numbers 4401–2)
Page 96   *Mary Anne* at Deptford (1815). Passengers.

*ADM 108/27 (reel number 4402)
Pages 33–8   *Lord Melville* at Deptford (1816). Female convicts and their children,
                  wives of convicts and their children, free women and their children.
Pages 64–5   *Fame* (1816). Male convicts (sentences given).
Page 66   *Sir William Bensley* (1816). Male convicts (sentences given) from
                  Woolwich, Sheerness and Portsmouth.
Page 86   *Morley* (1816). Male convicts from the following hulks: *Bellerophon* and
                  Retribution at Sheerness.
Pages 98–9   *Shipley* (1816). Male convicts from the following hulks: *Justitia* at
                  Woolwich, *Captivity* and *Laurel* at Portsmouth.

THE NATIONAL ARCHIVES, LONDON

MISCELLANEOUS RECORDS OF CONVICTS AND SETTLERS FROM COLONIAL OFFICE CORRESPONDENCE RELATING TO AUSTRALIA

1. **Correspondence of the Secretary of State** (CO 201)
   *CO 201/1 to 629 (1783–1900)
   (Reel numbers 1 to 411, 619 to 681: 1806–1906)

Subjects covered include: convicts, despatches, Hobart Town, individuals, Navy Office, Norfolk Island, Port Dalrymple, Port Jackson, settlers, Tasmania, crimes in Australia, list of free persons and convicts, applications for government service, licences for carts, watermen, bakers, etc., lists of pardons, female prisoners and their children (stating who living with), births, marriages, deaths and funerals (includes Roman Catholics).

Baptisms state if parents are married; children are recorded under either parent's name. Marriages give ages, whether free or convict and by what ship came, whether marrying by banns or special licence. Funerals give age, whether free or convict, and by what ship came, when deceased, and sometimes when interred. Deaths sometimes give additional information such as cause of death.

There are three indices to CO 201. The first two are held at The National Archives, London. The third is held at the Somerset Heritage Centre, Taunton.

   1.   **Subject Index** CO 714/118 [IND 18582] covering the period 1812 to 1870.
   2.   **Name Index** covering the period 1823 to 1833; bound in one volume but in several sections. This index is for CO 201/146 to 9, 159 yo 60, 170, 180, 190, 199, 208, 217, 237.
   3.   **Dwelly's Australian Emigrants**, Index 3, C1 and C2 (Somerset Heritage Centre). Alphabetical slip index; slips arranged by the first letter of the surname (2 boxes: A–L and M–Z). Each reference gives the name of the emigrant, date and place from.

2. **Land and Emigration Commission** (CO 386)
    CO 386/10 to 176
    (Reel numbers 310, 986 to 7, 865 to 75, 1493 to 7, 2127)

*CO 386/10, 11	Letters from the South Australian Association, 1833 to 1835
*CO 386/12 to 18	South Australia, 1836 to 1842
§CO 386/19 to 23	Letters from Agents for Emigration, 1837 to 1839
CO 386/24 to 42	Letters from Agents for Emigration, 1846
§CO 386/43 to 72	Letters to Colonial Office, 1837 to 1871
*CO 386/76	New South Wales, 1854 to 1869
*CO 386/77	Western Australia and Tasmania, 1854 to 1869
*CO 386/78	New South Wales, Queensland, Western Australia and Tasmania, 1870 to 1876
*CO 386/79	South Australia, 1854 to 1870
*CO 386/80	Victoria, 1854 to 1871
CO 386/126	Paid Passages to Adelaide, 1849 to 1850
*CO 386/128 to 130	Australia, Tasmania [and New Zealand], 1854 to 1860
CO 386/131	Australia, Tasmania, etc., 1861 to 1862
CO 386/132 to 133	Australia, etc., 1866 to 1868
*CO 386/141	Proceedings of South Australian Conversazione Club, and of the Officers of the Colony, 1840 to 1846
*CO 386/142	Orders and Land Regulations of the South Australian Colonization Commission, 1835 to 1840
*CO 386/145	South Australia, Land Selection
*CO 386/148	Embarkation Register; Land Purchasers and Labourers (purchasers but not labourers named)
CO 386/149 to 151	Register of Emigrant Labourers Applications for Free Passage to South Australia, 1836 to 1841
CO 386/152	Alphabetical Index to CO 386/149 and 150 (it appears that only part of 150 is covered)
*CO 386/154	Register of Applications for Passages to Colonies for Convicts' Families, 1848 to 1873
*CO 386/156	South Australia, Register of Correspondence, 1840 to 1842
CO 386/170	Register of Births and Deaths of Emigrants at Sea, 1847 to 1854
CO 386/171 to 172	Register of Deaths of Emigrants at Sea, 1854 to 1869
*CO 386/175 to 176	Register of Acts and Ordinances of Australia [and New Zealand], 1847 to 1855

3. **Convicts** (§CO 207)
    (Only pieces 9, 10 and 11 are on microfilm)

CO 207/1 to 3, 9	Alphabetical list of convicts with particulars, 1788 to 1842
CO 207/4 to 6, 10	Convicts' Savings Bank Books, 1824 to 1827
CO 207/7 to 8, 11	Letters from Superintendent of Convicts, 1854 to 1867

APPENDIX 19

THE NATIONAL ARCHIVES, LONDON, AND THE NATIONAL MARITIME MUSEUM, GREENWICH

SHIPS' CORRESPONDENCE, SHIPS' LOGS, SURGEONS' JOURNALS AND MEDICAL HOSPITAL MUSTERS

THE NATIONAL ARCHIVES, LONDON

Despatches and correspondence from ships' officers are sometimes found in TNA document class CO 201. There is no general index, but many individual volumes have a name index to the correspondence, and if the date of sailing for a particular vessel in known it is a relatively easy matter to locate any surviving ships' despatches.

Table App. 19.1: Location of captains' despatches and logs, ships' logs and masters' logs (note that only a selection of material is available for each of these series of records).

Description	TNA reference	Reel numbers
Captains' despatches (subject and name index in ADM 12)	*ADM 1	3281 to 3431
Captains' logs	*ADM 51	1762 to 1764 1550 to 1571 2900 5712 to 5721 5736 to 5778

Description	TNA reference	Reel numbers
Ships' logs	*ADM 53	2901
Masters' logs	*ADM 52	1603 to 1609 1615 to 1625 1762 to 1763 2900
	*ADM 54	1610 to 1614

Note: Captains', ships' and masters' logs are listed chronologically in their respective class lists by name of ship. Transportation vessels are listed under Transports.

Surgeons' journals   *ADM 101 (reel numbers 3187 to 3216). Listed by name of ship.
*MT 32 (reel number 3181). Listed by name of ship.

Admiralty hospital musters   ADM 102 (real numbers 1740–1860).
Journal of the *Mandarin*   HO 20/13 (c. 1840).

THE NATIONAL MARITIME MUSEUM, GREENWICH

Lieutenants' logs   Many logs from the eighteenth and early nineteenth century are held at the National Maritime Museum, Greenwich (ref ADM/L). It should be noted that these logs are filed under the lieutenants' names and not the ships' names.

THE NATIONAL ARCHIVES

SHIPS' CREW LISTS AND PERSONAL DETAILS

1. **Merchant Navy crew lists**
   Series I (up to 1860)
   1.1 BT 98/1 to 4758

Aberdeen and Cardigan	1800 to 1856
Bristol	1831 to 1856
Dartmouth	1770 to 1856
Dundee	1835 to 1856
Drogheda, Montrose and Newport	1838 to 1856
Greenock	1845 to 1856
Lancaster	1800 to 1856
Liverpool	1772 to 1856
Lynn	1850 to 1856
Plymouth	1761 to 1856
Portsmouth	1847 to 1856
Shields and other northern ports	1747 to 1858
Whitby	1800 to 1856

Lists for all other ports not listed above date from 1835 to 1856. Up to 1856 the lists are arranged chronologically by home port and then by name of ship.

   1.2 BT 98/4759 to 6932 (1857–60)
        All ports. Arranged by ships' official numbers.

   Series II (1861–1938) BT 99/1 to 4502.
        All ports. Arranged by ships' official numbers.

The National Archives hold only a 10 per cent sample. Other lists from this series are held at the National Maritime Museum, Greenwich; the Memorial University, Newfoundland; various county record offices in Great Britain; the Public Record Office of Northern Ireland, Belfast; and the Public Record Office of Ireland, Dublin.

2. **Registers of merchant seamen**

    2.1 BT 113/1 to 283 Registers of seamen giving personal details
         These are arranged by Ticket Number. A seaman's Ticket Number can be found
         be referring to BT 114, which is an alphabetical index of seamen. These numbers
         run from 1 to 546,000 and cover the period 1845 to 1854.

    2.2 The following do not give personal details. The names are arranged alphabetically.
         Registers of Seamen – Series I   BT 120 (1835 to 1836)
         Registers of Seamen – Series II   BT 112 (1835 to 1844)
         Registers of Seamen's Tickets   BT 114 (1845 to 1854)
         Registers of Seamen – Series III   BT 116 (1853 to 1857)

3. **Royal Navy crew lists**

The crew lists or 'muster rolls' are to be found in document classes ADM 36 and ADM 37.
The lists are arranged chronologically by name of ship.

THE NATIONAL ARCHIVES, LONDON, AND THE NATIONAL MARITIME MUSEUM, GREENWICH

SHIPS' DETAILS

THE NATIONAL ARCHIVES, LONDON

Merchant Navy
1.   Transcripts and Transactions
  Series I BT 107/1 to 112 Ships whose home port was London (1786–1854)

The records provide the following details:
  i.   Number of port of registry
  ii.   Name and home port
  iii.   Date and place of registration
  iv.   Names and addresses of owners and their occupations
  v.   Names of masters
  vi.   Place and date of construction or place and date of capture as a prize
  vii.   Name and employment of surveying officers
  viii.   Nationality of building (British, Plantation or Foreign)
  ix.   Number of decks and masts
  x.   Depth of hold, and tons burden
  xi.   Type of vessel
  xii.   Whether possesses a gallery or figurehead

  Series II BT 108/1 to 386 (1855–89)

Details as in Series I, together with the following:
  i.   The ship's previous port number
  ii.   The builder's name and address
  iii.   Particulars of the ship's engines
  iv.   Number of shares held by each owner
  v.   The ship's official number (allotted to all newly registered ships following an Act of 1854)

Series III BT 109/1 to 943 (1856–84)

Details as in Series I and Series II.

Series IV BT 110/1 to 1953 (1891 onwards)

From 1889 the organisation of ships' records was changed. Henceforth all papers relating to a specific ship were kept together (regardless of date) and were filed at the date of the closure of the ship's registration. If, therefore, a convict ship or emigrant ship was still in existence after 1888 its record should be found in this series.

Indices to Series I and II

BT 111/1 to 52. These are arranged under Home Port and then under the name of the ship. BT 111/53 to 72. These are arranged by Ship's Official Number.

A ship's official number is found by referring to the Mercantile Navy Lists, in which the ships are listed alphabetically with the official number given against each ship's name.

THE NATIONAL MARITIME MUSEUM, GREENWICH

2. **Lloyd's Ship Surveys** (1839–1914)
These give a detailed description of ships, with tonnage, number of sails and precise details of the size of timber and bolts used in its construction.

3. **Royal Navy**
Royal Naval Vessels (eighteenth and nineteenth centuries)
    i.   ADM 168 Contracts for building Royal Navy vessels in merchant yards
    ii.   ADM 170 Specifications
    iii. Detailed plans and drawings of Royal Navy ships

THE NATIONAL ARCHIVES

HATTON PAPERS

These papers were presented to the Public Record Office in 1942 by Miss Bessie Hatton. They had been purchased by her father, Joseph Hatton, in 1868. Most are apparently Home Office papers and include petitions on behalf of convicts. The following lists those documents that relate to criminals. The few that cover other topics have been excluded from the list. Documents that have been transcribed and appear in Chapter 20 are marked with a *.

TNA reference PRO 30/45/1 covering the years 1779–90, 1805–41 and 1854

f1–2*	14 July 1779	Grey Elliott pleads for the release of John Evans of Hammersmith who is on the hulk at Woolwich.
f3–4	27 July 1780	Death sentence on John Gibbons alias David, commuted to 4 years hard labour. John Green, John Tebbott, Benjamin Viccars and William Smith should serve in the Navy.
f5–6*	28 May 1784	Petition of Samuel Parker sentenced to transportation.
f7–8	2 June 1784	Thomas White servant to Baroness Forrester convicted of robbery.
f9–10	5 June 1784	John Carty, Joseph Hall, Thomas Brown, John Jones.
f11–12*	27 March 1786	William Piggott
f13–14	5 April 1786	John Mears, death sentence.
f15–16	April 1786	John Lockley – death [commuted to transportation for 7 years – First Fleet]
f21–22	14 Aug. 1789	John Gewalt, a Swede – death.
f23–24	Nov. 1789	John Pitt – petition.
f25–26	26 January 1790	John Hetherington
f27–28	24 Dec. 1790	Thomas Hollyoak
f29–30	15 March 1805	Edward Evans, pardon.
f31	not dated	ditto
f32–33	22 Aug. 1806	Husband of Jane Bachelor
f34*	not dated	George Batchelor
f35–36	11 Nov. 1806	ditto
f37–42	18 Nov. 1806	ditto

f43–44	1 Aug. 1810	Wm Taylerson
f45–46	11 April 1812	Mr Jemott
f47–48	13 May 1812	George Hammon
f49–50	2 June 1812	ditto
f51–52	26 Dec. 1812	Thomas Brown, debt.
f53–54	29 Dec. 1812	ditto
f57–58*	21 Sept. 1813	John Fanthom
f59–60	6 Dec.1813	Wm. Hughes
f61–62*	6 Feb. 1813	Wm. Jemott
f63–64	6 April 1813	Lars Segerstrom
f65–68	9 April 1813	Lewis Smith
f69–70	10 April 1813	L. Segerstrom alias Lewis Smith
f71–72	3 May 1813	Joseph Ewbank
f74–78	1813	Robert Kennett
f79–83	26 May 1813	Robert Kennett
f87–88	20 June 1813	Mr Petersen (led into crime by his wife).
f89–90*	9 July 1813	Wm. Sandoe
f91–92*	18 July 1813	ditto
f93–94*	19 July 1813	Mr Sandoe
f95–96	20 Aug. 1813	Salvadore Sano
f99–100	23 Aug. 1813	ditto
f101–102	23 Aug. 1813	Thomas Ball (death).
f105–106	21 Sept. 1813	James Isaac
f109–110	1 Dec. 1813	G. Hammon
f111–112	31 Jan. 1814	— Lentz
f113–114	11 March 1814	Joseph Horseby
f115–116	13 March 1814	Stephen Lister
f119–120*	14 July 1814	Jane Stanfield
f121–122	19 Aug. 1814	Thomas Williams
f123–124	9 Nov. 1814	Wife of Wm. Blake
f125	not dated	Francis Lloyd
f127–128	14 Feb. 1814	Rev. Bingham
f129–130	14 April 1814	Sgt. John Barlow of 48th Foot.
f133–134	21 Sept. 1814	John Binstud, forgery.
f137	17 Dec. 1814	Three convicts: George Cook, James Dunbar, and Malcolmn Brodie.
f138–139	Jan. 1815	Robert Butcher
f140–141	2 Feb. 1815	A convict (not named).
f142–143	16 Feb. 1815	Widow of Anthony Swinton
f146–147	11 March 1815	James James
f148	7 March 1815	James James, Death – Newgate.
f149–150	16 April 1815	Wm. Sweetman of Wilton, Death – Newgate (Charlotte Clark, Sweetman's mother).
f151–152	1 June 1815	(Convicts; not named)
f153–154	30 May 1815	Charles Frisby – request for his wife to accompany him on transportation.
f155–156	2 June 1815	Thomas Nix, transportation.
f157–158	19 June 1815	Jane Brown
f159–160	23 June 1815	John Gilham on *Discovery* at Sheerness.

f163–164	22 Aug. 1815	Thomas Turner
f165–166*	16 Sept. 1815	Sarah Boneham [is husband Joseph a convict in New South Wales still alive?].
f167–168	16 Oct. 1815	A convict (not named).
f169–170*	21 Nov. 1815	Young man named Bradford now in Newgate.
f171–172	23 Nov. 1815	Thomas Schofield, Chester Assizes, Aug. 1812 – Luddites.
f173–174	4 Dec. 1815	A man, not named – Suffolk Assizes.
f175–176	1815	Suffolk Assizes, Prussian sailor – Death.
f177–178	4 April 1815	Mary Ranson
f179–180	8 April 1815	Stephen Monk
f181–182	16 April 1815	Mary Smith
f183–186	7 June 1815	Mary Smith's real name Chapman.
f187–188	17 April 1815	Robson; stealing hay; Durham Q.S.
f189–190 2	7April 1815	A petition from Shrewsbury.
f191–192	30 May 1815	Mrs Gollicott and family; Mr and Mrs Capon and child. Recommended by Admiral Bligh on the *Mary Anne*.
f193–195	1815	Letters to John Beckett – passage to New South Wales.
f196–197	13 June 1815	A petition.
f198–199	not dated	Wm. Bagnall
f200–201	not dated	ditto
f202–205*	6 Oct. 1815	Wm. Jemott, a convict in New South Wales.
f206–207	30 Oct. 1815	Thomas Martin
f208–209	31 Oct. 1815	James Hardware
f210–211	14 Dec. 1815	2 men and George Lyon executed, March Assizes. (Place not given.)
f212–231	3 April 1815	Charles de Hamel to 24 Aug 1815.
f232–233	19 March 1816	Benjamin Beardsley
f234	5 April 1816	Edward Morrill at Horsham.
f235–236*	14 April 1816	George Wheeler alias Ayres
f237–238*	12 April 1816	ditto
f239–240	2 May 1816	Philip Street
f241–242	12 June 1816	Mrs Steel the widower mother of a convict under sentence of death.
f243–244	16 July 1816	José Peru, a Spanish Sailor – Death.
f245–248	23 May & 18 July 1816	Joseph Cowdray – Petition.
f249–250	19 Sept. 1816	S. Hulse, his father.
f251–252	7 Oct. 1816	Charles Desroches – Death.
f253–254	12 Oct. 1816	James Crow
f255–256	30 Oct. 1816	House of Correction at Wilton.
f257–258	27 Nov. 1816	Thomas Hughes
f259–260	27 Nov. 1816	A prisoner (not named).
f261–262	19 Dec. 1816	A petition (no names).
f263	7 March 1816	Edward Ford
f264	9 April 1816	Wm. Green; sheep stealing – Death.
f265	14 April 1816	Wm. Mallett

f267–268	10 May 1816	Wm. Burton, Wyndham Bridewell.
f269–273	16 May 1816–18 June 1816	Thomas Jones
f274–275	24 Sept. 1816	Taylor & Austin at New Bethlem Hospital.
f276–277	17 May 1816	Barnes
f280–283	not dated	John Trudgett; Horse stealing; Death.
f284–285	24 May 1816	John Street at Newgate; Death.
f286–287	28 May 1816	Mary Walker
f288–291*	1 June 1816	Wm. Jemott in New South Wales.
f292–293	2 July 1816	A woman (not named).
f294–295	5 July 1816	A convict (not named).
f296–297	7 July 1816	Convict rioters.
f298–299*	15 July 1816	John Hickman
f302–303*	20 Sept. 1816	Henry Hitchman on *Justitia*.
f304	14 Dec. 1816	Patrick Robinson
f305–306	25 Nov. 1816	Alexander Aitkins
f307 308	28 Nov. 1816	Mary Buxton
f309–310	28 Nov. 1816	Benjamin Willis
f311	not dated	son of Edward Morrell
f312–313	8 Feb. 1817	Wm. Elliott
f314–315	13 Feb. 1817	Wm. Hartland of Grafton Flyford, Worcestershire.
f316–317	5 March 1817	Ann Jones of Worcester.
f318–319	11 March 1817	Cashman's hanging.
f322–323	12 April 1817	Ann Edwards
f324	12 May 1817	ditto
f325–326	24 April 1817	Thomas Ramsay
f327–328	23 May 1817	Richard Williams, Benjamin, Evans, Richard Lloyd, Samuel Davies, John Brookes, Francis Prosser.
f329–332	5–14 July 1817	Release of 2 convicts on Hulks at Portsmouth; Silas Harris and John Maidment; Sentenced to Transportation.
f333–336	5–7 Aug. 1817	Thomas Feming condemned to Death for Rape.
f337–340	1–3 Sept. 1817	Thomas Castle and John Box.
f341–342	3 Sept. 1817	Wm. Amisbury, Wm. Norris, John Sims, Wm. Brooks and George Barton.
f343–344	6 Sept. 1817	Wm. Child; Life Transportation.
f345–346	28 Sept. 1817	A Youth (not named) sentenced to Death.
f347–348	27 Oct. 1817	Petition of Thomas Egan and Mr Winn, a solicitor.
f351–352	20 Dec. 1817	'The Prisoner moved to Millbank.'
f353	28 Jan. 1817	John Henry Goodinge's conduct in Newgate.
f355–356	6 Feb. 1817	Isaac Clarke on the hulks at Sheerness.
f357–358	25 March 1817	Joseph Clarke; Death sentence.
f359–360	27 March 1817	Convict in Tothill Fields Prison (not named).
f361–364	28 March– 5 May 1817	J. Lamb to I.H. Capper in favour of Wm. Cowper, on *Captivity*, sentenced to Transportation.
f365–366	17 May 1817	Anne Edwards, sentenced to Transportation.
f367–368	21 July 1817	Private James Pitfield
f369–370	13 Aug. 1817	Respite for two soldiers.

f371–372	26 Aug. 1817	George, Joseph, Wm. and Henry England, imprisoned in St. Albans. To be released in time for the harvest.
f373–374	7 Sept. 1817	Wm. Cryer Gidswell and Mary Sutcliffe, sentenced to Transportation.
f375–376	10 Dec. 1817	Petition (no names).
f395–400	21 Feb. 1818	Socy for the Improvement of Prison Discipline and for the Reformation of Juvenile Offenders. Two boys, Wm. Kelly and Thomas Spicer convicted of uttering forged notes and sentenced to Death.
f401–406	12 March–14 April 1816	Edward Mills
f407	27 March 1818	Harriett Shelton; Petition.
f408–409	13 April 1818	Mary Ingram and Wm. Cook; Petition.
f410–413	12 & 15 April 1818	Baines – forgery – Death.
f414–415*	16 May 1818	Solomon Cohen on *Bellerophon* at Sheerness.
f416–418	14 to 18 July 1818	John Bromley, bigamy.
f419–424	25 Aug. & 5 Nov. 1818	Broomfield, Winchester Gaol – Transportation.
f425–426	30 Sept. 1818	Joseph Bake Betterston
f427–428	30 Sept. 1818	Wm. Davis
f429–430	14 Dec. 1818	Driscoll, Weller & Cashman – Death.
f431	20 Jan. 1818	Prisoners
f432–435	2 & 27 Jan. 1818	Anne Masner
f436–437	20 March 1818	James Cobbett alias Coppack and J. Wilkins Jay.
f438–439	26 March 1818	A prisoner (not named) to be executed.
f440–441	1818	Samuel Leatherland; York Castle. Death.
f442–443	3 April 1818	Harriett Shelton, Newgate. Death.
f444–445	7 April 1818	John Ward
f446–447	14 April 1818	Richard & Wm. Moseley. Imprisonment to be remitted.
f448–449	22 April 1818	Honesty of James Adie.
f450–451	28 April 1818	John Newington; imprisonment for assaulting Anne Hewlett. Asks for remission.
f452–453	1 Aug. 1818	Lawrence Davoren's case.
f454–455	25 Aug. 1818	Papers relating to Park.
f456–457	29 Aug. 1818	George Canning to H. Hobhouse.
f458–459	8 Oct. 1818	George Colly now at Sheerness.
f460–461	16 Oct. 1818	George Carlmer alias Emanuel. Has been Transported before.
f462–463	7 Jan. 1818	Biddlecomb's confession.
f464–465	5 April 1819	Petition of James and Elizabeth Dorer in favour of their son James Dorer Junior, sentenced to Death for horse stealing.
f466–467	3 May 1818	John Newsome sentenced to Transportation.
f468–469A	12 May 1819	Thomas Dicks, imprisoned in Ilchester gaol.
f469B–469C	14 May 1819	Thomas Dicks, sentenced to 1 year hard labour in Ilchester.

f470–471	31 July 1819	Petition in favour of John Coghlon.
f472–473	29 Aug. 1819	Edward Morgan for mercy.
f474–475	11 Sept. 1819	Petition in favour of Elias Brown on the hulks at Woolwich.
f476–477	18 Dec 1819	Joseph Burke; Petition on behalf of his son.
f478–479	21 Dec. 1819	Mary Connor in favour of her husband Wm. Connor.
f480–481	Dec. 1819	Petition; Joseph Bush, sentenced to Death in Newgate.
f482–483	15 Feb. 1819	Petition from M. Taylor.
f484–485	10 March 1819	Petition; Thomas Rice.
f486–490	25 & 30 March & 8 April 1819	Petition; James Gibbs sentenced to Death for stabbing George Gibbs.
f491–492	30 March 1819	Petition; James Proud.
f493–494	5 April 1819	Papers relating to Belcham.
f495–496*	10 April 1819	Petition; John Horseman Drake, sentenced to Death.
f497–499	29 & 30 April 1819	Petition; Thomas Jeffcott sentenced to Death.
f500–501	not dated	Jeffcott's statement stealing letter containing money from Post Office.
f502–507	not dated	2 Petitions. Thomas Jeffcott of Richmond, gardener and Hannah his wife in favour of their son Thomas Jeffcott.
f508–509	17 May 1819	Petition from Mark Masterman Sykes.
f510–511	19 June 1819	Petition; Col. Drinkwater.
f512–513	29 July 1819	Samuel Loundes in Newgate (Swindler's case: Hadley, Jones and Dalton).
f514–515	15 Aug. 1819	Petition; Thomas F. Heathcote.
f516–518	16 & 17 Aug. 1819	Letters from John Piper asking for mercy.
f519–520	5 Nov. 1819	Petition; M. Taylor (prisoner not named).
f521–522	24 Feb. 1820	Petition; Mr Connor; sentenced to Death.
f523–526	2 March 1820	Petition; James Wright; embezzlement.
f527–528	29 April 1820	Petition; Henry Aisthrop alias Henry Hawkins.
f529–530	3 June 1820	Petition: H. Lindsey from his constituents at Perth.
f531–532	27 May 1820	Petition; Alexander Reid.
f533	10 June 1820	Petition; William Baylis and George Keene.
f534–535	6 July 1820	Letter from Keeper of Cambridge Gaol.
f536–537	4 July 1820	Petition; Charles Green.
f538–539	21 July 1820	Petition; Thomas Comber.
f540–541	17 Oct. 1820	Letter; Ducat.
f542–543	11 Oct. 1820	Petition; Adam Ducat.
f544–545	17 Nov.1820	Petition from Mr Hassale, Sheriff of Bristol.
f546–547	4 Dec. 1820	Petition; John Burke.
f548–549	19 Dec. 1820	Petition; John French Burke.
f550–551	22 Feb. 1820	Petition; A convict in the hulks (*Ganymede*).
f552–553	11 March 1820	Petition forwarded from M. Taylor.
f554–555	18 March 1820	William Bell
f556–557	16 March 1820	'The Convict' (not named).
f558–559	— 1820	Petition; William Weedon.

f560–561	2 May 1820	Nathaniel Davis in Newgate.
f562–563	24 July 1820	Thomas Cumber, sheepstealing – Death.
f564–565	not dated	Petition; Thomas Cumber.
f566–570	29 Sept. & 10 Oct. 1820	Petition; Edward Charles Tierney. Newgate.
f571–572	19 Oct. 1820	— Fowler; Transported.
f573–574	1821	James Addaway for robbing James Ware.
f575–576	2 April 1821	Wm. Hancock
f577–578	10 April 1821	Marquis of Lothian and Dr. Somerville.
f579–580	not dated	Wm. Mercer, assaulting Wm. Dore.
f581–582	27 March 1821	Dr. Somerville in favour of Wm Mercer.
f583–584	16 April 1821	Wm. Harris
f585–586	5 May 1821	Wm. Grant
f587–588	9 June 1821	Son of Dorothea Sharp
f589–590	1 Aug. 1821	Alexander M. Girr
f591–292	5 Oct. 1821	Allan Carswell, forgery.
f593–594	19 Oct. 1821	Warrant removing 39 male convicts from Edinburgh Gaol to the hulks.
f595–596	20 Jan. 1821	Hannah Smith
f597–598	26 Feb. 1821	Edward Parsons, forgery.
f599–600	1 March 1821	Wm. Powell and Wm. Robinson, Newgate, Death.
f601–608	28 March —	James Addoway
f609	19 April 1821	Wm. Leonard Swan
f610–611	14 May 1821	James Pendleton
f612–613	4 June 1821	Sylvia Morgan and Mary Willis
f614–615	14 June 1821	John Jackson, rape, Death.
f616–617	16 June 1821	Patrick Robertson and John Jackson.
f618–619	18 June 1821	John Jackson
f620–621	30 June 1821	Mary Shepherd; John Jackson.
f622	not dated	Capper
f623–626	29 & 30 July 1821	Mary Watts, Leicester Gaol.
f627–648	23 June to 2 Oct. 1821	Alan Carswell, Ayr Gaol, forgery.
f649–650	not dated	Mary Smith and daughter
f651–652	not dated	W. Nash; Death
f653–654	April 1829	William Mercer
f655–656	not dated	A woman; forgery; Death.
f657–660	not dated	Convict insane.
f661–663	[Sunday night]	Joseph Peru
f664–665	not dated	Frederick Woronzoff
f666–667*	not dated	Frederick Salmon; Life Transportation.
f668–669	24 March 1818	John Outridge in Bedford Gaol.
f670–673	16 & 22 April 1819	William Sage; Execution respited.
f674–675	22 May 1820	James Spokes
f676–677	26 July 1820	Petition from Benjamin Blomfield.
f678	25 Aug. 1820	Mr Froude
f679–680	7 Sept. 1820	Samuel Shole
f681–684*	22 Jan & 28 March 1821	Edward Parker on *Retribution* hulk after coming from the *Justitia*.

f685–686	6 April 1821	William Brown; forging.
f687–688	3 April 1821	Petition for W. Jameson.
f689–690	4 April 1821	W. Jameson re Brown.
f691A–691B	3 April 1821	William Brown alias William Morley Stubbs.
f692–693	2 April 1821	William Brown
f694–695	28 May 1823	Seven female prisoners recommended for mercy.
f696A–696B	7 Aug. 1823	George Hugett
f696C–697	7 Aug. 1823	Henry Knight former Vice Consul at Boulogne.
f698–699	16 March —	[C. Grant forwards papers.]
f700–701	19 Oct. 1822	Stephen Toole; burglary – Death.
f702–703	11 Jan. 1823	Lilias Gualter in favour of her brother Jacob Wagner – Life Transportation.
f704–705	5 Feb. 1823	John Fleming in favour of two youths.
f706–709	5 & 12 March 1823	Philip Fargher
f710–711	2 April 1823	Edward Bray in Monmouth Gaol.
f712–713	10 April 1823	Thomas Ricking
f714–715	18 April 1823	Letter from Rev. Ruffles of Liverpool.
f716–717	18 April 1823	John Camaish & Catherine Kinrade, executed.
f718–719	20 May 1823	Letter from Dalton.
f720–721	17 May 1823	John Dalton; petition in favour of neighbours.
f722–723	25 Jan. 1823	John Bennett
f724–725	16 Aug. 1823	Petition from Newcomen Edgworth.
f726–727*	10 May 1817	Thomas Edgcombe and Christopher Savery.
f728–729	19 Aug. 1823	John Harris now in Van Diemens Land.
f730–732	13 Sept. 1823	John Bacon, prisoner in Norwich Castle for debt.
f733–734	6 Oct. 1823	— Bacon
f735–736	11 Nov. 1823	— good character of the prisoner's family.
f737–760	1823	Samuel William Miles. Forgery/Death.
f761–762	8 Sept.1822	James Schofield late of 48th Regiment.
f763–764	4 Feb. 1823	— Baldo
f765–766	8 Feb. 1823	— Sirett
f767–768	14 Feb. 1823	Ratford in favour of his nephew John Syrett.
f769–770	31 March 1823	James Banting in Winchester Bridewell.
f771–772*	3 April 1823	Isaac Simpson
f773	10 April 1823	Petition – no names
f774–775	11 April 1823	Giles Jolly
f766–777	30 April 1823	Henry Grace
f778–779	30 April 1823	Richard Grace
f780–783	14 May 1823	Robertson and Hanslow
f784	14 June 1823	John Jackson
f785	12 July 1823	Shields alias Stuart
f786–787	24 July 1823	Wild; stealing/ Death.
f788–789	28 July 1823	Turvey; burglary/ Life Transporation.
f790–791	11 Aug. 1823	Thomas Short
f792–793	11 Sept. 1823	William Bird
f794–795	14 Sept. 1823	Petition
f796–797	3 Nov. 1823	Papers
f798–799	7 Nov. 1823	James Scott/Death.

f800–801	25 Feb. 1824	Childs alias Stuart.
f802–803	10 July 1829	Convicts/ families – no names.
f804	29 Dec. 1841	Grace Netherwood and Richard Gardiner.
f814–815	not dated	William Barlow aged 30, William Bailey aged 29, James Piper aged 21, John Clarke aged 48, Richard Suphton aged 21; all of Liverpool.
f820–821	not dated	A man in Dorchester Gaol/ poaching/sentenced to 3 months.
f822–823	not dated	2 men – execution postponed.
f824–825	not dated	Dean

BIBLIOGRAPHY

Adams, K.M., *Australia: Gaol or Colony* (London: Angus & Robertson, 1970).

Barnard, Marjorie, *A History of Australia* (London, Sydney and Melbourne: Angus & Robertson, 1962).

Barrington, George, *A History of New South Wales* (London: 1810).

Bassett, Marnie, *The Governor's Lady* (Melbourne University Press, 1956).

Bateson, Charles, *The Convict Ships 1787–1868*, 3rd edn (Glasgow: 1983).

Branch Johnson, W., *The English Prison Hulks* (Chichester: Phillimore, 1970).

Brown, Martyn, *Australia Bound* (Bradford on Avon: Ex Libris Press, 1988).

Campbell, Charles, *The Intolerable Hulks*, 3rd edn (Tucson, Ariz.: Fenestra Books, 2001).

Carter, Paul, *The Road to Botany Bay* (New York: A.A. Knoff, 1987).

Chambers, Jill, *Buckinghamshire Machine Breakers* (Jill Chambers, 1998).

Chapman, Don, *The People of The First Fleet* (North Ryde, NSW: Cassell Australia, 1981).

Chuk, Florence, *The Somerset Years* (Victoria: Pennard Hill Pubs., 1987).

Clark, C.M.H., A History of Australia, vols I, II, III (Melbourne and Cambridge: Melbourne University Press, 1962, 1968, 1973).

Clark, Manning, *Select Documents in Australian History*, vol. I 1788–1850, vol. II 1851–1900 (London, Sydney & Melbourne: Angus & Robertson, 1950, 1955).

Cobley, John, *Sydney Cove, 1788* (Sydney: Hodder and Stoughton, 1962).

——, *Sydney Cove, 1789–1792* (Sydney: Angus & Robertson, 1963).

——, *The Convicts, 1788–1792* (Sydney: privately published, 1965).

——, *The Crimes of the First Fleet Convicts* (London, Sydney, Melbourne, Singapore, Manila: Angus & Robertson, 1982).

Colledge, J.J., *Ships of the Royal Navy*, vols 1 and 2 (Newton Abbot: David and Charles, 1969, 1970).

Crowley, Frank, ed., *A New History of Australia* (Melbourne: Heinemann, 1974).

Erickson, Rica, and O'Mara, Gillian, *Convicts in Western Australia, 1850–1856* (Perth: University of Western Australia Press, 1994).

Fidlon, P.G., and Ryan, R.J., *The First Fleeters* (Sydney: Australian Documents Library, 1981).

Fitzhardinge, L.F., *Sydney's First Four Years: Port Jackson, 1788–1791* (Sydney: Library of Australian History, 1979).

Flynn, Michael, *The Second Fleet* (Sydney: Library of Australian History, 1993).

Gibson, J.W.S., *Quarter Sessions Records*, 5th edn (Bury: History Partnership, 2007).

Gillen, Mollie, *The Founders of Australia* (Sydney: Library of Australian History, 1989).

——, *John Small – First Fleeter* (Sydney: Library of Australian History, 1985).

Hawkings, D.T., *Criminal Ancestors*, 2nd edn (Stroud: The History Press, 2009).

Hughes, Robert, *The Fatal Shore* (London: Collins Harvill, 1987).

Kerr, James Semple, *Design for Convicts* (Sydney: Library of Australian History, 1984).

Kerr, Joan, and Falkus, Hugh, *From Sydney Cove to Duntroon* (London: Victor Gollancz, 1982).

King, Jonathan, *Australia's First Fleet* (London, Sydney and Auckland: Fairfax & Robertsbridge, 1987).

Lee, R., *Adventures in Australia* (London: Grant and Griffiths, 1851).

MacMillan, David S., *Scotland and Australia, 1788–1850* (Oxford: Caledonian Press, 1967).

Madgwick, R.B., *Immigration to Eastern Australia, 1788–1851* (Sydney University Press, reprint 1969).

Mann, D.D., *The Present Picture of New South Wales* (London: 1811).

Miles, T., *The Chronicles of Crime*, 2 vols (London: 1887).

Moore, John, *The First Fleet Marines* (Brisbane: University of Queensland Press, 1987).

Mudie, James, *The Felonry of New South Wales* (Melbourne: Lansdowne Press, 1964).

Oldham, Wilfrid, *Britain's Convicts to the Colonies* (Sydney: Library of Australian History, 1990).

Phillip, Arthur, *The Voyage to Botany Bay* (London: Hutchinson, reprint 1968).

Rees, Sian, *The Floating Brothel; The Extraordinary True Story of an Eighteenth-Century Ship and its Cargo of Female Convicts* (London: Headline, 2001).

Reid, T., *Two Voyages to New South Wales and Van Diemen's Land* (London: Longmans, 1822).

Roberts, Stephen H., *History of Australian Land Settlement, 1788–1920* (Melbourne: Macmillan, 1924)

Robson, L.L., *The Convicts of Australia, 1787–1852* (Melbourne University Press, reprinted 1976).

Ryan, R.J., *The Second Fleet Convicts* (Sydney: Australian Documents Library, 1982).

——, *The Third Fleet Convicts* (Sydney: Australian Documents Library, 1983).

Scott, Reg, *The West Country's Australian Links* (published privately, 1988).

Shaw, A.G.L., *Convicts and the Colonies* (London: Faber & Faber, 1966).

Sweeney, Christopher, *Transported in Place of Death* (South Melbourne: Macmillan, 1981).

Vine Hall, Nick, *Tracing Your Family History in Australia* (Dee Why West, NSW: Rigby, 1985).

Ward, Russel, *The Australian Legend* (Oxford University Press, 1977).

Watts, Christopher T., and Michael J., *My Ancestor was a Merchant Seaman* (London: Society of Genealogists, 2nd reprint with addendum, 2004).

Weidenhofer, Maggie, *Port Arthur: A Place of Misery* (Oxford University Press, 1981).

——, *The Convict Years; Transportation and the Penal System* (Melbourne: Lansdowne, 1973).

Woolcock, Helen R., *Rights of Passage* (London, New York: Tavistock Publications, 1986).

Worgan, George B., *Journal of a First Fleet Surgeon* (Sydney: Library of Australian History, 1978).

Reference books and specialist lists of convicts and free settlers

Baxter, Carol J. (ed.), *Muster Lists: New South Wales and Norfolk Island, 1800–1802* (Sydney: Australian Biographical and Genealogical Record, 1988).

——, *Musters of New South Wales and Norfolk Island, 1805–1806* (Sydney: Australian Biographical and Genealogical Record, 1989).

——, *General Musters of New South Wales, Norfolk Island and Van Diemen's Land, 1811* (Sydney: Australian Biographical and Genealogical Record, 1987).

——, *General Muster of New South Wales, 1814* (Sydney: Australian Biographical and Genealogical Record, 1987).

——, *General Muster and Land Stock Muster of New South Wales, 1822* (Sydney: Australian Biographical and Genealogical Record, 1988).

——, *General Muster List of New South Wales, 1823, 1824, 1825* (Sydney: Australian Biographical and Genealogical Record, 1999).

Butlin, N.G., Cromwell, C.W., and Suthern, K.L. (eds), *General Return of Convicts in New South Wales, 1837* (Sydney: Australian Biographical and Genealogical Record, 1987).

Chambers, J., *Criminal Petitions Index, 1819–1839*, from TNA document classes HO 17 and HO 18, Part 1 HO 17/40–79; on CD ROM (Stamford, Lincs).

Fidlon, P.G., and Ryan, R.J., *The First Fleeters: A Comprehensive Listing* (Sydney, 1981).

Genealogical Society of Victoria, *Index to Convicts Who Arrived in New South Wales, 1788–1842, and the Ships that Transported Them* (Melbourne: 2000).

Gillen, Mollie, *A Biographical Dictionary of the First Fleet* (Sydney: Library of Australian History, 1989).

Griffin, Ken, *Transported Beyond the Seas: An Alphabetical Listing of Criminals Prosecuted in Hertfordshire Who Received Transportation Sentences to Australia, 1784–1866* (Hertfordshire Family and Population History Society, 1997).

Hawkings, David T., *Somerset Criminals, 1805–1830*, a list of all criminals in TNA document class HO 27 for Somerset, which includes convicts given a transportation sentence; in two parts (The Somerset and Dorset Family History Society, 2003).

Palk, Deirdre, *Prisoners' Letters to the Bank of England, 1781–1827*, vol XLII; includes some who were transported (London Record Society, 2007).

Sainty, M.R., and Johnson, Keith A. (eds), *Census of New South Wales, November 1828* (Sydney: Library of Australian History, 1985)

Tamblin, Stuart, *All English Counties: Indices of the Criminal Registers at TNA*, in document class HO 27 for the period 1805–16; also for 1817–28 for Cornwall, Dorset, Bedfordshire, Devonshire, Leicestershire and Bristol; 1829–40 for Cornwall and Dorset (Northampton: available on micro-fiche).

Wyatt, Irene, *Transportees from Gloucestershire to Australia, 1783–1842* (The Bristol and Gloucestershire Archaeological Society, 1988).

LIST AND INDEX SOCIETY

Volume 304	Pardons and Punishments: Judges Reports on Criminals, Part 1, Part A, 1783–1790 (HO 47/1-12) (2004)
Volume 305	Pardons and Punishments: Judges Reports on Criminals, Part B, 1783–1790 (HO 47/1-12) with Index to Parts A and B (2005)
Volume 312	Pardons and Punishments: Judges Reports on Criminals, Part 2, 1790–1795 (HO 47/13-18) (2006)
Volume 330	Pardons and Punishments: Judges Reports on Criminals, Part 3, 1785–1800 (HO 47/19-24) (2009)
Volume 337	Pardons and Punishments: Judges Reports on Criminals, Part 4, 1800–1805 (HO 47/25-37) (2010)

INDEX OF PERSONAL NAMES

INDEX OF PLACE NAMES

INDEX OF SHIPS AND PRISON HULKS